HOW TO WRITE ABOUT MUSIC

HOW TO WRITE ABOUT MUSIC

Excerpts from the **33⅓** Series, Magazines, Books and Blogs with
Advice from Industry-leading Writers

Edited by
Marc Woodworth and Ally-Jane Grossan

Bloomsbury Academic
An imprint of Bloomsbury Publishing Inc

B L O O M S B U R Y
NEW YORK · LONDON · OXFORD · NEW DELHI · SYDNEY

Contents

This is another way of saying that music writing in the twenty-first century is more adventurous, more idiosyncratic, and more personal than at any point in the last thirty years, and in this way it has a lot in common with the wild-west ethos of the first generation of rock critics, writers like Richard Meltzer, Lester Bangs, Gary Giddins, and Greil Marcus.

And: one of the greatest redoubts of this adventurous contemporary spirit in music writing has been the **33⅓** publishing enterprise, which the present book celebrates prominently. From its very first publication (*Dusty in Memphis*, by Warren Zanes, from the year 2003, a work I read avidly and voraciously upon publication), to its current crop, the **33⅓** series has featured not only great albums, but great and unusual writers writing about these great albums (Joe Pernice on *Meat Is Murder*; Colin Meloy on *Let It Be*, by the Replacements; Drew Daniel on Throbbing Gristle's *20 Jazz Funk Greats*; Jonathan Lethem on *Fear of Music*, and so on), and, even more than this, the series has boasted great writers writing about great albums in *extremely unusual ways*. For example, try reading John Darnielle's work on the subject of Black Sabbath, from 2008, or Carl Wilson's extremely erudite treatment of Céline Dion (2007), both of them excerpted herein.

These **33⅓** books, in their handsome (almost old-fashioned now) CD-style trim sizes revolutionized contemporary rock criticism, making it again (as it had been back in the '60s) *creative work*, instead of second-order writing. These are works of imagination and exegesis and joy. And in this way **33⅓** served and continues to serve as a leaping off point for a lot of the unusual writing about music that is to be found out there these days, in that unruly and unregulated world of contemporary digital media. The Talkhouse, to take one obvious example, probably would not be what it is, if not for the artists-and-musicians talking about music formula that has driven the success of **33⅓**.

As befits an anthology that uses **33⅓** as its point of origin, the book you hold in your hands, *How To Write About Music*, is an enthusiastic hard-to-contain assemblage of this unruly present in music writing, and naturally therefore its tendency is to concentrate on the fanciful rather than on the conventional orientation of the sort we might have seen in the bygone era of *Rolling Stone* or *Spin*. *How To Write About Music* alleges that there are particular kinds of approaches that could conceivably be hierarchically organized (artist interview, artist profile, track-by-track analysis, and so forth) into a discussion, and it appears to have some actual practical advice about how to perform these particular tasks. But believing that these how-to moments are an exhaustive set of principles necessary for music writing is perhaps just as fanciful as the book itself. *How To Write About Music*, with its emphasis on the slant approach, the creative, the recondite, the wry, the historically obsessive, probably amounts to an advice book assembled by people who themselves avoided all the advice anyone ever gave them.

I certainly did. I avoided all the advice. I am lucky enough to be included in these pages, and I will say that I personally started writing about music only because I loved music, and, by and large, I have written only about music I love (well, okay, once I did write about how much I dislike Taylor Swift, and there was also an uncharitable paragraph about Daft Punk), because if I can't write when *moved* to write, then as far as I'm concerned, I might as well go sell PVC tubing somewhere. Therefore, I say to you, read this book as a manual on how to write about music, if you must, but also as an example of how to bury a manual on how to write music *in subterfuge*, replacing it instead with a series of examples of how to think *against* a tradition of responsible and reliable criticism, in order that this tradition might be replaced with the literary traces of the human passions. Because: the answer to the question of how to write music criticism in the twenty-first century is to write it in exactly the same way that you would write a series of profane haikus to your love object, or in exactly the same way you would write a suicide note—as if the language of your music writing were extremely important to you, as if this were the only way to make contact with your readership.

Frank Zappa may have been right about his era, but this book is proof that writing about music in the present can be, and is, so much more.

Rick Moody's music writing is collected in the volume *On Celestial Music: And Other Adventures in Listening*. His music column, "Swinging Modern Sounds," appears regularly on The Rumpus (therumpus.net). He is the author five novels, three collections of stories, and a memoir.

ACKNOWLEDGMENTS

We would like to thank all of the writers in this book and their publishers for graciously allowing us to reprint their pieces.

To everyone at Bloomsbury: Michelle Chen, Danny Cooper, Michael Elmets, Kaitlin Fontana, Kim Muranyi, Evan Arev Pivazyan and Clare Turner.

Special thanks are due to our panel of brilliant writers who took time out of their lives to answer our insane and uncomfortable interview questions: Kyle Anderson, Pete Astor, Nick Attfield, Michael Azerrad, Michael Barclay, Joe Bonomo, Franklin Bruno, Bryan Charles, Kim Cooper, Phillip Crandall, Drew Daniel, Marty Davis, Jim DeRogatis, Kevin Dettmar, Bruce Eaton, D.X. Ferris, Jim Fusilli, Matthew Gasteier, Rob Harvilla, Tony Herrington, Anthony Kwame Harrison, Richard Henderson, Jessica Hopper, Sam Inglis, Casey Jarman, Matt LeMay, Jonathan Lethem, Marvin Lin, Paul Morley, Simon Morrison, Evie Nagy, Chris Ott, Oliver Primus, Mark Richardson, Luis Sanchez, Rob Sheffield, Ross Simonini, Ben Sisario, Scott Tennent, Luke Turner, Marc Weidenbaum, R.J. Wheaton, Carl Wilson, Douglas Wolk, Alex Young and Lindsay Zoladz.

Marc: Thanks to my students at Skidmore who have taught me a lot about music and helped to shape the workshop over the years and to the English Department for the chance to teach this class. Thanks to my family—Emma, Calla, and Ryder—for (most of the time) supporting my music habit and joining in for the fun stuff (what's *New*, Calla?). Thanks to Ally-Jane Grossan for her editorial acumen, friendship, and the chance to make this book together. Thanks to Rick Moody for his Foreword and his visits to my Writing Rock class on a number of occasions.

Ally-Jane: Thanks to Marc for finding me in full panic mode all those years ago in the English Department at Skidmore College when my summer internship had fallen through. Thanks to Marc also for calling his "quirky British editor" at 33⅓, David Barker, and asking him to take a chance on an intern he had never met. Thanks to David for taking that chance and for his many years of guidance since. I feel incredibly lucky to be at the helm of the 33⅓ series and wish to thank all the wonderful people who have spent countless hours pitching ideas and writing for it. Also, thanks to my baby sister Madison Rose for always being *a little bit cooler than me*.

music writing increasingly occupies a place in the classroom, we've tried to compile a useful and various archive of work that takes music as its occasion. There's enough here to see you through an in-depth apprenticeship—and well beyond it. We hope what we've collected will inspire, encourage, energize and even vex you as you find your own way to respond to the music.

During the six years I've been teaching a workshop called "Writing Rock" at Skidmore College, I've taken a lot of pleasure in working with young writers who care passionately, often obsessively about music. We may love different music and we may have learned what a song is under vastly different circumstances, but we always start on the first day with a compatible desire to devote ourselves to the project as listeners, talkers and writers. No one who signs up for the course thinks of music as anything less than crucial to his consciousness, her life. That said, it's often the case that many musically sophisticated students who have listened intensely to a variety of music have not written much about it—or read widely beyond the most readily available kinds of music writing. The workshop gives them the chance both to write extensively about a subject they care about and also to do so with models by accomplished writers in front of them. *How To Write About Music* gathers those models in one place. There's plenty in this book to provide for writers who want to work toward publishing reviews, writing profiles for magazines or posting on music sites, but there's also work collected here that goes well beyond standard journalistic categories: personal essays that experiment with form; cultural analysis that sees the significance of even the seemingly insignificant in high social and political relief; irreverent, loving and off-beat responses to songs and lyrics that fit no established genre. And there's also a lot of practical advice from critics and writers solicited expressly for this volume to help with everything from placing your work to interviewing musicians—all with the intention of providing a context that will enable you to make yourselves better music writers.

But even as you come into your own, even when you hit it right, your sentences don't necessarily serve to replace or even parallel the music that is your subject. That's not what writing about music does—or should do. The "writing about music is like dancing about architecture" canard may be witty enough to stick. It may even suggest something of the difficulty of the job. Still, I'd welcome rather than dismiss a priori a good dance about architecture, just as I'd welcome a masterful film made from a book, or an opera based on international diplomacy. Unlike expressions cross-pollinate and bring unexpected forms into being. The idea that dancing about architecture is impossible, or even pointless, isn't a convincing dismissal of the project of writing about music. It's precisely in that gap between arts that the possibility of making something worthwhile might best be realized. The most affecting and effective writing sometimes shares and exemplifies the heart of the subject it takes up in a more direct way—lifts into the light what's central so we can see it again or perhaps see it differently. But even when it stays closest to the subject, the writing, obviously enough, doesn't speak to music in its own language (even as the sound language makes is a music of its own that creates atmosphere and carries emphasis and meaning). The differences between music itself and language make for the difficulty and the pleasure of writing. Art leads to art but not necessarily to the art you expect. Despite all the distance between mediums—and all the allowances we might make for that distance—there's an undeniable pleasure when language comes closest, on its own terms, to the music. We could look at any number of examples, but here's Alex Ross's description of Radiohead performing "Airbag":

> At the mention of war, Colin let loose a jumpy bass line, giving a funky spin to the hymns in the treble. The music cut through a jumble of verses and choruses, then held fast to a single chord, as Yorke fell into synch with O'Brien's chiming lines. Just before the end, Colin grinned, leaped in the air a couple of times, and seized hold of his brother's tune, the one that had set the song in motion. The doubling of the theme had a kind of thunderous logic, as if an equation had been solved.

"Hymns in the treble" and "chiming lines" get us somewhere, but it's the arrival of that final claim and simile that articulates a musical reality without trying to approximate it. If *hymns* and *chiming* give us a way to imagine what the music sounds like, the claim that "Airbag"'s conclusion hits with the "thunderous logic" of solving an equation is not so much about describing sound as it as about describing the impact of the sound, its way of reaching us beyond what's physical. The simile sees inside the sound and makes us feel what the writer feels when listening to it. We don't know if Alex Ross arrived at this image easily or after a lot of toil, but the claim reads like the inspired dividend of immersion, patience, good ears, and well-developed descriptive muscles. We don't expect mathematics to provide the cognate for this moment in the song, but it does, and with flawless emphasis: the language of numbers as a way to convey the impact of music. It may not be dancing about architecture, but writing like this communicates what's at the heart of another form of expression, a confirmation of what's possible for music writers and an example, like so many in the pages that follow, that serves to guide and inspire.

HOW TO USE THIS BOOK

The foundations of this book were laid down in the fall of 2008 at Skidmore College where Marc Woodworth taught a workshop called Writing Rock. A college sophomore at the time, I enrolled in the course. During our first class meeting, Marc had us listen to an early clip of The Who (when they were still The High Numbers) playing a show at a nondescript hotel. They looked like kids. They *were* kids. We watched the clip and then he asked us to start writing about it. He didn't reveal to us that it was The Who we'd been watching until we had all read our page of musings out loud. Some students struggled with the immediacy of the assignment and had barely written a sentence. Others jumped right in and wrote astoundingly clear assessments of the clip. My piece was mostly gobbledygook about youth culture but I was completely in awe of how this simple constructed exercise had forced a room full of students to write *something* about music.

But writing can't be forced and many might argue that it can't be taught. With a little instruction, inspiration and structure, however, music writing CAN be encouraged, fostered. That's what we hope to accomplish with this volume.

Whether you have been assigned this book in a class or are reading it alone you will find all the tools you need to start writing about music.

There are many different ways to write about popular music. We have carefully chosen 13 different types of writing to demonstrate and teach. From a short album review to proposing a full book of music criticism, you will learn different styles and approaches, some of which you may have never even considered.

Each chapter contains the following:

INTRODUCTION: Each chapter begins with an introduction that will briefly explain its purpose and significance.

EXPERT ADVICE FROM OUR WRITERS: This section is unique to this book. We have asked over 40 working music writers and editors a series of questions about their work as music journalists. Their answers provide invaluable advice to start pitching stories, launch your blog or embark on your music writing career.

EXCERPTS: Each chapter contains 3–5 examples of music writing by a wide range of authors. Some you'll find inspiring and want to emulate—others might make you cringe.

Bryan Charles is the author of the novel *Grab on to Me Tightly as if I Knew the Way*, the memoir *There's a Road to Everywhere Except Where You Came From*, and *Wowee Zowee*, a book about Pavement written for the **33⅓** series.

Longtime *Scram* editrix **Kim Cooper** wrote the bestselling **33⅓** series volume on Neutral Milk Hotel's *In the Aeroplane over the Sea*, and co-edited the anthologies *Bubblegum Music is the Naked Truth* and *Lost in the Grooves*. She runs offbeat L.A. bus tour company Esotouric, and successfully campaigned to save the Union 76 gas station signs from destruction.

Phillip Crandall lives in South Florida and is a former editor for *FHM Magazine*. His freelance writing has appeared in *ESPN The Magazine, Maxim*, and whatever other publications at which his scattered friends have taken up shop.

Marty Davis writes and draws his own comic books. He's got a tumblr under the handle "brushpen," and has published a couple volumes of his drawings under the title "Brushpen Breakfast." Look for his new comic book "FUME" (fumethecomic. com) at your local comic retailer!

A full-time lecturer in the English Department at Columbia College Chicago, **Jim DeRogatis** spent 15 years as pop music critic at the *Chicago Sun-Times*. He continues to write about music for WBEZ.org, the Web site for the public radio station that hosts *Sound Opinions*, the national radio show he helms with Greg Kot. He has written several books about music, including *Let It Blurt: The Life and Times of Lester Bangs, America's Greatest Rock Critic*.

Kevin J. H. Dettmar is W. M. Keck Professor and Chair of English, Pomona College. In popular music studies, the author of *Is Rock Dead?*, editor of *Reading Rock & Roll: Authenticity, Appropriation, Aesthetics* and *The Cambridge Companion to Bob Dylan*. He's a contributor to *The Atlantic, LA Weekly*, and the *Chronicle of Higher Education*.

Drew Daniel is the author of *Twenty Jazz Funk Greats* (Continuum) and *The Melancholy Assemblage; Affect and Epistemology in the English Renaissance* (Fordham). His articles have appeared in *The Wire*, Pitchfork, *Shakespeare Quarterly, Film Quarterly, Opera Quarterly, Parkett, Frieze, Criticism, Journal of English Studies, Early Modern Culture*, and the *Journal of Early Modern Cultural Studies*. He lives in Baltimore and is one half of the electronic band Matmos.

Writer and jazz concert producer **Bruce Eaton** is the author of Big Star's *Radio City*. A member of Western New York's first new wave band, he is a longtime contributor to *Buffalo Spree*. His work has also appeared in *DownBeat* and *The Oxford American*.

D.X. Ferris is an Ohio Society of Professional Journalist Reporter of the year. **33⅓**'s *Reign in Blood* on Slayer was his first book. His credits include RollingStone.com, the [*Onion*] A.V. Club, the *Village Voice*, Cleveland *Scene, Ohio Magazine, Decibel*, the Pittsburgh *Tribune Review*, and numerous other newspapers, magazines, websites and alt-weeklies.

Jim Fusilli is an American writer. He serves as the rock and pop music critic of the *Wall Street Journal* and is the author of eight novels. He is the founder and editor of ReNewMusic.net, a website about contemporary music for grownups. He lives in New York City.

Matthew Gasteier was a music reviewer for *Prefix Magazine* and the *Boston Phoenix* among other publications before writing the **33⅓** entry on Nas's *Illmatic*. That same year, he also published a humor book, *FU Penguin*, based on a hit website. He lives in Cambridge, MA, with his family.

Anthony Kwame Harrison is Associate Professor of Sociology and Africana Studies at Virginia Tech. He is author of *Hip Hop Underground: The Integrity and Ethics of Racial Identification* and has published widely in the academic field of Popular Music Studies. He is also a hip-hop recording artist and member of the groups Forest Fires Collective (SF) and The Acorns (DC).

Rob Harvilla has been a theoretically professional music writer for nigh on 15 years; formerly music editor at the *Village Voice* and deputy editor at *SPIN*, he's also written for Pitchfork, *Blender, Entertainment Weekly*, and many other fine publications.

Richard Henderson, born in Detroit, MI, is a music editor and sometime music supervisor for films, including *Borat, The Life Aquatic, Into The Wild* and *Whiplash*. He has written for *The Wire* (U.K.), *Billboard, LA Weekly, The Beat, Escape* and *Murder Dog*. His **33⅓** book *Song Cycle* appeared in 2010.

Jessica Hopper is a music and culture critic whose work regularly appears in *GQ, Rolling Stone, The Village Voice,* and the *Chicago Tribune*. She is a senior editor at *The Pitchfork Review* and the music editor at *Rookie*. Her essays have appeared in *Best Music Writing* for 2004, 2005, 2007, 2010 and 2011. Hopper was the longtime music consultant for *This American Life*. Her book, The *Girls' Guide to Rocking* was named one of 2009's Notable Books For Young Readers by the American Library Association. She lives in Chicago with her husband and young sons.

Sam Inglis is a writer, folk singer and recording engineer. He is the author of *Harvest* in the **33⅓** series, and *Teach Yourself Songwriting*. He used to be a songwriter, but eventually decided that centuries of tradition usually produce better songs.

Carl Wilson is a Toronto-based writer who is currently the music critic for Slate.com, and has written for the *New York Times*, the *Los Angeles Times*, the *Atlantic*, Salon. com, *Bookforum, Blender, The Globe and Mail* and many other publications. His book *Let's Talk About Love: Why Other People Have Such Bad Taste*—first published as part of the **33⅓** series, but reissued in expanded form in 2014—has been called a "cult classic" by the *New York Times Book Review*.

Douglas Wolk is a freelance arts journalist in Portland, Oregon. He is the author of **33⅓**'s *Live at the Apollo* and *Reading Comics: How Graphic Novels Work and What They Mean*, and contributes to *TIME*, the *New York Times, Rolling Stone* and the *Believer*, among others.

Alex Young founded Consequence of Sound in 2007 and remains as the publication's Publisher and CEO. He oversees the website's daily content output and is actively involved in all business decisions. He currently lives in Chicago with his fiancée Kelly and his two cats Zooey and Dorian.

Lindsay Zoladz has been writing for Pitchfork since 2011. Her writing has also appeared in *The Believer, Slate, Bitch, Salon*, the *Washington City Paper*, and more. She lives in Brooklyn.

OVERTURE: EXPERT ADVICE FROM OUR WRITERS

We asked our panel of experts about their careers as music writers and here's a bit of what they had to say:

Do it for love or not at all. Keep your overhead low and your expectations lower. The only reward you can ask from writing is the chance to keep doing it. If you attract the attention of readers or editors, all the better, but that's extra—you can't make other people's attention your goal. If you do it for love, you have spent your writing time wisely whether anybody reads it or not.—**Rob Sheffield**, writer, *Rolling Stone*

I wish I had more confidence at a younger age. It's always been decent, but my male peers who totally suck are about a zillion times bolder at pursuing things than even the cockiest women I know working in this field. What's kept me employed is that I have always stuck to my guns, written with integrity, tackled tough subjects, held unpopular decisions, did the homework no one wants to and put out consistent work. I have had a total of 5 pieces killed in the last 20 years; I counted this morning.—**Jessica Hopper**, Music Editor at *Rookie Magazine*, and Senior Editor, the *Pitchfork Review*.

I can't overemphasize the importance of self-motivation, timeliness, meeting deadlines/quotas, and being open to change and adapting when needed. I think too that keeping tabs on all types of music and trends, whether or not you like them on an aesthetic level, is a good quality to possess, as well as the ability to think critically and conceptually.—**Marvin Lin**, Editor-in-Chief, Tiny Mix Tapes

I'm a fairly kamikaze writer—I don't have a set process other than to listen and read and research until I've well overdone it and then to write frantically. Most recently I wrote a fairly long essay (3,000 words) for Slate about the merits and faults of "The Star-Spangled Banner" as a national anthem, which involved spending a day listening to dozens of national anthems from around the world, reading about the history of the song and the arguments that have been made for other songs to replace it, etc., then passing out for six or seven hours, getting up and trying to put myself in a jaunty enough frame of mind to riff on all those ideas without becoming too dry or academic. With most of a draft done that day, the next day was spent revising—first on my own, then in cooperation with my editor. Since I write semi-weekly for Slate, a two- or three-day process is usually all I can afford; for a larger reported feature or profile the methodology would be different, of course.—**Carl Wilson**, Toronto-based writer and Slate.com music critic

There's only one part of my routine, or practice, or habituation, whatever it ought to be called, that's admirable and worth emulating—only one part that matters, in the end, and I'll gladly promise great things to anyone who adopts it. Two tenets comprise my wisdom. First: write every day. Doesn't matter how long. For me, I can usually barely cross the three-hour mark, I quit committing anything useful to the page somewhere well before the fourth hour, even if I sit there through it. Some days I write for only half an hour or forty-five minutes, but by god I add something to the project each and every day, like a law. Second: write before the world wakes up and announces its clawing demands. This is more important than ever, given the way our typewriters and telephones have converged. Whenever you start, start earlier. Start while the coffee is still brewing, start while NPR is still playing BBC World News, start half asleep. Get it done first, and you'll be someone another human being might be willing to live with, at least eventually.—**Jonathan Lethem**, novelist

I became a music writer because I was incredibly shy, and awkward, and lonely, and incredibly enthusiastic about music—and took it very seriously, so I think seriousness was a factor as well—and I used my enthusiasm for music, and pop stars, Bowie, Bolan, Roxy, Sparks, and musicians, to try and find a place for me in life, to overcome my shyness, and along the way I managed to earn money, which helped me find a place in life as well—as a music writer I became an expert in something, which helped my confidence and self-esteem, and I found company through music, so I was less lonely, and was paid for actually loving music and wanting to find out about it and what its power was, which I would have done anyway. I think also what first employed me and then kept me employed was that I loved writing, and writing about new things, and writing about music gave me a chance to write that I would not have had anywhere else, and then because of the nature of how music changed gave me a chance to write about new things.—**Paul Morley**, writer and critic

I stayed in the game by taking every assignment that anyone offered me. I never said "Oh, I don't *knooooow*, I'm not *passionate* about that band" and begged my way out of work—as I saw countless aspiring writers do over my years as an editor, writer, coach, and mentor. Everybody wants to be a music writer, but it's amazing how few people will take an assignment to cover a group they're not personally interested in. If you can't/won't take an assignment to cover an act you're not personally interested in, you have no business being in the game.—**D.X. Ferris**, Ohio Society of Professional Journalists Reporter of the Year, Professor, **33⅓** author

I am going to steal the words of one of my favorite writers, Cheryl Strayed:

> Don't lament so much about how your career is going to turn out. You don't have a career. You have a life. Do the work. Keep the faith. Be true blue. You are a writer because you write.

The useless days will add up to something. The shitty waitressing jobs. The hours writing in your journal. The long meandering walks. The hours reading poetry and short story collections and novels and dead people's diaries . . . These things are your becoming.—**Lindsay Zoladz**, Associate Editor, Pitchfork

I think it's unfortunate when critics seem to be writing mostly for other critics. I would like to change criticism so it's clearly about communicating with readers and is based on listening to and experiencing music, as fans of music first.—**Mark Richardson**, Editor-in-Chief, Pitchfork

I write quite a few news stories a day, however, the writing process is pretty bare bones: a strong lead identifying the topic of the story and then I try to write as succinctly as possible while also incorporating a bit of personal voice. For me, news writing isn't so much talent as a learned experience: the more practice, the better you'll become. I'd also recommend the following exercise: have someone give you a topic, then write everything that possibly comes to mind over a five-minute span. Do not think, just write. That way you'll train you brain to write and think simultaneously. When I do write a more long form piece, I typically map out what I want in my head, jot down bullet points on paper, and then just start writing. Again, I like to take more of a personal angle with my writing, one that'll keep the reader entertained as well as informed.—**Alex Young**, founder and publisher, *Consequence of Sound*

Aspiring music writers should involve themselves in the music-making process whenever possible. Get in a van with some punk band so you can find out just how boring it is; hang out in the studio with some rappers so that you can see how different production ideas come about; spend some time backstage with jazz players to hear how they talk about their set. Learning the emotional truths of making music is pretty much important no matter who you're writing for or what you're writing about, and I think spending time with musicians makes you a more empathetic and understanding music journalist.

Songs still bring me to tears all the time. Great albums still completely fuck my whole life up. And when I feel passionate about something, I will work really hard to explain to people why that thing matters. That's pretty much what I have going for me.—**Casey Jarman**, Managing Editor, the *Believer*

I've always been a fan of writing that's a visceral reaction to music, and I think approaching it with open, almost naive ears helps with that.—**Luke Turner**, Associate Editor, The Quietus

I have never lost track of the fact that writing about music for a living is a great job, and that no matter what my situation, it's still better than real work. That appreciation is important, and it keeps me humble and hungry.—**Kyle Anderson**, Senior Writer, *Entertainment Weekly*

CHAPTER 1
THE ALBUM REVIEW

INTRODUCTION

How do writers show up in their reviews? Ann Powers' keen eye for the gender politics of rock gives her review of Daft Punk's *Random Access Memories* a characteristic perspective: "There is one glaring omission from Daft Punk's foray into vintage pleasures. Where is the female voice representing those who truly defined that liberatory spirit?" (She's just limned out the album's relationship to the music of the 70s, its hedonistic nature and "promiscuous eclecticism.") The lack of a "feminine presence," she concludes, makes "the satisfactions *RAM* offers . . . incomplete." It's a fair and telling point. Powers identifies a shortcoming to which another reviewer might have been blind. How the critic sees and hears a record, Powers' caveat reminds us, isn't neutral or objective, but determined by their own experience, passion, and focus.

We often learn more when we come across a knee-jerk review that strikes us the wrong way than from one we agree with, learn more not only about the record under consideration but about some aspect of our own response to music, especially if that aspect isn't yet entirely clear to us. The "Dean of American Rock Critics," Robert Christgau first published his "Consumer Guide" capsule reviews in 1969. They've served to define the nature of record reviews ever since even as they remain largely inimitable, marked by a fiery critical intelligence and an immediately identifiable style. For all the critical stances he takes that are utterly convincing however, an important aspect of reading his reviews is the way the ones you disagree with get under your skin.

His B– for Guided By Voices' *Bee Thousand* isn't a particularly low mark in the pre-grade-inflation reckonings of the Dean even if the grade itself doesn't entirely jibe with the damning consonance-rich sentence that caps the review: "this is pop for perverts—pomo smarty-pants too prudish and/or alienated to take their pleasure without a touch of pain to remind them that they're still alive."

Even if you're invested in the record or the band, those over the top 'p's are fun to hear coming from the lips of the master reviewer but they tend to leave sticky traces of his spittle on your face. Taking a second to wipe them off gives you pause to think about whether or not you *are* a prudish, perverted pomo smarty-pants and whether that's why you like the record after all. Once you decide you're not really any of those things, you become almost grateful for the fact that the critic has given you a chance to confirm what you know about yourself and the music you love.

Reading that sentence reminds me of Christgau's early reviews of Sonic Youth. The fact that there was an audience out there which liked this stuff seemed more of a disincentive to the critic than the music itself: he sends up the preciosity of the kind of store where you can by an EP like *Death Valley '69* by calling it a 'shoppe' and suggests that if you actually pay for such bootless product you might as well be sexually servicing (his language is less polite) the "Boho poseurs" in the band. Are the *Boho poseurs* who constitute Sonic Youth (a band that consistently received As from Christgau for much of its later career) and its fan base predecessors of the Guided by Voices listeners he imagines to be perverted *pomo smarty-pants*? They must be. The critic's allergy to the image of the fawning hipster makes his eyes swell up so quickly that he can't see the music isn't postmodern or enervated at all but an example of brilliant, even lovingly rendered songs made by regular guys—OK, so one of them's a regular guy who happens to be a genius—with a full-blooded love of rock and very limited recording equipment. Christgau may have identified accurately a portion of the band's audience in New York who lionized Guided by Voices for the wrong reasons and found this demographic as repellent as early Sonic Youth fans, but once he has these cardboard cutouts in his sights, he can only dismiss the music without really taking it in.

I'm not dwelling on this review merely to settle scores with a famous critic about a beloved record (though there's that), but to suggest a couple of things that might prove useful to a writer of album reviews. First, the critic both uses and is sometimes blind to his prejudices and ideals—the more you know about yourself and how you process what you're writing about given that self-knowledge, the better. Second, don't write as someone who doesn't care about what you care about. Don't be hipper or more sanguine, less cranky or suspicious than you are. Show up on the page as yourself. There's nothing cautious or second-guessing about Christgau's GBV and Sonic Youth reviews—and that's the pleasure of reading them: his verbal intelligence, desire to sniff out a bad deal for the "consumer," and concern that what he's hearing may not be authentic are all palpably real aspects of his response to music. You, on the other hand, might be more inclined to draw out nuance than spit fire—or even praise—so use what you've got. And as Rob Sheffield writes about what proved to be a dead wrong review he wrote of a Radiohead album (*The Bends*) that became one of his favorite records by one of his favorite bands, "getting things wrong is part of a music critic's life ... That's probably the most crucial advice I could give a young critic—plan on getting a lot of things wrong." Just make sure when you're wrong, you're wrong on your own terms.—MW

EXPERT ADVICE FROM OUR WRITERS

With album reviews, there was a time when writers got advance albums two or three months before the general public ever heard it. So you could spend some time crafting a meaningful argument that was really unaffected by the fan reception of a record, or by the promotional campaign of that record. That landscape has changed so dramatically that writers don't have much of an advantage over anyone else. Everyone has an opinion the moment an album is leaked or released, and editors are going to (understandably) demand that their writers join that chorus as quickly as possible so their outlet's coverage doesn't feel stale. When you're under that kind of deadline pressure, as a writer, I think it's much harder to write something personal and meaningful and structurally sound, so readers often get something half-cooked or something that pretty much repeats the safe status quo opinion that's floating around out there. The democratization of this stuff is a lot better than the old "gatekeeper" system in so many ways, but I think serious criticism is really struggling right now, because even the stalwart voices have the ability to see what everyone else is saying, and we wind up in a weird feedback loop.—**Casey Jarman**, Managing Editor, the *Believer*

I listen to music as I would "in the wild" before I approach it critically. That means listening to it regularly on headphones to and from work usually.—**Matt LeMay**, senior contributor, Pitchfork

I begin by listening to the disc in question several times. Even as a young sprog reading magazines like *Crawdaddy!* and *Fusion*, I could tell when the reviewer had only listened to something once, especially if I already owned and enjoyed the record. There's research for record reviews, too. Most reviewers, at least the majority of those I've read, seem to think that the music to which they're listening and the accompanying liner notes are sufficient data from which to build a review. A little research, especially beyond the immediate realm of music, goes a long way towards enriching both one's opinion of a record and the ability to express that opinion with allure.—**Richard Henderson**, music writer and 33⅓ author

When I reviewed Oneohtrix Point Never's *R Plus Seven*, which was voted Tiny Mix Tapes' favorite album of 2013, I already knew the album intimately, since I had listened to it many times before knowing that I'd be writing about it. But in general, it's crucial for me to immerse myself in the music first, then, depending on the artist, do as much research as possible by reading interviews and articles. This research is not only for fact-gathering purposes, but also to understand how meaning is created and reinforced throughout the media, how publicity might have affected how people are writing about the music in question, and whether or not any of it aligns with my personal beliefs.—**Marvin Lin**, Editor-in-Chief, Tiny Mix Tapes

I've realized that I try to make everything I write, even reviews, into some sort of narrative—there has to be a story or I don't know what to say. And then I just smooth it all together into a legible story.—**Michael Azerrad**, author, journalist and Editor-in-Chief of the *Talkhouse*

I wrote a 1500-word review about the Slint boxset (multiple LPs, book, and DVD) in the *Wire* magazine. I listened to the music, watched the film several times, and started by simply thinking about exactly what struck me as most significant about the band, their reputation, their album *Spiderland* and the historical gap between the time of its creation and the present. Once I had a lot of sentences more or less worked out in my head, I wrote a preliminary draft. Then I revised it many times, adding and expanding and cutting back and reshuffling certain key points. Then I sent it to the editor and we had several back-and-forth edits and changes. He wanted me to add some things and I thought about how I would do that effectively. It's not just about "your voice" or "inspiration"—to write is to work with editors, to revise, and to sometimes change your mind and your emphasis.—**Drew Daniel**, Assistant Professor, Department of English, Johns Hopkins University

The short form is hard for me—especially the really short form. Like I don't know what I'd do if I had to write one of those 200-word album reviews. I guess I'd adapt. Short for me would be in the 2,500-word range. And even then things spill over. But I like revising and editing a lot. Those are my favorite things about writing.—**Bryan Charles**, writer and **33⅓** author

When I'm assigned an album for review, the first thing I do is contact the publicist to try and track down a promo copy of the album (if I don't have one already; sometimes my editor will provide me with a promo, or I'll have pitched the album for review having already listened to it).

Then, I listen. A lot of people ask me how many times I try and listen to an album before reviewing it, and the truth is that there is no magic number. It really depends on how far in advance I'm given a record; sometimes I'll live with a promo copy of a record for months before I have to sit down and organize my thoughts about it, and in other cases—especially with bigger, major label releases—I'll hear an album for the first time a day or two before I have to file the review. I prefer situations between these two extremes. If you have *too* long to marinate on an album, you can sometimes overthink your opinion and second-guess your gut reaction—specifically if you see a lot of people arguing about it a lot on the internet. But of course, you don't want to feel rushed, either. A lot of my favorite albums are "growers" that didn't immediately grab me on first listen, but I came to appreciate them over many consecutive listens, and I try to consider this when listening and writing.

One thing I try to do consistently, though, is listen to an album I'm reviewing in a variety of contexts. A lot of people might think of a music critic pensively listening to a record alone in a silent room and through huge, state-of-the-art headphones … and true, sometimes I do that. But that's not the *only* way people listen to music, and I try to remember that when I'm writing about a record. I want to take it out for a test-drive—to try it out in real life. I try to listen on speakers *and* on headphones. I try to give it a few spins (pen and notebook in hand, usually) focused specifically on the music *and* when I'm playing it in the background of doing something else. Sometimes I'll listen alone and sometimes with other people. Music filters into our lives in a variety of ways, and I try to keep this in mind when I'm evaluating it.

Then, once I feel like I'm ready to say what I want to say (or when my deadline is unavoidably looming), I'll sit down at my computer and write. Usually I'll have already jotted down some phrases or observations on a napkin, or my hand, or the notebook I'm always carrying with me, and I'll consult these notes if I have them, but sometimes I like to start the review as a blank slate. Even when I think I have a handle on how I feel about an album, I don't really know exactly what I'm going to say until I sit down to write, and I think the trick is finding that uncertainty exhilarating rather than terrifying.—**Lindsay Zoladz**, Associate Editor, Pitchfork

I would make it illegal to review a record sooner than a month after release. I think it's impossible to have the proper perspective on a record when you've sat with it for just a few weeks—sometimes even a few days for bigger records. There are so many reviews I've written that I would change almost completely because how I felt about the record after a handful of listens changed significantly even a few months after I wrote my review. This happens in both directions, too. Some records seem like potential classics and then totally fade from memory, while a few of my favorite records ever didn't even make my year-end list when they came out.—**Matthew Gasteier**, writer and **33⅓** author

In 1995, when I was the music columnist for *Details* magazine, I got the new advance cassette called *The Bends*, from a British band who were already forgotten two years after their fluke MTV hit "Creep." I gave the new album a negative review, saying "Radiohead are back trying to prove they're not one-hit wonders. Unfortunately, they are." (That was the *entire* review, by the way.) Needless to say, *The Bends* went on to be one of my favorite albums, from one of my favorite bands. Getting things wrong is part of a music critic's life. Fortunately, this went down before the Internet existed. That's probably the most crucial advice I could give a young critic—plan on getting a lot of things wrong.—**Rob Sheffield**, writer, *Rolling Stone*

I'd love to free myself from the album-release hype cycle, where there are 3–5 artists/albums of current interest that everyone "has" to write about, which leaves very little time to both write about or even listen to anything else, even way better stuff we'd enjoy writing about way more.—**Rob Harvilla**, Deputy/Culture Editor, *Deadspin*

I would get rid of the "star" rating system. We're dealing with music, not a skating competition. It's a cheap gimmick that encourages unimaginative writing and discourages readers from actually reading the review and learning if the writer had something insightful to say about the music. With the star rating, it's almost inevitable that a writer decides first on the rating for an album and then writes an opinion to match the rating.

I think readers are far more likely to read a review if there's no rating attached. My eyes glaze over when I see a long string of 3 to 3½-star reviews. I'm most likely to read a 1-star review on the chance that either the artist is doing something interesting that went past the writer or that the writer is deservedly trashing a record with some comedic flair.—**Bruce Eaton**, author, *Radio City* (**33⅓**)

Most of my preparation is in the listening; I listen to the record many times, and over time, the ideas and point of view start to gel in my mind. When it comes time to finally write the review, I usually have most of it pretty well sketched out in my head. But the listening is where the hardest work happens. **Mark Richardson**, Editor-in-Chief, Pitchfork

ANN POWERS ON DAFT PUNK'S *RANDOM ACCESS MEMORIES*

Robots In Ecstasy: Daft Punk's *Memories* Embraces The Pleasure Principle*

"Give life back to music," coo the robots on the first track of Daft Punk's new album, *Random Access Memories*, which showed up yesterday on iTunes after a long period of near-hysterical anticipation and advance marketing. Does the veteran Parisian dance music duo succeed in doing this on its first album in eight years? Your answer will depend on how you view music's relationship to the central human experiences: pleasure, the tangible satisfaction of body and soul.

For purists, *Random Access Memories* may instantly disappoint because it abandons EDM's tried-and-true routes to body-mind fulfillment: accelerating machine beats, busy noise and that roller coaster effect, the drop. "It's confusing. There are no drops," declared a writer for the site White Raver Rafting, referring to the moments when a fast computer-generated beat suddenly breaks and shifts its rhythm. Instead of tightly focused tracks shaped through such electronic manipulations, *RAM* features relatively loose live jamming, pop-operatic balladry and the Bach-quoting keyboards of progressive rock.

On one level, these changes seem to serve nostalgia instead of the current dance music ideal of rapidly accelerating progress. Daft Punk's choice to sink deeply into protoplasmic mud where contemporary dance music was born will strike some as less conservative than contrarian. The most active collaborator on *RAM* is Nile Rodgers, the producer and guitarist whose work with his band, Chic, and many other artists built the bridge between funk/rock and disco. Also prominently featured are the blockbuster songwriter Paul Williams, best known for his baroque rock opera *Phantom of the Paradise*, and Giorgio Moroder, Eurodisco's Adam, who fabricated a distinctly dirty Eden with his Eve, the late great Donna Summer.

These 1970s luminaries define the sound and the substance of *RAM*. While plenty of younger collaborators surface—including Pharrell Williams, Julian Casablancas of The Strokes and Animal Collective's Panda Bear—none makes a contribution as

---

*Powers, Ann. "Robots In Ecstasy: Daft Punk's *Memories* Embraces The Pleasure Principle." NPR, May 14, 2013. Printed with permission.

crucial as Williams's scenery-toppling vocal on the eight-minute long ballad, "Touch," or Rodgers's guitar riffs throughout, which run like ground wires through the album's grooves. Moroder is mostly on board as a patron saint, but his dictum to "free your mind" is important. This 74-minute excursion into a re-imagined past seeks to rewire the brains of Daft Punk fans by forcing an encounter with a central principle of 1970s popular culture: the pleasure principle. Its songs suggest that by understanding how pleasure felt then, we might better pursue pleasure now.

On the surface, songs like the florid "Touch" or the pleasantly ecstatic "Lose Yourself To Dance" seem to celebrate a 1970s defined by hedonism and self-indulgence. But that's only one layer. Disco was explicitly tied to gay and (as writers like Alice Echols have shown) women's liberation—the way bodies moved on the dance floor inspired liberation movements in the streets. Not much later, soft rockers responded by offering new versions of masculinity that were more sexually expressive and free. Funk, too, played a major role, taking cues from the civil rights movement to free the mind—and as Funkadelic famously said, the ass followed. 1970s music described and fueled this pleasure revolution.

Musically, *RAM* harkens back to another 1970s pleasure source—the promiscuous eclecticism of the pop scene. Though the image of disco hardened into its Top 40 version after the success of *Saturday Night Fever*, in reality the genre made room for everything from Florida soul to Italian synth suites to jazz fusion and futuristic take-offs on classical chestnuts. On a purely musical level, *RAM* defines pleasure through these oozy encounters among sounds—a prog rock keyboard line blending with some guitar boogie or a wandering New Age melody finding focus in a pulsing house beat. The problem with exploring how pleasure worked in earlier times is that some people now just won't relate. "My dad had an incredible time dancing to this Daft Punk album at his law school prom," tweeted the writer Jeff Weiss after hearing *RAM*, expressing the views of many who find any version of fun that even remotely smacks of the parental not just dull, but embarrassing. (Weiss did later add that he thinks half of *RAM* is great.) Yet while some within the EDM scene may reject *RAM* as old-fashioned, the album fits very well within the larger world of pop. After all, rock bands like Fleet Foxes, and divas like Solange have been mining the past for something that feels more personal for a while.

But what does it mean to be "personal," anyway? What is a real man? That, too, was a central question of the 1970s, and it's a central one on *RAM*. It's couched in science-fiction terms here, suiting the central conceit of Daft Punk—the masked identities that allow two musicians who "look not unlike a couple of guys in a rock band," as Zach Baron recently wrote in *GQ*, to remain both private and mysterious. Like the 1970s band KISS, Daft Punk exists through its disguise and is trapped by it. And like the sci-fi films of the 1970s that reconsidered humanity through the lens of the all-too-human robot or alien, *RAM* plays with the idea that machines might experience pleasure as well as pain.

There is one glaring omission from Daft Punk's foray into vintage pleasures. Where is the female voice representing those who truly defined that liberatory spirit? Donna Summer, who died last year, may not have been available, but plenty of others could have filled that role. The body and soul satisfactions *RAM* offers are many, but without that feminine presence, they remain incomplete.

JIM DEROGATIS ON SIMON & GARFUNKEL'S *BOOKENDS*

Old Friends Never Sounded Better*

By 1968, it had become obvious that there was a dark flip side to the sunny ideals that characterized the first half of the decade—the boundless optimism of the Camelot era and the intoxicating freedoms ushered in by the psychedelic explosion.

With riots in the streets, the mounting toll of a bloody war and a flurry of assassinations filling the headlines, it seemed as if the center wasn't holding, as New Journalist Joan Didion famously observed. America was lost and "getting loster," and few artists captured that vibe of anxious uncertainty better than genteel crooners turned melodic folk-rockers Simon & Garfunkel.

"America," one of several standout tracks from the duo's fourth and best album, *Bookends*, can be heard as a baby-boomer's update of the central crusade that was the theme of many of the Beats' best writings, starting with Jack Kerouac's immortal *On the Road*. The song starts with some introspective humming, and then quietly introduces two playful, daydreaming lovers who set out to find "the heart of America" by hitchhiking through Michigan and taking the Greyhound bus out of Pittsburgh. The tune builds to a beautiful, tastefully orchestrated climax as Paul Simon and Art Garfunkel's vocals join together for the ultimate verse.

> 'Kathy, I'm lost,' I said, though I knew she was sleeping
> I'm empty and aching and I don't know why
> Counting the cars on the New Jersey Turnpike
> They've all come to look for America.

Nothing is resolved, but the musical coda of Garfunkel's amazingly pure and soaring vocals and Simon's soothing guitar and organ indicate that maybe, just maybe, our heroes and their many peers will eventually find what they're looking for.

Childhood friends from Forest Hills, N.Y., Simon & Garfunkel began recording together in 1957 as an Everly Brothers-style duo called Tom & Jerry. They scored one minor hit, "Hey, Schoolgirl," before splitting up after the act went nowhere.

The two reunited in the early '60s during the height of the Greenwich Village folk boom, split up again, then came together most successfully to join a wave of folk-rockers that included West Coast artists such as the Byrds, and the Mamas and the Papas.

---

*DeRogatis, Jim. "The Great Albums: Old Friends Never Sounded Better." The *Chicago Sun-Times*, October 19, 2003. Reprinted with permission.

Simon, who wrote the vast majority of material, was always capable of crafting a memorable melody a la early hits such as "The Sound of Silence" and "Homeward Bound," and Garfunkel's high-tenor harmonies were never short of amazing. But the pair could also be annoyingly twee and cutesy—witness "The 59th Street Bridge Song (Feelin' Groovy)"—or unbearably smug, pretentious and self-important. With "A Simple Desultory Philippic (Or How I Was Robert McNamara'd Into Submission)," Simon lampooned Bob Dylan, who he clearly thought was an—*harrumph*—inferior songwriter.

Recording technology had been improving steadily through the mid-'60s, and under the influence of psychedelic drugs (or simply the spirit of experimentation that they represented), many artists had begun to use the studio to create imaginative new worlds that existed only in the listeners' imaginations. Released during the height of 1967's fabled "Summer of Love," the Beatles' *Sgt. Pepper's Lonely Hearts Club Band* represented the new standard for other ambitious artists to emulate. Simon & Garfunkel certainly benefitted from this new, ambitious but playful attitude.

The duo recorded *Bookends* with producer Roy Halee, a trumpeter who had become a staff engineer at Columbia Records, recording "Like a Rolling Stone," among other Dylan songs. "It was never a challenge to get that blend as long as they were singing on one microphone," Halee said in 1990 of working with Simon & Garfunkel two decades earlier. "The blend of their sound hitting that microphone was very unique; it changed it, and it sounded separated when they didn't do it together. It was never quite the same."

Though *Bookends* was, in fact, a collection blending previously released singles with new material, the album, like *Sgt. Pepper*, was perceived as a concept effort—at least through the first half. After opening with the quiet "Bookends Theme" (which also closes what would have been Side 1 in the vinyl days), the songs chart the life cycle, from birth and early childhood ("Save the Life of My Child") through the teenage years ("America" and "Overs," which finds the couple portrayed in the previous song splitting up) through old age ("Old Friends," which features the line, "How terribly strange to be 70"—odd to ponder at a point when Simon & Garfunkel are 61 and 62, respectively).

The album's most famous track hails from Side 2: The rhythmically galloping and wildly hummable "Mrs. Robinson" became a smash hit after it appeared on the soundtrack for *The Graduate*. But even beyond the theme of sexual tension, it is timelessly poetic in its evocation of lost innocence: "Where have you gone, Joe DiMaggio?" Simon sings of an icon from the previous generation. "A nation turns its lonely eyes to you." (The notoriously cantankerous baseball legend was said to have been offended by the line, but Simon has disputed this, citing a meeting several years after the song's release. "I said that I didn't mean the lines literally, that I thought of him as an American hero and that genuine heroes were in short supply," Simon wrote in an op-ed piece for the *New York Times*. "He accepted the explanation and thanked me.")

The album's third undeniably great track is "A Hazy Shade of Winter," which stands not only as an indelible East Coast answer to "California Dreamin'," but as a production tour de force, with electric rock instruments joining symphonic touches to create a psychedelic-rock classic. (Psychedelic popsters the Bangles recorded a memorable cover in the '80s, just as progressive-rockers Yes claimed "America" as their own in the '70s—two diverse testaments to the enduring strength of these tunes.)

With Halee cheerfully indulging them, Simon & Garfunkel continued the psychedelic experimentation throughout the album, and the results are mixed. Odd synthesizers enhance "Save the Life of My Child" (one of the weirdest songs the duo ever recorded), and Simon's flair for surrealist wordplay flourishes on "Punky's Dilemma" (*"Wish I was a Kellogg's cornflake/Floatin' in my bowl, takin' movies,"* he sings while banging on a toy piano).

But "Voices of Old People" serves as a pointless collage of sounds and conversations that Garfunkel taped on the street, and Simon's tendency to overreach as a lyricist comes to the fore on the album-closing "At the Zoo," a wannabe Orwellian allegory. (*"Zebras are reactionaries/Antelopes are missionaries/Pigeons plot in secrecy/And hamsters turn on frequently."*)

After "Bookends," Simon & Garfunkel began to drift apart. Halee was heartbroken when they started insisting on recording their vocals separately. Simon wanted to strike out on his own without a collaborator, and Garfunkel was branching out into acting.

After one last great studio album, *Bridge Over Troubled Water* (1970), they took a "break" that has been interrupted only occasionally for reunions such as the 1975 single "My Little Town," a 1981 concert in New York's Central Park and their current concert tour.

The pair's rivalry and animosity has become legendary—an earlier reunion tour in the early '80s was supposed to culminate in a new studio album, but that was canceled, due to the infamous "artistic differences"—so it's anybody's guess whether the pair will move forward after their sold-out shows Friday and Saturday at the United Center. On *Bookends*, though, the strength of their collaboration is apparent, and neither has ever topped it.

LAURIE ANDERSON ON ANIMAL COLLECTIVE'S *CENTIPEDE HZ*

Laurie Anderson TALKS Animal Collective's *Centipede Hz**

First of all, I hate to admit it but you might as well know it right off: the more it sounds like "Grass" (my favorite Animal Collective song) the more I like it.

"Grass" is ecstatic. A huge football game that goes haywire. The players suddenly running in circles, insanely chirping cartoon birds, clouds billowing, the marching band spelling out arcane words in quickly shifting formations, the scoreboard in fast forward, the crowd going "Rah! Rah! Rah! Rah! Rah! Rah!"

As a musician I know that's not the most generous approach to a new record that has ambitions and lots of great sounds and dangerous harmonies and new constructions. It's not fair to hope it sounds like something from the past. But I just can't help it. "Grass" is so full of joy and freedom, all that manic humming and rattling and chirping. Are there more of you out there like that?

That said, I'm not even sure how I feel about *Centipede Hz* since every time I listen to it I change my mind. I mean really change my mind. Take "Monkey Riches." It went from unlistenable to one of my current favorites. Dense and flexible, great bunches of sound, emerald isles. Or the transitions. The transitions are beyond lovely. Listen to the way the music slips into "Father Time."

Other things jump up at me with each listening. "Amanita"'s big chunky moves, its triumphant lyrics. There's nothing to do! There's nothing to do! And the way the song marches away double-time at the end, restlessly around and around the field, then just breaks down in a heap. "Grass" redux. Lots of sounds like sputtering and wheels or cards flapping against bicycle wheels. Did they actually attach cards to bike wheels and mike it? I've done things like that—tried to record the clicking of false teeth inside the mouth. Why? To put things into sounds. The opposite of putting things into words but still hard to do without sounding like something from your SOUNDFX collection.

Centipede Hz is a record with lots of things in it—motors and propellers, a giant samba band with the massive surdo drum. A record that's going somewhere, inventing its own form of transportation.

And it's in the transitions where you can hear the method, the sounds of large structures breaking down into pieces, chunks, the metal springs still trembling, the

---

*Anderson, Laurie. "Laurie Anderson TALKS Animal Collective's Centipede Hz." The *Talkhouse*, March 7, 2014. Reprinted with permission.

spent batteries. And it's from these pieces that are lying around that the next song is swiftly deftly assembled. In "Pulleys" the initial construction is half techno, half organic. Big bundles of hollow rushes through Indonesian filters mix with big, thick chords and a massive, pointy bass line, hooting smoky vocals that curl and twist. Once in a while a vocoder.

"Mercury Man," restless in the challenging third spot, is the only one that gets a little lost, aimlessly anthemic, until the groove line appears and takes over. "New Town Burnout" starts off differently with an authoritative, compelling beginning, then a cool groove and spectacular drone. One of the few pieces where I felt the vocals added nothing made up for the large moves of history, the mechanical birds that flap through it. More broken equipment, metal things. Equipment damaged in transit.

But today, "Applesauce" is my favorite. Largely because I can see large manatees driving, twirling, and spinning in the most playful way and I like "Rosie" too, with its sophisticated harmonies and "Today's Supernatural"'s knocking, stuttering accordion, jittering monkeys, and big, banging punctuation. I'm in the red zone, wherever that is, a world that's falling apart in the most delightful way, a place with a mountain view. Fragmentary lyrics.

And there's "Moonjock" muttering with a great groove, again the great crashes and the tangled masses of notes that roll out in swoops, the song that's most like the world of "Grass" and then the winding down, the blurry descent into the world of dark chant.

And back to "Grass." It's still one of my favorites, but listening to *Centipede Hz*, like many ambitious, multifaceted new works of art, takes some time and every time I hear it, I hear it more. It's a work in progress. Dynamic. I wish I could comment on it like it was a thing but it's too alive for that.

There are more contradictions on "New Slaves," where he says "Fuck you and your Hamptons house." But God only knows how much he's spending wherever he is. He's trying to have it both ways—he's the upstart but he's got it all, so he frowns on it. Some people might say that makes him complicated, but it's not really that complicated. He kind of wants to retain his street cred even though he got so popular. And I think he thinks people are going to think he's become one of *them*—so he's going to very great lengths to claim that he's not. On "New Slaves," he's accusing everyone of being materialistic but you know, when guys do something like that, it's always like, "But *we're* the exception. It's all those *other* people, but *we* know better."

"New Slaves" has that line "Y'all throwin' contracts at me/ You know that niggas can't read." Wow, wow, *wow*. That is an amazing thing to put in a lyric. That's a serious accusation in the middle of this rant at other people: an accusation of *himself*. As if he's some piece of shit from the street who doesn't know nothing. Yeah, right—your mom was a college English professor.

He starts off cool on that track but he winds up yelling at the top of his voice. I think he maybe had a couple of great lines already written for this song but then when he recorded the vocal, he just let loose with it and trusted his instincts. Because I can't imagine actually writing down most of these lines. But that's just me.

But musically, he nails it beyond belief on "New Slaves." It's mainly just voice and one or two synths, very sparse, and then it suddenly breaks out into this incredible melodic . . . God knows what. Frank Ocean sings this soaring part, then it segues into a moody sample of some Hungarian rock band from the '70s. It literally gives me goosebumps. It's like the visuals at the end of the new Superman movie—just overwhelmingly incredible. I played it over and over.

Some people ask why he's screaming on "I Am a God." It's not like a James Brown scream—it's a real scream of terror. It makes my hair stand on end. He knows they could turn on him in two seconds. By "they" I mean the public, the fickle audience. He could kill Taylor Swift and it would all be over.

The juxtaposition of vocal tones on "Blood on the Leaves" is incredible—that pitched-up sample of Nina Simone singing "Strange Fruit" doing a call-and-response with Kanye's very relaxed Autotuned voice. That is fascinating, aurally, nothing short of spectacular. And holy shit, it's so gorgeous rhythmically, where sometimes the vocal parts are matched and sometimes they clash. He's so sad in this song. He's surrounded by everyone except the one he wants—he had this love ripped away from him, before he even knew it. "I know there ain't nothing wrong with me . . . something strange is happening." Well, surprise, surprise—welcome to the real world, Kanye.

It's fascinating—it's very poignant, but there's nothing warm about it, sonically— it's really electronic, and after a while, his voice and the synth are virtually the same. But I don't think that's a statement about anything—it's just something he heard, and then he made it so you could hear it too.

At so many points in this album, the music breaks into this melody, and it's glorious—I mean, *glorious*. He has to know that—why else would you do that? He's not just banging his head against the wall, but he acts as though he is. He doesn't want to seem precious, he wants to keep his cred.

And sometimes it's like a synth orchestra. I've never heard anything like it—I've heard people try to do it but no way, it just comes out tacky. Kanye is *there*. It's like his video for "Runaway," with the ballet dancers—it was like, look out, this guy is making *connections*. You could bring one into the other—ballet into hip-hop—they're not actually contradictory, and he knew that, he could see it immediately. He obviously can hear that all styles are the same, somewhere deep in their heart, there's a connection. It's all the same shit, it's *all music*—that's what makes him great. If you like sound, listen to what he's giving you. Majestic and inspiring.

WRITING PROMPT: THE BLIND REVIEW

Album reviews should not be limited to music you know you love or know you hate. Challenge yourself to explore the unknown. Write a review of an album that you know absolutely nothing about by an artist you have never even heard of, music that has never crossed your path before. Try looking to genres you are unfamiliar with.

Write an album review of approximately 1000 words that describes your impressions of an album by an artist you are completely unfamiliar with.

How to find an album you've never heard of? Go outside. Go to a record store, library, Goodwill or garage sale and find something that catches your eye. Maybe it's the album artwork that draws you in. Maybe it's a band name. If exploring in the real world isn't an option, dig on iTunes, Spotify, Pandora or other sites.

First listen to the record from start to finish at least twice and begin to write down your first impressions. How does it feel? What does it sound like? What does it remind you of? Then write up your notes into a short paragraph that just describes the music.

Okay, now you can Google. Use the incredibly vast resources available to you to find out about this artist. Where are they located? What's their story?

Now revisit the paragraph you wrote about the music and combine what you've learned about the artist with your first impressions.

Consider these questions while writing:

1. How will you succinctly introduce this record?

2. How does this record fit within its genre or, more broadly, pop or rock history?

3. Where would you want to listen to this record?

WRITING PROMPT: MAKE IT BETTER

Do you get infuriated when an album you love is trashed by a critic? Is your knowledge of the artist and their influences superior? Do you disagree with almost everything the critic writes?

Find a negative, wrong-headed review of an album you love and make it right.

First think of a recent album that you love. Then search for album reviews on sites like *Rolling Stone*, Spin and Pitchfork. Keep reading reviews until you find one that rubs you the wrong way. You may not find something on your first try so keep a few albums in mind. Once you've located the piece that truly raises your hackles, read it three times through so you know it well enough to use as the scaffolding for your positive review. Take notes about what's wrong with it. Look at your notes and begin formulating your response. Your review should mirror precisely the structure and tone of the original piece but the language, observations and opinions should be your own.

THE GO-BETWEENS

HOW TO MAKE CONTACTS

Now more than ever, people are readily accessible, and rare is the writer worth listening to or the editor worth writing for who is not open to hearing from young talents. In fact, it has been my experience that the most talented writers I've met have been the most open and nurturing (while mediocre talents often are threatened and not at all eager to share with their peers, young or old). As for pitching an editor, the golden currency remains the idea that nobody else has given them. This always will get a good editor's attention, if not the first time, than the second, or third. Give them something they didn't know they needed or wanted until they got it from YOU.—**Jim DeRogatis**, author, co-host of *Sound Opinions*, and lecturer at Columbia College Chicago

I know nobody ever wants to hear this, but the publishing world is one of the few places where internships remain super-valuable. Getting your work in front of an editor (or any employer) is one thing, but getting your personality in front of them on a regular basis is infinitely more valuable.—**Kyle Anderson**, senior writer, *Entertainment Weekly*

Know your stuff—stay informed. If you are interested in working for a publication, make sure that you know all about it. Fundamentally this is something that if it's the right fit, you won't have to even think about it—that's just how it'll be. However it is amazing the amount of people who say they like a magazine/blog/band when they actually have taken no time at all to find out anything about it.—**Pete Astor**, writer, academic, musician

Go to a lot of shows. You'll inevitably meet people. And do a lot of interviews. And talk to background sources. That's how you meet people. And go to parties.—**Michael Azerrad**, author, journalist and Editor-in-Chief of the *Talkhouse*

Call them. Because no one thinks to do that anymore, and email is too easy to ignore. Otherwise, festivals are an obvious place to schmooze. Attend the panels, chat people up afterward.—**Michael Barclay**, freelance writer/broadcaster, co-author, *Have Not Been the Same: The CanRock Renaissance 1985–1995*

I was often put in touch with key figures during interviews. Either the subject might say, "You know, you've really got to talk to so and so, I've got his contact info," or you can ask who you're interviewing if there's anyone else she or he thinks you should talk to.—**Joe Bonomo**, music columnist, *The Normal School*, and Associate Professor of English at Northern Illinois University

I'm far too timid and full of self-doubt for blanket hustles. I'd wholeheartedly recommend approaching those you truly admire, however. With people I respect and whose work I have genuine affection for, it never feels like I'm ever blowing smoke for the sake of a paycheck. As for how to reach them, you have to look for and respect the procedures that are in place at that individual's establishment; if he or she is publicly active in any social media outlets, I'd consider that an acceptable route. Be specific with any compliments, and be ready with relevant ideas should the opportunity to share them arise. Sincere warmth and enthusiasm are attractive in any interaction.—**Phillip Crandall**, author of the **33⅓** book on Andrew W.K.'s *I Get Wet*

This is undoubtedly the hardest part of the job, and it's what eventually tired me out. The hustle is vital to your success. You need to cold call, pitch, send samples, and then cold call, pitch, and send samples. If that doesn't work, try cold calling, pitching, and sending samples. Don't get discouraged until you'd rather have a real job.—**Matthew Gasteier**, **33⅓** author

Twitter seems particularly invaluable in this sphere—the quickest way to be a smart, funny, perceptive writer and get your stuff in front of people in a way that doesn't seem forced or pandering. But generally start your own blog, Tumblr, etc., hone your own voice, and gradually mix into the circles you're looking to infiltrate.—**Rob Harvilla**, Deputy/Culture Editor, *Deadspin*

If you live in one of the fleshpots, hang out with music geeks and network through them. It has worked for me in New York and Los Angeles. Beyond that, in spite of my own reservations and innate diffidence I've submitted pitches to magazines I enjoy, without the benefit of an introduction or recommendation. I've been ignored often enough, but occasionally (as with The *Wire*, mentioned above) it leads to a lengthy and mutually profitable relationship.—**Richard Henderson**, music writer and **33⅓** author

There's nothing wrong with the direct approach, as long as it's done sensibly. I've commissioned many pitches that have arrived out of the blue, because they were well written, well thought-out and potentially interesting. Come up with some feature ideas that are tailored to the editor or publication you want to write for. Phrase them so that your chosen editor can say 'yes' without committing him or herself to anything. ("It looks as though I'll be visiting Snorksville, Arizona next month. If I can get an interview with legendary dronecore kazooist 'Knees' McLeod while I'm there, would this be of interest?") An editor you don't know will want to see the completed feature before he or she makes a firm decision about publishing it. You're much less likely to get a positive response if you simply send out an email telling people you're a writer looking for work, especially if you blind copy it to everyone from Jazzwise to Metal Hammer. If you think up a great idea for a feature, most editors will think it fair to let you have a crack at writing it, even if they don't know you. But good ideas are valuable and scarce, and no editor is likely to hand out their own ideas to an unknown author.—**Sam Inglis**, Features Editor, *Sound On Sound* magazine

Flatter them! Find their email address, let them know you like what they do—and seriously, there's never any reason to contact an editor unless you like what they do—and ask if they'd be willing to meet up for coffee or beer. These are not rock stars. These are generally lonely people who would love to meet you and shoot the shit. I think that so long as you're not pushy and annoying, but just legitimately interested in what someone is doing, then most of the time they'll be happy to make your acquaintance. Also: internships.—**Casey Jarman**, Managing Editor, the *Believer*

I've taken a risk on an unsolicited email, simply because of the writer's enthusiasm and drive. (Though, if the email sounds like a cookie-cutter letter sent to various publications, I tend to ignore unless I feel there's something they can offer specifically to TMT.)—**Marvin Lin**, Editor-in-Chief, Tiny Mix Tapes

My original technique, done without any really thought other than a form of desperation, was to write something that I thought no one else in the world could write, and send it off to the places and people I wanted to work for. The first thing I wrote—a fanzine called *Out There* I wrote, designed and edited myself—I sent to the editor of the *NME*, a great journalist called Nick Logan who later went on to invent *Smash Hits, The Face* and *Arena*—with a note saying "I can do better than you." He actually contacted me, probably to check if there was any truth in this ridiculous boast. The *NME* was then the greatest music paper in the world, in terms of its energy, wit, photography, taste, influence, idealism etc.—**Paul Morley**, writer and critic

I work quite a bit for a website called Silent Radio. They have a fabulous resource of live and recorded music to review and have a very egalitarian, open approach to new writers. It's Manchester-focused in terms of the live side but they review recorded music from all over the world. They're a wonderful bunch of music lovers—as many music teams are. Tell them Simon sent you.—**Simon A. Morrison**, music journalist and Programme Leader for Music Journalism at the University of Chester

First, I can tell you how not to do it. Do not reach out to editors you don't know at all via email or social media and say "I'd love to write for your publication, here's my resume," or "can you give me some advice on how to break into music writing," because they are very, very busy people and have no incentive whatsoever to spend their limited time on helping someone they've never heard of out of the goodness of their hearts. It would be great if just expressing passion for music writing was enough, but it's just not. The number one way to get an editor's attention is to have a *good idea*. This does NOT mean "X artist has an album coming out, I'd like to interview them." It's astonishing how many times writers new and old make pitches like this to editors they've rarely or never worked with, and an editor has no reason to award that story to someone unproven. Make a real pitch with a time hook, an interesting angle, a reason people should want to read about it, and a reason people should want to read about it from you specifically. Editors are always hungry for ideas, not just warm bodies. Practically speaking, the reality is that it's always better to have a personal recommendation or connection, rather than sending cold emails, which editors may not even read if they don't recognize your name. This doesn't mean you have to have gone to college with an editor or know their sister. It means you should be willing to do the work to earn the recommendations— spend time in your local scene and interview smaller artists on your own site, pitch smaller publications and do a good job, apply for jobs in related fields and earn your contacts.—**Evie Nagy**, *Fast Company* staff writer, former Editor at *Billboard* and *Rolling Stone*

Join the fray, hope to get noticed, but don't make a point of self-promoting. Offer things to the stream, hope people recognize them, but don't advertise.— **Chris Ott**, 33⅓ author

Publications have a clear idea of what their identity is, and for the most part writers are used to strengthen that identity.—**Oliver Primus**, Site Editor, *The 405*

There are many, many music websites that don't pay that are open to anyone, and these can be good places to learn your craft. I work with many great writers who started out writing for free for these sites. With a smaller item, I've taken chances on unknown writers many times.—**Mark Richardson**, Editor-in-Chief, Pitchfork

Write. It's the only way. Write as much as you can, then send out the links to people you hope will read. Assume most of them won't have time to read it, because most of them won't. But keep writing. Even if you never accumulate any readers, you'll always have your writing.—**Rob Sheffield**, writer, *Rolling Stone*

There's nothing better than a polite, well-worded email that's full of original ideas, and that demonstrates an awareness of the publication that the writer is contacting. Trying to write an email that (you think) makes you the next Lester Bangs—bad idea. An email full of spelling and grammar errors—bad idea. Contacting a site like The Quietus suggesting that you want to cover landfill indie—bad idea. Pitching the same opinion piece as you've read elsewhere ten minutes before—bad idea. It's amazing how many people make these mistakes. Oh, and don't have a wacky email address. It looks really unprofessional.—**Luke Turner**, Associate Editor, The Quietus

Think of something you're genuinely, deeply interested in writing about. Start a blog. Write about it there on a regular basis: every day or every week. Make it known to your friends. Keep to your schedule for a few years, and you will either get bored of it or get really, really good. If the latter happens, employers will find you.—**Douglas Wolk**, freelance arts journalist

Join Twitter, follow editors and writers of major publications, tweet them when you have something relevant to say.—**Alex Young**, founder and publisher, Consequence of Sound

CHAPTER 2
THE LIVE REVIEW

INTRODUCTION

Meeting the deadline for daily newspaper print reviews by rushing into the newsroom and commandeering a formerly futuristic-looking desktop computer with a convex aquarium screen and sad, blinking green cursor sounds awfully quaint these days. But it wasn't so long ago that music reviewers scrambled into the office late with a handful of scrawled notes, fed copy into a machine and put a piece to bed by midnight before the presses started rolling. Even if the image of a reviewer on deadline in the middle of the night conjures up nothing so much as an exotic dead past—the moody black and white newsroom of the *New York Mail* in *It Happened One Night*—rather than the present reality of posting from home or a handheld, the job is nevertheless much the same. Here's Kevin J.H. Dettmar to provide continuity: "I got back from the gig at midnight; I had to sit down and write the full thing (~ 650 words) in one sitting, in a couple of hours, before going to bed; it had to be uploaded to the *LA Weekly* online editing site before 8:30 a.m. the next morning." The routine of seeing a show and writing a review on deadline brings out the old school journalist in many music writers: "I have carried a notebook in my back pocket since I was a child—I'm always writing *everything* down if I want to remember it. I do not turn on my phone during a rock show, for any reason—the very idea of glowing screens at a rock show makes me weep." I like Rob Sheffield even more, if such were possible, picturing him scribbling with an actual writing utensil in the dark and especially for keeping his phone off during a show.

Two of the three live reviews collected here were written and published before *everything changed*, but the most recent one, by Zach Schonfeld on Spiritualized at Webster Hall in 2013, doesn't look much different in this era of the virtual and remote than strong live reviews from the pre-digital decades before it. These writers did their homework before the shows—or knew enough about their subjects not to need to do much homework at all—and provide context for the review that takes account of everything from the arc of a given artist's career to the psychological place-holding an artist does (or doesn't do) for their audience. You can put down parts of a live review beforehand—the facts, the album, the history, the personalities—but what makes a live review spark is the unexpected formulation at which the writer arrives *because* of the experience itself. You can hear that arrived-at language in Paul Morley's description of Joy Division as a "powerful act of make believe." Or in Charles Aaron's brutal but well-turned come-back as he reduces Courtney Love's debacle in Cleveland to this sharp and terminal barb: "Hole came off like a skinny-tie bar band fronted by Nancy Spungen." Best of all might be a view of something essential that can only be the dividend of seeing a band live, like this perception from Zach Schonfeld: "It's just the tenderer songs where the band sometimes runs into trouble live—it's too big to approximate the tortured intimacy Spaceman manages on record, so it settles for sentimentality instead."—MW

EXPERT ADVICE FROM OUR WRITERS

My most recent piece wasn't entirely typical: it was a concert review, which meant that when I got back from the gig at midnight, I had to sit down and write the full thing (~650 words) in one sitting, in a couple of hours, before going to bed; it had to be uploaded to the *LA Weekly* online editing site before 8:30 a.m. the next morning. The process proper started early in the concert: thinking about organizing concepts, what the performer (Neil Young) was doing with his set list, what the show, at this point in his career, meant. It quickly became clear that he was doing solo acoustic versions of his own work, and that of his contemporaries whom he admires. So that was my lede ("Neil Young conducted a master class on (North) American songwriting last night . . ."), and I mentioned a few of the more salient examples from the show.—**Kevin J. H. Dettmar**, author, 33⅓ book, Gang of Four's *"Entertainment!"*

Have fun. Pay attention. If it's worth remembering, you'll remember it later. Stay sober.—**Michael Barclay**, freelance writer/broadcaster, co-author, *Have Not Been the Same: The CanRock Renaissance 1985–1995*

I'm at the point where I can enjoy a beer or two at a show and still get the job done. I'm always taking copious notes, especially if it's at a festival. I try not to write while tipsy, but I never have any trouble doing reporting while tipsy.—**Kyle Anderson**, senior writer, *Entertainment Weekly*

When I reviewed live shows I would occasionally make notes surreptitiously, as I probably felt like it was disrespectful to what one should 'do' at a show. Drinking, yes, partying at a show is something I think of as involving lots of talking and hanging out and missing the band—there are several fantastic bands that I "saw" but didn't actually watch! One thing I do remember once when The Weather Prophets were playing in Nottingham was seeing the journalist who'd come up from London to review one of our out of town shows, dancing manically at the front, clearly in some kind of transcendent trance-like state (or so we thought). Anyway, we looked forward to the review in the next week's *NME* only to find a very sober and positive review of our show, but one which bore no traces whatsoever of the reviewer's behavior and transport at the gig itself. Odd!—**Pete Astor**, writer, academic, musician

I don't take notes, but prefer to use the show to formulate impressions, responses, even sentences that I then try to remember. It's important to remain alert to what's going on, and not to try and capture it in (usually inadequate) written form.—**Nick Attfield**, music academic

I do take notes. I think it was Robert Christgau who described the various zones of the audience at a show. I'm generally in the second zone—not right up front, but close enough that I can feel like I'm in the moment, as opposed to being at the back, looking on. But you won't see me slam-dancing in the pit or anything.—**Michael Azerrad**, author, journalist and Editor-in-Chief of the *Talkhouse*

I'd be the roving reporter with a Moleskine notebook and self-imposed two-drink limit. I wouldn't want to read the dreck I'd come up with if I let reckless abandon reign. I probably wouldn't want to read anyone else's for that matter either.—**Phillip Crandall**, author of the **33⅓** book on Andrew W.K.'s *I Get Wet*

I let the evening "wash over me." It's nice if I can make sketches, but usually that's pretty difficult (darkness, colliding bodies, etc.).—**Marty Davis**, comic book creator

I try to experience the same emotions as the rest of the audience on the assumption that my readers would have too had they been there.—**Jim Fusilli**, Rock and Pop Critic, *The Wall Street Journal*, Editor, ReNewMusic.net

I think live shows are a difficult thing to write about, because you have to formulate a thesis from something very fleeting and often underwhelming. I try to have the exact experience I would have if I was going to the show on my own dime and think about what I would want to know about the concert if I was reading the review.—**Matthew Gasteier**, 33⅓ author

I take notes on my phone, typing out stage banter verbatim in particular, which makes me look like a clod, it's true. I started writing for the daily Columbus paper, overnight reviews, which means I'm full-on writing the review in real time on my phone as it's happening, which is not the best way to experience a show, but oh well.—**Rob Harvilla**, Deputy/Culture Editor, *Deadspin*

My favorite show reviews read more like embedded journalism. A list of songs played and what the band wore is not very compelling, but a great narrative piece about the crowd, the space, and the energy of a room can be wonderful to read.—**Matt LeMay**, senior contributor, Pitchfork

In a live setting, I'm more interested in my perceptual reaction to the surrounding environment than the technical aspects of the musical performance, which in turn allows me to enjoy some beers, as I normally would. But this certainly isn't how I think everyone should cover a live show—it just works for me.—**Marvin Lin**, Editor-in-Chief, Tiny Mix Tapes

I never took notes, as I always thought that first of all I was there as a fan, observer, witness, and my review was always about what I remembered about the night after the fact, rather than what I recorded at the time. I always thought that memory was a much about what music was about as anything, and even if you could not remember the facts, figures and songs played, the fact of not remembering was as much a comment on the show as anything. If you drank, partied, collapsed, went missing, invaded the stage, etc, that is what happened, and what is what you are reviewing—again, the context of the music more than the music itself, and it is these other things, the moments around the music, the experience of the fan and audience, that has made pop music what it is. The music is the beginning, it is the soundtrack, it reflects, and inspires, changes in social and individual behavior, and the best music writing is about the other things that happen around and because of the music.—**Paul Morley**, writer and critic

For live reviews, I tend to open an Evernote page on my iPhone. Then I jot down things that occur to me during the gig—things about the set list, the crowd, the venue, moments that happen, just things that interest me. I may also try to put together some phrases, or descriptions that occur to me, that might pin down the music. When I get home the Evernote will be on my MacBook in my study, via the magic of the cloud, and I will usually hit play on the artist's work, perhaps via Spotify. Then I will use my notes as the skeleton around which to construct the body of the review. That way there's never a blank page. The blank page is the enemy of the journalist. I always saw the process like a potter at the wheel. You need to chuck some clay onto the wheel, any old how. *Then* you can start to sculpt it into something worthwhile.—**Simon A. Morrison**, music journalist and Programme Leader for Music Journalism at the University of Chester

I treat it like any other show. Anything you can't remember the next morning wasn't important. And that may mean the entire show was unimportant.—**Chris Ott**, 33⅓ author

I don't think it's impossible to strike a balance between critical observation and being present in the moment. If I do take notes on a show, it's usually right after, in a mad scramble before the mood wears off, and the notes mostly consist of impressions, passing thoughts, and as thorough a setlist as I can remember. It's more important for me to put something about mood and atmosphere before it wears off.—**Luis Sanchez**, 33⅓ author

I'm always taking notes, whether I'm planning on writing or not. I have carried a notebook in my back pocket since I was a child—I'm always writing *everything* down if I want to remember it. I do not turn on my phone during a rock show, for any reason—the very idea of glowing screens at a rock show makes me weep. I do not necessarily believe in keeping a remote distance from the show—I think you can probably get a truer account if you enter into the spirit of the festivities. But obviously you want to be careful what you indulge in, whether you're writing or not, and you need to think in terms of your writing energy, e.g., you don't want to get dehydrated at a festival, or in the sunlight, or if you have to get up to write or travel or function in the morning. So it depends on the show. One thing I have learned though: once you turn 23, stay the hell out of the pit.—**Rob Sheffield**, writer, *Rolling Stone*

I do take notes at live shows, but I take notes everywhere—at dinner, in movies, on the bus. I always have a pad and paper, and I use it a lot. I sometimes take notes on my phone, too. There's been plenty of good writing about music and culture by people who have been inebriated, but I just haven't done that myself.—**Marc Weidenbaum**, author of *Selected Ambient Works Volume II* (**33⅓**, 2014)

It depends. I do usually prefer going to an event I'm covering alone; that way it's a lot easier to eavesdrop, have a casual conversation with a stranger, or generally take the pulse of the crowd. Your sense of observation is more heightened when you're alone.—**Lindsay Zoladz**, Associate Editor, Pitchfork

PAUL MORLEY ON JOY DIVISION AT UNIVERSITY COLLEGE LONDON

Joy Division, University of London (8 February 1980)*

I didn't know which way to turn. In every corner of the second floor of the anonymous university building there seemed to be some group demanding attention.

Blackpool's Section 25 I missed—PiL-Lite, somebody said, whether as insult or not I don't know. And Honey Bane's Fatal Microbes I couldn't stand, though I wanted to. The Smirks I forgot all about. Killing Joke were the worst, heroically adding nothing at all to the latent seventies post punk beats and bashings one or two turned into their art.

I wandered around looking for a time machine. There's one. The sign said the future was none of my business, but I found the present for the first time all evening.

I walked through a door and Joy Division had started their first song. Live entertainment. Start here.

Joy Division at the University of London was a sell out. The guest list was huge. Their impact was substantial.

Seeing Joy Division, if you are properly tuned, is a jarring experience. The music keeps coming, trenchant, serene, steady, hard, almost an orgiastic celebration of the decent fact that Joy Division have arrived at a noise and form that is distinctive, instinctive and immeasurably dynamic. The introversion and singularity of the four musicians is fitfully held under control, and private music is forced out into the open. The tension is startling.

The presentation is as grey and bland as the noise is volatile and deeply black— singer Ian Curtis' comical trapped butterfly flapping the only real stage movement, a visual representation of the struggle inherent in Division's music. As Richard Jobson said, Division's music is genuinely violent, and it's the violence of beauty rooted in beastly desire, the violence of breakdown, inhibition, failure, fatalism . . .

It could be vanity, it could be impatience, even nervousness, but during a Joy Division set, outside of the songs, you'll be lucky to hear more than two or three words. Hello and goodbye. No introductions, no promotion. Good or bad? Inside the songs, careful words—setting, situations, dilemmas, images that are primitive and anxious. Joy Division are a powerful act of make believe, their songs like desperate bits of nightmares, clearly drawn, potent and personal. But Joy Division's dreams

*Morley, Paul. *Joy Division: Piece by Piece: Writing about Joy Division 1977–2007*. London: Plexus, 2008. 514–521. Reprinted with permission.

are the inescapable places where we live. It's all suggestion rather than direction or dogma.

Joy Division sped through their early songs, with intensity of feeling and concentration, and without totally relenting the shadows and suspense. The group pointedly proved that they still work well away from the re-established mainstream, forging ahead down the same slippy corridor of experimentations. They played more new songs than old (untitled but I guessed two were 'Sound of Music' and 'Colony'— they didn't play 'She's Lost Control' or 'Transmission' or 'Disorder' or . . . name your favourite) and these new songs give no suggestion of Division stagnation.

These new songs show that Division's music is as natural as PiL's, not held down by the grey hand of limitation and expectation. Division aren't conforming to pressure or pattern. The songs revealed a new extension of their language and possibility, and considering that live the songs are true caricatures of recorded versions, how these new ones will end up is a good mystery. But Joy Division are still coming up with new ways to alter the shape, emphasis and texture of their music. The new songs are as organized, hostile and spacious as the last set, but there's all round intensification, further emphasis on the lead bass and the active drums, even an overall simplification.

The songs have extreme, para-melodies, and some have no bass, some no guitars. Synthesisers and bass with the drums, or two guitars. The new single 'Love Will Tear Us Apart' is one hell of a 'classic'—bass, synth, drums, voice, Curtis hugging a white guitar up to his chest but rarely using it. The song's mobility and fluidity shows how much potential there is in the simple contrasting and connecting of instruments that Division use. It's a staggeringly melodic and momentous piece.

For 'Isolation' they have the same instrumentation, but it's more withdrawn and estranged; a song they wrote only days before that reveals Numan and Foxx as true fools.

The full new introduction of synthesiser has not damaged the coherence and balance of the music in any way, it simply increases the amount of mood, atmosphere, ephemeral terror Division are capable of achieving. The encore is a confident, compelling utterly withdrawn ballad, something like a dislocated and depraved improvement upon Bowie's 'Heroes'. So impressive.

Part of Joy Division's 'success' is the breadth and certainty of the reactions they inspire. For this performance there were three obvious ones: love, penetration and stimulation is one all in its own, and if I wasn't tied down by language and responsibility I could attempt to explain. Simple frustration; that the group didn't lay out for selfish delectation their eloquent standards. How ironical! And old fashioned derision. A dissenter behind me, with a spiteful snort, reckoned Joy Division are the new Pink Floyd.

Joy Division's music is physical and lucid, music about uncontrollable emotions, impulses, prejudices, fears. The group have turned inarticulacy and vagueness into concrete, disturbing impressions of the most degenerate, deepest desires.

It's simple music, but not simple-minded; cryptic but not impenetrable.

As Danny Baker said to me, Joy Division are due some sort of backlash, but he's not the one to do it. If the group had shown the slightest indication of slackening or straightening out I would have attacked. But they are now better than they have ever been.

Joy Division will tear you apart. Still.

ZACH SCHONFELD ON SPIRITUALIZED AT WEBSTER HALL

Spiritualized at New York's Webster Hall (10 September 2013)*

It's easy to forget, given all the strings and pomp and pleas to a higher power, but Spiritualized is a rock band. Not the way, say, Vampire Weekend is a rock band, but a *rock* band—the bracing, psychedelic kind, given to brash, ear-splitting freakouts and thickly coated drones and harmonica squalls. You know, the blues—fed through a gospel choir and beamed down from Mars.

That side of J. Spaceman and Co. was largely absent from 2008's otherwise solid *Songs in A&E*, a literal recovery effort. It made a return to the group's live shows the following year, when they began performing 1997 masterpiece *Ladies & Gentlemen We Are Floating in Space* in its entirety. And it highlighted the group's lengthy Tuesday night set at Webster Hall, deafening 2,500 or so fans with recent cuts ("Hey Jane"), '90s epics ("I Think I'm In Love"), and much in between. Spaceman may be a comically uncharismatic frontman (seated on a stool, he neither removed his dark shades nor spoke a single word to the audience). But his command of musical texture, of the sheer potential of sonic expression to capture the familiar extremities of human emotion, was of far more interest.

Curiously, *Songs in A&E* seems to have been purged from the group's (frustratingly rigid) setlist altogether. Its material was replaced by three of the more raucous cuts from last year's *Sweet Heart Sweet Light*. "Hey Jane" was the best of the bunch, a fiercely energized guitar-rock number buoyed by a steady Krautrock groove and Doggen's nagging lead riff. So, too, did a surprising amount of material from 2003's *Amazing Grace* make the cut, perhaps in the knowledge that that album's passable attempt at stripped down garage-rock fares better onstage than on record—"Rated X" made for a thrillingly eerie interlude and "Cheapster" positively surged, though two back-up vocalists weren't quite enough to capture the gospel-tinged grandiosity that "Lord Let It Rain On Me" demands.

Speaking of which, *Ladies & Gentlemen We Are Floating in Space* continues to garner the biggest crowd reactions: "Electricity" offered just what its title promises, amply fulfilling J. Spaceman's scorched-earth blues fantasies, and a marathon-length "I Think I'm In Love" made me wish I hadn't missed the *Ladies & Gentlemen* tour, despite some needlessly cornball blues flourishes on the guitars. It's just the tenderer

*Schonfeld, Zach. "Live Review: Spiritualized at New York's Webster Hall (9/10)." *Consequence of Sound*. September 11, 2013. Reprinted with permission.

songs where the band sometimes runs into trouble live—it's too big to approximate the tortured intimacy Spaceman manages on record, so it settles for sentimentality instead.

Then again, you can't fault J. Spaceman for not quite capturing those astounding vocal harmonies on *Ladies & Gentlemen*'s heavenly title track—no one can, except a brokenhearted J. Spaceman in 1997. Acknowledging his applause after an encore that offered a lovely detour into 1995's *Pure Phase* ("All of My Tears"), the frontman kept his silence and simply applauded at the crowd—perhaps because music of such labored scope and drama demands an equally vast audience to take it all in and echo it right back.

Setlist:

Here It Comes (The Road, Let's Go Down)

Hey Jane

Electricity

Home of the Brave

Lord Let It Rain On Me

Perfect Miracle

Rated X

Oh Baby

Ladies and Gentlemen We Are Floating in Space

She Kissed Me (It Felt Like a Hit)

Let's Dance

Cheapster

I Am What I Am

So Long You Pretty Thing

I Think I'm In Love

Take Your Time

Encore:

All of My Tears

CHARLES AARON ON HOLE AT
NAUTICA STAGE

Courtney Love at Nautica Stage, Cleveland, Ohio (29 August 1994)*

Pale arms outstretched, offering herself up for crucifixion, or a pie in the face, or a big hug, Courtney Love exclaimed, "Fuck with me, fuck with me. It's the only thing I like!" The audience members, who had been standing in a snaking, endless line with visions of Trent moshing in their dyed-black dread heads, murmured. A few hoots. A desultory heckle. We were only three songs into Hole's first American show since the suicide of Love's husband, Kurt Cobain, and since the heroin overdose of bassist Kristen Pfaff; the band's first gig as opening act for Nine Inch Nails' sold-out, post-Woodstock tour, and already the ride was getting bumpy.

Nobody wanted to play Love's co-dependent game of "I'm rubber, you're glue, fuck you." The few Hole fans—high-school girls huddled together to the right of the mosh pit—were simply awestruck. Everybody else acted like the band's appearance must be a gesture of mercy. Few seemed familiar with the album *Live Through This*. And the setting, a concrete outdoor amphitheater in a riverfront development mallplex, only further deadened the atmosphere. There was no moment of silence for Kurt, as there had been at Lollapalooza in Philadelphia. Just silent curiosity as Love sauntered onstage, wearing a black car-coat and carrying a small black handbag. Hole immediately roared into "Beautiful Son," a punk rant about how Cobain looked great in a dress, and how moms are the biggest starfuckers. Mid-song, Love quit playing guitar and took off her coat with a flourish, revealing a gray, clingy top, gray minidress, and gray stockings that stopped mid-thigh. The band lurched a bit, but her voice quickly regained its raging wail and the high-school girls pogoed madly.

Unfortunately, it turned out to be a promising opening to a sordidly sad B-movie. After the feedback subsided, Love nervously blurted out, "You know, I punched a guy on the plane." The crowd tittered, confused. Love wandered away from the mike. "Miss World" was a tentative, raggedy mess, and when she changed the coda from, "I am the girl you know / Can't look you in the eye" to "I am the girl you want / So sick that I'll just die," it was obvious that she was not just nerve-wracked, but wracked in general. Playing so little that the soundman eventually turned her down and cranked up impassive guitarist Eric Erlandson, Love looked totally lost. She frantically took off her stockings during "Jennifer's Body," and after "Asking for It," cried out pitifully,

*Aaron, Charles. "Hole Rock Cleveland: Read SPIN's Somewhat Dismayed 1994 Live Review." *SPIN*. August 29, 1994. Reprinted with permission.

"Where are my boots?" With neither Erlandson nor new bassist Melissa Auf Der Maur, a timid 22-year-old from Montreal, able to take up the slack, Hole came off like a skinny-tie bar band fronted by Nancy Spungen.

The crowd got increasingly impatient, but Love staggered on. "So, you guys wanna talk to me for awhile? Trent'll be out here in a minute with his black rubber, so why don't you guys just talk to me, go ahead." Waiting for a tragicomic rimshot, she added, "How many of you have read *Valley of the Dolls*?" A guy yelled, "I wanna fuck you, Courtney!" She shot back, "I wanna fuck you, too, but only if you're a water sign." The band jerked into "Gutless," with Love barely struggling through the first verse before the chorus overran her. Then, without a word, she put down her guitar, yanked up her top, and began to pose in her black bra. As the crowd looked on, stunned, she tore off the bra, thrust out her chest, and slurred, "Now you know why I get all the guys, you fucking shitbags." The Trent teens were too flabbergasted to catcall. And there she stood, for what seemed like an eternity—a voluptuous car wreck, a pathetic fuck-doll, a body to die for. It was like watching your sister strip for a stag party. From then on, the show was a long, painful non sequitur. "I just got offered the Guess? jeans campaign … That's so retarded, those stupid pants." Later, as if gazing at the ghost of Kurt hovering above the audience, she said: "I give you a morning blow job, I make your fucking breakfast, so leave me alone."

As "Softer, Softest" fell apart, she reverted almost completely to her stripper days, sticking out her belly and writhing in spazzy circles. Threatening to play Echo & the Bunnymen covers, she cracked, "So, do you guys think Trent is a top or a bottom?" During "Doll Parts," after moaning, "He only loves those things because he loves to see me break" (instead of "them"), she wobbled back from the mike almost punch-drunk. It was horrific and mesmerizing. By this time, the band had bailed, and Love was alone, strumming slower and slower, singing "Someday you will ache like I ache," again and again, her voice a faint sob. Roadies milled around. She finally took off the guitar, stumbled over to a huge speaker, and leaned into it like she was about to pass out. Then, while being led off by an assistant, she stepped back, pulled up her top one last time, and flipped us off with both hands. A guy with a video camera zoomed in. A kid near me yelled, "That's why they call you a whore!" His friends, girls and guys, giggled sheepishly.

If you cared at all, it was devastating. And there was nobody with whom to share your dismay, just a lot of oblivious zitfaces waiting around for Nine Inch Nails to erase Love's tits and pathos with their precisely packaged anguish. I thought about what I'd say to her if I had the gall to get angry. Melodramatic junk like: Jesus, Courtney! What? What?! Do you want us to feel every single fucking wince of your pain on every single fucking song to the point where we don't even remember which song is which anymore? Do you want us to have nightmares about pulling you off ledges weeping and naked, and staring into your eyes and seeing our own? Do you want all your reviews to read like half-assed scripts for a punk-rock *A Star Is Born*? Is too much sadness never enough?

But melodrama is a luxury most of us don't have. And besides, maybe we do want Love to stick her ring finger in our mouths so we can suck her dry. I hope there's more to it than that. But right now I'm not so sure.

WRITING PROMPT: THE LIVE REVIEW ON DEADLINE

1. Find out what local shows are scheduled over the next couple of days and commit to going to one even if it features a band or artist you don't know or even particularly like.

2. Research the band or artist and listen to as much music as you can before you attend the show.

3. Tell your mother, significant other, or special music friend you'll be writing a review and see if he or she is willing to be on the receiving end of your review when it's done. If you're writing for a class, your professor/lecturer/teacher will play this important role (and grade you down if you're late).

4. Clear your evening entirely to attend the show and write about it afterwards.

5. Attend the show as if you're *on assignment.*

6. Immediately following the show, set yourself up to write at home, at a coffeeshop, or elsewhere, allowing yourself only the most enabling distractions as you work.

7. Set an alarm for two hours and write a 650-word review of the concert. Make sure you've met your word count without exceeding it. When the alarm goes off, you're done: no more writing or editing.

8. Email your piece to your chosen or assigned recipient from #3, completing the illusion that you've met a hard and fast deadline for a demanding editor.

THE GO-BETWEENS

**THE FIVE THINGS EVERY MUSIC WRITER
OR EDITOR NEEDS**

Brain, pen, paper, computer, tea.—**Pete Astor**, writer, academic, musician

Every writer, no matter the genre, needs two qualities that are often at odds with each other: endless patience and a relentless drive to get better.—**Bryan Charles**, writer and **33⅓** author

A reliable internet connection, a distraction-free workspace, good headphones, access to an all-you-can-eat streaming service like Spotify or Google Play All-Access (I've found this incredibly helpful for quickly absorbing an artist's stated influences), and a functional and up-to-date to-do list or deadline calendar.—**Matt LeMay**, senior contributor, Pitchfork

Too subjective. I dunno what works for anyone else. Brain. Hands are helpful. A Trust fund. A way to play music? A way to escape from music?—**Jessica Hopper**, Music Editor at *Rookie Magazine*, and Senior Editor, the *Pitchfork Review*

Humility is one, and not bullshit Hollywood humility either. That's gotta be genuine. A good pair of headphones will take you far. Comfortable shoes. The willingness to be wrong, and also the drive to go to bat for stuff you believe in.—**Kyle Anderson**, senior writer, *Entertainment Weekly*

Just one, really: don't be conservative in your definition of "music." It seems that there's an easy answer to the question "what is music?", but this answer tends to fall apart on close examination, and disperses into all kinds of facets of experience and different stimuli. A favorite album, for instance, might be split into lots of meaningful fragments (the recorded sounds, the lyrics, the cover design, the images of the band, the reception of the band to that point, etc. etc.), all of which might be said to constitute the musical experience, and all of which are worth your inquiry.—**Nick Attfield**, music academic

1. An AP or Chicago style guide
2. Diligence

3. Integrity

4. Empathy

5. A trust fund

—**Michael Azerrad**, author, journalist and editor-in-chief of the *Talkhouse*

Curiosity. Poetry. Discipline. Punctuality. Shelving.—**Michael Barclay**, freelance writer/broadcaster, co-author, *Have Not Been the Same: The CanRock Renaissance 1985–1995*

Curiosity. Self-confidence. Patience. Tape or digi recorder. Ear plugs.—**Joe Bonomo**, music columnist, *The Normal School*, and Associate Professor of English at Northern Illinois University.

1. In this day and age, you need to be able to count to five ... maybe 10. Because the dominant form of the age isn't reviews or previews or features or interviews; it's listicles. Even newspapers' arts coverage is degenerating into list-age like "three new albums you need that were released today" and "six things you need to know about the Spappaly Borbly concert."

2. I think every really good music writer has a band or two or become their primary case study that eventually explains for them how the music industry works. Your fandom becomes your *de facto* master's thesis. Me, I love the Misfits. So if you want to understand the band's convoluted history, it leads to a lot of issues about record deals and how labels work, performance rights vs. publishing rights, the long tradition of bands continuing on well after the classic lineup shatters, etc. You always need to understand a lot to truly explain the circumstances that made the art possible. So look deeper into your favorite group's story and understand why it took all the weird twists, turns, and bounces it did.

3. Similarly, have an area of expertise. I'm not saying go to Wikipedia and memorize every fact about late-1980s crossover. But just learn something about the music you love. I love 1980s hardcore, but I was young at the time, and I didn't spend more than a few minutes passing through a scene. But I love that music, so I have researched it a lot. Even if you're not from a scene or of a scene, it's good to have a case study as a frame of reference. Eventually, whether it's socially or professionally, you will meet someone whom you really connect with because you care about the same thing. When you're dealing with artists, that share reference is often the difference between getting the same old interview, or really

hitting it off with a source, even if it's just for 20 minutes on a phone interview.

4. Have some standards. Everybody around you is going to do the job wrong. If you do it right, you will go places. And you'll have a portfolio that becomes a parachute when you get older and don't care about music as much, and you want to write about something else.

5. Have a vocabulary. Certain words and terms mean certain things—and this point is lost on many editors and writers and readers. "Out of print" generally means "no longer commercially produced in the country we live in"—not "extinct and not available in any way, shape, or form anywhere."

Know what "one-hit wonder" means. It doesn't mean "a band who had a big hit once, and where are those guys now?" From alt-weeklies to MTV, that term is abused with regularity. "Thrashy" doesn't mean "kinda fast and sorta, like, punkish." And don't describe metal fans as "pit-thrashin'," because nobody talks like that, especially metal people, who have never used that term in the history of the known universe. "Comeback album" does not mean "a pop star's first album since her last one, which was two years ago." And "unplugged" doesn't mean "acoustic."

And, again, have some damned standards: Traditionally, language is used to make specific points and convey information. In the age of driving web traffic, usage is increasingly vague and misleading. Whether they're acts of clickbaiting or dumbness, internet headlines routinely mischaracterize quotes, inaccurately paraphrase statements, and misuse specific terms, all to make readers click. Editors say they're doing what they need to do, or they argue it's a valid way to interpret the facts; I call it "lying."—**D.X. Ferris**, Ohio Society of Professional Journalists Reporter of the Year, Professor, **33⅓** author

Empathy, perspective, humility, an insatiable thirst for new music, and a cheap apartment.—**Matthew Gasteier**, **33⅓** author

I really don't know. You need tools to write but other than that I don't want to get too specific. I'm tempted to say ears. But on the other hand, I think you can understand a lot by not listening, just watching.– **Anthony Kwame Harrison**, popular music scholar, Virginia Tech

I believe Stephen King, ordinarily a writer not even on my radar, has supplied at least twice the five rules requested. "Adverbs are not your friend," that's a good one from him. Otherwise, a solid thesaurus/dictionary, not just whatever's bundled with your word processor. Humility is a must, by which I mean willingness to draw the curtain between yourself and your published words. Good lighting and a chair with decent lumbar support. I don't believe deathless prose is forged on the couch.—**Richard Henderson**, music writer and **33⅓** author

Some means of taking notes or recording interviews. A good editor. Luck. Time. Ears.—**Sam Inglis**, Features Editor, *Sound On Sound* magazine

1. Patience
2. Empathy
3. A sense of humor
4. A mean streak
5. An addictive personality

—**Casey Jarman**, Managing Editor, the *Believer*

Five things every writer needs? Music writer or otherwise, how about we start with: love. Do it for love. You'll spend too many hours stashed away from all humanity in an ill-furnished room, sitting plumped unhealthily—fatally, they tell us lately!—on your ass, immersed in compositional ennui and editorial minutiae, nibbling your fingernails until they bleed, wishing you could go outside and play with the other kids, to choose this life for any other reason. Love your instrument as much as a musician does. Love the words. Love the objects to which you apply them. Even if in disappointed love, even if in betrayed love, begin at least with the yearning, the adoration, the utopian hunger for something bigger than yourself, something outside yourself, something connected to everything else and willing to bring your tiny consciousness aboard, like P-Funk's mothership. Love is all five things you need, actually: if you follow it and sustain it will bring you, not easily, not automatically, but assuredly in the longer run, to the other four, whichever they happen to be for you (an ear for rhetoric and persuasion; the ability to conceive the lie that tells the truth; a doggedness in describing what's indescribable; a district attorney's brilliance at grilling the interviewee; the capacity to open your eyes underwater; whatever). Love what you love and the love will follow. Who knows, you might even get paid at some point.—**Jonathan Lethem**, novelist

A: a manifesto—there must be change! notice the magical! eschew all clichés implying a herd mentality! learn more! action defines history!

B: time.

C: space.

D: the coiled anger of the lone leader, the isolated collective, the individual battler, the pure dreamer.

E: long for something missing. There is always something missing.

—**Paul Morley**, writer and critic

1. Patience 2. Enthusiasm 3. Drive 4. Passion 5. Coffee—**Oliver Primus**, Site Editor, *The 405*

Self-knowledge, thick skin, good headphones, a wall full of books on music, reliable wi-fi.—**Mark Richardson**, Editor-in-Chief, Pitchfork

Simon Le Bon, Nick Rhodes, John Taylor, Roger Taylor and Andy Taylor. Those are the gentlemen of Duran Duran, a lifelong obsession for me. Every music writer needs a twisted obsession or two, and it helps if your friends fail to understand, so you have to keep explaining why it matters. It doesn't matter what band or singer or style of music you obsess over—you just need to have that *aficion*.—**Rob Sheffield**, writer, *Rolling Stone*

Talent, audacity, patience, empathy, ears.—**Ben Sisario**, reporter, the *New York Times*

1. Art first. Know the record before the biography. Let the artists (not PR or other writers) lead you to other art.

2. Be as obsessive about reading good writing as you are about listening to good music.

3. Be brave enough to let the whims of your taste guide you to new things.

4. When you find something you like, go deep. Then go deeper.

5. Know that the albums or songs you love most will likely not lead to lucrative jobs.

—**Scott Tennent**, 33⅓ author

To read George Orwell's *How To Write*, an iPhone for its dictaphone and note-taking capabilities, originality, a loathing of consensus, willingness to work hard and not grumble—it beats most jobs.—**Luke Turner**, Associate Editor, The Quietus

Taste. Sorry, there's no way around that. I don't mean "taste" objectively, obviously. Just that you need to have an opinion on which types of music, which artists, which techniques, are better than others. You need to have an opinion on why. And you need to be able to explain or imply that in an compelling and interesting way. Without that, your writing will lack passion and you yourself will lack the drive to explore the new, whether it's actually new or merely new to you in the service of deepening your enthusiasms. So that's the first. Second: a reliable note-taking system. 'System,' not device, because if taking notes on your phone is your go-to technique, you need a fallback for when you drop it or your battery dies. Which will happen. You're a professional in a low-paid and competitive field, so unreliability or poor work will wound your ability to earn. Third: a recording device, rather obviously, but of particular importance for interviews. Fourth: if you're freelance, some system to organize contacts, opportunities, and assignments. Cultivate a reputation of turning in good work on time and your career will be a great deal easier. Fifth, a routine. Whatever works for you; but something to keep you honest. It's always an ungovernable temptation to keep listening or to seek the next thing you haven't heard yet. Yet you still need to pitch, research, write, and submit. Routine is the successful sum of effective habits.—**R.J. Wheaton**, Publisher, *Hazlitt* magazine; author of **33⅓**'s *Dummy*

Clear ethical boundaries. Curiosity. An understanding that you're serving your readers and not anybody else. Negotiation skills. Patience.—**Douglas Wolk**, freelance arts journalist

A notebook, a recorder, a Twitter account, caffeine pills, and a thesaurus.—**Alex Young**, founder and publisher, *Consequence of Sound*

CHAPTER 3
TRACK-BY-TRACK

INTRODUCTION

Sometimes an album's lyrics are so rich that each track deserves its own lengthy analysis. In her best-selling **33⅓** on Neutral Milk Hotel's *In The Aeroplane Over the Sea*, Kim Cooper devotes an entire chapter to "The Songs." It's an album steeped in history, filled with sad stories of loss from the first half of the twentieth century. The songs feel like short lessons in a new mythology; the song titles could easily be the titles of short stories. Instead of speculating, Kim Cooper asked Jeff Mangum and others exactly what the lyrics meant and provides fans with detailed insight into the story of the album. In this short chapter Cooper guides us through each track, analyzing the sounds and lyrics and tells us what to listen for. She explains that the most popular track from the album, "Holland, 1945," is about Anne Frank's family hiding from the Nazis. Cooper's work reminds us of how important it can be when writing your own track-by-track analysis of lyrics to seek out the artists themselves who wrote the songs or find interviews in which they explain their lyrics.

Or perhaps a song means something profound to you and so it doesn't matter what the artist's intended meaning was. Take Mary Gaitskill writing about B-Movie's 1981 track "Nowhere Girl." She uses her brief but memorable encounters with the song to talk about the general effect and formula of pop songs. She writes "maybe all good pop songs have this deceptively light ability to touch and awaken multiple associations that blend with the wordless, innocent and completely non-hierarchical sense of dreams." When writing about a single song consider why it works and why others might experience the same feelings you do when listening to it.

Because music is such a personal experience, it's likely you'll find yourself defending something you like to others who claim to hate it. If you're a fan of pop music, this is likely to happen often. Taylor Swift doesn't have to be a guilty pleasure, as Tavi Gevinson shows us in her essay on Swift's lyrics for *The Believer*. Tavi's conversational tone is candid and you can almost imagine her sitting in a chair across from you, sternly and successfully defending every one of Swift's songs. This kind of song-by-song focus leavened by a chatty tone can accomplish a lot of work in the right context.—AJG

KIM COOPER ON NEUTRAL MILK HOTEL

33¹/₃ Volume #29 *In the Aeroplane Over the Sea*

The Songs*

When I first proposed writing about *In the Aeroplane Over the Sea*, I told the folks at Continuum that I wasn't interested in subjecting the album to a literal-minded line analysis, sucking all the mystery out of the lyrics and spoiling their effects. Nevertheless, as I spoke with the musicians and their associates, interesting stories, details and connections emerged. I found these added to my enjoyment of the album. If you love Neutral Milk Hotel, then these songs mean something particular to you, and no writer's ruminations can negate that meaning. Consider the following as a series of cover versions, a layering of possible and partial interpretations that are intended to be transparent; the album remains the primary text, and your reaction to it the secondary one.

The King of Carrot Flowers Pt. One

In the Aeroplane Over the Sea begins with an aggressive acoustic strum, punk's energy filtered through traditional troubadour strings. From the outset, the singer addresses a first person listener, reminding him what he was when young (the titular monarch) and listing horrors and pleasures of that distant time. The royal parents menace each other while singer and subject form a union that seems as holy as it's carnal. There are hints of incest (who is this singer/lover who observes so intimately, if not a sibling?), of cannibalism (mom sticks the fork into daddy's shoulder, and presuming he's a cooked carrot how smoothly it would slide), of Southern religious mania (holy roller rattlesnakes) and of the gypsy Tarot (the tower tumbling through the trees). If this is your first experience with Neutral Milk Hotel—and for most, who've had the second album recommended to them by an acolyte, it is—what's immediately clear is that Neutral Milk Hotel is no ordinary pop band, riffing redundantly on stock topics of love, aggression and consumption. There's more heart, imagination and eclecticism here, and a singing style that fuses holy cantor song with the hysterical expressions of schizophrenics compelled to communicate. And yet it's all so gloriously catchy that even the most startling elements rest comfortably among the whole.

---

*Cooper, Kim. "The Songs." *In the Aeroplane Over the Sea*, 68–76. New York: Continuum, 2005. Reprinted with permission.

Robert Schneider says this song has the feeling in it of the woods behind Jeff's house in Ruston.

The King of Carrot Flowers Pts. Two & Three

"Pt. One" ends with a spacey drone that oozes into this track's initial gutsy cry "I love you Jesus Christ," which is the spot where aggressively non-Christian listeners have to make a conscious decision to stay with the music. But is the expression one of love for the Savior or for another person, punctuated by the emphatic invocation of J.C.? Jeff repeatedly made it clear that he was singing about Jesus, but the alternative interpretation is there for those who need it. Either way, it feels real and raw and fearless, and soon Jeff's voice is running away with him, a swirl of disjointed imagery culminating in the loving union of a dead dog and a synthetic flying machine, an idea that obliquely recalls the proto-surrealist writer Lautreamont and his celebrated phantasm of the fortuitous encounter of a sewing machine with an umbrella on a dissection table. On the lyric sheet, Jeff omits the words of this song in favor of a run-on message declaring that the song seems to confuse people, but that he means what he sings, and further that the theme of "endless endless" on the album doesn't stem from any one religion, but reflects his belief that all things contain an eternal white light.

When asked if there were any happy accidents in the recording process, Robert Schneider immediately mentioned this song, and the part where Julian's amplified, fuzz-pedaled banjo comes in, right after the drums, in a woozy effect achieved by bowing the strings. "It really bugged me that it was out of tune. But Julian really liked it and Jeff liked it. And Jeff's not looking for tuning and stuff like that. But now listening to it, I hear that it has a raw, almost Eastern quality of *being* out of tune. That's its little tuning, but I didn't recognize it at the time. Now I hear it as being noisy. At the time, I went for a walk with Jeff and said, 'I can't stand hearing this in the song.' And he's like, 'Yeah, but you know, Julian likes it, and I think we'll leave it.' It overrode my sensibility, which was that it was out of tune, but if Jeff is happy with it, it doesn't matter, that's all I wanted."

With the title track we find the first hints of Anne Frank's posthumous presence, and she's everywhere ("Anna's ghost all around"). Briefly in this album dotted with darkness, love and beauty are celebrated—but mainly for their effervescence. The singer treasures these gentle graces, but must introduce the inevitability of death into the equation. This aeroplane delivers ashy remnants into the sea. (I can't think of cremains thrown from a plane without being brought into real-time South American horror: in Argentina the Junta flew dissidents out over the Atlantic and pushed them out alive, while Pinochet's Chile more neatly dumped weighted corpses into the Pacific. Perhaps not coincidentally, plenty of ex-Nazis lived out their dotage in Argentine villas.)

The singer animates his beloved, a flesh puppet maybe already dead, by putting his fingers in her mouth. In this way he even manifests a voice. One is reminded that the most precious things pass out of living memory and are lost, but also that the dead can live on in those that loved them. And Anne Frank, already immortalized by her diary's survival and the cult of the lost girl genius with the goofy-pretty face, gains new levels of posthumous being from Jeff Mangum's work with Neutral Milk Hotel. Picture the Franks in their Dutch hidey-hole, 1944. Picture the Elephant 6 gang fifty years later, rock'n'roll and road trips and DIY. Incongruous worlds, but the sets collide, and somehow fit perfectly together. If Anne were alive today, what would be her favorite band?

This scans like a song for a carnival punk—one of those freaks of nature preserved in formaldehyde, yet somehow animate, cognizant and full of love for she who waits outside the jar for the radio he's building her. And here's starved Anne again, with the lover's—or are they the killers'?—fingers that trace her meatless spine. Maybe the jar is a metaphor for impermeable time, a transparent barrier between souls. Maybe the title is an off-color reference to every man's (woman's, too) eternal struggle, which head do you think with? The song closes with words of comfort for the jar-baby, singing him to silence, or the sinking into poison fluid oblivion that he resists no more.

Scott Spillane notes that it took him six or seven years to realize that the two-headed boy was tapping on a jar in a darkened lab somewhere, as someone asks, "Where are you? Tap on the jar and I'll follow the sound."

The Fool

The origins of Scott Spillane's soundtrack piece are discussed in the section on the *Aeroplane* sessions.

Holland, 1945

Halfway through the album, hints of Anne Frank's presence give way to direct biographical references. Frank and her family went into hiding in occupied Amsterdam in July 1942. In August 1944, an informant alerted the Gestapo to their presence and the Franks were captured and sent to internment camps. Anne and her sister Margot arrived at the German camp Bergen-Belsen in October 1944, where they died of typhus in February or March. So while Anne was not physically in Holland in 1945, the association of the country with the year of the war's ending nonetheless suggests her presence. And it was in Amsterdam in 1945 that Anne's father Otto, himself liberated from Auschwitz, learned of his daughters' deaths and received Anne's secret diary from family friend Miep Gies.

In "Holland, 1945," the singer proclaims his love, marveling at the awful randomness that sees his darling in the ground just weeks before the Allies liberated her camp. But mourning makes a metaphysical leap as the promise of reincarnation is introduced in an image (perhaps borrowed from avant-garde Chilean filmmaker Alejandro Jodorowsky's 1967 *Fando & Lis*) of a young Spanish boy playing a flaming piano. This is a blessed relief, for if she can be this little boy in Spain, why mourn the teenage Jewess in the mass grave? Can life and consciousness and identity maybe mutate to survive human evil and corporal rot? Those who survive war's traumas are advised to pick up all they can of their old, shattered life so that they can continue on to what's next. This suggests Otto Frank's protection, editing and publication of his daughter's journal, which would become the most powerful personal document of the Holocaust.

But to read "Holland, 1945" or *In the Aeroplane Over the Sea* as being "about" Jeff Mangum's fantasy love affair with Anne Frank is far too literal and limiting an interpretation. The second verse introduces a circus/fate wheel on which rides a dead brother who refuses to be reincarnated, happier in the cosmos above than down on troubled earth, where human actions and emotions trigger such suffering. That image of a dead brother, which *Boston Phoenix* critic Carly Carioli connected with a suicide in the family of one of Jeff's close friends, will recur powerfully in the Neutral Milk Hotel mythos.

The closing couplet, "That they'd rather see their faces fill with flies/All when I'd want to keep white roses in their eyes," is curious. When he wrote the song, Jeff had never heard of the White Rose movement, the anti-Nazi Munich based student group whose main members were jailed and martyred in the early 40s. Somehow he must have heard the name without consciously realizing it, or he simply plucked the phrase out of the universal mind in one of his creative channeling sessions. The White Rose was famous for the leaflets they secretly printed in one of their bedrooms and mailed out to random Germans whose names they found in the telephone book; the parallels to the Elephant 6 DIY scene are obvious and fascinating.

Communist Daughter

Simple, brief and lovely, this song introduces itself with delicate cricket-like oscillations. The imagery is South American and at the same time elemental, with semen and seawater and powerful drugs. Cars careen from the clouds, fusing the earthly and heavenly worlds. Meanwhile, to prove she still exists, the title character masturbates and walks on the water, a hermaphroditic fusion of man/woman, human/god, body/spirit. All things are present within the selves painted here.

Oh Comely

"Comely" is an old world word, Middle English for someone pleasing and wholesome. But in Jeff's song, the one who's called comely seems to roll in filth. The narrative is unclear, but disturbing, suggesting obligations and desires that can pull one down into dark, dangerous parts of oneself.

It seems there are four separate songs fused here: "Oh Comely" itself; then the part about the father/betrayer which slides so elegantly into plant-body-machine metaphor; a verse (the most direct of all, with a hopeful heartbeat rhythm as accompaniment) about Anne Frank's death; and finally a verse from the lost song "Goldaline." Then there's a shadow/companion song, the relentless, unreleased "Oh Sister," which Jeff introduced at the Aquarius instore as being connected to "Oh Comely." "Oh Sister" is full of bits that ended up elsewhere: a character called Rose Wallace Goldaline; the "moves herself around her fist" lyric that found itself in "Communist Daughter"; and the "bright and bubbly" bit that went to "Oh Comely."

In interviews, Jeff has identified the characters in "Goldaline" as Siamese twin sisters, lost and freezing in the woods. The narrating sister sings to Goldaline not to worry, that they two will be eaten but it's not so awful, for they'll be warm and one again in the belly of some beast. In this spare little fairy tale narrative, death is accepted as inevitable and possibly improving.

Ghost

A song about spirits moving between bodies and the memories the living keep alive. Anne Frank was born in 1929, so maybe she's the one who was born in a bottle rocket. If so, then the lyrics obliquely trace the contrast between America and the old world, between different sorts of tragedies and the ways in which souls can overcome them. Jeremy Barnes remembers witnessing a fire in a tall building near the apartment in the West Village, standing down on the street with all his friends watching the fire engines and the smoke up high—he always thinks of this scene when he hears "Ghost."

10

The untitled tenth track is a carnivalesque jam recorded at the end of the sessions, featuring Michelle Anderson's uilleann pipes, an Irish instrument akin to the Scottish bagpipes.

Two-Headed Boy Pt. Two

There's a weary quality to Jeff's vocal on this closing song that makes the tender sentiments especially moving. Even with the lyrics changed to mask Anne Frank's presence, there really is no lovelier moment in pop than when he sings "and in my dreams you're alive and you're crying." The dead brother reels through, his head burning, his skull broken by what might be a suicidal bullet, as the living who love him seek to undo the destruction and put him back together. At the end, the twin boy in the glass jar appears. Now he has a lover who gives him tomatoes and radio wires (he's building a magical radio for her, down in the wetness where he bobs). "But don't hate her when she gets up to leave" is a gentle, somehow humorous warning, as if to say "what else can she do but leave—you live in a jar!" God is there too, as a place, as every place. Whatever the trials these characters confront, in closing they find a peaceful spot where miracles can be awaited.

MARY GAITSKILL ON B-MOVIE

"Nowhere Girl"*

I don't know why this song touched me. I heard it at a small Manhattan club in '81; it came tingling through the crowded dark and lightly touched me with an indefinable feeling that was intense almost *because* it was so light—and then disappeared into whatever song followed. It was in no way the best song I heard during that time; it did not "save me." I did not even go out and buy it, though if I'd been able to afford anything to play it on, I might've. *Might've.* I was not a fan by nature and it was a slight, slightly ridiculous little song. But it touched me in a way I could not quite forget. I heard it randomly maybe three more times; I didn't go out that much and apparently it wasn't popular. But each time I heard it, it touched me in that peculiarly light and emotional way, with the quality of something small that is trying to get your attention, though unconfidently, from somewhere off in a corner. Or from nowhere. *Nowhere girl in self-imposed exile/Nowhere girl in martyr-like denial.* That was part of what touched me; the word "nowhere," and the idea of someone living there, a picture of mysteriously seductive loneliness, a delicate and melancholy thing expressed in manic synth-pop. (Maybe it unconsciously reminded me of a fantasy story I'd written when I was fifteen, in which some space-traveling teenagers come across a beautiful woman confined in a transparent false world that moves fluidly with her movements, in which she lives a hallucinatory non-life, unaware of "real world" people who can watch her delusional existence but who cannot help her.)

Nowhere girl, you've never gone outside/Nowhere girl cause you prefer to hide/ Everyday, every night, in that old familiar light: the words "everyday" and "light" activated this phrase, and, put together with the music, made multiple pictures that blended and flashed through me. Everyday light: the light in a basement, streetlight, club light, imaginary light; something as mundane as a lamp and as sinister as the glow of a hypnotizing dream that the girl has become lost in, yet which is at the same time the only thing keeping her alive.

The music evokes delight, longing, urgent melancholy and fun: *And I try to get through/And I try to talk to you/But there's something stopping me from getting through.* The sincere, slightly exasperated, actually pretty happy voice is that of a guy in cheap fashionable clothes that look good as long as it's dark; he's no prince, and he's more bemused than ardent—still the song has the enchanted feeling of Sleeping Beauty, though in this case the enchantment will not break.

---

*Printed with the permission of the author.

So much association and imagery is a lot of weight to put on such a small song, and I didn't think any of that at the time; I just felt it sort of speeding past. But the wistful sound that translated as a kind of emotional touch entered my system with all of that somehow encoded, and it bloomed in my subconscious imagination like the artificial sea shell somebody gave me when I was a kid which, when dropped into a glass of water, opened and bloomed into an elaborate flower.

This is a quality that many, maybe all good pop songs have, this deceptively light ability to awaken multiple associations that blend with the wordless, innocent and completely non-hierarchical sense of dreams. (For someone else's fantastically rendered dream of this song, in a more tarted-up and sentimental version than the one I first heard, see the video posted by somebody called "davidapa" on YouTube; its a beautiful mash-up with the mad scientist scene in Fritz Lang's *Metropolis*, in which the theme of awakening is demonically moving.) It's a quality that I felt more complexly in many other songs from the same time which I find better and more delicious, songs by Crime and the City Solution, Talking Heads, Joy Division, Roxy Music, The Ramones, Patti Smith, Sonic Youth, the Psychedelic Furs among others. It is a quality that can make pop music appear ephemeral to the point of cheap, exceptionally vulnerable to changes in fashion, attachable to dumb things like ads for cars or pizza, dependent on its period of time for its language of shared associations to make sense. It is also a quality that makes pop music exceptionally powerful in its ability to artlessly enter a person's most private schema and whisper to that person in secret.

It makes sense if this song wasn't popular; what night-clubber in NYC wants to identify with some retard sitting by herself in the basement, staring into space? At the same time, it also makes sense that this retard and the guy trying to get her out of the basement appeared in NYC in 1981, a time of costuming, pretense, fancy-shaped, day-glo colored hair. Costuming is a romantic way of giving shape to something previously inchoate inside you, of trying to discover, to become. It can also be a way of obnoxiously parading the self while simultaneously hiding it, especially if the costume is socially agreed on. The song is about a person who "prefers to hide" in a physical place, such as a room, but also perhaps in the self, in a construction of personality in which something essential and vulnerable remains hidden and undeveloped. When I heard "Nowhere Girl," I was lost in a self-created nightmare that had become a terrible reality I was trying desperately to get out of, and instead was getting more lost in by the moment. I think the song in its light passing gave me a strange glimmer of hope just because in it I could hear that other people saw and felt this lostness too, and rather than despising it, someone had considered it worth writing a song about.

By '86, I was starting to find my way. I could sort of talk to people. I remember though a particular moment when I couldn't. I was spending an afternoon with this guy I liked, not sexually, just liked, and we were walking around doing something I no longer recall. I just remember that at one point we sat down outside somewhere and he said "I really like you and I want to get to know you. But it feels like there's all these obstacles and I don't know what they are and I don't know how to get around them." I was so astonished that I could not reply. I knew exactly what he meant. At the same time, *I* didn't know what the obstacles were either. I crossed my hands over my lap and looked down. I have no idea what I was thinking. Maybe I was trying to come up with something smart to say and realizing that it was beyond me. Maybe I was just weirded out. Probably I thought he was saying there was something wrong with me. He put his hand on my arm, then took it away. The moment passed. We talked about something else, then said good-bye.

Because I knew I was going to write about this song, I told this anecdote to someone recently and she said "It just sounds like he was coming on to you." My mind snagged on the word "just"; I seldom think that anyone "just" comes on. I don't know what he wanted or what he was doing. I remember the moment because I felt he was trying to get through, trying to talk to me and that something was stopping him—and yet he succeeded. It is still moving to me that he saw something real that most people wouldn't bother to see, and that he said something about it; that he helped me, in a tiny way, to wake up.

By '87 I had gotten somewhere in the social sense; I had sold a book and it was about to be published. I remember going to a club for the first time in a while and being kind of appalled. There were no costumes, no sense of discovery or romance; there were mostly a lot of expensive clothes, and I was wearing them too. The best thing was the DJ, who for some reason made me remember a song I hadn't heard in years; I went up to her and asked, "do you have 'Nowhere Girl' by B-Movie?" She did. She played it and for a moment the room was drenched in feeling from the past: the feeling of something unknown trying to get your attention, of not quite being able to see what it is; of somebody trying to awaken somebody else; of trying to wake. Banal somewhere was suddenly and beautifully infused with mysterious nowhere. It was a very small moment, but it was a lovely one. As this is a small but lovely song.

TAVI GEVINSON ON TAYLOR SWIFT

Just Kidding, Love Sucks: Notes on Taylor Swift*

The general public has managed to make Taylor Swift's greatest strength seem like her greatest weakness, and it makes me feel sad and angry and like people are really missing out on something great.

By "general public" I mean email-hosting sites and sometimes Fancier Publications, and by her "greatest strength" I mean Taylor's unique ability to focus in on one detail or exchange and magnify it completely in this way that makes it feel at once universal and deeply personal. I don't want to devote too much of this holy ink and paper to haterz, but I do want to free your mind from any reservations about the Swift Power in order to fully prepare you for a MAGIC CARPET ROLLER-COASTER RIDE across this CANDY LAND BOARD of a DECLARATION OF INDEPENDENCE from BRITAIN (= NOT LIKING TAYLOR SWIFT).

Swifties see the characteristic at hand for what it is: writing. Her songs are her point of view, making it her job to blow up the most minor event into something that more accurately represents the way *she experienced it*. As Tay quoted Neruda in her *Red* liner notes, "Love is so short, forgetting is so long." This is basic Nabokov shit, right? Everything hits harder in memory. Everything changes color. Her first album will tell you she is a natural crusher, daydreamer, hopeless romantic. Obsessing over the briefest of encounters is *what we do*. She was just born to translate it for millions of people. And I don't think her commercial responsibilities detract from her genuine passion for her craft. Have you ever watched her in interviews when she gets asked about her actual songwriting? She becomes that kid who's really into the science fair. Her hands go crazy and she explains all the different categories she breaks emotions into and how they all have their own individual sounds. Then the interviewer totally doesn't get it because it's *60 Minutes* and they were hoping for a pleasant little soundbite instead of, like, an Andrew Kuo-style verbalization of the human psyche. And Taylor smiles, perfectly aware she just weirded them out, perfectly aware it's the same weirdness from which she pulls all these beautiful songs.

So the fact that people think they're, like, Nancy Drew for claiming that none of her relationships have lasted long enough for her to be able to write a song about them really proves only that she has this uncanny talent for dressing up an experience until what *happened* matches how it *felt*.

---

*Gevinson, Tavi. "Just Kidding, Love Sucks: Notes on Taylor Swift." The *Believer*, July/August 2013. Reprinted with permission from the author.

I don't care that her relationships aren't long-term—she's a little busy running a goddamn empire! I don't care if she only dates guys to write songs about them, like people say—she dates people, she writes songs about her life, naturally many of these songs are about people she's dated, and many of them *aren't*, as well. Mostly, basically: I DON'T CARE, I LOVE IT.

These are some of my favorites, severely edited down for word count. I almost didn't want to publish it, because her music is so close to my heart, but I also really wanted to publish it because her music is so close to my heart. Please handle with care.

Album: *Taylor Swift*

"Our Song"

Somewhere in the dark depths of deleted YouTube videos is a circasixth-grade recording of my childhood best friend and me singing this while I play guitar. Taylor's one of the reasons I learned guitar (along with some vague image I had of ROCK STARS and PEOPLE IN COOL HATS), and I was very serious about imitating her country twang. While Taylor is not technically an exceptional vocalist on this first album, she knows exactly how to make each word sound on an emotional level. Her instincts are just *right*, her cadence is so *her*. Like, it's not just that her lyrics perfectly match up with the music and together they accurately capture a certain emotion— you can also just *hear* it when she's smiling, or looking up, or thinking. This, I would argue, is more important than technically good vocals, and it's also very rare.

"Picture to Burn"

So much sass! Pickup trucks! Dads who are gonna beat up ex-boyfriends! I'LL TAKE IT.

"Stay Beautiful"

This song KILLS me because I only ever listened to it a few times way back when, which means rediscovering it was like seeing someone you didn't even know you missed but you're suddenly so grateful they're in your life. The lyrics totally apply to young Taylor: "Don't you know, you're really gonna be someone. / Ask anyone." UGHHH. I think I get so emotional listening to her first album because it's just so heartening to think about where she was when she wrote these songs (lonely, bullied, awkward phase, bad at boys, country-music nerd) and where she is now (BFF to PLANET EARTH). She's a prime example of how you can turn a middle-school rooted inferiority complex into beautiful, relatable art. She's like Chris Ware, except not, except *totally*.

"Should've Said No"

PERFECT for singalongs. There's a great live performance where she starts out seated, wearing a black hoodie, angstily banging it out on a guitar and looking at the ground, and by the end she's become this beautiful butterfly, like a really emotional deodorant commercial.

"Tied Together with a Smile"

Whenever people are like, "Ugh, ew, Taylor Swift, stop acting like you know pain when you are beautiful/famous/etc.," I want to play them this song. It reminds me of really bad school hallway art of girls looking in mirrors and feeling sad but in a way that makes me love everyone and want everyone to love themselves.

Album: *Fearless*

"Fearless"

This song is *made* for daydreaming; when I listen to it, it's OK that I'm alone in my room and not with some boy, because I'm exactly where I'm supposed to be. There's a great liner note in this album where she says fearlessness isn't being totally fearless, it's owning up to having fears and being flawed and being OK with life anyway, which is sort of just like very basic Fiona Apple theory for twelve-year-olds.

"Fifteen"

I'm not going to touch on the feminist argument as it applies here (in short: girls who have sex "early" with people who don't love them will feel broken afterward), because this album came out five years ago and since then she's put out two albums that give a total seal of approval to sexytimes. Plus, I mean, these lines: "In your life you'll do things greater than dating the boy on the football team." "Back then I swore I was gonna marry him someday but I've realized some bigger dreams of mine."

That blew my mind when I first heard it! But I will touch on the feminism debate in *general*, because I am both a feminist and a seventeen-year-old girl who feels empowered by Taylor.

I think the "fairy-tale-obsessed" and "slut-shaming" criticisms just aren't relevant anymore, since there's no hint of either on the latest album. As for her writing so much about boys, that's just a lazy summary of her body of work. And, frankly, I would *love* for every girl to aspire to be Patti Smith, but for the ones who don't relate to that, let them still have a role model who displays her own version of strength and does dole out some sage advice. As for her supposedly acting all weak and self-victimizing, I don't think she acts that way at all. She's just a gracious interviewee, a paranoid hard-worker, and a cautious prodigy. If you watched any of her tour movies (*Journey to Fearless; Speak Now World Tour Live*), you would see that she makes it pretty clear that she thinks she's awesome and wants you to think *you* are also awesome. If you looked at any Swifty tumblrs, you would see that her young female fans admire her not because she seems weak and submissive, but because they admire her wit, her sense of humor, how much control she still has over what she does, and her passion for her fans and for making good music. From the Kathleen Hanna school of thought: "Some of the themes she writes about are stuff I wish was there for me when I was in high school, and I'm so happy she really cares about her female fans. She's not catering to a male audience and is writing music for other girls. I don't care if she calls herself a feminist or not. There is something that she's doing that feels feminist to me in that she really seems to have a lot of control over what her career is doing."

"Love Story"

Taylor's parents wouldn't let her date some guy, so she stomped into her room and wrote this in twenty minutes. The intro sounds like footsteps and whispers and secrets in the woods.

"White Horse"

Seriously important to this album as her moment of being like, "Maybe the fairy-tale Romeo and Juliet shit doesn't always happen and maybe other things will make me happy?" (Paraphrasing.) The whole song swings between her blaming herself and her wild heart to her being like, "Wait, maybe I can go have my own life now." Essential counter to the songs of hers that are just total fairy-tale lovefests.

"Forever and Always"

This was introduced on her *Fearless* tour with a video of her giving an interview, and the interviewer asking her, "Why do you think any guy is going to date you?" and Taylor saying, "If guys don't want me to write bad songs about them, then they shouldn't do bad things." Then she and the interviewer rise from below the stage on a platform, and Taylor says, "No more questions!" and THROWS A FUCKING GIANT RED CENTRAL PERK ARMCHAIR OFF THE PLATFORM. Then the phrase "They shouldn't do bad things" shows up, like, eighty times on each Jumbotron.

"You Belong with Me"

I once listened to this song on repeat while driving to Michigan with my family and it was the kind of melancholy that you're secretly so into despite fully committing to the vignette of an angry teen wearing headphones in the backseat of a minivan.

Album: *Speak Now*

"Sparks Fly"

If Britney or anyone who we think of as damaged by pop-star sexytimesrepression had just been allowed one song with the hormonal power of "Sparks Fly," they might have turned out OK. "Drop everything now. / Meet me in the pouring rain." "Give me something that'll haunt me when you're not around." Staaahhhhhp! (Sidenote: recently I've been writing out, color-coding, and diagramming Stevie Nicks lyrics, and there are a LOT of similar motifs between hers and Taylor's.)

"Back to December"

I used to listen to this song ALL THE TIMEEEE. Sad and powerful and guhhhhh. Also a good example of her taking the blame for a relationship ending even though the common misconception is that she always blames the guy.

"Speak Now"

Next time you are stressed out just listen to this stoned and you will be OK because there have been times when listening to Taylor Swift stoned was the only thing keeping me from becoming a combination of Vincent Gallo and both Edie Beales. P.S.: don't do drugs. P.P.S.: you are probably older than me and can do whatever you want and thank you for reading this article.

"Dear John"

Has there ever been a revenge love song that cuts this deeply? It has the equal parts classy and witchy SECRET BITE I love so much about her. I mean, come ON: "All of the girls that you've run dry / have tired, lifeless eyes / 'cause you've burned them out. / But I stole your matches before fire could catch me, so don't look now, / I'm shining like fireworks over your sad, empty town." The imagery! The metaphor she draws out as long as possible before it just explodes in a moment of triumph! This song is one of her absolute best, lyrically. Another ingenious layer to this one: John Mayer–esque guitar farts in the background. (It is about John Mayer.)

Oh, and she said this is the one where, when she looks out during her tour, girls are crying the most. How did she write a song that's both such a GIANT BURN to her ex AND a victory bonding moment for girls who have been in toxic relationships?

"Mean"

Famously wrote this after a critic turned his back on her and people get mad that she seems to victimize herself in it but HER ART IS HER TRUTH, MAN, JUST LAY OFF.

"The Story of Us"

Listening to this song is the only time I can ever see myself fist-pumping.

"Enchanted"

The very beginning shows how aware she is about the bullshit parts of her job, though she never sounds like she's whining about how hard it is to be famuzz. "There I was again tonight, / forcing laughter, faking smiles. / Same old tired, lonely place." Then, what's this? A fixation on a flirtation as a creative way to distract from the mundanity of the Kids' Choice Awards or whatever toilet flush of stupidity was going down at the time? "Your eyes whispered, 'Have we met?' / Across the room, your silhouette / starts to make its way to me." At last, the chorus just SLAYS ME: "This night is sparkling, / don't you let it go. / I'm wonderstruck, / blushing all the way home. / I'll spend forever / wondering if you knew / I was enchanted to meet you." God, just typing it out makes me remember hearing it for the first time and feeling like absolutely nothing else in the world existed or mattered. SO jealous if it's new for you.

"Long Live"

This was my number one before *Red*. The way you can hear her smiling when she says, "You traded your baseball cap for a crown." The simultaneous football homecoming victory/fairy-tale king-and-queen imagery. The joy that must exist in the world when she plays this live, as she wrote it for her band and fans.

"If This Was a Movie"

Another cathartic moment of her sort of questioning her own daydreams.

Album: *Red*

"State of Grace"

"We are alone, just you and me, / up in your room and our slates are clean. / Just twin fire signs, / four blue eyes." By the end of this album you will have a complete visualization of her world.

"Treacherous"

The hopeful and in-love energy is at "Sparks Fly" levels of intensity. Almost too much for me to handle. "Put your lips close to mine /as long as they don't touch. / Out of focus, eye-to-eye, / till the gravity's too much." Every time I hear this line I just shake my head repeatedly until I feel I know what it's like to be a .gif.

"I Knew You Were Trouble"

Like "Forever and Always," begins with the lyric "Once upon a time" and goes on to be like "JUST KIDDING, LOVE SUCKS," only this one is in 4-D and with dubstep.

"All Too Well"

"You call me up again just to break me like a promise. / So casually cruel in the name of being honest." Aiiiieeee! The song's structure, the visuals, EVERYTHING IS PERFECT. She revives a Stevie-esque "Did I scare you with my FEELINGS and my HONESTY?" kind of haunting (daunting? taunting? all of them?) challenge that makes me feel less bad about my bad feelings.

From her recent *Vanity Fair* interview: "For a female to write about her feelings, and then be portrayed as some clingy, insane, desperate girlfriend in need of making you marry her and have kids with her, I think that's taking something that potentially should be celebrated—a woman writing about her feelings in a confessional way—that's taking it and turning it and twisting it into something that is frankly a little sexist."

"22"

OMG OMG OMG. Perfect "Girls Just Wanna Have Fun"–type jam about going out with your friends and dancing and flirting haaaaay. I wanna jump around to it all the time. Also: "It feels like a perfect night to dress up like hipsters." WHAT DOES THAT EVEN MEAN? Whatever, I totally get it on a cosmic level.

"I Almost Do"

Classic cinematic walk-in-the-rain Taylor goodness.

"We Are Never Ever Getting Back Together"

ALREADY EASILY ONE OF THE BEST POP SONGS OF ALL TIME *OF ALL TIME*. Here's where she's like, "I know I'm not some fucking hip, tortured indie artist and also I don't care, OK, cool": "I'm really gonna miss you picking fights, and me / falling for it, screaming that I'm right, and you / would hide away and find your peace of mind, with some / indie record that's *much* cooler than mine." I reeeeally didn't want to bring any exes' names into this—her music is more enjoyable when all that gossip is ignored—but apparently this song is about Jake Gyllenhaal and I can just *so* see Donnie Darko being like, "Can't you see how FUCKED UP the world is, man? I don't have time for your bullshit teen tiger beats!" Wait—OMG—is this why there are furries in the music video? TAYLOR, YOU CARD. I hated *Donnie Darko* so much that I looked it up on Facebook to see which of my friends liked it and then silently judged them and then probably got food and went to sleep.

"Stay Stay Stay"

"I just like hanging out with you / all the time." Taylor is a big fan of *Girls* and I wouldn't be surprised if this song was inspired somehow by the speech Hannah delivers at Adam's door in the fourth episode of season one. I also think this song shows her sense of humor about herself and her own lovesickness/crazy-girlfriendness: "I threw my phone across the room at you" is sung so cheerfully! Over, what, a ukulele?! All-around delightful. The very beginning sounds like some happy commercial with cartoons bouncing around because it's spring and you need new laundry detergent or something.

"Holy Ground"

This feels like drinking every energy drink at every gas station from every Lana Del Rey song ever. By the end it has a "Long Live"–esque kind of HUZZAH feel that I'm sure will make it amazing in concert.

"Sad Beautiful Tragic"

HER VOICE. All of it. So delicate and fragile and then the bridge is absolutely heartbreaking. "Could you just try to listen?" *kills me.*

"The Lucky One"

Taylor is a smartypants about fame some more.

"Everything Has Changed"

The little bit about the butterflies is just perfect. The whole thing is perfect. This is a perfect song.

"Begin Again"

"He didn't like it when I wore high heels. / But I do." This is the last track on the album, like her parting words with us are just an FYI that she's growing up and she does things for herself now and she's BEGINNING AGAIN and changing. In "You Belong with Me," from ye olde *Fearless* phase, she goes, "She wears high heels, / I wear sneakers." I feel like now she's established herself as both a sneakerwearer and a high-heels-wearer and I am totally cool with that. Beautiful and famous and good at performing, but capable of feeling lonely and small, and unafraid to talk about it.

One of my most passionate waves of TS love hit when I had been working for thirty hours straight without sleep and just wanted something that was so HIGH SCHOOL and NORMSIES and made me feel part of that demented girl culture that I was left out of in middle school because I looked like a boy/grandma and that I eventually stopped wanting because It Gets Better™ but that I still desire in a corner of my soul when I'm doing my adult job. This is not supposed to read like one of those weird side comments people make for pity, because #WritingAnArticleAboutTaylor SwiftForTheBeliever #Summer2013 #NoRegrets. But for a long time, I did use her music to feel part of a teen experience that I just wasn't meant for, and to feel connected to something so many people like in this way I had become rather opposed to due to my own middle-school inferiority complex. Those first three albums helped me believe I was still someone who could relate to something that had no irony to it, who could genuinely enjoy a completely earnest expression of desire and love. Letting myself geek out over Taylor's music was legit good for my mental health.

In the time since then, however, two things have happened and fucked me over completely. For one, I embarked on a relationship with a person I love, meeting my once-harmless wistfulness with a scary, real thing that I care about. For another, *Red* was released—an album free of any fairy-tale bedazzlement, set outside the high-school vacuum of the other three, sung in screams and whispers and nothing in between. It's not daydream material; it hits too hard. It's not just catchy chemical power satisfying my perpetually slight yearning for an adolescence I just wasn't cut out for; it's a musical manifestation of my very own brain and soul and blood and tears.

It almost makes me angry, having to deal with these dumb, real feelings now. I feel like a Kevin James character, middle-aged and moderately depressed because I thought I was just picking up a lady at a sports bar but we ended up getting married instead. I feel like TAYLOR SWIFT HERSELF dated me and "tricked" me into staying in it long enough for a relationship and then wrote a song about me that GETS ME COMPLETELY, whether I like it or not.

But one thing you become shockingly OK with when you do reach this scarier understanding of the music of Taylor Swift is these dumb, real feelings. You start to see each one, no matter how painful, as just another layer of your emotional spectrum, another experience, another inexplicable circumstance valuable in itself because it's another thing you get to feel. It is suggested, perhaps, that her music is less about being in love or mourning the loss thereof, but how incredible it is that we can know what it's like to have these emotions at all.

This facet of Taylor Swift's strength I spoke of four thousand words ago, the most heart-stopping one of all, can be best summarized with this sentence from a letter Frida Kahlo wrote Diego Rivera: "It's not love, or tenderness, or affection, it's life itself."

Long live.

JONATHAN LETHEM ON TALKING HEADS

33⅓ Volume #86 *Fear of Music*

What Was the Fate of the *Fear of Music* Songs in Live Performance?*

The *Fear of Music* tour, the one I glimpsed with Tom in New Jersey, was the band's swansong as a performing quartet—that's unless you count the moment in the *Stop Making Sense* enactment when the original foursome are alone on the stage. (It's "Found a Job"—precisely what these four human beings did together when they signed their first record deal.) But that moment is more like an eloquent tombstone for what had been, isn't it?

Almost the whole album was tried on stage at one point or another, in 1979 and 1980. Only "Drugs" would wait for the expanded band (and that song, as we'll see, had a secret early life in live performance, under another name). Even "Animals" and "Electric Guitar" were given air. Some of the songs are tough to work up—not because they necessarily demand extra players (though "Life During Wartime" misses its bongos), but because Eno-aura, those treatments to which he'd subjected voice and instrument, needed an equivalent on other terms.

"Life During Wartime," knowing it has the obligation of becoming a classic, nevertheless sounds, in Boston in August 1979, tentative and roller-rinky, much as Bob Dylan's "Like a Rolling Stone" did at the Hollywood Bowl in 1965, mere months before it became the song that destroyed European civilization. Yet at that same Boston show "Memories Can't Wait" appears with a new guitar part, scudding and nervous, to simulate the Enoreverb—the result has the skeletal ferocity of Gang of Four. (An even better 1979 version, at the State Theater in Sydney, Australia, is introduced by Byrne as "Memories," reducing the title to its noun-essence.) Once in a while, the singer's psycho-killer one-man-theater makes too much a cartoon of "Mind" or "Cities." Yet the band's total commitment, to what you'd think must still have struck them as an astonishing new burst of songs, rides over any limitations. These recordings, which fortunately circulate pretty widely, are essential. They halt the album in time and gaze at it in wonder.

On that 1979 tour, in Peoria, Illinois, Jerry Harrison invited Adrian Belew onstage, to add a guitar solo to the band's encore of "Psycho Killer." A year or so later, faced with the thrilling prospect of putting across live versions of the layered, polyrhythmic, diffuse *Remain in Light* tracks—themselves constructed out of things like Belew's solos, and Nona Hendryx's vocals—Harrison took the job of recruiting a larger band:

---

*Lethem, Jonathan. *Fear of Music* 117–122. New York: Continuum, 2012. Reprinted with permission.

Belew, a bass player named Busta Jones, a drummer named Steve Scales, and Bernie Worrell, a Julliard-trained architect of the Parliament-Funkadelic sound.

You must change your band.

By the time the nine- or ten-person ensemble working under the name Talking Heads had finished touring to support *Remain in Light* they were one of the greatest, most compulsively danceable, and certainly most unprecedented, live bands in the history of pop music. Many thousands of people knew this at the time.

Three years later, the successive evidence offered by *The Name of This Band is Talking Heads*, and the film and album *Stop Making Sense*, which documented the subsequent "Big Suit" tour, and the spotlight focused by "Burning Down the House," the band's first top-ten hit, ensured everyone knew it.

The boy in his room—well, by this time increasingly out of his room—was aboard this bus. At the Forest Hills tennis stadium in Flushing, NY, in August, 1982, the "evolved" Talking Heads dragged the boy bodily through transformations he couldn't have known to invite but didn't remotely care to resist. At that concert, undergoing a state of rapture that easily rekindles in memory, the boy turned to his best friend Joel and gave the simplest and most unguarded expression possible to a feeling nearly anyone has had at least once (I hope), perhaps most often at the perihelion of some sexual experience, or drug experience. I don't remember the exact words the boy used, but the gist was, "We must never, ever, miss a chance to do this again." To be fair, this was a drug experience as well. And the boy was a week or two from leaving for his first days at college, which is to say at the door of his first departure from his city, from the city of prideful fear. Yet to doubt that recollection would be to doubt pleasure itself. If we all have two or three moments to which we'll forever ache to return, this is one of mine.

At that concert the band debuted a song from the album that would become *Speaking in Tongues*. I couldn't make out the title the singer announced (he may only have said "a new song"), nor much of the lyrics, which anyway prominently consisted of a nonsense phrase: "High, high, high, high, high, hiiiigh—woo-hoooo!" The song would turn out to be "Swamp." It scared me at the time, and I liked that. David Byrne sounded devilish. Maybe Talking Heads were headed to an (even more) fearful place, on my behalf, as a lover of my own fear. *Fear of Music* remained my sentimental favorite, but you'd have been an idiot to argue with *Remain in Light*.

In fact, it was easy to congratulate yourself in 1982 that you'd chosen your favorite band perfectly, for its capacity to grow at a rate that outpaced your wild expectations.

Some of the *Fear of Music* songs were swept up in this apotheosis: "Life During Wartime," of course, and "Cities," but also "Mind." "I Zimbra" appeared, sometimes mated to "Big Business," a *Remain in Light* style Byrne solo track. "Heaven" went on to play a special role as semi-ironic interlude, its simplicity more and more in contrast to the dance-oriented swirl of the set-list. "Drugs" makes some surreally jubilant appearances. If you'd asked me then, I'd have sworn the songs had grown with the band, responding to their globalized treatments by evolving too, unfurling new avenues and implications only glimpsed on the original album.

Listening to these concerts now, and even watching the undeniably joyous *Stop Making Sense*, I'm not so sure. By now I will have plainly disqualified myself as anything but a *Fear of Music* purist and partisan, so I may as well go ahead and say that from the first time Adrian Belew stepped onstage—or maybe the first time Busta Jones stepped onstage—something was lost as well as gained, for these songs especially. *Fear of Music*'s special aura and tension seem to me now absolutely defined within the four-person band that held the name Talking Heads when they made the album. The negotiation of solitude with companionship, located in the space between those four players, activates the deeper forces in the *Fear of Music* songs. David Byrne had been struggling with the format of "rock band," and with the (implicitly confessional) role of "lead singer." In *Remain in Light* and beyond, and in the expanded band's performances, he solved it. But the sound preceding, the sound of that struggle just before it was solved, generated a field of meanings with an unstable but permanent power.

Not to be overly dramatic, but *Fear of Music* sounds to me now to have been almost instantly renounced. Its door closed. The anxiety, claustrophobia, and dread, but also the fascination, the solipsistic delight, all bound within a suite of internal self-references, has exploded. The pieces will never be put back together. In fact, David Byrne sings the *Fear of Music* songs beautifully with the larger band—sings them urgently, as if the songs are wildly alive to him. How could he do otherwise, in musical surroundings as fervent as any singer's had the luck to inhabit? But the air isn't close around him, generating the pressure of dread these songs once dramatized. He's gained elbow room, room enough for him to learn to be a hilarious dancer, room enough to declaim and preach as the *Remain in Light* songs need him to do, room enough for a big suit and some groovy back-up singers. And fear is drained, like a snake's venom.

Up to *Fear of Music*, the name of this band is Talking Heads. After, Talking Heads is what they're called. It's as though the original band was both too lonely and not lonely enough for the singer and songwriter of *Fear of Music*.

Cities have a lot of people in them, more than families do, but we go to them, often, to be unknown.

And then our cities become our families, and we might find we have to venture forth from those as well.

In the film *Stop Making Sense* it is during "Life During Wartime" that David Byrne begins running in circles around the stage, around the band, even behind Chris Frantz's riser. The gesture is paradoxical—mute and eloquent, a singer running away from his microphone and at the same time seeming to say *look at all I can encircle. Look at all that the alchemy of my fear and desire has brought into being. My wartime has become a party in my mind and yours.* It is the running of a proud curator racing through the rooms of his museum gesturing at the wonders in his collection, implements from a war, once dangerous and ugly, but now transformed into Dada "readymades," decanted into myth and symbol. It is the running of an animal measuring the limits of its cage.

WRITING PROMPT: TRACK-BY-TRACK

Come up with a representative "album" comprised of 10 –15 tracks that you feel best represent a single artist's or band's career. After compiling the track list, read liner notes from several compilations that consider the songs track by track (for example, Alec Palao's "A Certain Magic: Track Notes" for the Big Star box set *Keep an Eye on The Sky* or Andrew Sandoval's notes to the Reprise deluxe reissue of the Bee Gee's *1st*). Then write your own liner notes for your album, discussing the significance of each track you've chosen, no more than 250 words each. If you find that undertaking this assignment is making you feel acutely solipsistic, have a look at the *Onion*'s post "Area Man Proud Of Liner Notes To Self-Burned Compilation CD."

THE GO-BETWEENS

HOW DID YOU LAND YOUR JOB?

Every job I've ever got was because I knew somebody who recommended me to a third party. On any given day, I'll be responsible for two or three news-based blog posts, one or two reviews for that week's issue, and whatever reporting I have going on for future projects. (I also frequently host radio shows on Entertainment Weekly's SiriusXM station, which averages out to about a half hour to an hour a day.) It varies wildly depending on the time of year and where we are in a production cycle.—**Kyle Anderson**, senior writer, *Entertainment Weekly*

I'm an academic, so I came through the Ph.D. route having originally studied for a BA in Music. I lecture, run seminars, and write articles and books—as well as reviews of academic articles and music performances, and programme notes.—**Nick Attfield**, music academic

I wrote a story, and they liked working with me on the story, so when a position with The *Believer* opened up, they asked if I'd like to apply for it. This all happened very quickly. But it was my favorite magazine, so I could hardly say no. Still can't really believe I'm here (seriously, no pun intended). My daily tasks are probably 33 percent emailing with editors and writers and business folks, 33 percent editorial tasks and reading, and 33 percent design or paperwork stuff. Something like that. Mostly I look at a computer screen.—**Casey Jarman**, Managing Editor, The *Believer*

I created Tiny Mix Tapes with a friend in 2001, and after six years, it became an official business. A couple years later, it became my full-time job. I started the site just as a place to write, purely for fun, but nowadays, I write very little since I have a lot of business, managerial, and administrative tasks day in and day out.—**Marvin Lin**, Editor-in-Chief, Tiny Mix Tapes

Without being flippant, I got the "job" because I really, really wanted it. My daily tasks have changed over the years but remain the same—right now I have my first full-time writing (non-editor) job, but it's not strictly music, as I write for the business/culture publication *Fast Company*. I do cover music business frequently, and I definitely got the *Fast Company* job because I had been working for *Billboard*, a trade publication, meaning that while I had been focusing on one topic, I had the familiarity and comfort with business writing that would be necessary. *Fast Company* also has a very pop culture slant to it, so many of the people who work there come from entertainment journalism, even as they cover tech or marketing or design, etc.—**Evie Nagy**, *Fast Company* staff writer, former editor at *Billboard* and *Rolling Stone*

It took four years of working part time jobs and getting up at 5 a.m. before I could actually pay myself some money and ditch non-music work. I'm now coming up on two years of full-time work, and even though I could get a job working at a fast food restaurant and get more money for half the hours I currently work, I'm happy.—**Oliver Primus**, Site Editor, *The 405*

I'm a writer for *Rolling Stone*, so I'm always writing about music. I started in the late 1980s, when I got out of college and started freelancing, sending out Xerox copies of my clips to editors around the country and hoping for that one-in-a-thousand response. My day job was shelving books at a science library at Harvard, then I went to grad school in Virginia (English Department) and wrote rock criticism in my spare time. I freelanced for years, writing for places like *SPIN* and the *Village Voice* and the *Boston Phoenix*, as well as my friends' zines. In 1994 I took my first full-time contract, to write for *Details*. Three years later, my editor Joe Levy went to *Rolling Stone* magazine and I followed him there.—**Rob Sheffield**, writer, *Rolling Stone*

CHAPTER 4
ANALYSIS

INTRODUCTION

I devoted a substantial part of my **33⅓** book on Guided by Voices' *Bee Thousand* to "an unfinished dissertation" by Nolen Twinn-Johnson, an English graduate student who had suffered an untimely death before he could finish his degree.

The fact is the passage wasn't from a dissertation at all, finished or unfinished—I'd made up the conceit so that I could include my own long-form analysis of the lyrics under cover of a pseudonym. I wanted the book to reflect the ad hoc nature of an album which is wildly various and marked by a spirit of open experimentation (plus I got to make anagrams of the names Robert Ellsworth Pollard and John Winston Lennon for the occasion). Offering up the work behind a screen also allowed me to distance myself in some way from a literary analysis of the lyrics. Analyzing popular music seems to many readers unnecessary at best and self-indulgent at worst. Maybe that's in part why I was hiding out behind the putative prose of a dead student.

I don't know how many of those who feel *any* extended analysis of rock is pretentious can tell illuminating analysis from the jargon-ridden prose of third-rate academic writing (often, if the writing is at all challenging or employs a vocabulary that requires more than a 6th grade education, the backlash begins). When was the last time those who seem allergic to ideas and elaboration read a substantial literary essay? Are we only supposed to write for the most boorish fanboy with a chip on his shoulder about high culture?

As the work in this chapter suggests, analysis of music is alive, well, and at least in these instances, very worthwhile. It's been that way at least since the publication of Richard Meltzer's *The Aesthetics of Rock*, a 1970 work of ersatz, manic brilliance that came out of nowhere and, perhaps, everywhere, at just the wrong time. As Greil Marcus writes in his introduction to the Da Capo edition of the book, many thought Meltzer's book was a joke upon its publication, but that was no more than a knee-jerk reaction to the way it challenged readers whom it made "feel queasy" and "creepy" because it was "so out of tune with the mandated optimism of late '60s pop culture." Readers today don't necessarily feel queasy when they come upon extended analysis for the same reasons, but there's still plenty of resistance to eccentric, extended, or ambitious writing.

Maybe we've traded out the enforced optimism of the '60s for an illusion of authenticity that relies on a lowest common denominator version of "keeping it real." Or maybe the culture as a whole has just dumbed it way down. Marcus writes that in "1966 bedazzled college students like myself were helplessly dumping quotes from Plato on Beatles hits and Dylan albums, attempting to make sense of the emotions the music was provoking, trying to talk about the world the music seemed to be changing—changing forever, it seemed, and forever for the better." If we're duly chastened now regarding such illusions, we're also a great distance from the ambitions that generated them. To accede to such resistance is to radically limit the scope of possibility for music writing. We may not wish to return to the naiveté of an earlier time even if such were possible, but we hope this chapter will serve to encourage complex and ambitious responses to music in a way that may appear anathema to the current climate's strains of anti-intellectualism and forced simplicity.—MW

RICHARD MELTZER ON EVIL
AND ROCK 'N' ROLL

The Aesthetics of Rock*

A survey of the evil done by rock people themselves is vastly revealing. With Leadbelly there is almost a straight unity between the content of his life and his songs, although he often exceeds "in life" anything he would have described verbally, even if his "Ella Speed" mentions "first degree murder with a Colt 41." A rapist and murderer, he was more publicly evil than Genet without the latter's objective glory (while still young) and with much less merely literarily enviable punishment. In "Rock Island Line" he half-jokingly bewails the triviality of his tragedy: "Jesus died to save others' sins,/ Glory to God we're gonna need him again." This could almost be a laughing reply to Joseph Wood Krutch, who opines about tragic man, "His passions are important through all time and all space; the very fact that he can sin (no modern can) means that his universe is watching his acts; and though he may perish, a God leans out from infinity to strike him down."[1]

Chuck Berry is later able to surpass Leadbelly, for he can do no better than commit a violation of the Mann Act with a fourteen-year-old Apache girl. For a long while rock 'n' roll, motorcycles, and juvenile delinquency were correlated as part of a common evil. Movies like *Blackboard Jungle* and *Rock & Roll Generation* reported and created this connection and were even impressive.[2] Elvis Presley and such groups as the Elegants easily could be labeled "evil" in appearance. Teen-agers beat up adults and fought with policemen outside Alan Freed rock 'n' roll shows in the middle and late 1950's. But even with the eventual diminution of evil in rock, the summer of 1965 saw a crowd outside the Bridgeport, Connecticut concert of the acceptedly innocent Herman's Hermits throwing rocks at cops, who by this time had become the new evil; a cult of innocence is now perfectly within rock's context.

But leading up to this eventuality is a period of sociological reduction in rock, in which the evil one is viewed as the victim of circumstance. The Crystals' "Uptown" and "He's a Rebel" are Manhattan sociology of a Michael Harrington variety, viewable as significant only for their destructive effect upon the visceral quality of rock evil.

---

*Meltzer, Richard. *The Aesthetics of Rock*. New York: DeCapo, 1987. 192–197.
[1] Joseph Wood Krutch, "The Tragic Fallacy," from *The Modern Temper*, Harcourt, Brace & World, 1929, on p. 180 of a xeroxed anthology. The Bonzo Dog Doo Dah Band's "Death Cab for Cutie" is the rock contextualization of both Krutch and the old tragic cats: "Someone's gonna make you pay your fare."
[2] One remnant of this era is the record series entitled "Mr. Maestro's Bad Motorcycle Golden Oldies," a proper consideration for original context without diminution of evil.

Martha and the Vandellas revel in evil but somehow see the need to rely on sociological apology, as in "Wild One" where they rant, "You're the victim of circumstance." Fortunately the new (and new-old) wave of rock 'n' roll has brought with it a system of random ethical values, of even a system whereby sociological protest can be cool, just as Dylan makes (real-live) hate cool in "Positively Fourth Street."

Sociology, all the way up to Zappaesque articulate babble about sexual repression and Hank Ballard and the Midnighters,[3] is an obvious functional drag, particularly when it subverts the move qua move by means of opaque non-magical causality. The Stones have always had a super-easy time mocking this dilly-dally and all linguistic manifestations of it. On *Between the Buttons* three tracks, "Something Happened to Me Yesterday":

No one's sure just what it was
Or the meaning and the cause . . .
He don't know if it's right or wrong,
Maybe he should tell someone;
He's not sure just what it was
Or if it's against the law

"Let's Spend the Night Together" ("But I just can't apologize, oh no") and "Ruby Tuesday" ("Don't question why she needs to be so free,/She'll tell you it's the only way to be"), go to the point of kicking rationalistic ethics in the groin, rightfully demonstrating that philosophical delineation and actual moral ascription are radically divergent problems. And metaethics too comes into play, with explanatory metaethical grounds varying from track to track. In "She Smiled Sweetly" it's "nothing in why or when." "Something Happened" asserts "Someone says there's something more to pay/ For sins that you committed yesterday," using perfectly clearly two ambiguous referents (someone, something) while being convincingly "superstitious." "All Sold Out" angrily rejects reductionist psychological ethical groundwork. Inconsistencies, eclecticism. But above all, dilly-dally before and after the entrance of the ethical language game convention, ritualized chaos-and-back with the omnipresent over-riding assumption of the ritualized what-the-hell-does-evil-innocence/good-bad-mean-anyway?[4] So of course the reentry of just these terms as presenting the most obvious crucial (dippy) inapplicable meat of all.

---

[3]Zappa, "The Oracle Has It All Psyched Out," *Life*, June 28, 1968, p. 85.
[4]In "My Back Pages" Dylan uses this as an obvious backdrop for the clarification of assumed out-of-context clarify: "Good and bad, I define these terms, quite clear, no doubt, somehow."

And on an even more invulnerably flimsy level is the extension of ethical whimsy to intra-art interpretive byplay, as is manifest in the Stones' "Ride On Baby":

You walk up to me an' try an' look shy,
The red round your eyes says that you ain't a child,
Get out and ride on, baby, ride on, baby, ride on, baby,
Well I seen your face in a trashy magazine,
You know where you're goin' but I don't like the places you been.

If you could only recapture the times when you were just a creep and your responses to other creeps were just creepy, man that's where primal innocence is at. Go back to the days when you could really get something out of "Can I Get a Witness" and "Walkin' the Dog," an innocence that you still had all the way up to "Last Time" but not "Satisfaction," when you spread it on too thick and lost your vulnerability. Innocent even when you know *completely* where Cassius Clay was at and even Feuerbach but *not* Feuerbach as a *post*-religious guy. Man once upon a time you *knew* that the Cowsills ate it but somehow could be listened to, you know it *without* resorting to calling them a pack of freaks. Man the Stones were *always* happy don't you see? But now you see the Doors are like Cowsills and their world view is irrelevant. And the rest of this mamby pamby nostalgia (a priori nostalgia, easily generated) only makes it when the flash is gone and the recollective penis is limp and silent. But like there were the days when you wanted to be Hud and now you respect him as a freak and deal with yourself as implicitly about the same as the guy, and who knows where *that* is at?

LUKE TURNER ON ENYA

The Uncanny Valley: Enya's *Watermark* Revisited, 25 Years On*

I was never really into pop music as a kid, and would sometimes watch *The Chart Show* or *Top Of The Pops* with the volume turned right down. My dad used to listen to Capital Gold in the car, occasionally banging the steering wheel and exclaiming "great number," and there were any number of Wesleyan hymns (magnificent), contemporary praise music (less so) and, always, Leonard Cohen. My deep, enduring, entirely non-ironic love for Enya's gazillion-selling, buy-myself-a-castle-across-the-valley-from-Bono LP *Watermark*, a record that I still find deeply affecting to this day, probably connects elements of all the above.

Enya Ní Bhraonáin's first music came with her family as part of the hugely successful Clannad. Dissatisfied with her role in the group, she quit in 1982 and teamed up with the band's former manager Nicky Ryan and his wife Roma, a poet. Although there was little commercial interest in what they were doing—the trio were broke and recording in a garden shed—their songwriting swiftly began to develop. "I started writing instrumentals but Roma pointed out they were very visual, so she started writing lyrics," Enya told *The Times* in 2005. "And Nicky had this idea of creating a wall of sound and started multi-tracking my voice." This led to commissions to provide music for 1984 film *The Frog Prince* and TV series *The Celts*, which attracted the attention of Warner Music chairman Rob Dickens, who signed her, saying "Sometimes the company is there to make money, and sometimes it's there to make music. Enya's the latter."

As I was buying *Watermark* digitally yesterday, my colleague (and fellow Enya fan) Rory Gibb joked "sure you can't pick it up on Boomkat? They've loads of that sort of thing these days". And he's a point. I've actually been planning to write an In Defence Of Enya feature for the Quietus since the very day we started the site. For years, saying you liked Enya was enough to get you laughed out of town. Recently, though, her implicit presence has been everywhere (whether intentional or not). A recent example would be Julia Holter's "Horns Surrounding Me," a kissing cousin to *Watermark*'s "Cursum Perfico." Or how about early Laurel Halo, Julianna Barwick, Grouper; even new Burial track "Rival Dealer" has an Enya passage, as if his night bus had got lost up a country lane. She's surely ripe for a reappraisal.

Perhaps much of the derision directed at *Watermark* over the years has come thanks to the millstone around its neck—the entirely un-representative "Orinocho

*Turner, Luke. "The Uncanny Valley: Enya's *Watermark* Revisited, 25 Years On." The Quietus, December 13, 2013.

Flow," with it's icily plinking keys and lyrics "from the North to the South, Ebudæ into Khartoum/from the deep sea of Clouds to the island of the moon" that my brain used to get muddled up with and bootleg the "Scaramouche, Scaramouche, will you do the Fandango" from Queen's "Bohemian Rhapsody." (An unpleasant consequence). For all its hundreds of thousands of sales, and the *Top Of The Pops* performance that made them, that track distracts from the quiet, clever grace of much of the rest of the album, which recalls traditional Celtic folk, sacred early music and world music—which, let us not forget, was then held in its stuffy, separate ghetto. To label and denigrate this as new age is lazy too—Enya herself dismissed the term as "marketing," and I'd argue that *Watermark* is no more crystals and wind charms and whimsy than much of Sigur Ros' output. While a record with clear Celtic origins and Enya always proud of her roots, there's no misty-eyed evoking of some shamrock 'n' leprechaun "auld country" here, with songs delivered in English, Irish and Latin.

"On Your Shore" and "Exile" are both gorgeous hymns, the latter gliding downstream on flute and organ drones. "Storms In Africa" has a great loom, the curvature of the earth appearing from Mir, that sort of thing, ending with great rattling drums and chants. It's not a million miles from the section of Fuck Buttons' current set where Ben Power starts clobbering away on a tom. The finest track of all is "Cursum Perficio," with its strident, thundering chant.

Looking back, perhaps some of this clear pomposity (and I see nothing wrong with pomposity) comes from overproduction, with sometimes just a little too much 80s gloss and sheen on the strings and Enya's vocals. Yet, essentially, *Watermark* is a deeply weird album in the context of its bright and garish era, and as well as that a strongly and confidently female album. It also stands out as a record inspired by spiritual music in a mainstream pop world that has in recent years chosen to end the centuries-old musical dialogue between the secular and religious, the sacred and profane.

I find it fascinating that *Watermark* was released on the same day as Talk Talk's superlative *Spirit Of Eden*. Arguably, they're records cut from a very similar cloth, with similar evocations and textures, though *Watermark* was of course at heart a pop album, and *Spirit Of Eden* the sound of a group tacking ever further into the avant-garde.

Listening back to *Watermark* now is a strange experience. Like any music from childhood, it has a powerful ability to take me back: to car journeys through the British landscape, the orange baked beans of traffic lights over the moors, trees caught in the headlights, or enduring the prosaic surroundings of my satellite town and dreaming of being in a place of wind and water, mountains, marsh and sky. The gunmetal paint and blobs of glue that disfigure that old cassette case also recall endless plays while applying toxic paint and cellulose dope to model aircraft—I suspect *Watermark*'s more psychedelic qualities might have been revealed during those innocent headrushes. I don't really believe in the separation of music into false binaries of credible and authentic versus naff and hollow pop, and guilty pleasures are a nonsense. Musical taste is an aesthetic continuum, and listening back to *Watermark* now I can trace the evolution of my interests from Enya not to Julia Holter and her ilk, but through The Cure's *Disintegration* and Slowdive to the living other worlds of Coil, Carter Tutti, Grumbling Fur and These New Puritans. Looking back with hindsight, W*atermark* marked the beginning of my own journey, from otherworldly pop to entirely stranger musical pastures.

The Enya *Watermark* piece was a bit of an itch that needed scratching, something that I find is the case with a lot of articles that I've written over the years, especially think pieces. The idea is there, won't go away, and eventually appears, rather chaotically, over my computer screen. I don't really have a set workflow for my music writing, but that Enya piece was probably fairly typical—a scattering out of ideas that are eventually corralled into a narrative, then leaving the piece overnight before revisiting for a final check before publishing the next day.—**Luke Turner**, Associate Editor, The Quietus

BRIAN MORTON ON COMPUTER MUSIC

Metal Machine Musings: Composing With Machines*

Machines can't laugh, but will they sing? Back in the Dream Time of any culture there is a persistent fantasy about things that make music—singing rocks, "sea organs" that pipe sound out of fissures, naturally interwoven branches that groan their "cool" harmonics as the evening sun moves off them. Only a step from there to artefacts that make their "music"—is it?—without further intervention.

The Aeolian harp is only a distant Mediterranean ancestor of "environmentally interactive" works of the 60s and after, pieces like Detlef and Tauschi Kronberger's, which combined environmental change (like rain or wind) with photo-electric cells and pressure pads, to create a musical ambience that couldn't be controlled because the parameters were always too changeable. Step back into that corner of the room, where the baby gurgled, and the pad triggers something different. The wind changes and the harp falls silent, or produces a new, warning hum. Terry Riley drew his inspiration for a music of equal temperament from the image of a harp left on a headland, subject to the movements of time itself.

The "technology" goes back even further. There are rain drums, tuned to patter out a quiet accompaniment to the redemption of the desert. There are wind chimes. There's even the bushman who traps bees in a gourd and drifts off to sleep to a minimalist New Age hum, confident too that their stinging anger has been contained. And isn't all music about either containment or release?

That's certainly true of the longest-standing music machine, the bird-in-cage. If a Weather Report sleeve is to be believed, a bird doesn't fly because it has wings; it has wings because it can fly. If so, a bird in a cage isn't a bird any more. Blind it with a hot wire to make it sing better, and it becomes a thing. Harrison Birtwistle's Mad King has a rack of tuned finches to accompany his wandering.

The technology begins to assert itself and establish its own "event horizon" with the arrival of mechanical clock-bells, musical boxes, fairground calliopes, perfect, controllable events that nonetheless appeal to a certain distant animism in our make-up. There was a soldier in the King's Guard at Windsor in the 1930s who tried to prove he hadn't nodded on duty by claiming that Big Tom had struck thirteen. They banged him off to jankers and had him talk to the chaplain. And then the bell did it again, for no discernible mechanical reason, just for the sheer hell of hearing its own voice one more time. It's the most dangerous fantasy of all, that machines might actually be

---

*Morton, Brian. "Metal Machine Musings: Composing With Machines," *The Wire*, #96, February 1992.

trying, not just to communicate, but to *express*. Do we dare to believe that the Tin Men really want hearts?

As we've got further down the road, towards the generational leap that might let a machine make up its own mind about something, we've also got further from the animistic self-confidence that lets us share the world with things that might tap our quintessence. It's somehow OK to have a computer or a robot run amok, but the thought that one might sit down and write a piece of music (more dangerous even than randomizing colors or words into "accidental" realism or metaphor) is utterly, unutterably unacceptable.

And so, we've got to the stage where we preen our tattered and outmoded humanism with the idea that it's all down to us anyway, computers-don't-make-errors-people-do, GIGO ("garbage in, garbage out"), you-can-always-pull-the-plug, and so on. The machine demands an interface.

The history of music and machines has always been started too late. The first score to be written through the offices of a digital computer was LeJaren Hiller's and Leonard M. Isaacson's 1956 string quartet *Illiac Suite*. Serialists soon found that they could save quite a lot of "paper time," hell, quite a lot of paper, by getting the idiot savant box to rattle through the permutations and inversions in a tenth of the time, with the comforting thought that they know not what they do and you-can-always-pull-the-plug.

Xenakis used computers with a refreshing pragmatism to save the labor of working out every last detail of those huge stochastic masses, and no one dismisses as bogus his music any more than one might dismiss a Piero della Francesca because an unknown apprentice "did the sky bits" or colored in an edge of curtain.

In the wake of Hiller's and Isaacson's beautifully documented experiment, there was increasing activity in digital sound synthesis. Max Mathews, with the blessing of Bell Telephone, devised complex arrays of "compilers" that allowed all the quantifiable parameters of a "musical event," as he described it, to be determined by machine. A decade later, he was operating with the optimistically-titled GROOVE (Generation of Real-Time Operations on Voltage-controlled Equipment) which gradually gave way to digital synths, and lead by an inexorable progress of intellectual machination and raw cash to IRCAM and the much-vaunted polyphonic 4X.

That skips quite a lot of the history and much of the arithmetic, because at the same time there was a countervailing resistance to the idea of technology as a primarily analytical and synthetic tool. Cage, with or without a dose of Zen, perceived that there was a music in and of the environment which had to be understood before we risked the hubris of making our own. Cage has had remarkably little truck with computers. He has been content to explore the external and inner space we occupy for the music that it yields.

And at the same time as Hiller and Isaacson were making their experiments, Percy Grainger was working on his Heath Robinson [or Rube Goldberg, for an American audience] "free music machine," which followed a dark-field ink trace to produce great swooping glissandi, not dissimilar to Xenakis's, and concentrations of sound inaccessible to a human performer. Down in Mexico, the now vastly over-rated Conlon Nancarrow was punching out "scores" of fanatical denseness for an Ampico player piano. It's interesting that Kurt Vonnegut Jr's first full length science fiction tale took the player piano as the informing metaphor for a world whose alien inhumanity still depended on a piece of domestic kitsch.

What all of these men share, to adapt the words of Xenakis's mentor and collaborator Le Corbusier, is that music has become a machine to be inhabited. That is very different from the belief that we can be possessed by music. The mutuality of music within and without is the impossible harmony. As long as we are trapped with the weaselly conception of instruments as things that stand between us—sometimes neutrally, sometimes obstructively—and the music, then we cannot realise that the instruments are the music.

This isn't nature mysticism, and has nothing to do with the "natural" resonance of gut and wood, brass or ebony, but with a basic metaphysical misconception at the heart of technologised music-making. We've never been closer to or further from understanding it.

The problem with GROOVE is that it didn't. Computer music, all mediated music, is painfully cumbersome, even when it seems most graceful. Our obsession with silence and music's aspiration to silence is explained by our persistent belief that music is etched on silence the way a circuit is etched on a board. There is very little interactive freedom in the direction musical technology has taken us. Watching and hearing George Lewis in "conversation" with a computer, as attentive to its gestures (and as politely blind to its limitations) as it is responsive to his trombone, is one of the most significant experiences in contemporary music, for it allows the possibility that technology allows us to be responsive to the made environment as we might be to other improvisers or to the weather or to a particular configuration of alpha waves (though we wouldn't know about that).

The dream has faded into a programme of research. But it really isn't over till the Tin Man swells his skinny ribs and sings.

JORDAN FERGUSON ON J DILLA'S *DONUTS*

33⅓ Volume #93 *Donuts*

The New*

As Dilla's final work, *Donuts* will always carry extra significance in the minds of many listeners. There's something about an artist's last work that seems to bring added resonance. According to the novelist John Updike, "[W]orks written late in a writer's life retain a fascination. They exist, as do last words, where life edges into death, and perhaps have something uncanny to tell us."[5]

If the presence of death and dying can be felt and heard throughout *Donuts*, if hidden messages are scattered throughout it, they don't explain why they're delivered in the ways in which they are. As the end point of a career that spanned over a decade and went through at least a quartet of distinct styles, it's hard to deny that *Donuts* is, at its most basic, *really weird*. To try and glean a sense of why that is, one must consider what it means for artists when they're faced with their expected or untimely end, and what that means for their art.

In 2006, the same year *Donuts* was released, the literary theorist Edward Said published *On Late Style*, a book that sought to explore why great artists and composers late in their lives (meaning near the end, not necessarily elderly) frequently produce work in one of two styles: a sort of creative final summation, the period at the end of the sentence as found in Shakespeare's *The Tempest*, or works that suggest not, "harmony and resolution but ... intransigence, difficulty and unresolved contradiction."[6] With those moods at either end of the continuum, *Donuts* clearly falls along the latter.

Said draws heavily on the work of German philosopher Theodor Adorno, specifically what he had to say in a 1937 essay on the late works of Beethoven:

> For Adorno . . . those compositions that belong to [Beethoven's] third period . . . constitute . . . a moment when an artist who is fully in command of his medium nevertheless abandons communication with the established social order of which he is a part and achieves a contradictory, alienated relationship with it.[7]

*Ferguson, Jordan. *Donuts*. New York: Bloomsbury, 2014, 100–105. Reprinted with permission.
[5]John Updike, "Late Works," *The New Yorker*, August 7, 2006, http://www.newyorker.com/archive/2006/08/07/060807crat_atlarge.
[6]Edward W. Said, *On Late Style: Music and Literature Against the Grain* (New York: Vintage, 2006), 7.
[7]Said, 2006, 8.

Like Adorno's Beethoven, J Dilla was also an artist at the height of his powers, struck down by forces he could not control just as he ventured out into what would be the last phase of his career. The move to L.A., collaborations with Madlib, and an easy working relationship with Stones Throw seem to have given Dilla the freedom to move his art wherever he wanted. As a musician he had nothing left to lose, no limits or rules to concern himself with. And, if what Kübler-Ross suggests is true, he was acutely aware his window to do so was rapidly closing.

"I think mentally [moving] just kind of freed his mind, you know? It's a better way of life out here compared to where we were. I think it just freed him up to kind of think like, 'man, I can do whatever I want to do,'" said Frank Nitt.[8]

Since the publication of Said's book (written during his own late period as he battled leukemia and published posthumously), critics and scholars have been engaged in a sort of tug-of-war regarding the validity of his ideas. The most common criticism is that, considering each individual encounters death in his or her own way, one cannot shoehorn a universal theory of late style into all circumstances, there are too many variables at play: some artists have no idea death is imminent, some are aware of its possibility for years; some endure physical disabilities or diseases, some do not; some are elderly, some are taken tragically young. It's unreasonable to think that any theory of late style is applicable in all scenarios. Even the term itself falls under criticism: "[It] can't be a direct result of aging or death, because style is not a mortal creature, and works of art have no organic life to lose,"[9] writes Michael Wood in his introduction to Said's *On Late Style*.

But just because critics can't agree on a unified aesthetic for late style doesn't mean that late style, as a phenomenon, does not exist. One doesn't need to be a classical music scholar to notice the sweeping sonic and structural changes between Beethoven's "Moonlight Sonata" and the *Ninth Symphony*, first performed three years before his death and long after he started losing his hearing. Late style has been applied to Stravinsky, Strauss, and Schumann, and is equally applicable to J Dilla. Look at the adjectives frequently incorporated to describe what is considered "late style": fragmentary, difficult, irascible, nostalgic, and introspective. *Donuts* can be legitimately described with an identical vocabulary. So where does Dilla's late style come from?

According to the scholar Joseph N. Straus, the one unifying characteristic among authors working in a late style is disability, not impending death, as death cannot typically be predicted accurately, but non-normative bodily functions are something the artist endures every day: "[i]n the end *there may be nothing late about late style* in the sense of chronological age, the approach of life's end, or authorial or historical

---

[8]Stussy—J Dilla Documentary Part 2 of 3, YouTube Video, posted by "Stussy Video," May 25, 2011, https://www.youtube.com/watch?v=b7d-uMSsklc

[9]Michael Wood, "Introduction," *On Late Style: Music and Literature Against the Grain* by Edward W. Said (New York: Vintage, 2006), xiii.

belatedness ... late style may be less about anticipating death than living with disability, less about the future hypothetical than the present reality" (emphasis in the original).[10] Certainly, Dilla's present reality during the mixing of *Donuts* could be considered non-normative, and was bound to have a psychological and physical impact on the music he made.

Ronnie Reese echoed Peanut Butter Wolf's comment to Egon before *Donuts* entered production, that a project of its sort was maybe the only thing Dilla *could* produce. "I think that it was the album that it was most feasible for him to make. You know, it's not like he can go to studios and master things or had access to a tremendous amount of equipment or gear when he was working on *Donuts*. So what he gave is the most he was able to give us at that time."

Like the Kübler-Ross model, late style theory is not intended to be a catch-all for all works by dying artists, and not every dying artist's work conforms to every aspect of late style: "It would be unlikely for any single work to exhibit all of these characteristics, but a late style work would necessarily have most of them."[11] This is certainly true of *Donuts*.

Contrary to Said's argument regarding the late artist's contradictory relationship to the present, though, *Donuts* doesn't abandon the present social order as much as tilts its head at it in a "what's up?" moment of acknowledgment, not just in its use of classic breaks and sounds but in specific response to the larger hip-hop landscape. "Dilla Says Go" takes the same sample source as "Hate It or Love It," a chart-topping single by L.A. rapper The Game released in early 2005, and makes something that sounds entirely different. More interestingly, "Stop!" uses the same Dionne Warwick sample as "Throwback," a 2004 song by the R&B singer Usher produced by Just Blaze. The song, like many contemporary R&B songs, features a rap break on the bridge, in this case provided by Jadakiss. In the opening moments of "Stop!" it's Jadakiss's voice that's manipulated to ask, "Is (death) real?" Is it a coincidence that Dilla took the same sample used on a song that came out the year before *Donuts* and even sampled the voice of that song's featured rapper? It's a question that can't be answered but it certainly seems too coincidental to be an accident. The choice may have been more intentional than anyone thought.

An online message board post attributed to Questlove, dated 2007 (its authorship is unverified, though it has a voice extremely similar to Questlove's writing from that time), alleges that the 2005 beats, including *Donuts*, were Dilla's "Kanye Batches" just as the process that led to the "Little Brother" beat came from the "Pete Rock Batches." They were the result of Dilla taking inspiration from what he was impressed by in hip-hop, and trying to put his own stamp on it.

"He told me that 'Spaceship' [from West's debut *The College Dropout*] fucked him up cause for the first time he couldn't hear that interpretation of [Marvin Gaye's]

---

[10]Straus, Joseph N., "Disability and 'Late Style' in Music," *The Journal of Musicology*, 25, 1 (Winter 2008), 6.
[11]Straus, 2008, 11.

'Distant Lover' in his head when he heard 'Distant Lover.' Kind of fucked him up a li'l [sic]."[12] If the post is to be believed, for the first time in years, Dilla was actually taken aback by something he heard in hip-hop, a flip he never would have considered. So he tried not only to approximate the style popularized primarily by West and Just Blaze, he looked to master it, taking their soulsampling approach, annihilating it, and reconstructing it into something wholly his own.

For all of these reasons, *Donuts* continues to exist as a late work in all its irascible, confrontational glory, continuing to challenge and irritate new listeners looking for insight into mortality with its occasionally impenetrable contradictions.

As the cultural critic Terry Teachout writes, "[m]ost of us want to know what to expect at the end of our own lives, and look to art to shed light on that dark encounter. But true artists, unlike the Hollywood kind, don't always tell us what we want to hear."[13]

[12]"Questlove on Dilla's Inspirations," Stones Throw Message Board, http://webcache.googleusercontent.com/search?q=cache:9VrxiWumegsJ:www.stonesthrow.com/messageboard/index.php%253F showtopic%253D4357+&cd=1&hl=en&ct=clnk& gl=ca

[13]Terry Teachout, "Facing the Final Curtain," *The Wall Street Journal*, September 18, 2009, http:// online.wsj.com/article/SB10001424052970204518504574418790035029918.html

WRITING PROMPT: LATE STYLE

Using Jordan Ferguson's examination of Edward Said's concept of "late style," discuss a song or a handful of songs from a late album by a deceased artist in a 1,000–2,000 word essay.

Consider writing about late albums by Johnny Cash, Queen, or Elliot Smith (or choose your own).

Alternately, use another theory or concept to discuss a single song or album: Harold Bloom's concept of "the anxiety of influence" from his book of the same title; the idea of "the male gaze" from Laura Mulvey's essay "Visual Pleasure and Narrative Cinema"; a new historicist approach as exemplified by literary critics like Stephen Greenblatt (see his *Practicing New Historicism*, edited with Catherine Gallagher). Choose a passage from the work of the author who articulates the concept you're considering then quote and discuss it in your essay (note how Ferguson offers and discusses a passage by Adorno early in his piece) before turning the idea to an analysis of the song you've chosen.

THE GO-BETWEENS

OFFBEAT ADVICE

Don't listen to anyone who tells you that whatever subject you're exploring is pointless, lacking a market, and/or a waste of your or his time.—**Joe Bonomo**, Music Columnist, *The Normal School*, and Associate Professor of English at Northern Illinois University

Lighten up a little—but only a little! I was kind of hard on myself, always castigating myself for not working hard enough or not getting enough done. But, particularly when you're just starting out and maybe don't have too many people in your corner yet, you need this kind of drive. You have to take your work seriously before anyone else will.—**Bryan Charles**, writer and **33⅓** author

I've had to admit that I'm an idiot many times. It's kind of crazy how often no one says it, really.—**Casey Jarman**, Managing Editor, the *Believer*

In the comics business, they say "you need to have two out of three things to make it in this industry: you need to be brilliant, you need to be the easiest person in the world to work with, and you need to be on time every single time. Any two of those will do." Same goes for this business. I try to be timely and I try to be easy to work with. I am also pretty decent at negotiating; that helps.—**Douglas Wolk**, freelance arts journalist

Having started out as an editor first, I always file on time. It's amazing how many people think that's not a big deal.—**Michael Barclay**, freelance writer/broadcaster, co-author, *Have Not Been the Same: The CanRock Renaissance 1985–1995*

I try to have a clear picture in mind of who reads what I write. I work the beat hard, and I trust my conclusions, so I can write with confidence and respect for the reader.—**Jim Fusilli**, rock and pop critic, *The Wall Street Journal*, Editor, ReNewMusic.net

In an Austrian Death Machine piece, I mistakenly identified the drummer, because the band's singer mistakenly identified the drummer. You can't be too careful with fact-checking. Double-source everything. Sources mis-speak all the time. If I'm not paying attention when I'm talking, I might mistakenly identify myself as being 42 years old, not 41. Don't assume anything. If you're doing an email interview and the subject's Facebook page says they live in Boston, Mass, then don't assume a wrong detail into existence and write "Ferris answered questions from his home office in Boston." I've had that happen. Verify every little fact.—**D.X. Ferris**, Ohio Society of Professional Journalists Reporter of the Year, Professor, **33⅓** author

I would ban the word "ethereal."—**Michael Azerrad**, author, journalist and Editor-in-Chief of the *Talkhouse*

I can only think of writing pet peeves not at all exclusive to music writing, the big one being the "Insert Joke Here" punchline. I find writing about music thrilling and fun and intimidating and rewarding . . . and I can't imagine wasting an opportunity for merriment and hilarity in the fertile music ecosystem by copping out like that.—**Phillip Crandall**, author of the **33⅓** book on Andrew W.K.'s *I Get Wet*

I find unhelpful the romantic idea that music writing is a calling to which people are drawn by a burning passion for music. If it's an art form at all, it's a very minor, secondary, parasitic art form. Writers who recognize that they are basically hacks with a job to do usually write much better. If I was Supreme Leader, I would also purge music writing of the cliches with which it's plagued. There would be no more 'sophomore albums'. Use of the word 'seminal' would bring about show trial and a slow death.—**Sam Inglis**, Features Editor, *Sound On Sound* magazine

A return to more ferocious and arbitrary discrimination would be nice. Less polite, cautious, narrow minded, neo-educational writing in mainstream journals would be nice.—**Paul Morley**, writer and critic

I'm not a fan of the shift in journalism of all kinds to light, list-focused click bait that people enjoy but don't have to think about, but I also think people should come away from a piece thinking "that was a good read that I think others should read too," not just "well now I know what reviewer X was obsessed with in the '90s—**Evie Nagy**, *Fast Company* staff writer, former editor at *Billboard* and *Rolling Stone*

I was more confident, better at pitching, and perhaps a little less shouty. On occasion—generally I think being shouty is a good thing.—**Luke Turner**, Associate Editor, The Quietus

Turning off the internet is a must. If you want to have a writer's output, you need to be aggressive managing your input. I have one computer on my desk that's hooked up to the internet, and another one that's a green 1998 iMac with no modem. When I need to concentrate, I write on the internet-free one, then use floppy disks to transfer it to the new computer. The two-computer method works for me. God only knows how I'll get any writing done when that 1998 iMac finally bites the dust.—**Rob Sheffield**, writer, *Rolling Stone*

CHAPTER 5
THE ARTIST INTERVIEW

INTRODUCTION

I was anything but a seasoned music writer when I had the good luck of interviewing a number of successful artists for the first music book I edited, *Solo: Women Singer-Songwriters In Their Own Words*. The writers who give advice about conducting interviews in this chapter have much to say about how to do it well. I'm in no position to gainsay any of that advice, the product of a lot of experience, trial and error, success. Much of what they advise jibes perfectly with what I've found: don't offer questions that will be likely to trigger prefab responses, follow the conversation with great focus and imagination rather than sticking to your question list, know your subject and his or her work cold. Having come from the smaller and more belletristic world of literary magazines, I approached the interviews for *Solo* as conversations with writers, thinking more about the *Paris Review* interviews than celebrity Q and As. From Sheryl Crow to Lucinda Williams, the women I talked with responded in fresh and generous ways to what was anything but a typical music journalist interview. The full, often revealing answers they gave suggested that these artists were eager to engage in an extensive, thoughtful conversation. Sometimes with a particularly in-demand subject, an assistant would arrive at an appointed time to signal the end of the interview, but the artist would wave him away and we'd go on talking. That's undeniably a great feeling for an interviewer: it's going so well that even the musician wants to keep going, push back other commitments, forgo a little downtime before a show. If such sessions were a point of pride, I felt a lot less proud when I listened back to those interviews and heard myself *not paying attention* as I stopped a response dead—whether from nerves or eagerness—instead of patiently letting the answer develop, encouraging it to continue on its way to wherever it had been so promisingly headed. Heeding the advice implicit in the interviews and explicit in the tips from the music writers that follow will help you stay clear of that pitfall and, I hope, have fewer regrets that you missed out of what might have been the really good stuff.—MW

EXPERT ADVICE FROM OUR WRITERS

Whoever it is—actor, writer, musician, rookie, veteran, legend, hype—they have a story. So I try to look for questions that will tell or illuminate their story.—**Rob Sheffield**, writer, *Rolling Stone*

Rock critics and music geeks love lists (see: *High Fidelity*), so let me put in list form the knowledge I've synthesized during 33 years of interviewing (my first two interviews: rock critics Robert Christgau and Lester Bangs, when I was a 17-year-old senior at Hudson Catholic Regional High School for Boys in 1982).

1. Prepare exhaustively. Read everything you can get your hands on about the person you're about to talk to: new stuff, old stuff, ancient history, the phone book in their area code. And then throw it all away!

2. You need to have that background on file in your brain, so you can reference it at a moment's notice if the subject gives you an opening. ("Funny you should say that, because I read that as a kid, your hobby was breeding goats, isn't that right?") But above all, you want to have a conversation! You know, just like the person across from you is a normal human being, even though he or she almost certainly is not. (If they were, why would you be interviewing them? And human nature being what it is, even the person in the street is probably way more complicated and unrepresentative of "normal," whatever that may be, then you might assume at first.)

3. Whatever you do, do not compile a list of "great questions" and then ask them in order, one to ten. Have a few questions ready as emergency fallbacks, but listen to what your subject is saying. Be flexible enough to go in the directions that he or she is taking you. Unless . . .

4. They're one of those subjects who just want to sell-sell-sell you. Some interviewees, particularly celebrities on the road with new product to hawk, do not listen to your questions; they simply hit "play" on the tape recorders inside their pea brains. You may ask, "How was the weather in Cannes last week?" and they may answer, "My new album is available in stores now, and the movie opens next week!" So be ready to derail the hype express if warranted. As long as you're heeding point three above, don't be afraid to jump in with an aggressive or digressive question. Get in their faces if you have to, as we used to say in Jersey.

5. In case the importance of point three hasn't become clear as yet, let me say it again: Listen. Listen, listen, listen, listen. LISTEN!

6. And, finally, despite the empathy of all that listening, remember that you are not there to have this person like you. Be respectful or congenial, yes. But do not (do not, do not) kiss ass. Do not try to impress. Do not make the mistake of thinking your subject likes you or is a real person just like you! (See point two again.) You are trying to get at some small sliver of the truth, and to expose some possibly hitherto unseen aspect of the subject's personality, philosophy, or life's work. As Phillip Seymour Hoffman-as-Bangs says to Patrick Fugit as the young Cameron Crowe in the director's autobiographical film *Almost Famous*: "You can't make friends with rock stars. These people are not your friends!" Substitute "rock stars" for "interview subjects" in any situation—actor, Nobel Prize winner, congresswoman, revolutionary, cartoon character, or America's Next Top Model—and you will never, ever go wrong.—**Jim DeRogatis**, author, co-host of *Sound Opinions*, and lecturer at Columbia College Chicago

I never prepare questions; I just have a conversation with someone. I might think up two questions. Sometimes it works to know less about them so that they can tell you and also so you do not ask whatever everyone else asks.—**Jessica Hopper**, Music Editor at *Rookie Magazine*, and Senior Editor, the *Pitchfork Review*

When I interviewed Pete Rock, I was most interested in how his legendary status was sitting with him as he continued his career in a wildly different musical landscape. I picked a few questions that I thought set up this concept but would be positive, ego-boosting set-ups that would make him feel comfortable with me and stuck those at the front of the line (along with some questions about his new record to make it clear to him I actually cared about what he was promoting). Then I eased into the bigger questions.—**Matthew Gasteier, 33⅓** author

If I can get at why they are making music, that helps to shape the direction of my questions, to flesh that out and learn from them.—**Mark Richardson**, Editor-in-Chief, Pitchfork

Learn the subject's tone. Do they evade certain types of questions? Do they have a series of standard answers they give? Are there questions they've been asked way too many times already? What have they never discussed? What subjects excite them? What questions will lower their defenses? Why? Then, listen as hard as possible.—**Ross Simonini**, writer, Editor at The *Believer* magazine, musician

I once conducted 75 percent of an interview into a cassette recorder that was on Pause. There was no fixing it; the artist was on a plane to another continent by the time I realized the tape was lost. I was sorry not to have the interview, but after beating myself up for a few minutes, decided it was going to have to be enough that we'd had a great conversation. That's one benefit of editing your own magazine: the only boss who can chew you out is you.—**Kim Cooper**, Editrix, *Scram*

Ask yourself what really interests you about the subject, and ask that person a question in a clear, honest way. I've found that people respond to that approach because they can tell it's something you really care about and not just a perfunctory question.—**Ben Sisario**, reporter, the *New York Times*

I'll write down all the questions I want to ask on a piece of paper, glance at them a couple of times and—for me this is the most important part—put that piece of paper away and never look at it again. Interview subjects want to be engaged in natural, flowing conversation with someone who's making eye contact with them; they don't want to talk to somebody who's looking down at a piece of paper every five seconds and reading off stilted questions verbatim. Try your best make the flow of conversation as natural as possible, like you're having a chat with a friend.—**Lindsay Zoladz**, Associate Editor, Pitchfork

First I think about who my audience is and what they will want to learn from the subject. Is it just a personality piece? A business piece where practical lessons should be drawn out? Then I read interviews that have already been done with the subject, if they exist. This helps me determine not only what ground has been covered in the press, but what I'd like the subject to expand on. It's not a crime to ask a subject a question they've been asked before if necessary, but a better way to do it is to acknowledge that you know they've said X, how has that evolved or how does it apply to a particular new angle or context? And then there are just the left field questions—anything you want to know about their personal life or free time that you decide would be appropriate to ask about and that readers would enjoy knowing.—**Evie Nagy**, *Fast Company* staff writer, former Editor at *Billboard* and *Rolling Stone*

As an ethnographer—ethnography is a research process that involves spending time within a community as a way of understanding it—ideally, I strive to get to know a community and its members before I start asking questions. I prefer to ask open-ended questions, which allow people to tell me what's most important to them.—**Anthony Kwame Harrison**, popular music scholar, Virginia Tech

In some senses it is better to go into an interview needing to find things out because you can't do a quick check and instantly know things. I still try and do an interview without doing too much checking, or basing it on my own, possibly inaccurate, or subjective, information, so that I have a need to find out. The problem is, though, that if you write stuff that cannot be easily checked and clarified—i.e. it is not part of what is already out there—there is a tendency for people, editors and readers, to not believe it or trust it, to think that what you are writing is dead wrong. For me this interferes with the essential myth-making qualities of music writing—the best music writing generates great, billowing lies, elaborates the effective fantasy of great music, rather than confirming facts and meekly agreeing with dates, descriptions and existing classification.—**Paul Morley**, writer and critic

The nice thing about talking to artists is that you can tackle shit like love and death and they generally won't be freaked out by it. The main thing is just to not give them any opportunity to give you the standard spiel about their new album or whatever. You don't want that, and however secretly, they don't either.—**Casey Jarman**, Managing Editor, the *Believer*

I try and keep the questions as open as I can; try and remember not to speak very much and let the interviewee do all the talking, remembering to really give them time to get to answers—this can mean letting silence happen. This can be very helpful in terms of unlocking what the interviewee is really concerned with.—**Pete Astor**, writer, academic, musician

The most important quality in an interviewer is the ability to listen: when interviewing, don't worry about your next question; allow whatever answer's being given to steer the conversation. You can always get back to your original list of questions—and you should make sure that you do that before the interview's over—but leave yourself open to surprises and turns. The best "answers" usually come to questions that I hadn't originally conceived. Sometimes, once an interview subject gets comfortable, they will end up steering the conversation. It's important to let that happen naturally, as long as the subject isn't steering only toward their agenda.—**Joe Bonomo**, music columnist, *The Normal School*, and Associate Professor of English at Northern Illinois University

Try to surprise your subject. Sometimes talking about something tangential reveals something about their own art they've never even thought about before. It also means you'll get quotes that won't appear in every other article that month.—**Michael Barclay**, freelance writer/broadcaster, co-author, *Have Not Been the Same: The CanRock Renaissance 1985–1995*

I try to learn something about the subject's interests beyond music and work those topics into the conversation early on.—**Bruce Eaton**, author, *Radio City* (33⅓)

The closest I've seen to a formula for interview magic is from Nardwuar The Human Serviette; he gives incredibly thoughtful gifts to spark conversation, which he then complements with incredible research. He's the best for a reason.—**Phillip Crandall**, author of the **33⅓** book on Andrew W.K.'s *I Get Wet*

LIZZY GOODMAN WITH KIM GORDON

Kim Gordon Sounds Off*

The last time I saw Kim Gordon, she was preparing a chicken for roasting. This was several years ago, and I was working on a piece about the bohemian style of Northampton, Massachusetts, home of indie rock's most powerful couple, Kim Gordon and Thurston Moore, of legendary noise-rock band Sonic Youth. Moore gave me a tour of the veritable record store that was his basement, and Gordon showed me her art studio and racks of vintage clothes. I saw the rumpled sheets on the couple's bed, the *Buffy the Vampire Slayer* box set in their den, and the refreshingly girly bedroom of their teenage daughter, Coco. But later, to my friends, what I described was sitting at their kitchen table watching Moore assemble cassette tapes for an upcoming release on his Ecstatic Peace! label while his wife of some 20 years was elbow-deep in poultry stuffing. In that moment, Gordon was the ultimate hipster Renaissance woman I aspired to be, a feminist rebel who could make avant-garde art all day, then cook a killer dinner for her family at night.

Since forming Sonic Youth with Moore in 1981, Gordon has come to personify two qualities generally considered incompatible: rebellion and maturity. She played bass and guitar, wrote songs, and sang for Sonic Youth, a band whose mission—infiltrate the mainstream with dissonant, defiant guitar noise—shaped '90s alternative rock. Gordon coproduced Hole's debut album, *Pretty on the Inside*; nurtured a young Kurt Cobain; put a teenage Chloë Sevigny on-screen for the first time, alongside the infamous collection for Perry Ellis by then up-and-coming designer Marc Jacobs; and, via the band's album-cover art and videos, helped popularize the work of such visionaries as Spike Jonze, Todd Haynes, Gerhard Richter, Mike Kelley, and Richard Prince. Over the past 30 years she's been considered an indie sex symbol, an iconoclastic performer, and a de facto professor of modern feminist pop mystique (her interest in Karen Carpenter, Madonna, and, more recently, Britney Spears lent them depth).

And yet, as scrutinized as she has been, Gordon has always been considered a mystery. A typical Sonic Youth interview featured Moore waxing philosophical while Gordon, in sunglasses, sat by his side, nearly silent. Aloof, remote, and intimidating are often used to describe her. After decades in the public eye, it seemed like this was the way things would always be. Then, in the fall of 2011, Gordon and Moore announced they were separating. The news called into question the future of Sonic Youth and devastated legions of music fans. Jon Dolan, one of the flintiest rock critics

---

*Goodman, Lizzy. "Kim Gordon Sounds Off." *Elle*, April 22, 2013. Reprinted with permission.

around, began a piece for Grantland about their breakup with this plaintive cry: "Whyyyyyyyyyyyyyyyyyyyyyyyyyyyyyyyyyyyyyyyyyy!"

"I can understand people being curious," Gordon says when I ask her about all the attention she's gotten since the split. "I'm curious myself. What's going to happen now?"

It's late afternoon on an unforgivingly cold winter day in New York City. Gordon arrives a few minutes early at Sant Ambroeus, the understated West Village restaurant she chose for our meeting. She's wearing eyeliner, a black-and-white-striped sweaterdress, and cognac-brown boots. I find myself dissecting her look so I can copy it later; such is the immediacy of her style. It would be rude to say Gordon doesn't look her age, which is 59. That's a line reserved for those who are desperately trying to appear young. There is nothing desperate about Kim Gordon.

When the subject of dating comes up, I'm not surprised to hear that younger men are vying for her attention, though the couple is not yet divorced.

"We have all these books, records, and art and are getting it all assessed; that's what is taking so long," she says after ordering a glass of rosé. But both have moved on. Among her suitors are a restaurateur, an architect, and an actor. "It's just weird," Gordon says of navigating new romance. "I can't tell what's normal." And Moore has regularly been seen with the same woman, fueling the rumor that his affair helped doom their marriage. (Thurston Moore declined a request for an interview.) "We seemed to have a normal relationship inside of a crazy world," Gordon says of her marriage. "And in fact, it ended in a kind of normal way—midlife crisis, starstruck woman."

Some years ago, a woman Gordon declines to name became a part of the Sonic Youth world, first as the girlfriend of an erstwhile band member and later as a partner on a literary project with Moore. Eventually, Gordon discovered a text message and confronted him about having an affair. They went to counseling, but he kept seeing the other woman. "We never got to the point where we could just get rid of her so I could decide what I wanted to do," Gordon says. "Thurston was carrying on this whole double life with her. He was really like a lost soul." Moore moved out. Gordon stayed home and listened to a lot of hip-hop. "Rap music is really good when you're traumatized," she says.

The first few months were rough. "It did feel like every day was different," she recalls. "It's a huge, drastic change." But slowly things improved. She adjusted to the framework of semisingle parenthood. (Coco, their only child, is now a freshman at a Chicago art school.) Gordon kept their Colonial filled with friends—a musician, a poet, and Moore's adult niece, with whom Gordon has remained very close. "Sometimes I cook dinner and just invite whomever," she says of her improvised family life. "Everyone helps out a bit with the dogs. It's a big house. It's nice to have people around." Things were stabilizing. Then Gordon was found to have a noninvasive form of breast cancer called DCIS. "I'm fine; it's literally the best you can have," she says of her diagnosis, which required a lumpectomy. "I didn't do radiation or anything, but I was like, Okay, what else is going to happen to me?"

Sitting across from Gordon, who has long been a role model for women who want to be tough without becoming hard, I'm struck by how well-placed in her our collective faith has been. "Kim comes off all cool and badass, but she's really sweet and gentle and feminine," longtime friend Sofia Coppola says, praising Gordon's ability to draw power from vulnerability. That trait is much in evidence when Gordon discusses the recent past. She's sad, and unafraid to show it, but she's also clear-eyed about how the dismantling of some areas of her life has freed her up in others. "When you're in a group, you're always sharing everything. It's protected," she says of being in Sonic Youth. "Your own ego is not there for criticism, but you also never quite feel the full power of its glory, either." She's done with that for now. "A few years ago I started to feel like I owed it to myself to really focus on doing art."

Gordon has been painting a lot, in anticipation of a forthcoming survey show at the White Columns gallery in New York. She also recently worked on a capsule collection with French label Surface to Air and, with Coco by her side, shot an ad campaign for Saint Laurent. She's been onstage quite a bit in the past year too, singing and playing guitar. She joined musician John Cale in his tribute to former Velvet Underground bandmate and muse Nico at the Brooklyn Academy of Music, toured Europe with the experimental musician Ikue Mori, and took part in the renowned "Face the Strange" music series hosted by the Museum of Contemporary Art Chicago. And Gordon, like Moore, has a new band. This year she'll tour in support of the forthcoming debut album of Body/Head, which she formed with longtime friend and collaborator Bill Nace. "I do have a lot of things going on right now," she says with a slight smile.

Gordon grew up mostly in Los Angeles; her father was a sociology professor, and her mother a homemaker with creative tendencies. "She'd make long caftans with hoods and sell them out of our house," Gordon remembers. Her mother and father had few traditional expectations of her. "They were from a generation of hands-off parenting," she says, and cultivated in her two traits that an artist needs to survive: intellectual curiosity and a near antiauthoritarian level of creative independence. "I've never been good with structure—doing assignments for the sake of them or doing things I'm supposed to do."

She attended a progressive elementary school linked to UCLA and loved it. "It was learn by doing," she recalls. "So we were always making African spears and going down to the river and making mud huts, or skinning a cowhide and drying it and throwing it off the cliff at Dana Point."

The way Gordon talks about the L.A. of her youth conjures the bleached-out, diffuse brutality of the city as portrayed in Joan Didion's classic collection *The White Album*. "I remember when we were young, playing on these huge dirt mounds that became freeway on-ramps," Gordon says. "And my mom pointing to Century City, saying, 'There's going to be a city there.' I have a lot of nostalgia for Los Angeles at a certain time—just the landscape, before it was overgrown with bad stucco and mini malls and bad plastic surgery. It wasn't like I was happy. I don't want to be back in that time, but it felt a lot more open."

If you had to describe the core sensibility of Gordon's work—painting, vocal performance, or dress—it would be that quintessentially Californian expansive desolation. It's a feeling, not an idea, and it's what first pulled Gordon away from fine art and toward rock 'n' roll. "When I came to New York, I'd go and see bands downtown playing no-wave music," she recalls of her arrival, after graduating from art school. "It was expressionistic and it was also nihilistic. Punk rock was tongue-in-cheek, saying, 'Yeah, we're destroying rock.' No-wave music is more like, 'NO, we're really destroying rock.' It was very dissonant. I just felt like, Wow, this is really free. I could do that."

So she did. The Sonic Youth discography includes 16 studio albums and numerous EPs and compilation albums, not to mention music videos and documentaries. Their 1988 LP, *Daydream Nation*, was added to the U.S. Library of Congress National Recording Registry in 2005. Sonic Youth is not just revered within the indie rock world; it's an indelible part of American pop-cultural history, a sort of byword for tasteful and progressive art that's also popular. "She was a forerunner, musically," says Kathleen Hanna, of the riot grrrl band Bikini Kill and later the dance-rock group Le Tigre. "Just knowing a woman was in a band trading lead vocals, playing bass, and being a visual artist at the same time made me feel less alone." Hanna met Gordon when she came to a Bikini Kill show in the early '90s. "She invited my band to stay at her and Thurston's apartment," Hanna says. "As a radical feminist singer, I wasn't particularly well liked. I was in a punk underground scene dominated by hardcore dudes who yelled mean shit at me every night, and journalists routinely called my voice shrill, unlistenable. Kim made me feel accepted in a way I hadn't before. Fucking Kim Gordon thought I was on the right track, haters be damned. It made the bullshit easier to take, knowing she was in my corner."

Gordon's anodyne vocals and whirling dervish stage presence are as much a Sonic Youth signature as Moore's and Lee Ranaldo's discordant guitars, but her pursuit of additional creative outlets helped others think more broadly about what it could mean to be in a rock band. "Kim inspired me because she tried all the things that interested her," Coppola says. "She just did what she was into." Hanna agrees. "I loved so many kinds of art besides music, and it sometimes made me feel torn, but Kim seemed very comfortable doing whatever she felt like at the time."

"I never really thought of myself as a musician," Gordon says. "I'm not saying Sonic Youth was a conceptual-art project for me, but in a way it was an extension of Warhol. Instead of making criticism about popular culture, as a lot of artists do, I worked within it to do something."

We've finished the dregs of our wine, and the sun has set. I'm interested in something Gordon was filmed saying about imprisoned members of the Russian activist punk band Pussy Riot: "Women make natural anarchists and revolutionaries, because they've always been second-class citizens, kinda having had to claw their way up." Gordon nods as I read back her quote: "I mean, who made up all the rules in the culture? Men—white male corporate society. So why wouldn't a woman want to rebel against that?"

Part of my own affection for Kim Gordon, I realize, is her association with an era when even boys thought it was cool to call themselves feminists. I'm not sure when exactly that changed, but I know that by the time I was aware of experiencing sexism firsthand I'd already gotten the message that to identify myself as a feminist would limit me. I envy and admire the way Gordon—and the pop-cultural heroes she helped shape, like Hanna and Coppola and Courtney Love—seemed unafraid of that word. But I am even more envious and admiring of the way the men in Gordon's orbit— from the Beastie Boys, who played with Sonic Youth over the years, to Moore to Cobain, who was very close to Gordon—seem to have taken cues from her about how to be good men.

It's easy to forget that the ideals Gordon championed are now taken for granted by a younger generation, a fact driven home when Gordon mentions Lena Dunham's *Girls*. Despite being a fan of the hit show ("I love that all of the sex scenes are awkward and kind of a failure"), she's troubled by what she calls a "misleading" scene in which Marnie sleeps with Hannah's gay roommate. At one point Marnie says no, but they proceed to have sex, and her objection becomes part of their sexual play. "It's a mixed message about what no means," Gordon points out. It's part of an "ironic Williamsburg hipster" pose, she goes on, that considers political correctness kind of square. "If you're going to do that [in *Girls*], you also have to—in some other instance—show that it's not cool." For a show that's been written about nearly to death, it's an observation that seems both totally obvious and underdiscussed.

"What the breach of generations shows is that there's more than one way to be feminist," Gordon says. Indeed, her admirers put her in the same hallowed category in which she puts such figures as Didion, Jane Fonda, and, now, Hillary Clinton. When Gordon recalls Clinton being grilled by Congress in her final hearings, it's with deep reverence. "It just showed how experienced she is and how inexperienced those other guys were—she was masterful, the way she handled them. She's a living embodiment of being pro-women."

THOMAS SAYERS ELLIS WITH
BOOTSY COLLINS

From the Crib to the Coliseum: Stretchin' Out with Bass Legend William "Bootsy" Collins,* The Rock and Roll Hall of Fame

For the sake of history, let's start at the beginning.

Well, my mom, she grew us up. No dad. No dad in the house, but I always felt responsible for the things that went on in the household. And Mama always had a belt, too! And she would wear us out. I never got a male perspective of that, so I was always out in the streets. Looking up to the males in the streets that did certain things I dug, like entertaining—the players on the streets—the hustling. But then I got interested in music, because I wanted to be like my brother, "Catfish" [Phelphs]. He was playing guitar. I really got interested in music, and I think that's what started it.

During the *Player of the Year* tour, a pre-concert cartoon told the story of a paperboy who was transformed into a superhero. Throughout your work, the lyrics and the licks seem to be referencing a silly seriousness. Growing up, did you watch a lot of cartoons?

Oh yeah, I loved them. That was the thing coming up. When we went to school, we'd have the subject book—English, whatever it was—that would be the book the teacher would see. Then you'd have your comic book inside of that book, ya know? The teacher would say, "Did you hear me, William?" "Oh yeah, I got it. I got it." And at the same time, I'd be reading Spider-Man or Batman. We was just into the comic thang, and I guess it just spilled over into the music. We just wanted to have fun with it—music. And since we looked like cartoons anyway, we just ran with it.

How did you end up at King Studios?

Oh, that was a blessing! Well, actually, a guy in Cincinnati was an A&R guy. His name was Charles Spurling and he would go out and look for new talent, new people to come in and record. So he came out to a club one night. We always played benefits. We never got paid and weren't looking to get paid. At that time, we was just looking to have fun and have a good time. That's pretty much what it was all about. So he came out and saw us playing and said, "Yeah, I want y'all to come over to King's and be my recording band." We was like, "Yeah, King's. Ain't that where James Brown is?" He said yeah. Our whole thing was, okay, if we get over in King's, we'll get to meet James

---

*Ellis, Thomas Sayers. "From the Crib to the Coliseum: Stretchin' Out with Bass Legend William 'Bootsy' Collins." *Wax Poetics*, August–September 2006, 103–108.

Brown, Hank Ballard, the Isley Brothers. We were cocky kids off the street, and, like, "Yeah, we bad!" And we really believed that. We got over there and a lot of the different producers that was producing top acts at that time wanted us to perform on their records. Once we started doing that, word start getting around. Then Mr. Brown heard about us. He didn't want to be left out. It was like, "Who are these young dudes over here making all this noise. Making all these records?" And it was like, "Yeah, that's Bootsy and them." He said at some point, "I'd like to meet them, send them out on the road with Hank Ballard and Marva Whitney." And, actually, that was our first professional gig.

Where were you when James Brown's band walked out on him? Do you remember the night in 1969 when that phone call came?
I'll tell you exactly where we were. We were on Gilbert Avenue at the Wine Bar playing a benefit for the door, and I think it was just us and the bartender. And we was just as loud as I don't know what. And everywhere we played, we just played loud, whether we had one person in the audience or a thousand people. It didn't matter, ya know? Then all of the sudden, the phone rang. The bartender came up to me and says, "Hey, Bobby Byrd wants to talk to ya. He wants to talk to you about playing with James Brown." We had took a little break. We was like, "Yeah right, Bobby Byrd want to talk to us about James Brown." So we kind of laughed it off, and he was like, "Nah, he's on the phone." So, I went and answered the phone and sure enough, it was Bobby Byrd. And he says, "How would you like to play for James Brown?" And we're like, "You're joking. You must be joking." And actually, we had kind of made friends with Bobby Byrd, because he was the only one we could get to back then. He really befriended us and brought us in before we even got with James. So, yeah, he was like, "James really want y'all to be the band. Actually, I'm going to fly y'all up." We was like, "No, no way. James's jet! No way." So we had never flown in a plane before. So we was like, "Okay, we'll be ready. We'll be right here when you get here. See ya when ya get here—yeah right." And he actually flew up there within about forty-five minutes. He was there at the club: "Come on, we got to go now." So we had on our tiedyed jeans, my Afro was leaning to the right. And we were wearing them little round eyeglasses from back in the day. Just cool. I said, "Well, can't we go get cleaned up? We don't want to go like this." He said, "No, we gotta go right now. James is waiting on stage." We said okay. Next thing you know, we was on an airplane, my Afro was in the back of my head and we was flying up forty thousand feet in a Learjet. And I had never been on a plane before. I'm seventeen years old, flying on the Godfather of Soul's plane and I'm like, what is going on? Talk about a kid trippin'. I didn't know what was going on. So when we get to Columbus, Georgia—I never will forget the look on the people's faces when we got there. We came through the back door. I already had my bass out, ready to throw down. And as we were walking in, people started hollering, "You're late!" We didn't know what that was about! They asked us, "Y'all James Brown's band, ain't y'all?" We didn't know we were James Brown's band yet! So Bobby Byrd says, "Let me take you

back here so you can talk to the Godfather." So we get back there in James Brown's office—I got to get y'all in James Brown mode. I'm going into his voice now. He says, "Look here, Bootsy, y'all some bad boys. But y'all playin' with the Godfather tonight. So when I drop my arm down like this here [*Bootsy motions*], I'm gonna call out the songs to you. Y'all ready?" We looked at each other and said, "Yeah, Mr. Brown, we're ready."

But y'all knew the songs already?
Oh yeah, inside and out. And he knew we knew them. So we hit the stage and sure enough, he calls out a song, drops his hand down, and we were on it! I mean, we were onstage with the Godfather of Soul! Man we were going to wear that mutha out! We thought we were wearing it out. We hit every move. We knew all of his moves. If you noticed, it wasn't so much about his singing and screaming, it was all about his body. His moves. You had to pay attention! I ain't never paid attention that much! I mean, every little move he made, if it was with his foot, you had to be on it. Wasn't no getting high, I'm sorry! If you were high on that set, you wouldn't have made it. Done. So that's the straightest time I've ever been onstage! And that's the truth!

So what did you learn from him? Jab'O said that your style of bass playing had the most movement he'd ever heard. But Brown had to focus you on "the One."
He was the one who brought that to my attention. Because I thought I was doing something different. It was like, I don't want to be like other bass players, just holding the foundation down. I wanted to play a lot of things. "Son, listen to me now. I'm the Godfather of Soul." He always had to lecture me, and it was cool because, like I said, I didn't have a daddy back home, so I guess he felt like he had to fill those shoes. And he was like my dad. "Son, you got to stop doing all them things and just give me the One." So when I started doing that, he started to like it and I could tell. So I figured, if I could give him this One and play all them other things . . . I think he'll like me. So I started giving him that One that he needed, and playing what I felt. See, a lot of people at King liked that we played what we felt. In fact, James's string arranger asked me and my brother if we could read music. And we said, "Oh, yeah, we got this!" So he counts it off and says, "Okay, play what's in your face." And so we said, "Just count it off and let us hear a little bit of it before we start. We want to make sure we're on point here." So they count it off and the rest of the band played. And then we said, "Okay, count it off again." We was on it. So after the session, the arranger called me and Catfish back in the room and says, "Everybody just loved what y'all did, but y'all can't read a lick." So we were like, "Yeah, you right." But I said, "We wanted to play with y'all so bad, and we knew we had to know how to read." And he said, "No y'all don't, because the feel y'all got—don't nobody else got a feel like that right now." He said, "Don't worry about it. I'll work with you." So that's how we got the gig of playing with the big orchestras. First, I lied, and then I came back and ate the lie, but at the same time, I gave them the something that they wanted.

But you did eventually leave. How did that happen?

Well, really, the reason I left was because of the older people that had been there—because I was the one who could get his way with Mr. Brown. Yeah, I was the young one. They'd say, "Let Bootsy do it!" You know, like that old commercial [for Life cereal] used to say, "Let's get Mikey to do it! He'll do anything!" "Let Bootsy do it! He'll do anything." So they kind of used that with me, with James. Like, "Tell Bootsy to tell Mr. Brown that we need so and so. That we need this." And I'm saying to myself, "I don't need nothin'. I'm just groovin'!" And it's like, "Okay. If y'all want me to go in there and do that, I'll just go in there and tell him and see what he says. And every time I would go in there, he'd do it, ya know. But this last time, they said, "We need a raise! You know, he should be paying our hotels and he should be doin' this that and the other. Bootsy, you need to go in there and tell him!" I'm like, "Okay. I'll tell him. All he can say is no." So I say, "Okay, cool." So I go in there, "Mr. Brown, everybody's feeling like they need some more money, you know." He said, "Now, Bootsy, let me tell you somethin', son. Now I know they puttin' you up to this." In other words, he knew I didn't have sense enough to go in there and do that! Which I didn't, 'cause I wasn't thinkin' about nothin' like that. You know, all I was doin' was havin' fun with the girls, watchin' the artists get off; it was just a great time in my life.

You traveled to Nigeria with James Brown's band. Talk about meeting Fela Kuti.

Africa, man—we got off the plane and they started bowing down to us: "Yeah, James Brown's band!" And I didn't really know how to take that other than, "Yeah, we James Brown's band," but I didn't feel worthy of the praise they were giving us, because I was just this knucklehead, long-haired sucker from off the street, and all of a sudden, I'm with James Brown's band, and then I got a bunch of people praising me. We go to the hotel, and we find out that Fela Ransome [Kuti] has invited us to his club. And he was like James Brown over in Africa, so we went. And, man, I told them to take all those praises back, because they were the ones that needed to be praised. 'Cause them mugs was so on it. They had some grooves there that I had never heard or felt in my life. And I couldn't believe it. I just could not believe it. I mean, you could be ten miles away and you could hear the drums. You could be carrying on a conversation and the next thing you know, your body starts movin and you can't control it! And you're like, "Damn, what's wrong with me? I know I ain't high!" So it was a whole other experience. And speaking of high—can I go there?

You got to.

We're in the car. It's me, Bobby Byrd, Vickie Anderson, Catfish, Clyde, and an African driver. And just so you know, they didn't have policemen, they had army men policing the place. And they did not play. For instance, this one guy came to the show. He was blind, couldn't see nothing, but he busts into the dressing room, run up the steps, yelling, "I want to see James Brown!" And then the army guys just fell out, laughing. And we were like, "What are they laughin' at?" The cat is blind, and they laughing, saying, "You wanna see James Brown? He can't even see!" And that really killed me. And then they clubbed him all the way back down the steps. So when I saw that, I thought these cats couldn't give a dang about me if they did that to him. So what I was thinking while we was riding in this car, and I got some dirty stuff on me, right? We're riding and all of a sudden we see the army men coming up. And I start getting a little nervous because we're in the car gettin' a little tipsy. And the Army guys are coming towards the car, and I'm like, "Uh oh." We got to put this stuff away. We got to roll the windows down and get this stuff out of the car. All of this is going on in split seconds. Dude comes up to the car and right before he gets there, I say, "Vickie, put this in your purse. They won't look in your purse." She said, "No, I'm not taking that stuff." She says, "Put it in your boot." So I put it down in my boot, right? So dude comes up to the car and says, "Okay. What's in the boot?"

Damn!

And I did exactly what you just did. I could not believe he saw that. I was saying to myself, "How did he know I had put that stuff in my boot?" So he kept talking and the guy was trying to explain to him. I don't know what they were saying. The two men were speaking an African language. So the army guy says, "Okay, but I want to see what's in the boot!" So, okay, I'm getting ready to give in now, because I know I'm busted. I start to go down to my boot and the driver gets out and walks to the back of the car . . . to the trunk. The *boot* is the trunk! Ah man. I mean, my heart was in my boot! So he goes back and checks the trunk and says, "Okay, you're good to go." I looked at Vicki and Bobby Byrd, and I was through! My high was gone. I said, "Here, y'all can have this stuff. Just take it!" I mean, it was the bomb too. That stuff over there was the bomb! And I just gave it away. I quit getting high for two days.

Do you think you changed the direction of the James Brown thang?

That's what people say. I think I brought what I did to the music. But I can't say that I changed James Brown's music. I can only say I was so glad to get an opportunity to be there. I mean, whatever happened, just as long as I was there and learned what I learned. I can't take credit for that. All I can say is that, that was probably one of the best times of my life. Clyde and Jab'O—I had some of my heroes behind me. I mean, they were just like heroes for real. Even when I got there and was able to really get to know them, they were still heroes. It's like, say you're with a chick; you think she's this way or that way, and you get to know her, and you say, "It's not exactly how I thought." But you know I can't say that about the James Brown experience. It was everything that I thought and more. So I would hope that I brought something to it because that was a great time.

Let's jump to Detroit circa 1971. Y'all thought you had your own style until Mallia Franklin says that you guys have the same vibe as Funkadelic and that you should meet George. Do you remember meeting George for the first time?

Yeah, I definitely remember that. Wow. Mallia had come down to this club called the Love Club. It was a place where all of the youth would get together; you know, the young bands would go on stage and kind of compete for the gig. And that's what we did a lot. That's where "Let's Take It to the Stage" came from. Competing and taking each other's gigs. So Mallia heard us, and the other bands heard us too, and they were like, "I don't know who these mugs are, but we're not going on before them and we're not going on after them." So the reputation started going around, and George started hearing about us. And then Mallia says, "You need to go talk to George, because y'all got so much in common. I think his band is gettin' ready to leave him. They're having all kind of problems over there. Not enough drugs, whatever. They have had it up to here with George." So she takes us over the next day. I remember walking in the house—I'm kind of semi-trippin' too. Walk in, and George didn't have no furniture; got about three rooms. When you look straight through the house, you could see all the rooms. No furniture in none of them. And he sittin' in the last room, in the corner, got his legs in like a Buddha thing—you know, with his head down. He got a star on one side and a moon on the other shaved in his head and the rest was bald. He got a sheet on. His feet—you know he got these big *Boy, I say, Boy* feet. You know who I'm talking about: Foghorn Leghorn! Actually, I nicknamed him that. Yeah, but y'all ain't heard that from me! But he had these big feet stickin' out from under his thing. And I'm like, "Dang, this is gonna be fun." So I walk in and started talkin' and next thing I know, we just started clicking. It was like, "We'll go out with you, but I gotta make sure I keep my band's name. The band name is the House Guests. But let me back up a li'l bit. Before that even happened, the Spinners had called us up to come to Detroit to play behind them.

Go back even further to Philippe Wynne.
Philippe was from Cincinnati and he was our lead singer in our first band, the Pacemakers. So when we got to Detroit, we go as the House Guests featuring Philippe. But when we get there, we said, "Okay, the Spinners done called us, so we going to have to play behind them."

You were going to have to play "Rubber Band Man" instead of "Stretchin' Out (In a Rubber Band)."
Yeah, and after coming from James, after being in a band wanting to do our own thing, we want to come on stage and act a fool. We don't want to be cool with suits on. We don't want to have our shoes shined. We want our 'fros over here, leaning. We don't want to get fined! If we get with the Spinners, it's going be the same crap! So we say, "If that's the only choice we have, then we'll play with the Spinners." So when we get to Detroit, and Mallia tells us about George, we're like, "Oh yeah, that would be the bomb. Funkadelic instead of the Spinners?" I wanted to tie that in so y'all know that. So we go over there and we talk to George and he says, "What are you going do with Philippe?" I was like, "Well, he could go with the Spinners." I mean, they needed a lead singer too. They wanted all of us. They wanted the band and the lead singer. Philippe would have a star spot with the Spinners, and we would have a star spot with

Funkadelic. Because then, we could get up there and act a fool like we wanted to. So it all worked out. It was kind of like written already. I mean, it was like, *wow*, when it went down like that. I talked to Philippe about a year later, and he was like, "Man, I'm so glad y'all did it like that." And it was almost like he thought that I thought of that. [I told him,] "Nah, it just happened like that."

The first Funkadelics got turned out. Did you guys get turned out?
That's why my hat goes off to George so much, so regularly, because everybody wanted to hang with George on the stuff—drugs—and I ain't met nobody yet who can hang with George—not James, not Sly, not [Little] Richard. No one. None of them could hang with George! But everybody in Funkadelic was like, "I'm a Funkadelic, man." You know, being a Funkadelic, you had to be one of the wildest, craziest mugs in the world. Brothers just didn't do the things that we did.

I heard George got blowjobs on stage and used to use the bathroom onstage.
I'll tell you a small story. George was known for always making the gig. Never late, even if nobody showed up. I remember one time: me, Catfish, and George showed up to a sold-out, outside gig. We were the only ones that showed up. George said, "Well, we gotta go on. We're here." We went up, killed them for three hours. No drummer or anything. Just a guitar, a bass, and George singing. Killed them! The crowd loved it. Then again, they were all blitzed out of their minds. George was never late. He was always on time. He also showed me how to promote myself. We would beat radio stations back when funk was a bad word, and they would be like, "We can't have y'all talking about funk." George would say, "Well, motherfunk y'all then." And the more he said that, the more we got interviews to talk about the funk. But it just goes to show his persistence—'cause people were like, "We want the funk. We don't care what y'all critics say." And that's where [the lyric] "we want the funk" came from. George didn't make that up. The people came up with that. George heard it and said, "Yeah, let's take that. Come on, Bootsy, let's go to the studio." We would give the people what they gave us.

You were about to discuss the outrageousness.
We had a gig in D.C., at Howard University, and everybody is like, "Where is George?" The gig started at eight o'clock and it's a quarter till. The rest of the band is getting frantic, because no one knows where George is. It's like, how high can you get before showtime? You know what I'm saying, because they're doing angel dust, and all that craziness. But then I thought, "I know where George is." Everybody's like, "Go find him, Bootsy, go find him." So I start going to all the different bathrooms at the school, and I look up under the stall and I see these chicken feet. Back in the day, George was known for wearing these big ol' chicken feet on stage. They were really big and had three toes! He use to wear these things, and I saw them sticking out from under the stall! I said, "George!" He didn't say nothing. I was like, "I know that's

you, man. Ain't nobody else going to have them feet on but you!" So, he ain't got no rap, right? I hear moans. I know what's up. So I say, "Okay, I'm going give you a few more minutes, but we got to hit it, man. We're supposed to be on the set." No rap. So I stand outside the bathroom, and a few minutes later he come out and I say, "Man, we gotta get on the set. Let's go, let's go." But I later learned what was happening. Two chicks had him in there, and they were wearing that mother out. Yeah, they was wearing him out bad. George don't miss no show. He ain't late. So y'all know he was getting wore out. And when he finally come out, we killed them. Yeah, that was a great show.

On the song "Be My Beach," your signature voice and persona come out for the first time, as well as your talent for punning silly double meanings.
With Bootsy's Rubber Band, I tried to attract a younger audience than Funkadelic had. I would take words like "funk" and expressions like "I got the munchies for your love" and challenge kids to use their imaginations. I wouldn't be like, "I want to F you." It was fun to take that kind of slang—street terms—and do something different with them. George and I had a constructive competition to see who could come up with the best one. It made it fun, and it really opened my lyric thing up. It gave me depth. Everything wasn't in your face. Actually, when we were doing "Be My Beach," I was in the studio, joking with George with that voice. I was doing it as a joke, and he said, "Yeah, I want you to put that on the record." And that's what George was real good at, and still is—good at hearing things and saying, "Yeah, that's different. Let's do that."

And even now I pick up stuff that I hear or even stuff I do—I make sure I put it down. I got my little tape recorder. When I was with James, a lot of things flew in and I never got a chance to put them down, but with George we had the availability to go into the studio all the time. With James you didn't have that. You had to keep it in your head, until you could get somewhere where you could put it down and that was hard, man. You're like, "What was I thinking five minutes ago? That was the bomb! You should have heard it, man!" "Yeah, well why didn't you record it fool?"

You gave up the funk, a lot of funk, in order to get a record deal and your own band. What made George keep his promise to you?
Well, I think, you know, it's because I did everything I said I was going to do. No matter how loaded we got at night, no matter how crazy the girls got, I was there at nine o'clock in the morning before the engineer was there, ready to roll. I was right there, and he saw the dedication that no matter what—I mean, all the rest of them cats were drugged out. I mean, I was too, but I had to get up. If you wasn't at the studio first, you may not have [gotten a chance to record] . . . because it was a hundred of us. And if you didn't get in there, your song was shot. I was like, "I'm gon' have as many songs as I can get. I'm a get up. Yeah, I'm gonna party as hard as y'all, but I'm gonna beat yo' ass to the studio tomorrow." And I did that.

Was that the James Brown discipline?

Yeah. That was the discipline. I learned that from James. Being on it. James had a saying. He'd say, "Bootsy, let me tell you something, son. If you ain't on heel and toe, you got to blow." And me and Cat used to look at each other: "What the hell is he talkin' about?" And after we left him, we figured it out. If you ain't on heel and toe, you got to blow. He meant you had to be on it, on everything. On top of it. And when we got with George, I kind of lost that for a minute. I lost it on purpose because I wanted to have fun. You know, when you on it like that, you can't really have that kind of fun. You got to be responsible. I didn't want to be responsible, man. I just wanted to play music for people, have a good time. I don't owe nobody, don't nobody owe me, we just havin' fun. That's the way musicians looked at it back then. Let's just go have a good time, I ain't gotta pay nobody, and everything is cool.

"Bootzilla." That's a monster moment. That was your first number-one single—in 1978. It's also a hell of an ego leap.

Yeah, from the crib to the coliseum. George actually pushed me. You know, once I developed the character, it was like, "Oh no. You ain't stopping now." I was cool with Bootsy. Bootsy get out there with his little star glasses on and did his thing. I wasn't like, trippin'. It was just a good time. But George was like, "Nah man, you got to be the rock star now. You got to be the Black rock star." And it was like, Bootzilla was going be the one to take me there. So I found somebody—the dude that made my star glasses. I brought him the design I wanted for my glasses. They had to be sparkling. When I walk out on the set, it's going to be bling everywhere. I wanted to add that flash to the funk.

You've said many times that you had to find something else, because Larry Graham was already the baddest muthaplucker that ever lived. Talk about the birth of your space bass.

Oh, he was *the* muthaplucker! When I was in school, I used to draw stick men with a star guitar and star glasses. And I never knew what it was, but I spent a lot of time doing that. Pretty much all my time besides reading comic books. So when I got with P-Funk and that time came, George says, "Okay, it's time for you to go do your thing now." I was like, "For real, man? Ah man, you going to let me? Ah man!" Okay, I got to go get me some star glasses and get me a star bass. George looked at me like, "Where are you going to get all that? You ain't got no money." But I went and found these mugs. And these people had so much, and they felt sorry for me because I had enough nerve to be in there talking about all of this bigness, and ain't have a pot to piss in! I'm telling this boy how to make my bass, and didn't even have a down payment. You know: "I want it like this. It's gotta be in the shape of a star." I had everything already drawn out. "I want the pick-ups here." And he's like, "Man, this is incredible." I took it to all the boys in New York, and they were like, "Ah, get out of here. Ain't nobody going to make no money with that crap." But it was all about finding the right person that wanted to be creative. And I found the dude in Detroit that wanted to take the risk, the risk at making this bass. His name was Larry Pless, and I got with him. He worked in an accordion music store. And I'm going show you how God works. Check this out. I see "Accordion Music Store," and I'm saying to myself, "Ain't no way there's someone in there who knows a thing about guitars." And something just kept saying, "Go in there. Go in there and tell them about your space bass." I went in there, and the guy who owned the place says, "I don't do guitars, but I got a youngster in the back . . . he makes guitars." So he sent me in the back, and I started talking to this guy. And we just started hitting it off.

I had to hype him up first because I didn't have any money. He was like, "Wow, this is incredible." So I sold him on the idea, how incredible it was, and he said, "Yeah, man. Let's do it." I say, "Well, just get started on it and I'll be back." But he says, "But you got to give me some kind of something to get the materials. I say, "How much you need?" "How about $150." I say, "I know I can get $150 from somebody." So I actually bummed around a little and got the $150 and brought it back to the guy. That taught me to always be a man of my word. If I say I'm going to give you $150, I'm gonna get that $150 from somewhere. I mean, I didn't go out and rob anyone. I talked to a few chicks that kind of liked me: "Baby, I'll pay it back to you next week." So they hooked me up.

How did you get Maceo Parker, Fred Wesley, and "Kush" Griffith of the Horny Horns to join the Rubber Band?

Oh, that was easy. When we were with James, I told them. I said, "Man, when I get out of here, when I leave James Brown, and I start making it, I'm going get you cats to come out with me. Would y'all be up for that?" Fred and Maceo was like, "He just talking." I say, "Nah man, I'm for real. I'm getting out of here and I'm going to get something happening." And they said, "Okay."

What happened after *Player of the Year*? There was a huge gap before *This Boot Is Made for Fonk-n* was released.

I couldn't get high off of what I was getting' high on. This ain't it. It ain't why I got out here. I got out here because of the music. And I started to see that we couldn't do anything without getting high. It was like the high came first. Getting high was first instead of the other way around. It used to be, first we'd play music, and then maybe we'd get around to getting high. Things reversed on us. For me, coming from James Brown, that was backwards. Something was wrong with this picture. It didn't feel good anymore. I found myself, instead of partying with people—and [at] all the gigs, that's all we did was party, party, party—instead, I was running from people, and trying to hide and trying to get a minute to just take a breath. Because when you start rolling like that, and everything you touch starts turning into gold, you don't get a minute to yourself. And I didn't know nothing about that. I was just acting a fool all my life, so I didn't know nothing about the responsibility of being there all the time, on call. I would wake up in the middle of the night and a mug would have a microphone to my mouth in the hotel room. And I'm wondering, "How did this mug get in my room?" So I started hiding from people, and that wasn't cool.

What is Bootsy doing now? Has the player settled down?

Yeah, in a good way. I got a beautiful wife now [Patti Willis]. She's helped me a lot with settling down, because when I was coming up, the streets taught me never to be attached to one person. I could be in a city and have four or five chicks coming to see me at the same gig. If I got down below four or five women, I was like, "Wait a minute, I got to add some more here." So I was all screwed up with that one. I had grown up with the intention of not getting married because I had seen all my friends get married, and the next thing you knew, their lives were screwed up. I got to be around forty-five years old before I started thinking about it. And guess why I start thinking about it? This is the sad thing. I started feeling like I was losing my mother. I'm saying to myself, "Okay, wow, if I lose my mother, who else is going to have my back? As far as everything that goes on here at the house while I'm out acting a fool. Somebody got to have my back."

You don't go out with P-Funk or your own band as much as you used to either.

I don't want to go out like everybody else. I want to be the one to make the choice. If I want to perform, I want performance, then I'll give it to you. Y'all know I came up with the "If you fake the funk, you nose will grow, baby."

So I can't go out there faking the funk. You know, if I ain't feeling it, I can't bring it to you. So how can I talk about it without being about it? And that's the problem now. Mugs out here talking about it, but they not being about it. People do it in the church. People are talking about it. And my whole thing is what you see today is I'm a book. Can you read me? And I wanna be a good book.

Damn, I wish I had said that!

I just feel like you can't tell anybody what to do. James used to tell me what to do: "You can't be up here getting high." And the more he told me not to, the more I wanted to do it—and the more I did it. So it's all in the way that you approach people. And I'm in search of that way. I don't know it, but I think I'm on the right path. And Snoop, all of them come to the Rehab. My studio is called Bootzilla Rehab, and we don't do the things we used to do. No. It's the Rehab. We do music. You get high on our terms. That's cool. I done did it all, probably much more than any of y'all. But it's just the fact that the young people come in, and they expect me to be getting high, they expect me to be doing this and that. And I get off by just seeing, "Oh, I know what y'all expect. But I'm gonna give you somethin' different." And that's been my whole thing. I want to give you something different. You know, now kids be talking about I'm different this and I'm different that, and they all got the same gym shoes on.

Casper, Bootsy, Bootzilla, Star Mon, the Player, Gadget Mon, Captain P Mo, Mug Push, Count Tracula, and Zillatron. Do you know who you are now?
Yeah, you want me to tell you?

Yes.
William Collins.

ALLEN GINSBERG WITH BECK

A Beat/Slacker Transgenerational Meeting of Minds*

Allen Ginsberg: What I heard first of yours were funky things, very interesting rhymes, stanzas in blues, very old antique sound. I said, how'd this young kid get so educated? Because you're really young and coming from these classic roots. I thought, geez, something great is happening!

Beck: Yeah, That was my world. Still is. I found myself rejecting so much new music, everything that is part of our culture. Then a couple of years ago, I just spun all around and decided to embrace it all. Y'know, the machines, the rap, the loud guitars, every sort of emotional level. And just go with it all, and maybe somehow...

Ginsberg: It's working out.

Beck: I guess so. It's an experiment. I really have to plead innocent on knowing anything really about the "slacker" thing. At the time "Loser" was recorded, it was, y'know, hearing so much rap, where it's very self-aggrandizing. Like, I'm so dope, I got more this and that, I'm so bad. I was trying to be ironic by saying, I completely suck, I'm the worst. Well, the irony's not obvious to everybody. It got hijacked somewhere along the way.

Ginsberg: The whole Beat generation got hijacked at first, except the intrinsic merit of the work came through over and over again, generation after generation, because we all believed in the art.

Beck: But at the time wasn't it really annoying?

Ginsberg: You know what I did? I went to India and dropped out completely, and learned something new. I went to learn the whole Eastern thing. I came back and found Kerouac was famous. I was famous. But no money. So I said OK, now time to go on to greater triumphs of the mind . . . So you had a reasonably good education then?

Beck: I left high school at about ninth grade, but as far as ideas and looking at things in different ways, my grandfather was around a lot when I was younger. Did you know Al Hansen? Do you remember that name?

Ginsberg: Painter?

Beck: Yeah, and he did collage stuff. Hershey . . .

Ginsberg: I have one of them.

---

*Beck, and Allen Ginsberg. "The Late Allen Ginsberg and Beck in Conversation." *A Beat Slacker Transgenerational Meeting of Minds, Allen Ginsberg, Shambhala Sun*, January 1, 1997. Reprinted with permission.

Beck: You have one?

Ginsberg: . . . of those Hershey Bar things, or collages.

Beck: Yeah. He was amazing. I learned a lot from his speech. The way he talked. He had the whole sorta '40's jazz/hipster talk. He was a zoot-suiter in the '40's.

Ginsberg: I had no idea you came out of Hansen's. He was one of the first of the great pop artists, because of the collage.

Beck: His stuff seems like garbage. And then after about ten years, it kind of . . . well, it is made out of garbage.

Ginsberg: This was one of the Hershey label series.

Beck: He did that for years. The other thing he used a lot were cigarette butts. And he did all the Venus figures.

Ginsberg: Made out of cigarette butts?

Beck: Yeah, the Venus figure made out of cigarette butts, or candy bar wrappers or match sticks or anything he found. The Venus of Willendorf, I think.

Ginsberg: I have a little poem about her. Did you ever see her? It's pretty amazing. Round head, round body, round thighs and feet with three big circles. Perfect symmetry. Much more beautiful than anything I imagined, based on these circles. Very amazing art. Magna Mater.

Beck: I remember when I was about five I had a rocking horse, sort of a cheap plastic one, from the supermarket or a K-mart. It was sitting in the garage and I remember he gave me five bucks for it. 'Bout 2 days later, I remember going out in the backyard, and he had severed the head, covered it with cigarette butts, and spray painted it silver. So that opened a door for me. I also remember driving around in the car with him about that same time. I was just getting into words, just learning how to read, and I remember him teaching me how to rhyme. I thought that was the greatest thing. You could make words sort of lock together.

Ginsberg: Well, your rhymes are interesting. I grew up on that, too. See, my father was a poet, and a rhymer. A rhyming poet. So I could rhyme anytime, make it spontaneous. First thought, best thought, what comes into your mind, so you can rhyme in your gut. Did you ever see Harry Smith's Folkways records? Three boxes, two records each, American folk music?

Beck: Yeah, it's a collection of a lot of the field recordings . . .

Ginsberg: Actually a collection of his old 78's, so it has some very early musicians. Uh, Texas Alexander, Richard "Rabbit" Brown.

[sings:] Things ain't now nothing like they used to be
things ain't now nothing like they used to be
I'd have a much better time but the girls now are so hard to please.
I'll give you sugar for sugar, but you'll get salt for salt
I'll give you sugar for sugar, but you'll get salt for salt
baby you don't love me, you won't get nuthin' at all.

Sometime I think that you're too sweet to die
sometime I think that you're too sweet to die.
Other time I think you oughta be buried alive.

Beck: That's what I love about the blues. That a lot of those refrains were spread out in a lot of different people's songs. They would take verses from different things, assemble them with . . .

Ginsberg: Dylan took "Don't the moon look good shinin' through the trees." He took that from Charley Patton.

Beck: It's almost like you can't take those, though. They just sort of become a part of you and then they just come out. I've done that a few times. It just becomes unconscious if you're playing that music long enough.

Ginsberg: It's tradition anyway.

Beck: Yeah.

Ginsberg: Did you study music?

Beck: Not really. I just listened to the records. Like I said, I didn't go to high school. I just checked out one day. And just got really heavy into the old music, from the Carter family to all the blues stuff, and the field recordings. Became fascinated by it.

Ginsberg: What did you hear? The Alan Lomax Library of Congress stuff?

Beck: Whatever I could get my hands on. We'd just sit, listening for hours, trying to figure out how to do this stuff. And wrestled with it for five, six years and then I came out to New York, and hung around for a little while. New York kind of kicked me back out.

Ginsberg: Where were you living out here?

Beck: I was living on the floor. I was doing that for a long time. I had a lot of bad luck. The spirits didn't want me to be out here, I guess. I'd love to come back.

Ginsberg: One of the last times I saw Dylan, he said the best music in New York is being played in the subways, or on the street.

Beck: Oh yeah. Yup. That's where I was playing. Not really on the subways, but on the streets and the parks and down around Avenue A. There was this whole sort of folk scene happening, "Anti-Folk," right. There was a bunch of kids, a bunch of crazy poets. Really good poets.

Ginsberg: Yeah, I knew some of them, I used to sing with them sometimes.

Beck: Well, I was playing the traditional stuff and first I was really down with "Anti-folk." That's basically what the term was. It was separating themselves from all the new-age sounding stuff. The safe, watered down stuff. That charged me up, and I came onto the idea of taking the traditional music and come up with different words.

Ginsberg: That was my idea. Except I was too old to do it, and I didn't know how to play guitar.

Beck: I was fascinated with the whole early '60's folk revival. Did you know Dave Van Ronk, Jack Elliot, and those guys?

Ginsberg: Jack Elliot I know from 1950!

Beck: I just saw him about three months ago at McCabe's. And it was a great show. A lot of spaces. He has a lot of spaces. He just stretches those spaces out.

Ginsberg: I know him from 1950. I was in a bug house and I had a girlfriend.

Beck: He's the cowboy from Brooklyn.

Ginsberg: And he stole my girlfriend. I was in a bug house for about eight months. And I was getting out, and I had this girlfriend, trying that out.

Beck: He stole her away?

Ginsberg: An idyllic romance, and it was my first, she was my cherry. I was totally in love, and she liked William Carlos Williams, and was literate, but I was just this wimp from the nut house. Then he came along, and made out with her. So we know each other from then. Are you on Geffen?

Beck: Yeah. I have a thing.

Ginsberg: What's he like?

Beck: Uh, the man himself?

Ginsberg: Yeah, I met him once.

Beck: Same here. I met him once, and he told some long story about Barbra Streisand.

Ginsberg: I was invited to meet Geffen at a party in the Rainbow Room. I was eager to say, listen we have this double album which is gonna come out finally, after ten years on Columbia, and I wanted to make sure we can get it distributed and blah blah blah blah blah. So I went up to him and started talking to him. And he says, listen, I'm standing here talking to Harry Belafonte, and you're interrupting me.

Beck: Really, he said that?

Ginsberg: Yes. He said, who is this character? Because I'm older than both of them. I mean Belafonte, he's a great singer, sure, but I'm the Poet Ginsberg.

Beck: Yeah!

Ginsberg: They got to have some respect!

Beck: That's show biz, I guess.

Ginsberg: Although Gregory Corso says, those who demand respect seldom deserve it. It's enough not to disrespect.

WRITING PROMPT: BE BOTH INTERVIEWER AND INTERVIEWEE

Interviews are difficult to pull off. New artists are constantly bombarded with interview requests and can easily be bored by generic run of the mill questions. Carefully read through the advice that begins this chapter and craft five questions to ask your artist. You never know what sort of responses you'll get. And often the only information you'll have is a short bio like the one listed below. In this exercise, try to imagine yourself as the subject. How would you react to these questions? Do they get you thinking? Interviews should feel more like a conversation than an interrogation.

Prepare five questions to ask an artist in a radio interview. Then respond to your own questions in the voice of that artist. Use the made-up band below or briefly invent and describe your own.

Interview subject: The Lazy Shrubs. The Lazy Shrubs are a five-piece psych rock band from Los Angeles, California. They formed in 2012 when bassist Ian Smith and lead singer Jules Yarbird met at a graveyard screening of *The Little Shop of Horrors* at the Hollywood Forever cemetery.

WRITING PROMPT: LEARN FROM THE BEST

Jessica Hopper says at the beginning of this section, "I never prepare questions; I just have a conversation with someone." Jessica is a very effective and experienced interviewer as her profiles for *SPIN* show, but not all of us are so gifted in the art of conversation that we can go into an interview without a safety net. Having a passionate conversation with a friend about their inspirations, hopes, dreams and fears over a beer might sound like a fun Saturday night but what if that conversation is with David Bowie? (Hey, it could happen!) What if you become star struck and instead of a free-flowing and fulfilling conversation you end up mumbling your questions or forgetting everything you meant to talk about?

Short answer: it's good to be prepared. Interviews are extremely popular with both print and online magazines. Often the interview format is preserved and the interviewer's questions are printed just above the answers. Look to these questions as your source for this exercise.

Read Thomas Sayers Ellis's interview with Bootsy Collins that begins this section and select some of his most effective questions. Scour other interviews in magazines for questions that spark the reaction "that's a great question." Make a list of 10 great interview questions, alter them to fit your subject as necessary, and try them out on a friend, classmate or willing local musician. Conduct an interview either over email, in person or on the phone. You should explain the exercise to your friend and perhaps ask him or her to play the role of a popular musician. The answers don't need to be real: the point of this exercise is to get you to notice the questions that get people thinking and produce the most compelling answers.

THE GO-BETWEENS

YOUR DREAM INTERVIEW SUBJECT

David Bowie. I obviously love his records, and he's a genuine genius who gets a ton of credit but I still think is slightly underrated. I would need no less than 43 hours with him just to discuss the second side of *Diamond Dogs*.—**Kyle Anderson**, senior writer, *Entertainment Weekly*

Billy Corgan, no question. First of all because I love a lot of his music—Smashing Pumpkins are one of my all-time favorite bands—and even the failures and missteps are interesting to contemplate. Second of all, the guy just says fascinating things. He's quite obviously insecure, and full of contradictions, but also really smart about stuff. Really an intriguing mix.—**Bryan Charles**, writer and **33⅓** author

I'd fire up the Ouija board for Judee Sill, the brilliant, conflicted, hermetic songstress who died in 1979, to ask her about the mystic underpinnings of her Southern California youth, and the underworld experiences that lend such a sense of anguished authenticity to her work.—**Kim Cooper**, Editrix, *Scram*

Who doesn't love a scientist who can simplify complex matters and still leave a shine of wonder on every topic under the sun? For me, it couldn't get much better than Richard Feynman, with his bongos at the ready, talking about living life to the fullest.—**Phillip Crandall**, author of the **33⅓** book on Andrew W.K.'s *I Get Wet*

Bob Dylan—for the challenge of asking questions that interest him and the possibility that the greatest living artist on the planet will provide an insight into his work that he hasn't shared before.—**Bruce Eaton**, author, *Radio City* (**33⅓**)

Thelonious Monk. To have an opportunity to explore with him his brilliance and his idiosyncratic approach to public life would be extraordinary.—**Jim Fusilli**, rock and pop critic, *The Wall Street Journal*, Editor, ReNewMusic.net

Well, I'll regret forever that I was unable to interview Nas for my book. Looking back, I should have pushed harder to make it happen—it would have made something I'm still proud of even better.—**Matthew Gasteier**, **33⅓** author

That's a tough one. Most of the really interesting characters put everything into their creations, with little left over for chat. The voluble, articulate types, like Leonard Cohen or Brian Eno, have been over-interrogated by half, though I'm certain each man could still rise to the occasion and deliver fresh, impressively sculpted thoughts were the questions up to snuff. If he wasn't most of the way blotto, as he seemed to be for much of his brief time following puberty, I would have enjoyed speaking to Gram Parsons, a conflicted but perhaps ultimately sensitive soul, better read than he let on. Then again, him being spoiled rotten, star-struck, heroin addicted and self-smitten might torch that conversation before it began.—**Richard Henderson**, music writer and **33⅓** author

I narrowly missed out on interviewing Gil Scott-Heron (I left a message or two on his machine), and I will always regret that. I just can't think of many musicians who were smarter, or funnier, or craftier than him.—**Casey Jarman**, Managing Editor, the *Believer*

John Lennon, because he was so completely full of shit and no interviewer ever properly tore him down, intellectually.—**Chris Ott**, **33⅓** author

Oscar Wilde. Just to listen to that man talk for a few minutes. I would so love to take him out to karaoke and watch him tackle the Miley songbook. I bet Oscar would torch up "We Can't Stop."—**Rob Sheffield**, writer, *Rolling Stone*

John Cage, because he has a sprawling, innovative mind that wouldn't allow for a boring response.—**Ross Simonini**, writer, Editor at The *Believer* magazine, musician

That would be Dennis Potter, I think. His use of music in his screenplays—most notably *Pennies from Heaven* and *The Singing Detective*—really registered with me, about the way music shapes people's emotions, their interactions, their sense of the world, about how music works in people's minds, how it becomes part of their thought processes. But I'm kind of glad I didn't interview him when he was alive, because I would have mucked it up. I wasn't ready.—**Marc Weidenbaum**, author of *Selected Ambient Works Volume II* (**33⅓**, 2014)

CHAPTER 6
THE PERSONAL ESSAY

INTRODUCTION

Please consider the following passages:

> Eventually, an evening came to pass that I understand as the moment during which my parents were discussing how to tell us they were separating. They were enclosed in that family room with the expensive hi-fi. The louvered drawing room doors were closed. There was an unsettling silence in the house. We (my sister, brother, and I) looked at these closed doors, from up the staircase, between the dowels supporting the banister. Something lasting and grim was taking place.

> "Sparrow" was about loving the forgotten, the marginalized, the sick, homely, and despised, and it was about how everything has to die, and if heaven is a locale wherein the injustice of earthly mortality is repaired, uh, for *eternity*, then "Sparrow," in its radical acceptance of the spurned little bird, points in the direction of heavenly music, what it might *do*, how it might make the case for the equalizing force of paradise.

The first passage, about the indelible moment when the writer and his siblings learn the "grim" truth that everything in their family is about to change, would not seem out of place in a contemporary memoir. We're familiar with the markers: details that recreate a physical environment to contain an emotional reality—louvered doors, the dowels supporting the banister, unsettling silence—along with a frankness and temporal remove from the recounted event that frame a pivotal moment of lasting import. Only the expensive hi-fi suggests the possibility that such writing might have something to do with music (the writer has already written about the hi-fi and the room in which it is housed in a previous paragraph, hence the language "*that* family room," my italics). It's not difficult to categorize such a passage as memoiristic or "personal."

The second passage, consisting of one sentence and concerning Simon & Garfunkel's song "Sparrow," on the other hand, isn't at all the kind of writing we might expect to read in a conventional personal essay or memoir. Long by nearly any standard and distinct from the style we might expect to find in such intimate forms, this sentence appears to be a variation on theological exegesis from an earlier century, replete with a moral cast and an appeal to categories of investigation not usually found in contemporary prose, let alone current music writing. The essential and unexpected deployment of "uh" almost precisely in the middle of the sentence is not only a cue for the imminent arrival of the concept of "eternity" (that "uh" seems to prepare us to take in the forthcoming concept, to warn us not to read blithely past it) but is also an acknowledgment that the writer is in the middle of an unconventionally long run and he, like us, could use a moment of reprieve during which to take a breath. Length aside, the inclusion here of assertions like "heaven is a locale wherein the injustice of earthly mortality is repaired" and questions such as how "heavenly music" might "make the case for the equalizing force of paradise" would be unlikely to find their way into either a conventional music magazine or a standard memoir.

So it may be surprising to learn that both passages, as different as they are, come from the same piece by Rick Moody, an ambitious and award-winning personal essay entitled "On Celestial Music" that provides a seamless context for each kind of writing (and several other kinds as well). As you'll find when reading the work collected in this chapter, the personal essay as practiced by writers interested in music is a big house that contains many rooms. These selections may also suggest what we suspect: that some of the most ambitious, exciting, and unconventional music writing is currently written in the form of the personal essay, one that these writers make look easy but is in fact deceptively demanding. The form is so capacious that the range of what's possible in a personal essay is as daunting as it is (potentially) liberating. When you read the following work in anticipation of writing your own personal essay, you might consider questions such as "how do I write about myself and the music I love without seeming solipsistic?"; "what makes my story as it attaches to a given piece of music worth telling for a reader who doesn't know me?"; "how can I balance the personal with an account of the music itself without becoming too self-indulgent, on the one hand, or too objective and neutrally descriptive on the other?" All the writers represented here have answered such questions as they've taken up this form. Each finds a way to write about what is perhaps the most fundamental experience of music: what happens when a song or record comes to define and inform who we are and how we understand ourselves.—MW

BRUCE EATON ON BIG STAR

33⅓ Volume #65 *Radio City**

The plight of the vinyl junkie is that most days you have to settle for something less than great. Like a true wax fanatic, it was psychically impossible for me to leave a record store empty-handed. Entering Play It Again, Sam, I'd conduct a ritualistic search, starting with a beeline for the new releases bin, hoping it contained heretofore unseen treasures of black gold. If there were a couple of hot new imports along with a rare bootleg to top off the haul, the day might be as good as Christmas. More often than not, there would be the same exact records as the day before. That meant that there was work to do.

Play It Again, Sam specialized in used records—sorted and priced by a combination of condition and desirability and marked accordingly by a colored dot sticker. You'd start by combing through the red dots—the primo records that sold for two dollars and fifty cents. Here you'd find the latest releases that had been traded in by a local record promo man for his pizza and gas money. If you didn't find anything in the reds, you'd slide over to the two-dollar blue-dot bins, maybe settling for a used J. Geils Band album you'd once owned in college and had passed over on your previous 34 visits. If you still weren't in the mood to hear *Full House* again, you'd have to take desperate action and thumb through the dollar-fifty yellow-dot bins. It was here you'd find the records that were one step from being put out to curb—either worn-out and abandoned college dorm hits of yore (Carole King and Cat Stevens lived here), albums that even an artist's hardcore fans couldn't swallow (Steve Stills was releasing direct-to-yellow-dot at that point), or records that for one reason or another never garnered a following (April Wine were the Led Zeppelin of the yellow dots).

On this particular day, I had made it all the way to the yellow dots empty-handed. Starting at the "A" bin, I flipped past Ace and April Wine, a worn copy of The Band's *Stage Fright*, beat-up Beach Boys and Beatles albums, and the first wave of Bee Gees trade-ins. Some of these albums had been there for months—I could almost tell you what was going to come next. And then there it was. An album I'd never seen before. Unless a record had been released just yesterday, this alone was reason to pause. Across the top it read in black letters "Radio City Big Star" in a way that made it apparent that album was *Radio City* and the band was Big Star.

If you spend enough time looking at records, you develop a sixth sense about how good a record might be just from looking the cover. On first glance, *Radio City* looked quite promising. The front cover featured a big photograph of a bare light bulb against

---

*Eaton, Bruce. *Radio City*. New York: Bloomsbury Academic, 2009, 2–11. Reprinted with permission.

a bright red room and struck me as being at least several notches above your typical album art. It would be a few years before I knew that the photographer—William Eggleston—was a world-renowned artist and a friend of the band. Curious—okay, desperate—I picked up the album. The sturdy cardboard cover sheathed a nice thick slab of wax. Like a vintage Blue Note jazz LP, it felt like a record made by people who cared about the music and knew what they were doing. On the back cover there was another color photo—this one an informal shot of three guys—presumably Big Star—hanging out in a club (the original T.G.I. Friday's it turned out). They had an air of cool and confident informality—a band that didn't bother with rock star poses. Below the picture was some minimal information: song titles and a few credits. Nothing rang a bell except the words "distributed by Stax," a de facto seal of approval for any self-respecting rock snob.

In the back of my mind I vaguely remembered having read something about Big Star in *Creem* a few years earlier—that their sound was somehow connected to The Beatles (who in 1976 seemed to be way more a thing of the past than they do today) and the Byrds, and that the reviews were positive. I had a good feeling *Radio City* might be worth the six quarters. Holding the record up, I caught the attention of the clerk behind the register. I was just getting to know Bill, a friendly fellow who looked like he had once been a roadie for Quicksilver Messenger Service and whose taste in music leaned toward raw Detroit rock and roll with a psychedelic edge. The sort whose opinion you might value even if you were inclined to believe that yours was the only one that mattered. I gave Bill a quizzical "what's the deal?" look. "You might like that," was his offhand response, one that would prove to be an understatement to say the least. "Take it, and if you like it, pay me next time." I secured the record under my arm and headed home.

That evening I put the record on my turntable and sat down to write a few letters. It would be dramatic to say that hearing *Radio City* for the first time altered my life but the redirection came later. What actually happened is that, song by song, it pulled me in until by the end of the first side I had stopped writing and was propped back in my chair with my feet on the desk, listening as the sun set behind the woods outside my window, feeling the June breeze blowing in through the window screen. I flipped the record over to Side Two and by the time the needle reached the middle of "September Gurls," five cuts in, I was riveted. The song was, on first listen, as perfect as any two minutes and fifty-six seconds of rock and roll that I'd ever heard. Three years later to the month I would be on stage at McVan's Rock Castle in Buffalo, playing that very song with Alex Chilton—the guy who wrote it, sang it, and played what sounded for all the world like an entire symphony of chiming guitars.

I played *Radio City* over and over for a few hours (it clocks in at just over 36 minutes—unlike the interminable CDs of today, listening to an album from start to finish back then wasn't a major life commitment). I stared at the jacket—wondering who Big Star was and why *Radio City* hadn't risen to the top of the charts, or even crossed my path. By the time I went to sleep, I had a new favorite band, albeit one

I knew nothing about. (For rock snobs, the more obscure your favorite band, the better.) All I knew was that I had hit the vinyl jackpot—I had found a great record in the garbage bin.

At the time I was somewhat frustrated about the lack of information about Big Star but I now look at it as a blessing. For the next eight months or so, the only in-depth information I had about the band was what was stamped in vinyl. The grooves contained everything the musicians wanted me to know—a direct line of unfiltered communication. I could let the sound speak to me without any interference or preconceptions, form my own opinions and let the music fill my imagination, taking me to unexpected places. I could listen without having to decide if Big Star was really the future of rock and roll or if *Radio City* was the most important album of the year.

It's sometimes hard to remember but there once was a time when sound—not image, gossip, and hype—was indeed first and foremost in rock and roll. When Memphis deejay Dewey Phillips spun a new 45 by a local teenager on the night of July 7, 1954, the listeners who jammed up the request lines had nary a clue about Elvis Presley. Phillips himself didn't even know if Elvis was black or white (he obliquely found out by asking him what high school he attended). Elvis could have been 300 pounds of sweating human sausage packed into a bejeweled white polyester casing and it wouldn't have mattered. All that mattered was the *sound* of "That's All Right."

Recorded less than 3 miles away from the Sun Studios where Elvis had recorded his first hit, *Radio City* also had a singular, almost otherworldly sound that exerted a mysterious pull.

Trying to describe how a record sounds and why it grabs you can be like trying to pick up a little blob of mercury off a tile floor. But here's where I would describe the visceral appeal of *Radio City* in a roundabout way. When I was a teenager in the 1960s, my family spent a part of each summer at the beach out on the northern fork of Long Island, 90 miles out from New York City. The sound of WABC–AM—the Top Forty titan in New York—was virtually everywhere, pumping out the Super Hits from the All-American Survey around the clock. Lying on the sand in the hot afternoon sun, half-drifting off to sleep, you could always hear it off in the distance amidst the sounds of bathers and motorboats. But when you tried to zero in and follow along, your ears and brain would play tricks on you—turning a song you knew inside out into something completely different. You might have started with what you thought was "Help!" and before you knew it there was an entirely new—and equally perfect—song coming to life in your head, taking unexpected twists and turns. And then, like a mirage in the summer heat, it would vanish at the first sound of the Yoo-Hoo jingle that inevitably followed.

Radio City captures the sound of those illusory moments on the beach. It's as if all of the music coming out of all the little transistor radio speakers—Beatles, Stones, Byrds, Beach Boys, Sam and Dave, Fifth Dimension, Lovin' Spoonful, Question Mark and the Mysterians, Supremes, Young Rascals, Sonny and Cher, Four Tops, Sam the

Sham, Napoleon The XIV—had somehow been beamed into outer space to some distant planet and then transformed by a band of musical alchemists into something both fresh and yet familiar and sent back to Earth in a stream of glowing super-charged electrical particles by a wizard of sound. In a very real sense though, that's exactly what happened. Even on first listen, *Radio City* sounded like pure magic.

If *Radio City* sounded like an album that had been created in the past and then beamed to a time and place somewhere in the future for the world to eventually discover, it never really did have much of a present. It sold few copies when it was released in March of 1974—somewhere under 10,000 is a reasonable guess. If you had a copy, the cover most likely had a promo sticker or a corner cut off. What copies that made their way out into the world found their way into the hands of people who played it over and over. *Radio City* became much sought after, and once secured, treasured. Odds are that if you had a copy, it wasn't just another record in your collection. It was a directive for a mission—you had to spread the word. You had made a point of playing it for your friends and gladly made a cassette copy when they shook their heads in amazement. When you met someone who already knew about Big Star, it was like a musical handshake that made you part of an underground of true believers. A lot of those handshakes were the beginning of new bands. Some of those bands went on to enjoy the success that their inspiration had optimistically hoped for—even expected—during its brief life. If influence could be measured, *Radio City* would have now gone platinum many times over.

Eventually *Radio City* was reissued on LP and then CD—enjoying progressively far better distribution than it ever did upon its initial release. Listeners across several generations around the world discovered the music—finding it to be as fresh and captivating as it was on the day it was recorded. And improbably, Big Star reunited with a retooled lineup in 1993, released a new album in 2005, and still performed on occasion before Alex Chilton's death in 2010.

The story of Big Star has been told from a lot of different perspectives—virtually all involving a familiar cocktail of tragedy, drama, Southern gothic mojo, mystery, drugs, personal chaos, sex, booze, bad luck, youthful recklessness, mental disorder, dashed dreams, and thwarted ambitions. If you're reading this book, you likely know all the stories, rumors, and outright slander repeated over and over as gospel truth in liner notes, books, and magazine articles. When offered an opportunity to correct any falsehoods, Alex Chilton responds, "I'm sure there are hundreds and thousands of misconceptions out there that I've just learned not to bother with." Bandmate Andy Hummel adds, "An awful lot of what you read in the press about over the past ten years or however long it's been since it suddenly dawned on them that Big Star existed is highly colored by who they're talking to. Generally speaking, they're not talking to anyone in the band—"anyone" being sort of the creative energy behind the band. They're talking to people who were involved on the periphery. That's the story that's out there. It's not the story of what happened with the band—it's the story about what other people say happened to the band."

What gets lost in the familiar telling of the Big Star story is how the music and the sound came to be in the first place. A record like *Radio City* just doesn't appear out of nowhere via total happy accident. Rock and roll is somewhat slave to the notion that anyone with enough desire can learn a few chords, somehow stumble into a hit record, and be a star. The reality is that great records are made by really talented people (even geniuses—although that word has been used enough to render it virtually meaningless) who work long and hard at their craft until the day when the magic suddenly enters the studio.

Talent—God-given natural ability—is an unpopular, even cruel, notion in a world where it's widely believed that anyone can make it to the top if they have enough ambition, blonde or otherwise. But most of us don't have great musical talent. Instead, we get to buy the records and the concert tickets, write books and reviews, and even play in bands that allow us to have fun and dream a bit (hopefully avoiding delusions of grandeur).

Beyond talent, there's the often dismissed importance of experience—in music and in life. Does an artist have something interesting to say and the ability to say it in a unique and interesting way? The answer is usually "not really." One of the chief reasons that rock and roll from the 1960s and early 1970s still looms large is that its creators had deep reserves of experience to draw upon when the time finally came to go to the well in the recording studio. Take The Beatles or The Stones, Bob Dylan or Bruce Springsteen. Each knew hundreds upon hundreds of cover tunes—a disparaged concept today but vital to learning how music works—and had played endless gigs trying to sell them to indifferent, if not downright hostile, audiences. That experience takes patience but it eventually can get you to a point where you can write songs of your own that become a meaningful and permanent part of other peoples' lives. Alex Chilton, with century-deep family roots in the Mississippi Delta and a dad who infused his youth with jazz, may have only been 22 years old when *Radio City* was recorded, but he'd hit the road at the age of 16—playing shows all across the country, surrounded by masters of the craft, soaking up everything he could. It doesn't require any stretch of the imagination to believe that a kid who grew up listening to *Mingus Ah Um* and *Birth Of The Cool*, learned how to play guitar from a Beach Boy, and got to watch Wilson Pickett and The Staple Singers burn down the house night after night is going to have a few more interesting colors on his artistic palette than a kid who grew up watching music videos in his bedroom while copping shred licks in dropped D tuning. You can't see them but you can definitely hear them.

My goal in writing this book was to shed light on how the *sound* got into the grooves of *Radio City* and why, to the confoundment of many, it never happened quite that way again. After all, the *sound* is why we care about *Radio City*, not any surrounding six-string soap opera. I love to pore over musical biographies and *MOJO* alike but one can take it to a point where the actual music becomes a mere soundtrack to an oft-repeated mythologized tale of dysfunction. Looking back some 35 years ago, I got heavily into the music of Nick Drake and Gram Parsons when their albums were being released for the first time—without knowing a thing about either of them. I don't really feel that all that's been subsequently detailed about their respective struggles has added much beyond a whit to my listening experience. If you can accept the premise that genius almost always comes with a price tag, then you're free to concentrate on why you ultimately care about the artist. In one word: music. Listen carefully and you'll hear all their personal stories buried in the grooves anyway.

Some pieces of the creative puzzle are obvious: how a song was written or a particular part recorded. Other parts of the story are below the surface or even in the distant past. When you read the words of the people who were actually in the room, in one way or another, for the creation of *Radio City*, you'll find a lot of dots to connect. You won't be able to draw an exact roadmap—that would be impossible—but you'll be able to sketch out a rough blueprint of how *Radio City* was built and why, improbably, it still stands tall nearly three and a half decades after the final note was nailed into place. The **33⅓** series doesn't use subtitles for individual books—none are necessary. But if pressed, I'd offer this one for *Radio City*: How To Make A Great Record—If Only You Could.

LESTER BANGS ON VAN MORRISON

Astral Weeks*

Van Morrison's *Astral Weeks* was released ten years, almost to the day, before this was written. It was particularly important to me because the fall of 1968 was such a terrible time: I was a physical and mental wreck, nerves shredded and ghosts and spiders looming and squatting across the mind. My social contacts had dwindled to almost none; the presence of other people made me nervous and paranoid. I spent endless days and nights sunk in an armchair in my bedroom, reading magazines, watching TV, listening to records, staring into space. I had no idea how to improve the situation and probably wouldn't have done anything about it if I had.

Astral Weeks would be the subject of this piece—i.e., the rock record with the most significance in my life so far—no matter how I'd been feeling when it came out. But in the condition I was in, it assumed at the time the quality of a beacon, a light on the far shores of the murk; what's more, it was proof that there was something left to express artistically besides nihilism and destruction. (My other big record of the day was *White Light/White Heat*.) It sounded like the man who made *Astral Weeks* was in terrible pain, pain most of Van Morrison's previous works had only suggested; but like the later albums by the Velvet Underground, there was a redemptive element in the blackness, ultimate compassion for the suffering of others, and a swath of pure beauty and mystical awe that cut right through the heart of the work.

I don't really know how significant it might be that many others have reported variants on my initial encounter with *Astral Weeks*. I don't think there's anything guiding it to people enduring dark periods. It did come out at a time when a lot of things that a lot of people cared about passionately were beginning to disintegrate, and when the self-destructive undertow that always accompanied the great sixties party had an awful lot of ankles firmly in its maw and was pulling straight down. So, as timeless as it finally is, perhaps *Astral Weeks* was also the product of an era. Better think that than ask just what sort of Irish churchwebbed haints Van Morrison might be product of.

Three television shows:
A 1970 NET broadcast of a big all-star multiple bill at the Fillmore East. The Byrds, Sha Na Na, and Elvin Bishop have all done their respective things. Now we get to see three of four songs from a set by Van Morrison. He climaxes, as he always did in those days, with "Cyprus Avenue" from *Astral Weeks*. After going through all the verses, he drives the song, the band, and himself to a finish which has since become

---

*Bangs, Lester. "Astral Weeks" from *Stranded: Rock and Roll for a Desert Island*. New York: Knopf, 1979. Reprinted with permission.

one of his trademarks and one of the all-time classic rock 'n' roll set-closers. With consumate dynamics that allow him to snap from indescribably eccentric throwaway phrasing to sheer passion in the very next breath he brings the music surging up through crescendo after crescendo, stopping and starting and stopping and starting the song again and again, imposing long maniacal silences like giant question marks between the stops and starts and ruling the room through sheer tension, building to a shout of "It's too late to stop now!," and just when you think it's all going to surge over the top, he cuts it off stone cold dead, the hollow of a murdered explosion, throws the microphone down and stalks off the stage. It is truly one of the most perverse things I have ever seen a performer do in my life. And, of course, it's sensational: our guts are knotted up, we're crazed and clawing for more, but we damn well know we've seen and felt something final.

1974, a late night network TV rock concert: Van and his band come out, strike a few shimmering chords, and for about ten minutes he lingers over the words "Way over yonder in the clear blue sky/Where flamingos fly." No other lyrics. I don't think any instrumental solos. Just those words, repeated slowly again and again, distended, permutated, turned into scat, suspended in space and then scattered to the winds, muttered like a mantra till they turn into nonsense syllables, then back into the same soaring image as time seems to stop entirely. He stands there with eyes closed, singing, transported, while the band poises quivering over great open-tuned deep blue gulfs of their own.

1977, spring-summer, same kind of show: he sings "Cold Wind in August", a song off his recently released album *A Period of Transition*, which also contains a considerably altered version of the flamingos song. "Cold Wind in August" is a ballad and Van gives it a fine, standard reading. The only trouble is that the whole time he's singing it he paces back and forth in a line on the stage, his eyes tightly shut, his little fireplug body kicking its way upstream against what must be a purgatorial nervousness that perhaps is being transferred to the cameraman.

What this is about is a whole set of verbal tics—although many are bodily as well—which are there for reason enough to go a long way toward defining his style. They're all over *Astral Weeks*: four rushed repeats of the phrases "you breathe in, you breath out" and "you turn around" in "Beside You"; in "Cyprus Avenue," twelve "way up on"s, "baby" sung out thirteen times in a row sounding like someone running ecstatically downhill toward one's love, and the heartbreaking way he stretches "one by one" in the third verse; most of all in "Madame George" where he sings the word "dry" and then "your eye" twenty times in a twirling melodic arc so beautiful it steals your own breath, and then this occurs: "And the love that loves the love that loves the love that loves the love that loves to love the love that loves to love the love that loves."

Van Morrison is interested, obsessed with how much musical or verbal information he can compress into a small space, and, almost, conversely, how far he can spread one note, word, sound, or picture. To capture one moment, be it a caress or a twitch. He repeats certain phrases to extremes that from anybody else would seem ridiculous, because he's waiting for a vision to unfold, trying as unobtrusively as possible to nudge it along. Sometimes he gives it to you through silence, by choking off the song in midflight: "It's too late to stop now!"

It's the great search, fueled by the belief that through these musical and mental processes illumination is attainable. Or may at least be glimpsed.

When he tries for this he usually gets it more in the feeling than in the Revealed Word—perhaps much of the feeling comes from the reaching—but there is also, always, the sense of WHAT if he DID apprehend that Word; there are times when the Word seems to hover very near. And then there are times when we realize the Word was right next to us, when the most mundane overused phrases are transformed: I give you "love," from "Madame George." Out of relative silence, the Word: "Snow in San Anselmo." "That's where it's at," Van will say, and he means it (aren't his interviews fascinating?). What he doesn't say is that he is inside the snowflake, isolated by the song: "And it's almost Independence Day."

You're probably wondering when I'm going to get around to telling you about *Astral Weeks*. As a matter of fact, there's a whole lot of *Astral Weeks* I don't even want to tell you about. Both because whether you've heard it or not it wouldn't be fair for me to impose my interpretation of such lapidarily subjective imagery on you, and because in many cases I don't really know what he's talking about. He doesn't either: "I'm not surprised that people get different meanings out of my songs," he told an interviewer. "But I don't wanna give the impression that I know what everything means 'cause I don't. . . . There are times when I'm mystified. I look at some of the stuff that comes out, y'know. And like, there it is and it feels right, but I can't say for sure what it means."

There you go
Starin' with a look of avarice
Talking to Huddie Leadbetter
Showin' pictures on the walls
And whisperin' in the halls
And pointin' a finger at me

I haven't got the slightest idea what that "means," though on one level I'd like to approach it in a manner as indirect and evocative as the lyrics themselves. Because you're in trouble anyway when you sit yourself down to explicate just exactly what a mystical document, which is exactly what *Astral Weeks* is, means. For one thing, what it means is Richard Davis's bass playing, which complements the songs and singing all the way with a lyricism that's something more than just great musicianship: there is something about it that's more than inspired, something that has been touched, that's in the realm of the miraculous. The whole ensemble—Larry Fallon's string section, Jay Berliner's guitar (he played on Mingus's *Black Saint and the Sinner Lady*), Connie Kay's drumming—is like that: they and Van sound like they're not just reading but dwelling inside of each other's minds. The facts may be far different. John Cale was making an album of his own in the adjacent studio at the time, and he has said that "Morrison couldn't work with anybody, so finally they just shut him in the studio by himself. He did all the songs with just an acoustic guitar, and later they overdubbed the rest of it around his tapes."

Cale's story might or might not be true—but facts are not going to be of much use here in any case. Fact: Van Morrison was twenty-two—or twenty-three—years old when he made this record; there are lifetimes behind it. What *Astral Weeks* deals in are not facts but truths. *Astral Weeks*, insofar as it can be pinned down, is a record about people stunned by life, completely overwhelmed, stalled in their skins, their ages and selves, paralyzed by the enormity of what in one moment of vision they can comprehend. It is a precious and terrible gift, born of a terrible truth, because what they see is both infinitely beautiful and terminally horrifying: the unlimited human ability to create or destroy, according to whim. It's no Eastern mystic or psychedelic vision of the emerald beyond, nor is it some Baudelairean perception of the beauty of sleaze and grotesquerie. Maybe what it boils down to is one moment's knowledge of the miracle of life, with its inevitable concomitant, a vertiginous glimpse of the capacity to be hurt, and the capacity to inflict that hurt.

Transfixed between pure rapture and anguish. Wondering if they may not be the same thing, or at least possessed of an intimate relationship. In "T.B. Sheets," his last extended narrative before making this record, Van Morrison watched a girl he loved die of tuberculosis. The song was claustrophobic, suffocating, mostrously powerful: "innuendos, inadequacies, foreign bodies." A lot of people couldn't take it; the editor of this book has said that it's garbage, but I think it made him squeamish. Anyway, the point is that certain parts of *Astral Weeks*—"Madame George," "Cyprus Avenue"— take the pain in "T.B. Sheets" and root the world in it. Because the pain of watching a loved one die of however dread a disease may be awful, but it is at least something known, in a way understood, in a way measureable and even leading somewhere, because there is a process: sickness, decay, death, mourning, some emotional recovery. But the beautiful horror of "Madame George" and "Cyprus Avenue" is precisely that the people in these songs are not dying: we are looking at life, in its fullest, and what these people are suffering from is not disease but nature, unless nature is a disease.

A man sits in a car on a tree-lined street, watching a fourteen-year-old girl walking home from school, hopelessly in love with her. I've almost come to blows with friends because of my insistence that much of Van Morrison's early work had an obsessively reiterated theme of pedophilia, but here is something that at once may be taken as that and something far beyond it. He loves her. Because of that, he is helpless. Shaking. Paralyzed. Maddened. Hopeless. Nature mocks him. As only nature can mock nature. Or is love natural in the first place? No Matter. By the end of the song he has entered a kind of hallucinatory ecstasy; the music aches and yearns as it rolls on out. This is one supreme pain, that of being imprisoned a spectator. And perhaps not so very far from "T.B. Sheets," except that it must be far more romantically easy to sit and watch someone you love die than to watch them in the bloom of youth and health and know that you can never, ever have them, can never speak to them.

"Madame George" is the album's whirlpool. Possibly one of the most compassionate pieces of music ever made, it asks us, no, *arranges* that we see the plight of what I'll be brutal and call a lovelorn drag queen with such intense empathy that when the singer hurts him, we do too. (Morrison has said in at least one interview that the song has nothing to do with any kind of transvestite—at least as far as *he* knows, he is quick to add—but that's bullshit.) The beauty, sensitivity, *holiness* of the song is that there's nothing at all sensationalistic, exploitative, or tawdry about it; in a way Van is right when he insists it's not about a drag queen, as my friends were right and I was wrong about the "pedophelia"—it's about a *person*, like all the best songs, all the greatest literature.

The setting is the same as that of the previous song—"Cyprus Avenue," apparently a place where people drift, impelled by desire, into moments of flesh-wracking, sight-curdling confrontation with their destinies. It's an elemental place of pitiless judgment—wind and rain figure in both songs—and, interestingly enough, it's a place of the even crueler judgment of adults by *children*, in both cases love objects absolutely indifferent to their would-be adult lovers. Madame George's little boys are downright contemptuous—like the street urchins who end up cannibalizing the homosexual cousin in Tennessee Williams's *Suddenly Last Summer*, they're only too happy to come around as long as there's music, party times, free drinks and smokes, and only too gleefully to spit on George's affections when all the other stuff runs out, the entombing winter settling in with not only wind and rain but hail, sleet, and snow.

What might seem strangest of all but really isn't is that it's exactly those characteristics which supposedly should make George most pathetic—age, drunkenness, the way the boys take his money and trash his love—that awakens something for George in the heart of the kid whose song this is. Obviously the kid hasn't simply "fallen in love with love," or something like that, but rather—what? Why just exactly that only sunk in the foulest perversions could one human being love another for anything *other* than their humanness: love him for his weakness, his flaws, finally perhaps his decay. Decay is human—that's one of the ultimate messages here, and I don't by any stretch of the lexicon mean decadence. I mean that in this song or whatever inspired it Van Morrison saw the absolute possibility of loving human beings at the farthest extreme of wretchedness, and that the implications of that are terrible indeed, far more terrible than the mere sight of bodies made ugly by age or the seeming absurdity of a man devoting his life to the wobbly artifice of trying to look like a woman.

You can say to love the questions you have to love the answers which quicken the end of love that's loved to love the awful inequality of human experience that loves to say we tower over these the lost that love to love the love that freedom could have been, the train to freedom, but we never get on, we'd rather wave generously walking away from those who are victims of themselves. But who is to say that someone who victimizes himself or herself is not as worthy of total compassion as the most down and out Third World orphan in a *New Yorker* magazine ad? Nah, better to step over the bodies, at least that gives them the respect they might have once deserved. Where I live, in New York (not to make it more than it is, which is hard), everyone I know often steps over bodies which might well be dead or dying as a matter of course, without pain. And I wonder in what scheme it was originally conceived that such an action is showing human refuse the ultimate respect it deserves.

There is of course a rationale—what else are you going to do—but it holds no more than our fear of our own helplessness in the face of the plain of life as it truly is: a plain which extends into an infinity beyond the horizons we have only invented. Come on, die it. As I write this, I can read in the *Village Voice* the blurbs of people opening heterosexual S&M clubs in Manhattan, saying things like, "S&M is just another equally valid form of love. Why people can't accept that we'll never know." Makes you want to jump out a fifth floor window rather than even read about it, but it's hardly the end of the world; it's not nearly as bad as the hurts that go on everywhere everyday that are taken so casually by all of us as facts of life. Maybe it boiled down to how much you actually want to subject yourself to. If you accept for even a moment the idea that each human life is as precious and delicate as a snowflake and then you look at a wino in a doorway, you've got to hurt until you feel like a sponge for all those other assholes' problems, until you feel like an asshole yourself, so you draw all the appropriate lines. You stop feeling. But you know that then you begin to die. So you tussle with yourself. How much of this horror can I actually allow myself to think about? Perhaps the numbest mannequin is wiser than somebody who only allows their sensitivity to drive them to destroy everything they touch—but then again, to tilt Madame George's hat a hair, just to recognize that that person exists, just to touch his cheek and then probably expire because the realization that you must share the world with him is ultimately unbearable is to only go the first mile. The realization of living is just about that low and that exalted and that unbearable and that sought-after. Please come back and leave me alone. But when we're alone together we can talk all we want about the universality of this abyss: it doesn't make any difference, the highest only meets the lowest for some lying succor, UNICEF to relatives, so you scratch and spit and curse in violent resignation at the strict fact that there is absolutely nothing you can do but finally reject anyone in greater pain than you. At such a moment, another breath is treason. That's why you leave your liberal causes, leave suffering humanity to die in worse squalor than they knew before you happened along. You got their hopes up. Which makes you viler than the most scrofulous carrion. Viler than the ignorant boys who would take Madame George for a couple of cigarettes. Because you have committed the crime of knowledge, and thereby not only walked past or over someone you knew to be suffering, but also violated their privacy, the last possession of the dispossessed.

Such knowledge is possibly the worst thing that can happen to a person (a *lucky* person), so it's no wonder that Morrison's protagonist turned away from Madame

George, fled to the train station, trying to run as far away from what he'd seen as a lifetime could get him. And no wonder, too, that Van Morrison never came this close to looking life square in the face again, no wonder he turned to *Tupelo Honey* and even *Hard Nose the Highway* with its entire side of songs about falling leaves. In *Astral Weeks* and "T.B. Sheets" he confronted enough for any man's lifetime. Of course, having been offered this immeasurably stirring and equally frightening gift from Morrison, one can hardly be blamed for not caring terribly much about "Old, Old Woodstock" and little homilies like "You've got to Make It Through This World On Your Own" and "Take It Where You Find It."

On the other hand, it might also be pointed out that desolation, hurt, and anguish are hardly the only things in life, or in *Astral Weeks*. They're just the things, perhaps, that we can most easily grasp and explicate, which I suppose shows about what level our souls have evolved to. I said I wouldn't reduce the other songs on this album by trying to explain them, and I won't. But that doesn't mean that, all things considered, a juxtaposition of poets might not be in order.

If I ventured in the slipstream
Between the viaducts of your dreams
Where the mobile steel rims crack
And the ditch and the backroads stop
Could you find me
Would you kiss my eyes
And lay me down
In silence easy
To be born again

—Van Morrison

My heart of silk
is filled with lights,
with lost bells,
with lilies and bees.
I will go very far,
farther than those hills,
farther than the seas,
close to the stars,
to beg Christ the Lord
to give back the soul I had
of old, when I was a child,
ripened with legends,
with a feathered cap
and a wooden sword.

—Federico Garcia Lorca

JAMES WOOD ON KEITH MOON

The Fun Stuff: Homage to Keith Moon*

I had a traditional musical education, in a provincial English cathedral town. I was sent off to an ancient piano teacher with the requisite halitosis, who lashed with a ruler at my knuckles as if they were wasps; I added the trumpet a few years later, and had lessons with a younger, cheerier man, who told me that the best way to make the instrument "sound" was to imagine spitting paper pellets down the mouthpiece at the school bully. I sang daily in the cathedral choir, an excellent grounding in sight-reading and performance. I still play the piano and the trumpet.

But what I really wanted to do, as a little boy, was play the drums, and, of those different ways of making *music*, only playing the drums still makes me feel like a little boy. A friend's older brother had a drum kit, and as a twelve-year-old I gawped at the spangled shells of wood and skin, and plotted how I might get to hit them, and make a lot of noise. It wouldn't be easy. My parents had no time for "all that thumping about," and the prim world of ecclesiastical and classical music, which meant so much to me, detested rock. But I waited until the drums' owner was off at school, and sneaked into the attic where they gleamed, fabulously inert, and over the next few years I taught myself how to play them. Sitting behind the drums was like the fantasy of driving (the other great prepubescent ambition), with my feet established on two pedals, bass drum and high hat, and the willing dials staring back at me like a blank dashboard . . .

Noise, speed, rebellion: everyone secretly wants to play the drums, because hitting things, like yelling, returns us to the innocent violence of childhood. Music makes us want to dance, to register rhythm on and with our bodies. The drummer and the conductor are the luckiest of all musicians, because they are closest to dancing. And in drumming how childishly close the connection *is* between the dancer and the dance! When you blow down an oboe, say, or pull a bow across a string, an infinitesimal hesitation—the hesitation of vibration—separates the act and the sound; for trumpeters, the simple voicing of a quiet middle C is more fraught than very complex passages, because that brass tube can be sluggish in its obedience. But when a drummer needs to make a drum sound he just . . . hits it. "The stick or hand comes down, and the skin bellows." The narrator of Thomas Bernhard's novel *The Loser*, a pianist crazed with dreams of genius and obsessed with Glenn Gould,

---

*Wood, James. *The Fun Stuff, and Other Essays*. New York: Farrar, Straus and Giroux, 2012, 3–17. Reprinted with permission from the author.

expresses the impossible longing to *become* the piano, to be at one with it. When you play the drums, you *are* the drums. "Le tom-tom, c'est moi," as Wallace Stevens put it.

The drummer who *was* the drums, when I was a boy, was the Who's Keith Moon, though he was dead by the time I first heard him. He *was* the drums not because he was the most technically accomplished of drummers but because his many-armed joyous, semaphoring lunacy suggested a man possessed by the antic spirit of drumming. He was pure, irresponsible, restless childishness. At the end of early Who concerts, as Pete Townshend smashed his guitar, Moon would kick his drums and stand on them and hurl them around the stage, and this seems a logical extension not only of the basic premise of drumming, which is to hit things, but an inevitable extension of Moon's drumming, which was to hit things exuberantly. In the band's very early days, the managers of clubs would complain to Townshend about his drummer. We like you guys, they would say, but get rid of that madman on the drums, he's too loud. To which Moon succinctly replied: "I can't play quiet, I'm a rock drummer."

The Who had extraordinary rhythmic vitality, and it died when Keith Moon died, on September 7, 1978. I had hardly ever heard any rock music when I first listened to albums like *Quadrophenia* and *Who's Next*. My notion of musical volume and power was inevitably circumscribed by my fairly sheltered, austerely Christian upbringing—I got off on classical or churchy things like the brassy last bars of William Walton's First Symphony, or the chromatic last movement of the *Hammerklavier* Sonata, or the way the choir bursts in at the start of Handel's anthem *Zadok the Priest*, or the thundering thirty-two-foot bass pipes of Durham Cathedral's organ, and the way the echo, at the end of a piece, took seven seconds to dissolve in that huge building. Those are not to be despised, but nothing had prepared me for the ferocious energy of the Who. The music enacted the Mod rebellion of its lyrics: "Hope I die before I get old"; "Meet the new boss, same as the old boss"; "Dressed right, for a beach fight"; "There's a millionaire above you,/and you're under his suspicion." Pete Townshend's hard, tense suspended chords seemed to scour the air around them; Roger Daltrey's singing was a young man's fighting swagger, an incitement to some kind of crime; John Entwistle's incessantly mobile bass playing was like someone running away from the scene of the crime; and Keith Moon's drumming, in its inspired vandalism, was the crime itself.

Most rock drummers, even very good and inventive ones, are timekeepers. There is a space for a fill or a roll at the end of a musical phrase, but the beat has primacy over the curlicues. In a regular 4/4 bar, the bass drum sounds the first beat, the snare the second, the bass drum again hits the third (often with two eighth notes at this point), and then the snare hits the bar's final beat. This results in the familiar "boom-DA, boom-boom-DA" sound of most rock drumming. A standard-issue drummer, playing along, say, to the Beatles' "Carry That Weight," would keep his 4/4 beat steady through the line "Boy, you're gonna carry that weight, carry that weight, a long time," until the natural break, which comes at the end of the phrase, where, just after the word "time," a wordless, two-beat half-bar readies itself for the repeated chorus. In that half-bar, there might be space for a quick roll, or a roll and a triplet, or something fancy with snare and hi-hat—really, any variety of filler. The filler is *the fun stuff*, and it could be said, without much exaggeration, that nearly all the fun stuff in drumming takes place in those two empty beats between the end of a phrase and the start of another. Ringo Starr, who interpreted his role fairly modestly, does nothing much in that two-beat space: mostly, he provides eight even, straight forward sixteenth notes (da-da-da-da/da-da-da-da). In a good cover version of the song, Phil Collins, an extremely sophisticated drummer who was never a modest performer with Genesis, does a tight roll that begins with featherlight delicacy on a tom-tom and ends more firmly on his snare, before going back to the beat. But whatever their stylistic differences, the modest and the sophisticated drummer share an understanding that there is a proper space for keeping the beat, and a much smaller space for departing from it, like a time-out area in a classroom. The difference is just that the sophisticated drummer is much more often in time-out, and is always busily showing off to the rest of the class while he is there.

Keith Moon ripped all this up. There is no time-out in his drumming, because there is no time-in. It is *all fun stuff*. The first principle of Moon's drumming was that drummers do not exist to keep the beat. He did keep the beat, of course, and very well, but he did it by every method except the traditional one. Drumming is repetition, as is rock music generally, and Moon clearly found repetition dull. So he played the drums like no one else—and not even like himself. I mean that no two bars of Moon's playing ever sound the same; he is in revolt against consistency, he is always vandalizing repetition. Everyone else in the band gets to improvise, so why should the drummer be nothing more than a condemned metronome? He saw himself as a soloist playing with an ensemble of other soloists. It follows from this that the drummer will be playing a line of music, just as, say, the guitarist does, with undulations and crescendos and leaps. It further follows that the snare drum and the bass drum, traditionally the ball-and-chain of rhythmic imprisonment, are no more interesting than any of the other drums in the kit; and that you will need lots of those other drums. Lots and lots. By the mid-1970s, when Moon's kit was said to be "the biggest in the world"—and what a deliciously absurd conceit, anyway!—he had two bass drums and at least twelve tom-toms, arrayed in stacks like squadrons of spotlights; he looked like a cheerful boy who had built elaborate fortifications for the sole purpose of destroying them. But he needed all those drums, as a flute needs all its stops or a harp its strings, so that his tremendous bubbling cascades, his liquid journeys, could be voiced: he needed not to run out of drums as he ran around them.

Average musical performance, like athletic prowess and viticulture—and perhaps novel writing?—has probably improved in the last century. Nowadays, more and more pianists can brilliantly run off some Chopin or Rachmaninoff in a concert hall, and the guy at the local drum shop is probably technically more adept than Keith Moon was. YouTube, which is a kind of a permanent Special Olympics for showoffs, is full of young men wreaking double-jointed virtuosity on fabulously complex drum kits rigged up like artillery ranges. But so what? They can also backflip into their jeans from great heights and parkour across Paris.

Moon disliked drum solos, and did not perform them; the only one I have seen is pretty bad, a piece of anti-performance art—Moon sloppy and mindless, apparently drunk or stoned or both, and almost collapsing into the drums while he pounds them like pillows. He may have lacked the control necessary to sustain a long, complex solo; more likely, he needed the kinetic adventures of The Who to provoke him into his own. His cheerful way of conceding this was his celebrated remark that "I'm the best Keith Moon-style drummer in the world." Which was also a way of saying, "I'm the best Who-style drummer in the world."

Keith Moon-style drumming is a lucky combination of the artful and the artless. To begin at the beginning: his drums always sounded good. He hit them nice and hard, and tuned the bigger tom-toms low. (Not for him the little eunuch toms of Kenney Jones, who palely succeeded him in the Who, after Moon's death.) He kept his snare pretty "dry." This isn't a small thing. The talentless three-piece jazz combo at your local hotel ballroom—dinner-jacketed old-timers hacking through the old favorites—almost certainly features a so-called drummer whose sticks are used so lightly that they barely embarrass the skins, and whose snare—wet, buzzy, loose— sounds like a repeated sneeze. A good dry snare, properly struck, is a bark, a crack, a report. How a drummer hits the snare, and how it sounds, can determine a band's entire dynamic. Groups like Supertramp and the Eagles seem soft, in large part, because the snare is so drippy and mildly used (and not just because elves are apparently squeezing the singers' testicles).

There are three great albums by the Who, and these are also the three greatest Moon records: *Live at Leeds* (1970), a recording of an explosive concert at Leeds University on February 14, 1970, and generally considered one of the greatest live albums in rock; *Who's Next* (1971), the most famous Who album; and *Quadrophenia* (1973), a kind of successor to *Tommy*, a "rock opera" that nostalgically celebrates the sixties Mod culture that had provoked and nourished the band in its earlier days. On these are such songs as "Substitute," "My Generation," "See Me, Feel Me/ Listening to You," "Won't Get Fooled Again," "Baba O'Riley," "Bargain," "The Song Is Over," "The Real Me," "5.15," "Sea and Sand," and "Love, Reign o'er Me." There is no great difference between the live concert recordings and the studio songs—all of them are full of improvisation and structured anarchy, fluffs and misses; all of them seem to have the rushed gratitude of something achieved only once. From which emerges the second great principle of Moon's drumming: namely, that one is always performing, not recording, and that making mistakes is simply part of the locomotion of vitality. (In the wonderful song "The Dirty Jobs," on *Quadrophenia*, you can hear Moon accidentally knock his sticks together three separate times while traveling around the kit. Most drummers would be horrified to be caught out on tape like this.)

For Moon, this vitality meant trying to shape oneself to the changing dynamics of the music, listening as much to the percussive deviations of the bass line as to the steady, obvious line of the lead singer. As a result, it is impossible to separate him from the music the Who made. The story goes that, in 1968, Jimmy Page wanted John Entwistle on bass and Keith Moon on drums for his new band; and, as sensational as this group might have been, it would not have sounded either like Led Zeppelin or the Who. If Led Zeppelin's drummer, John Bonham, were substituted for Moon on "Won't Get Fooled Again," the song would lose half its passionate propulsion, half its wild excess; if Moon sat in for Bonham on "Good Times, Bad Times," the tight stability of that piece would instantly evaporate.

Bonham's drumming sounds as if he'd thought about phrasing; he never overreaches himself, because he seems to have so perfectly measured the relationship between rhythmic order and rhythmic deviation: his superb but tightly limited breaks on the snare, and his famously rapid double strokes on the bass drum, are constantly played against the unvarying solidity of his hi-hat, which keeps a steady single beat throughout the bars. (In a standard 4/4 bar, the hi-hat sounds the four whole beats, or perhaps sounds eight beats in eighth notes.) That is the "Bonham sound," heard in the celebrated long solo—one of devilish complexity—in "Moby Dick," on the live album *The Song Remains the Same*. Everything is judged, and rightly placed: astonishing order. Moon's drumming, by contrast, is about putting things in the wrong place: the appearance of astonishing disorder. You can copy Bonham exactly; but to copy Moon would be to bottle his spilling energy, which is much harder.

The third great Moon principle, of packing as much as possible into a single bar of music, produces the extraordinary variety of his playing. He seems to be hungrily reaching for everything at once. Take, for instance, the bass drum and the cymbal. Generally speaking, drummers strike these with respectable monotony. You hit the crash cymbal at the end of a drum roll, as a flourish, but also as a kind of announcement that time-out has, boringly enough, ended, and that the beat must go back to work. Moon does something strange with both instruments. He tends to "ride" his bass drum: he keeps his foot hovering over the bass-drum pedal as a nervous driver might keep a foot on the brake, and strikes the drum often, sometimes continuously, throughout a bar. When he breaks to do a roll around the toms, he will keep the bass drum going simultaneously, so that the effect is of two drummers playing together. Meanwhile, he delights in hitting his cymbals as often as humanly possible, and off the beat—just before or after the logical moment—rather as jazz and big-band drummers do. The effect of all these cymbals being struck is of someone shouting out at unexpected moments while waiting in line—a yammer of exclamation marks. (Whereas his habit of entering a song by first crashing a cymbal and then ripping around the kit is like someone bursting into a quiet room and shouting: "I'm here!")

So alive and free is this drumming that one tends to emphasize its exuberance at the expense of its complexity. But the playing on songs like "Won't Get Fooled Again" or "Bargain" or "Love, Reign o'er Me" or "The Song Is Over" is extremely complex: in addition to the intricate cymbal work, Moon is constantly flicking off little triplets (sometimes on the toms, but sometimes with his feet, by playing the two bass drums together); using a technique known as the paradiddle to play one tom against another; and doing press rolls and double-stroke rolls (methods by which, essentially, you bounce the sticks on the drum to get them to strike faster notes), and irregular flams on the snare drum (a flam involves hitting the drum with the two sticks not simultaneously but slightly staggered, and results in a sound more like "blat" than "that").

New technology allows listeners to isolate a song's individual players, and the astonishing isolated drum tracks from "Won't Get Fooled Again" and "Behind Blue Eyes" can be found on YouTube. On "Won't Get Fooled Again," the drumming is staggeringly vital, with Moon at once rhythmically tight and massively spontaneous. On both that song and "Behind Blue Eyes," you can hear him do something that was instinctive, probably, but which is hardly ever attempted in ordinary rock drumming: breaking for a fill, Moon fails to stop at the obvious end of the musical phrase and continues with his rolling break, over the line and into the start of the next phrase. In poetry, this failure to stop at the end of the line, this challenge to metrical closure, this desire *to get more in*, is called enjambment. Moon is the drummer of enjambment.

For me, this playing is like an ideal sentence of prose, a sentence I have always wanted to write and never quite had the confidence to: a long, passionate onrush, formally controlled and joyously messy, propulsive but digressively self-interrupted, attired but disheveled, careful and lawless, right and wrong. (You can encounter such sentences in Lawrence's prose, in Bellow's, sometimes in David Foster Wallace's.) Such a sentence would be a breaking out, an escape. And drumming has always represented for me that dream of escape, when the body forgets itself, surrenders its awful self-consciousness. I taught myself the drums, but for years I was so busy being a good boy that I lacked the courage to own any drums. One could timidly admit to playing them, only if that meant that one never actually played them. At school, I did play in a rock band, but I kept the fact very quiet. The kids I played rock music with did not overlap with the world of classical music. Drumming was a notional add-on, a supplement to the playing of "proper" instruments, a merely licensed rebellion. At school, the classical music path was the scholastic path. Choir school was like being at conservatory—daily rehearsal and performance. And then, later, as a teenager, to work hard at the piano, to sing in the choir, to play the trumpet in a youth orchestra, to pass exams in music theory, to study sonata form in Beethoven, to sit for a music scholarship, to talk to one's parents about Bach (or even, daringly, the Beatles!), to see the London Symphony Orchestra at the Albert Hall, even just to fall asleep during *Aida*—all this was *approved*, was part of being a good student. Nowadays, I see school kids bustling along the sidewalk, their large instrument cases strapped to them like coffins, and I know their weight of obedience. Happy obedience, too: that cello or French horn brings lasting joy, and a repertoire more demanding and subtle than rock music's. But fuck the laudable ideologies, as Roth's Mickey Sabbath puts it: subtlety is not rebellion, and subtlety is not freedom, and sometimes it is rebellious freedom that one wants, and only rock music can deliver it. And sometimes one despises oneself, in near middle age, for still being such a merely good student.

Georges Bataille has some haunting words (in *Erotism*) about how the workplace is the scene of our domestication and repression: it is where we are forced to put away our Dionysianism. The crazy sex from the night before is as if forgotten; the drunken marital argument of the weekend is erased; the antic children have disappeared; all the writhing, passionate music of life is tuned off; and the excremental body is fraudulently clothed—a false bourgeois order dresses you, and the sack and quick penury await you if you don't obey. But Bataille might also have mentioned school, for school is work, too, work before the adult workplace, and school tutors the adolescent in repression and the rectitude of the bourgeois order, at the very moment in life when, temperamentally and biologically, one is most Dionysiac and most enraged by the hypocritical ordinances of the parental league.

So adolescents quickly get split in two, with an inner and outer self, a lawless sprite inside and a lawful ambassador outside: rock music, or your first sexual relationship, or reading, or writing poetry, or probably all four at once—why not?—represent the possibilities for inward escape. And playing rock is different again from playing classical music, or from writing poetry or painting. In all these other arts, though there may be trancelike moments and even stages of wildness and excess, the pressure of creating lasting forms demands discipline and silence, a charged, concentrated precision; mindful of Pascal's severe aphorism about the importance of staying quietly in a room, one does just that—one *did* just that, even at the age of sixteen—and stares at the sheet of paper, even if the words are not coming. Writing and reading still carry with them, beautiful as they are, the faintest odor of the exam room. (It is exam-silent in the room where I write these words, and how terrible, in a way, is this disjunction between literary expression and the violence of its content!) Rock music, though, is noise, improvisation, collaboration, theatre, exuberance, showing off, truancy, pantomime, aggression, bliss, tranced collectivity. It is not concentration so much as fission.

Imagine, then, the allure of the Who, whose vandalizing velocity was such an incitement to the adolescent's demon sprite: "I'm wet and I'm cold,/But thank God I ain't old," sang young Roger Daltrey on *Quadrophenia*, in a song about a "Mod" teenager (named Jimmy, no less) who gets thrown out of his home:

Here by the sea and sand
Nothing ever goes as planned
I just couldn't face going home.
It was such a drag on my own.
They finally threw me out.
My mum got drunk on stout.
My dad couldn't stand on two feet
As he lectured about morality.

It is no accident that punk got a fair amount of its inspiration from the Who (the Sex Pistols often performed "Substitute"), or that, a generation later, a band like Pearl Jam would devotedly cover "Love, Reign o'er Me." (Or that Chad Smith, the volcanic drummer of the Red Hot Chili Peppers, has cited Moon as an influence.) Here was a band that, in one obvious way, embodied success, but that, in a less obvious way, dared failure—I mean the large amount of improvisation in their songs, the risky, sometimes loose, excess of their concert performances, the violent earnestness of so many of the lyrics. And the epicentre of this successful failure, this man who wanted to pack as much of *the fun stuff* into his playing as humanly possible, was Keith Moon.

The Who was a kind of performance art band: there was plenty of calculation amid the carelessness. Pete Townshend was a graduate of the Ealing art school (whose other musical alumni from the 1960s were Freddie Mercury and Ronnie Wood) and has sometimes claimed that the idea of smashing his guitar onstage was partly inspired by Gustav Metzger's "auto-destructive" art movement. That high tone is quite Townshendian. But in one way, it is hard not to think of Keith Moon's life as a perpetual "happening"; a gaudy, precarious, self-destructing art installation, whose gallery placard simply reads: "The Rock-and-Roll Life, Late Twentieth Century." In a manner that is also true of his drumming, he seemed to live at once naively and self-consciously: utterly spontaneous in his scandalous misbehavior, and yet also aware that this is how one *should* live if one is a famous and rich rock musician. His parody is very hard to separate from his originality; his parody *is* his originality. This is one of the most charming elements of his posture behind the drum kit: he is always clowning around—standing up sometimes, at other times puffing out his cheeks like Dizzy Gillespie, grimacing and grinning like a fool in some opera buffa, twirling his sticks, doing silly phantom rolls just above the skins of the drums. A child might think that Moon was a circus performer. His drumming, like his life, was a serious joke.

Nowadays, Moon would probably be classed as both ADHD and bipolar disorder; fortunately for the rest of us, he grew up in postwar, nontherapeutic Britain, and medicated himself with booze, illegal drugs, and illegal drumming. Born into a modest, working-class household in north London in 1946, Moon had a paltry education. He was restless, hyperactive, and often played to the gallery. An art teacher described him as "retarded artistically, idiotic in other respects," and the authorities were doubtless relieved when he left school at the age of fourteen. "You never felt, 'One day he is going to be famous,'" a friend told Tony Fletcher, Moon's biographer. "You felt more likely that he was going to end up in prison."

He had little formal training on the drums. As Gogol's brilliant prose or Richard Burton's swaggering acting embodies the temperamental exhibitionism of its creator, so Moon's playing is an extension of his theatrical hyperactivity. His mother noticed that he got bored easily, and quickly lost interest in his train set or Meccano. Throughout his short life, he was seemingly addicted to practical jokes: he set off cherry bombs in hotels, dressed up as Adolf Hitler or Noël Coward, rode a wheelchair down an airport staircase, smashed up hotel rooms, drove a car into a swimming pool, got arrested for breaching the peace. On planes, Moon might do his "chicken soup" routine, which involved carrying a can of Campbell's chicken soup on board, emptying it, unseen, into a sick bag, and then pretending to retch violently. At which point he "would raise it, and pour the sicklike soup back into his mouth, offering up a hearty sigh of relief while innocently inquiring of fellow passengers what they found so disgusting." There was a relentless, a curious, drunken patience to this theatricalism, which often needed preparation and forethought, and certainly demanded a kind of addicted commitment. "Keith wore the Nazi uniform like something of a second skin, donning it intermittently for the next six or seven years," writes Tony Fletcher. *Six or seven years*. His alcoholism and coke snorting were certainly addictions, but perhaps they were merely the solvents needed to maintain the larger, primal addiction to joking and playacting.

Performance is a way of sublimely losing oneself, and there is a sense in which Moon as drummer was another role alongside Moon as Hitler, Moon as Noël Coward, Moon as arsonist, Moon as sick-bag buffoon, and Moon as crazy "rock star." ("I don't give a damn about a Holiday Inn room," he grandly said, after some act of vandalism. "There's ten million of them exactly the same.") But "role" suggests choice, freedom, calculation, whereas these roles don't seem to have been chosen so much as depended on. Or to put it another way: despite all the gaiety and partying, the only performance that seems to have truly liberated Moon was the one he enacted behind the drum kit.

I often think of Moon and Glenn Gould together, despite their great differences. Both started performing as very young men (Moon was seventeen when he began playing with the Who, Gould twenty-two when he made his first great recording of *The Goldberg Variations*); both were idiosyncratic, revolutionary performers, for whom spontaneity and eccentricity were important elements (for instance, both enjoyed singing and shouting while playing); both men had exuberant, pantomimic fantasy lives—Gould wrote about Petula Clark's "Downtown," and appeared on Canadian television and radio in the guise of invented comic personae such as Karlheinz Klopweisser and Sir Nigel Twitt-Thornwaite, "the dean of British conductors"; both were gregarious and essentially solitary; neither man practiced very much (at least, Gould claimed not to practice, and it is impossible to imagine Moon having the patience or sobriety to do so); and with both men, all the other performing (Gould's hand washing and coat wearing and melodramatic, pill-popping hypochondria) have the slightly desperate quality of mania—except the performance behind the instrument, which has the joyous freedom of true escape and self-dissolution: Gould becomes the piano, Moon becomes the drums.

For both Moon and Gould, the performer's life was short—Gould abandoned concert performance at the age of thirty-one; Moon was dead by the age of thirty-two, and had not played well for years. He had perhaps eight really great drumming years, between 1968 and 1976. Throughout this period, he was ingesting ludicrous volumes of drink and drugs. There are stories of him swallowing twenty or thirty pills at once. In San Francisco, in 1973, he had taken so many depressants (perhaps to come down from a high, or to deal with pre-concert nerves) that, after slopping his way through several songs, he collapsed and had to be taken to the hospital. When his stomach was pumped, it was found to contain quantities of PCP, a drug described by Fletcher as "a drug used to put agitated monkeys and gorillas to sleep." What magically happened onstage, while Moon was being carted away, was incised, years ago, on my teenage cerebellum. Pete Townshend asked the crowd if anyone could come up and play the drums. Scot Halprin, a nineteen-year-old, and presumably soon to be the most envied teenager in America, got onto the stage and played with the Who. "Everything was locked into place," Halprin later said of the gargantuan drum kit; "anyplace you could hit there would be something there. All the cymbals overlapped."

Both Moon and Gould were rather delicate, even handsome young men who coarsened with age, and developed a thickness of feature, an almost simian rind. At twenty, Moon was slight and sweet, with a bowl of black hair upended on his head, and dark, dopey eyes, and the arched eyebrows of a clown. By the end of his life, he looked ten years older than he was—puffy, heavy, his features no longer sweetly clownish but slightly villainous—Bill Sikes, played by Moon's old drinking friend Oliver Reed, the arched eyebrows now thicker and darker, seemingly painted on, as if he had become a caricature of himself. Friends were shocked by his appearance. He was slower and less inventive, less vital, on the drums; the album *Who Are You*, his last record, attests to the decline. Perhaps no one was very surprised when he died, from a massive overdose of the drug Heminevrin, a sedative prescribed for alcohol-withdrawal symptoms. "He's gone and done it," Townshend told Roger Daltrey. Thirty-two pills were in his stomach, and the equivalent of a pint of beer in his blood. His girlfriend, who found him, told a coroner's court that she had often seen him pushing pills down his throat, without liquid. Two years later, John Bonham died from asphyxiation, after hours of drinking vodka. He was less than a year older than Moon.

There are two famous Glenn Gould recordings of *The Goldberg Variations*: the one he made at the age of twenty-two, and the one he made at the age of fifty-one, just before he died. The opening aria of that piece, the lucid, ornate melody that Gould made his own, sounds very different in each recording. In the young man's version, the aria is fast, sweet, running clear like water. In the middle-aged man's recording, the aria is half as fast, the notes so magnetically separated that they seem almost unrelated to one another. The first aria is cocky, exuberant, optimistic, vital, fun, sound-filled; the second aria is reflective, seasoned, wintry, grieving, silence-haunted. These two arias stand facing each other, separated by almost thirty years, as the gates of a life. I prefer the second version; but when I listen to the second, how I want to *be* the first!

RICK MOODY ON OTIS REDDING, SIMON & GARFUNKEL, THE BEATLES, FUNKADELIC AND OTHERS

On Celestial Music*

1. Otis Redding as Purveyor of Celestial Music

Music has soul. We operate as though it does. In fact, music is one of the few areas of human endeavor where the word *soul*, even among secular types, is liable to go unchallenged. All kinds of music are occasionally imputed to have soul. Even music that doesn't have anything but volume or a tiresome double-kick drum sound will sometimes be described as having soul. Ray Coniff, to a listener somewhere, has soul. Who am I to say otherwise? Soul in these cases perhaps indicates earnestness, rhetorical force, and/or vocal polyps. Nevertheless, there are persuasive indications that the word *soul* does indeed manifest itself in music, and so maybe it's useful here at the outset to point to a recording that demonstrates why music belongs in a discussion about heaven. So, along these lines, I'm going to describe briefly the mechanics of one example of *soul music*, namely, a live recording by Otis Redding entitled "Try a Little Tenderness."[1]

Lyrically speaking, "Try a Little Tenderness" starts as an exhortation to do better at peeling away the layers of defensiveness in a lover, a woman (in this case) who is not only *weary*, in the general sense, but maybe also weary of the traditional role of woman. Her only job at the song's opening is selflessness. Her condition is more than apparent, for example, in the limpid lyrical perception, "I know she's waiting, just anticipating, the thing that she'll never possess." What to make of this? What exactly is "the thing she'll never possess?" Is it love? Is it justice, in the prejudicial landscape of the USA in the middle and late sixties? Or, as with the weariness in the first line, is some more general dissatisfaction implied? One thing it's obvious Otis Redding intends, in his role as purveyor of celestial music, is to make us conscious of our human frailty, our lack, our incompleteness. And he does so here not only with the lyrics but with perfect phrasing and with the kind of vulnerability that's all but absent from music in these troubled times.

Still, this is to avoid mention of the dynamically satisfying *freak out* at the end of the song. The big ending! If celestial music is the music of the spheres, then the big ending of "Try a Little Tenderness" proves that music here on earth can also be

*Moody, Rick. "On Celestial Music." *Salmagundi*, #153–4 (winter–spring 2007): pp. 19–31.
[1]From, e.g., *The Stax/Volt Revue, Vol. 2: Live in Paris*, Atlantic Records, 1991.

tuned to the interstellar realms, especially when the rhythm section kicks in, and the horns start, and Otis begins his passionate exhortation as to how, exactly, tenderness is meant to be practiced (holding, squeezing, never leaving), and the horns work their way up the scale, likewise the rhythm guitar, chromatically, while Redding commences his soul shouting, and the crowd goes wild, hoping that he'll play through the chorus just one more time! Yes, *try a little tenderness!* How could we resist! We have not tried sufficiently! So many areas of our lives remain unexplored! So many virtues seem to lie dormant in us! So much is failure and half-heartedness! Tenderness as opposed to oppressing the poor and disenfranchised, tenderness as opposed to military intervention in foreign countries! Tenderness as opposed to the amassing of money, power, and real estate!

What I mean to say is that this live performance of Otis Redding *enacts* the attempt at tenderness he promotes, and in this way his song proves itself, proves the validity of *soul* in music, by *exercising* the soul, and if you are not convinced by my recitation of these facts, get the *Monterey Pop* DVD and watch it, because I swear just as you can be absolved of your malfeasances by watching the pope on television, you can be made a better person by watching Otis Redding deliver this song; you will go into the next room, and you will look at your husband, or your wife, or your child, you will look at the people whom you have treated less well than you might have, and you will kneel in front of these people and you will beg for the chance to try a little harder and to make their burdens a little less burdensome. If those five minutes of grace are not an example of what lies out there, beyond what we daily understand, if those five minutes are not like unto a candle that glimmers in the unending darkness of life on earth, then I have no idea what paradise is.

2. Heaven and Premium Stereo Equipment

Music is of God, that is, and music is with God, and music is how God expresses Him-, or Herself, and music is everywhere, and music is a crafty art and is completed in places inside us, in the impossible-to-locate precincts wherein there is access to feelings that we might otherwise ignore. Or: the abstraction of music is how God conceals His or Her complicated plan. Or: the abstraction of music, its connection to deep feeling, has all the traces of the Holy Ghost, so it seems to me, and if I didn't understand this logically as a kid, I at least understood how moving music was, when I was first going to church in the suburbs.

Back then, I wanted to lay eyes on things. Because when you're a kid you're open to ideas, but you trust what's in front of your face. I remember feeling that the praying part of the religious service was deeply suspect. People would get this expression on their faces, something near to earnest self-regard. I was supposed to overlook this earnest mien, and I was meant to know intuitively the precise organization of hands for prayer, and then I was supposed to know what to murmur and to whom. And then there was the posturing *after* church. Forget about it! That was not what I associated with God, heaven, the sublime, the celestial. There was some talk, during Sunday School, about heaven, and it was always of the old-guy-with-beard variety, and I never believed any of that. I had a bullshit detector, where ideology was concerned. I resisted what I was told, even if it was good for me, even if it made the world a better place.

What moved me was the music. Music filled me with this intense feeling about the state of things, from my earliest recollections. Not only the organ music before and after services. The organ music was sublime, even when I didn't know anything about harmony and counterpoint. Organ music scared me and demanded something of me, by virtue of its grandiosity. (This would perhaps be the moment to say the obvious, that if earthly music is played in heaven, then J. S. Bach really must be the *cappellmeister*.) There was also the choir singing during church service. My mom was known to sing in the choir (later on I did a bit of it myself), and there was a lot of singing going on around my house generally. The human voice, raised in song, was important, was unearthly, gave access to the numinous. And obviously there are indications of this across the centuries of recorded time, almost wherever you look. In David's psalms, e.g.: "O sing to the Lord a new song; sing his praise in the congregation of the faithful."[2] I wouldn't have had any idea what this meant, back when I was first in church. But I knew I liked the singing.

At about the same time, my mother became highly partisan about the popular recording artists known as Simon & Garfunkel. We had a lot of their LPs. In fact, we had all of them. I could make a good argument about the sublime and the song known as "The Sound of Silence," which would then lead to a discussion John Cage and the theological importance of silence, but I'm putting that off for another time. Instead, I want to talk about a mostly forgotten Simon & Garfunkel tune on the album *Wednesday Morning, 3 A.M.*, entitled "Sparrow." This song, in the folk genre that characterized early Simon & Garfunkel recordings, unfolds as a series of sympathetic questions about a sparrow, addressed to the other preoccupied living things of the world: Who will love a little sparrow? Who will speak to it a kindly word? A swan is posed this question, a field of wheat, an oak tree, and yet all of these eminences decline the opportunity to become stewards of the common sparrow, himself adrift on the callousness of the world, where it is the fate of tenderness to be crushed. Then in the last verse the *earth* steps in, having been asked the same question. The earth responds with a forceful affirmative, in regards to the sparrow, quoting from scripture, "From dust were ye made and dust ye shall be."

This little song shook my earthly foundations, back in Connecticut, where my early music appreciation lessons were taking place. Not only because it had that mysterious, unearthly quality that English folk music had about it. Not only because of the harmonies, which were always pretty extraordinary in the Simon & Garfunkel

---

[2]And especially in psalms 146–150, "Praise him with the blast of the trumpet; praise him with the harp and lyre. Praise him with timbrel and dances; praise him upon the strings and pipe. Praise him with ringing cymbals; praise him upon the clashing cymbals. Let everything that has breath praise the Lord. Alleluia."

corpus. Above all, the song moved me because it depicted so much loss and so much weariness, and because the sparrow, it seemed to me, *had to die*. These days, "Sparrow" might sound a bit quaint to the average listener, owing to its self-evident allegorical scaffolding. But this is also what makes folk songs profound, that they are simple, unadorned, and eager to confront religious, philosophical, and political questions. They are modal, polysemous, difficult to pin down, they are fairy tales with melodies. This makes folk music ideal for a kid who's six or seven. I didn't have any defense against the emotional freight of the song, and it devastated me. What was "Sparrow" about for me? "Sparrow" was about loving the forgotten, the marginalized, the sick, homely, and despised, and it was about how everything has to die, and if heaven is a locale wherein the injustice of earthly mortality is repaired, uh, for *eternity*, then "Sparrow," in its radical acceptance of the spurned little bird, points in the direction of heavenly music, what it might do, how it might make the case for paradise.

I guess I'm covering up if I'm not saying that I admired this particular song at a troubling time, the time when my own parents were divorcing. I suppose it's obvious that I was identifying with the sparrow, feeling, like him, as though refuge from heartache was hard to come by. In this way, many of the songs I liked then seemed kind of sad. For example: another song I cherished was "Golden Slumbers" by the Beatles. It's the lullaby on a very complex, protean album, *Abbey Road*. Let me explain where I listened to it. My parents had this new stereo system, in a big wooden cabinet in the living room. It was a *hi-fi*, in the classic sense of the term, and it was maybe the expensive hi-fi that they bought to convince themselves, through amplification, that they were more allied and resilient than they were. My father, who never seemed to be home, was not there while we were making dinner, and so he probably wouldn't remember my mother putting on *Abbey Road*, whereupon we would dance around to the rock numbers, like "Mean Mr. Mustard" and "Come Together." Nor was he there when we sang along with "Golden Slumbers" and "Here Comes the Sun."

Eventually, an evening came to pass that I understood as the moment during which my parents were discussing how to tell us they were separating. They were enclosed in that family room with the expensive hi-fi. The louvered drawing room doors were closed. There was an unsettling silence in the house. We (my sister, brother, and I) looked at these closed doors, from up the staircase, between the dowels supporting the banister. Something lasting and sad was taking place. It was obvious. And soon my mother came to break us the news. Ever after, when I imagined this scene, I heard in my head, chief among other songs, "Golden Slumbers." Once, as the song suggests, there *was* a way to get back home. In the past tense. The song still calls forth that loss in me, that time after certainty. Does this melancholy resides in the lyrics, because the relationship between the singer of the song (Paul McCartney) and the children to whom he sings, is, arguably, not dissimilar to the relationship between the divine (from a perch in heaven) and the His beloved flock here on earth?

Actually, I probably liked "Golden Slumbers," because no one sang me lullabies as a kid. I had no idea about *agape* and *caritas*. I had no idea about heaven. I was skeptical.

Even a lullaby, from my point of view, would have been like a happy ending in a movie. Happy endings were for people who believed any nonsense that came along. So I liked "Golden Slumbers," from the newly released *Abbey Road*, because I secretly wanted somebody to sing a lullaby to me. Admitting such a thing makes me uncomfortable. And yet it was from unfulfilled longing that I formulated some ideas of that *elsewhere* of paradise, the place where no longing goes unfulfilled.

3. The Heavenly Jukebox

So far it sounds like I'm making a playlist for a heavenly jukebox. What would be the selections on such a jukebox? Is this jukebox any good? From an earthly point of view, I imagine that if there is music in heaven, it should celebrate virtues and ideals. Does the heavenly jukebox therefore contain only songs by Pat Boone or Deborah Gibson? Does God, whatever He, She, It is have some amazing celestial version of iTunes where you can hear the songs you like all day long as long as you have, as a virtuous individual, gained admission to the celestial realms? Could I, for example, hear "The Spirit of Radio," by Rush in heaven (assuming I'm virtuous), even though I won't allow myself to listen to it on earth because it is simply too embarrassing? What if hearing Rush would (arguably) make me happy for all eternity? Do people in this kingdom of the worthy get to play Whitesnake around the clock, just because they are good and deserving? Or have they transcended Whitesnake, having passed beyond the earthly realms? Do they allow Metallica in heaven? What about that Finnish band where the lead singer wears Satanic horns? Maybe he's a really good hardworking guy, despite wearing the horns, and is just trying to provide for his Finnish wife and child? Will he be admitted into heaven and be able there to play a big gig with Jimi Hendrix sitting in?

Does God allow celestial broadcasts of Led Zeppelin's "Stairway to Heaven?" Or "Heaven Is A Place On Earth," by Belinda Carlisle? Or "Just Like Heaven," by the Cure? Or "Heaven," by the Talking Heads; or "Pennies From Heaven," or the oft-covered "Knockin' On Heaven's Door," which seems to imply that the doorway to heaven is constructed of such a lightweight material that you *could* knock on it. These songs all have *heaven* in the title, but I don't think they are all good songs, except maybe the Dylan composition, and they don't teach me anything about what kind of music exists in heaven.

And what kind of musical instruments *do* they have in heaven? In the old days, they had trumpets and lutes. Many accounts substantiate this point. Are we to believe that heavenly instrumental groups stopped innovating a thousand years ago? Unlikely! So are there, in fact, electric guitars in heaven, or things that sound like electric guitars? Are there didjeridoos in heaven? What about synthesizers or digital samplers? Do they have the latest plug-ins for computer-based music in heaven? Does one have to clear his or her samples in heaven (because stealing is a venal sin), or can you go ahead and pilfer copyrighted music to your heart's content? What about all those exotic instruments? Tibetan bowls? Mouth harps? Are these instruments available to all who need them for the sake of expression?

Well, it's a real stretch to posit a jukebox in heaven, and I don't think God is a jukebox, and you cannot take your iPod with you when you are gone, and there is no digital sampler and no mixing board to connect it to. Music in heaven probably would not have lightweight lyrics, or even unimpeachably useful lyrics like "All You Need Is Love," and since it's unlikely that we will reach heaven in our corporeal forms, we may not have ears with which to listen to music, nor voices with which to sing it.

4. The Groove In Heaven

Common time is said to be the time signature that closely resembles the human heartbeat, and 4/4 is also the time signature with the best opportunity for the *groove*. If in my early life, I might perhaps have advanced the notion that the music in heaven would be noteworthy for lyrical exegesis on subjects like compassion and love, in my teens I would have thought it was all about the groove. Bass and drums, those were the things that made music heavenly, as when you are a teenager or a young adult, and you like the endless groove, for example, in "Sister Ray" by the Velvet Underground, and you are willing to hear that groove go around and around, and you do not exactly care what the lyrics say, if indeed you are able to decipher them. The view from rock club floors and dance clubs and mosh pits is that music is ecstatic, that the groove is ecstatic, and if music is ecstatic then heavenly music should be the acme of this ecstasy. It should be all about union and the sense of community, things that are self-evident at concerts and clubs. When I am in the groove, the groove is good. Thus, the teenage version of myself imagined that heaven, or paradise, was where there was always a good groove, and all kinds of people could dance around to it together, for light years at a time. When I was in the groove, wallowing in the one-four chord progression, let's say, or during a song by Funkadelic, then it was all about how many people you could get playing at one time, and the entire audience was on its feet and chanting along with some line like "Get Up on the Downstroke! Everybody get up!" even if many listeners were not exactly sure what the downstroke was nor why they should get up on it. At one time, I would have said that if heaven could not deliver on these things, on the promise of community, and on a music that has a good groove to it, then I didn't think heaven was heavenly.

Meanwhile, it would be logical and easy to make the argument that the groove has a sexual cast about it, and that people respond to the groove because it is suggestive of the pace and rhythm of sexuality. If this were the case, then again we might have to disqualify this music from heaven, on the basis that there is no corporeal resurrection, in my view, and thus no need for music that appeals to the carnal (or procreative) ecstasy of the flesh. Perhaps for similar reasons, Cotton Mather frowned upon dancing: "Their Children dance, and They go down the Grave into Hell."

In the vicinity of this notion of the sexual cast of the groove for me would be the related notion of intoxication in heaven generally. There is no need for intoxication in heaven. I suppose this is kind of obvious. Why would you need to be intoxicated there? Up there, you have not fallen short, you are not in a condition of wanting, you are theoretically happy, and so you are not looking for the music or drugs or spirits to intoxicate you in any way. You don't need to be bludgeoned by the music in heaven, you don't need to dance until you are exhausted, you don't need one more rousing chorus, because you don't need to be roused, and you are not going to get banged up in the mosh pit, nor are you going to suffer hearing loss, and no one is going to cough during the most beautiful part of the aria, and no one is going to climb over you to get to their seat during the opening measures of the second movement of the symphony.

5. Music For Canyons

I bring up this fact of intoxication because of how quitting drinking improved and defined my own spiritual life. I didn't have any genuine conviction about heaven, or God, or spirituality, or an afterlife, or anything else, really, between the ages of fifteen and twenty-six, when I was often busy doing other things, most of them not very good for me. This came to an end in 1987,[3] after which it occurred to me to go back to church, out of gratitude for my reprieve, and for the remission of the considerable pain I'd been living with.

Music also came back into my life in a number of ways. First, I started dabbling in it again. I'd taught myself guitar as a teenager, and so I bought a guitar anew and began practicing it, and I began writing songs, which I had also done when young. I also started listening to things in a new way. I can chart the subsequent metamorphosis in my musical taste with a number of recordings I first heard on a local new music program that was broadcast each night in New York City.

First among the discoveries of that time was the music of Arvo Pärt. While I can't remember exactly which piece I first heard by Pärt, I can remember the first album I bought, which was the ECM release called *Tabula Rasa*. On this recording, both the piece called "Cantus in Memory of Benamin Britten," and the orchestral piece "Fratres," genuinely moved me in ways that "serious" music rarely had. These pieces, which are said to have been composed as a way out of the dead end of serial music and academic atonality, are frankly spiritual and completely tonal, using elements of early music, like plainsong, for their raw material. Elsewhere, Pärt set liturgical texts. For these reasons, and because the pieces are *so* simple, there is some grumbling in classical music circles about Pärt's work. He's not serious, he's conservative, etc.

I didn't care about any of this when I first heard these recordings, and I still don't. Pärt's compositions split me open like I was an oyster, and the way they did it was by

---

[3]Committed to psychiatric hospital, got sober, etc.

exploiting the simple harmonies of ancient Western music, the kind of dignity and stateliness that I associated with the music of the church as I first heard it. In a way, I can't explain what it is about this simplicity and tonality that was so moving to me. And I'm not sure I want to. *Tintinnabuli* is the term that Pärt has in the past used to describe these pieces, meaning that they sound like bells or have the unadorned grace of bells.

Pärt led me to other things. Not just spiritually inclined classical music, but to kinds of music that were organized along similar principles, where there was simplicity and elemental harmonics, and where the devotion was to serenity and austerity and to the notion of music itself. That is, I wasn't as interested in the noise that was very moving to me as a young person, nor was I interested in virtuosity for its own sake. Rather, I was after a rather baroque idea that tonality *was* spiritual, and even divine. I was therefore moved by minimalism, by LaMonte Young, by Meredith Monk, by chamber music like the Penguin Café Orchestra, by early music, by Hildegard von Bingen, William Byrd, Purcell. It also seemed as if anything contemporary that I liked had a lot of echo in it, as if music that was made in canyons was somehow better than music that was made anywhere else. Music that celebrated or was illustrative of sound and nature, and the physicality of things.[4]

Maybe in this way I'm beginning to answer the question about *why music in heaven at all?* One thing that everybody always talks about in heaven is the *light*. Dante talks a lot about the light in *Paradiso*. Such a pleasing light! When other chroniclers have made it up there and reported back, there's always ecstatic light in their description. No paintings, no sculptures, no epic poems. No one in heaven is busy making installations or performing performance art. But there *is* music.

This goes all the way back, I imagine, to when there was music to the planets themselves, the heavenly bodies. It's an old perception, the music of the spheres, you find it as far back as Cicero, (in *De Republica*), and if he was writing it down, he probably wasn't the first to have remarked on the subject: "This music is produced by the impulse and the motion of these spheres themselves. The unequal intervals between them are arranged according to a strict proportion, and so the high notes blend agreeably with the low, and thus various sweet harmonies are produced." Music, according to this view, is an essential quality of creation, and we might mention especially the sublimity of harmony. And, as Cicero further observes, along with the ubiquity of heavenly music goes the tendency of men to want to imitate it: "Skillful men reproducing this celestial music on stringed instruments have thus opened the way for their own return to this heavenly region, as other men of outstanding genius have done by spending their lives on Earth in the study of things divine."

Why music then? Because when we sing it and play it, we are not only imitating the things that are, but we are praising them, praising the things that are, and praising is good, and you find it, too, in almost any account of heaven. The angels sing their

---

[4] I am not, however, a partisan of the music known as *New Age*. I do not endorse bland sheets of wallpaper over a machined bed of "exotic" percussion, even if I am in a spa or a yoga studio.

praises, and when we sing, according to, among others, the Levites, we are imitating the angels.

6. Heaven and Non-Being

Still, in the end, any discussion of heaven hinges on the injustice of non-being, and whether you are worried about this injustice. This seems to me the weakest link in the argument about heaven. That there must be some reward for living through this life in the first world? Living through the war and greed and hypocrisy and selfishness? Maybe, there *is* no reward, really, but having done a good job here! That is its own reward! The reward for living in a dignified way in the first world is dignified life in and of itself. Who isn't full of longing for a place better than this place? Who, driving through Elizabeth, New Jersey, or Omaha, Nebraska, or Indianapolis, Indiana, wouldn't long for an idealized heaven? And if the longing is good and human, what need for heaven? Longing, and compassion, and tenderness, *are* heavenly, and they make you better than you otherwise were.

If the whole belief in heaven depends on a fear of non-being, then it's no more realistic than the notion of naked people sitting around on clouds playing lutes. Myself, I have no fear of non-being. I fear mortal pain, which so often seems to precede non-being, but otherwise I don't fear the end of the author of these particular sentences, and I don't need, for his sake, everlasting life. There's enough hassle involved with the temporary life. Everlasting life would be closer to hell, for me, than any fiery lake clogged with politicians. Because what would one *do* with eternity?

Unless, for the sake of argument, we are simply talking about energy. Unless we are talking about the little spark calved off the big creative first cause. Maybe we are simply talking about our ability to unite with that first cause. Maybe we are talking about a union that might take place, in which I can be, ideally, some little spark, some match light in the mostly dark and empty universe, the thirteen dimensions of it, and my eternal match light would not necessarily require consciousness or lutes. And along with being this spark, I can imagine that I have a tone, and if I were going to pick one, I would pick something high in, in the treble clef, something I couldn't reach when I was a baritone pretending to be a tenor. As this note, or some other note, I can imagine a heaven where I get to play this tone, and to collide with other notes, as if I were a constituent in a John Cage piece, and here there are no entrances and exits, and I don't have to have perfect rhythm, nor do I have to know my scales, because I am all scales. Therefore I have no responsibilities, as a note, I just am, because I can't be entirely eliminated, because that doesn't happen—energy gets reused—and in this piece of music you can come in anywhere, and you can be a part of it, or not a part of it, and this composition has a long duration, an eternal duration, but you don't have to worry about this, because you are no longer a perceiving entity, you are just the note and the note is a good thing to be, in this composition, which has all the characteristics that good things have, namely it causes no harm, and believes only in its iteration as goodness, which is harmony and sublimity, and all kinds of other music are apparent in this music, even though they are lost, all possible music is contained in this infinite music, so Otis Redding is in there, and Simon & Garfunkel, and Funkadelic, and Arvo Pärt, maybe even Rush, because everything is in there, and in this way I am gone and gone is good, but I am also a very excellent musician and no one is any better, except the artful arranger of all sounds.

WRITING PROMPT: THE PERSONAL ESSAY

Write a 2000-word essay that explores your connection to a single song. The piece should describe and discuss the song in the context of showing your reader why this music is important to you. As you write, consider how focusing on this song allows you to write about emotion, aesthetic preferences, identity and experiences.

What you write should be candid, perhaps revealing or possibly even difficult (though you need not write about a "dark" or alarming subject). You should write in the first person directly about yourself and your own experiences as they attach to the song.

The song itself—its features, how it sounds, how it's made, the lyrics, its history—should appear significantly in the piece.

To get going, you might write a full description of the song or a detailed description of even a very small element of it. For this preliminary exercise, make your prose descriptive and objective rather than personal or analytical. Then write a personal, subjective paragraph about the same aspect of the song. Here you'll use description too, but you'll do so in the service of articulating your own experience of the song. By formally separating descriptive and objective writing from personal and subjective writing, you may begin to gain a clearer sense of how to move between the reality of the song itself and your own experience of it. Use that perspective to find the voice you want for the essay, complete a full draft and then revise it until it's in its final form.

WRITING PROMPT: OFF-THE-RADAR MUSIC THAT MATTERS

Write a 3000-word piece that considers off-the-radar music or a largely unknown musician. The subject might be a local band that fed you as a music-starved or -obsessed high-schooler, the experience of falling in love with an obscure LP or even a single song, or how a "local" experience of music was particularly memorable or important to you at a given point in your life. You can pursue any subject that this frame can accommodate or be stretched to accommodate. The piece itself should be some species of memoir written in light of a not-very-well-known musical interest of yours. One of the difficulties you face will be to write both about the music in question and yourself. How will you balance writing about both subjects? How can you best serve both requirements? Better yet, how can you *join* both requirements?

The trigger for this assignment came from reading the passage in Bob Dylan's *Chronicles* where he leaves the Dead's studio with no prospect of returning, maybe no prospect of singing again (however unlikely that possibility seemed then or seems now) and then slips off rainy Front Street into a little joint where a veteran singer in a mohair suit is performing standards. Dylan's forgotten the simplicity of putting a song across ("It was like I'd forgotten how to button my own pants," he writes) but emerges from that unremarked encounter with an unknown musician able to teach himself how to perform again, a not insignificant experience with a local musician.

Your piece might serve to remind readers that sometimes what we take in most deeply, what we learn from most centrally, isn't necessarily music as product that's shouting in the big and undifferentiated voices of commerce and fame but music that's off to the side, unknown to a mass audience, circumscribed by a given place and time. The piece you write might feel something like a secret history, a formerly unvoiced connection with music expressed in personal terms. And, along the way, maybe this personal essay will turn a few people on to music they haven't heard before.

THE GO-BETWEENS

HOW IS MUSIC WRITING DIFFERENT?

Music writing allows for the incorporation of hard journalism, autobiography, humor, academic criticism, and most everything in between.—**Kyle Anderson**, senior writer, *Entertainment Weekly*

Writing about music means writing about something that is basically abstract, immaterial: sound waves. That presents unique challenges. There's a famous quotation that is now attributed to the comedian Martin Mull: "Writing about music is like dancing about architecture." Personally, I would love to see someone dance about architecture. That's why writing about music has the potential to be so good.—**Michael Azerrad**, author, journalist and Editor-in-Chief of the *Talkhouse*

It's so unbelievably subjective, I think more so than any other arts writing.—**Michael Barclay**, freelance writer/broadcaster, co-author, *Have Not Been the Same: The CanRock Renaissance 1985–1995*

I try to resist taxonomy, and prefer to think of "music writing" as writing, period. If writing on music blends journalism and autobiography and profile and lyric abstraction and knotty formal experimentation, then so be it.—**Joe Bonomo**, music columnist, *The Normal School*, and Associate Professor of English at Northern Illinois University.

Music writing is thoroughly undisciplined. It always has been, and it's only getting worse. I'd like to see more people with some professional standards and better knowledge about culture, who didn't feel obligated to chase traffic. Increasingly, the business is like reporting about the weather: Everyone is writing the same stuff about the same people (and, yes, increasingly, the news is about the *people*, and not the art). And if you're dealing with weather, that's what you need to deal with. But commercial music-media needs more people who aren't afraid to look at a buzz band and say "This is stupid and does not warrant coverage or discussion." Too many music writers will write about anything.—**D.X. Ferris**, Ohio Society of Professional Journalists Reporter of the Year, Professor, **33⅓** author

No difference. You have to go at the job with as much guts and honesty as possible, and mercilessly separate the worthwhile from the wormy. Avoid the fashionable. Resist the immediate. Strive to offer some perspective.—**Marty Davis**, comic book creator

Though it is rather out of vogue in these troubled days for journalism, which is simply trying to survive, I very much still believe in the ideal of using the techniques of the novelist or short-story writer in music writing/cultural journalism. Not every piece will be this successful; not every piece needs to be. But we can and should aspire to the heights of a Lester Bangs, a Nick Tosches, or an Ellen Willis, to be sure.—**Jim DeRogatis**, author, co-host of *Sound Opinions*, and lecturer at Columbia College Chicago

It's a cliché, but I want to say "freedom." By which I mean, given its relative youth as a genre, and lack of settled conventions, it still feels to me like rock writing is a genre in which the writer is constantly discovering and evolving a form appropriate to its occasion.—**Kevin J. H. Dettmar**, author, 33⅓ book, Gang of Four's *"Entertainment!"*

I think that 98 percent of music writing is almost instantly disposable and primarily exists to fill space (record reviews and concert reviews most notably). One percent is a skilled rehash of what's already been written (the 93rd major profile piece on, say, Gram Parsons or the Sex Pistols). And 1 percent brings something new, insightful, and/or entertaining to the table that makes it worth plowing through the other 99%.—**Bruce Eaton**, author, *Radio City* (33⅓)

Anything goes in music writing, and that's not a good thing. You can't find another topic-specific field in which the writers, as a species, can't correctly use the most basic terms. Or in which writers are so steadfastly devoted to presenting their first impression as undisputable truth.—**D.X. Ferris**, Ohio Society of Professional Journalists Reporter of the Year, Professor, 33⅓ author

Music writing is the crack cocaine of non-fiction writing. Your work hits quickly and fades out and it's really easy to end up whoring yourself out to keep doing it if you aren't careful.—**Matthew Gasteier**, 33⅓ author

I don't know. I guess I think music writing has full license to be musical in form.—**Anthony Kwame Harrison**, popular music scholar, Virginia Tech

Music writing certainly shouldn't be elevated above 'straight' journalism. Writing well about politics or the news is just as difficult and far more important in the scheme of things.—**Sam Inglis**, Features Editor, *Sound On Sound* magazine

Music writing is, in many ways, fundamentally translational work. Telegraphing the way something makes you *feel* beyond simply describing it is a wonderful and daunting challenge.—**Matt LeMay**, senior contributor, Pitchfork

However great the music writing, it is never taken as seriously as the straight journalism or literary non-fiction—or even post-novel/post-cinema AMC/HBO television—even if it has influenced straight journalism, literary non-fiction and *Breaking Bad*.—**Paul Morley**, writer and critic

The freedom, which can be a positive, but also the lack of structural or critical accountability, which is more often a problem.—**Chris Ott**, 33⅓ author

I think music as a subject slots into different forms (reportage, criticism, reviews, essays) as well as anything else, and there is nothing that makes it fundamentally different.—**Mark Richardson**, Editor-in-Chief, Pitchfork

My favorite music writers—Robert Christgau, Greil Marcus, Lester Bangs—can take off from a piece of music and end up almost anywhere. They can hear a blast of noise on the radio and chase it into American history or politics or personal memories or theory or *anywhere*. I started reading those guys young, lucky for me. I first encountered Christgau in his Consumer Guide, which was reprinted in *Creem* magazine, when I was 15. I first read Greil Marcus in the *Village Voice* when I was 18 and swiftly became obsessed with his books, first of all *Mystery Train*. Lester Bangs, like Marcus and Christgau, is a major voice in *The Rolling Stone Illustrated History of Rock & Roll*, which came out in 1980 and which I found in my college library. I didn't get to see much of Bangs's other work until I was 21, which is when Marcus's anthology of his work came out, *Psychotic Reactions and Carburetor Dung*. Most of my favorite writers are fixated on music, whether it's James Joyce or Gertrude Stein or Thomas Pynchon or Emily Dickinson or Jonathan Lethem, but Christgau, Marcus and Bangs are the voices who really sum up (for me) why music writing is my favorite kind of writing.—**Rob Sheffield**, writer, *Rolling Stone*

Music is wonderful and difficult to write about because it's ephemeral and non-narrative in nature. It's not like a film or a novel that has a story with a beginning, middle and end. It's not like a painting or an illustration which is fixed in place and can clearly represent a subject. Music enters you through your gut, and from there makes its way to your heart and your head. It can be simple or abstract, and it's very malleable in interpretation. When it comes to pop music, I also think it's something that can sneak up on people—they don't always expect pop music to have the potential for a lot of meaning, so that meaning can take people by surprise.—**Ben Sisario**, reporter, the *New York Times*

Most of the things that differentiate music writing from other forms are bad habits (of which I possess a few): shorthand references that assume musical knowledge on the part of the reader, stupid puns, flippant attitude, dependence on slang or internet-speak as signifier for knowingness, inability to separate the art from the artist—or worse, from yourself.—**Scott Tennent**, 33⅓ author

There's the view that anyone can do it, something easily dispelled by reading most music blogs.—**Luke Turner**, Associate Editor, The Quietus

CHAPTER 7
THE BLOG PIECE

INTRODUCTION

It's now easier than ever before to publish your writing. All you need to do is start a blog. Of course, writing and maintaining a blog takes a considerable amount of time and energy and getting people to read it is practically a full-time job. If you have a particular passion or have an idea that doesn't exist just start writing blog posts. There are many free platforms like Wordpress and Tumblr that make it easy.

Almost every popular music blog you've ever heard of began with a simple idea and the sites with the strongest voices succeed. Take Sarah O'Holla, who started a Tumblr called "My Husband's Stupid Record Collection" in which she provides candid reviews of the many beloved and obscure albums in the collection of her husband. Her voice is innocent and skeptical. Her husband, clearly an obsessive record collector and music fan, acts as sort of a template of the male music nerd. Her blog is fascinating because it brings to light two distinct stereotypes: that of the male music nerd and his female counterpart who wants to love the music but perhaps can't name all of the founding members of Devo.

Which is to say, if you have a unique idea, go with it. And if not, focus on coming up with individual post ideas to pitch to existing blogs that you read to get your name out there. Visit the contact page of sites you frequent to find the email addresses of the editors. There are many different ways to pitch a story but a short email introducing yourself and your idea should do the trick. Blogs are always looking for fresh ideas and content from new writers. Editors might not respond to your email but if your timing is right and your idea is good or it's a slow week for them, you might just find yourself with an assignment. Some blogs will compensate and others will not, but it's absolutely worthwhile to pitch early on, especially as a student to get your name out there and to see how it feels to be given an assignment with a deadline. You may not hear back right away but as many of our experts have said, it's the right pitch at the right time that will get you that first assignment and therefore your foot in the door.

Blog writing is unique in that you are not limited by print deadlines or the layout limitations of a print publication. You can tell a story with YouTube clips and SoundCloud links to illustrate a point. You can react almost instantly to a news item and state your opinion or report an announcement within hours of it occurring. In March of 2014, *The Daily Beast* published a blog post by respected Jazz critic Ted Gioia titled "Music Criticism Has Degenerated Into Lifestyle Reporting." In it he criticized music journalists and critics for being ill-informed and easily distracted by celebrity. Within hours, those critics and journalists fired back with blog posts and for weeks the debate raged. On Twitter, a battle between Ted Gioia and *New York Magazine*'s Jody Rosen raged when Gioa tweeted a photo of his bookshelf to demonstrate he was well-read and Rosen tweeted a photo of his right back. Thus the term "shelfie" was born. It was fascinating to read and watch as the drama unfolded instantly.—AJG

Are you ready to start pitching? Here's a generic email template to help guide your story into the hands of an editor. Keep your first introduction short and sweet and don't attach samples until they are requested. You might include a link to a piece you've published elsewhere. It's likely that you won't get a response the first time. It's also likely that you won't get a response the second time. Carefully comb the "Contact Us" page of the site you want to pitch. Often there are instructions for submissions and editors are especially thrilled to receive a pitch that follows their prescribed protocol. Try to write to specific section editors if their email addresses are available. There's no perfect formula for getting an editor's attention. BUT sending out a few of these emails each week to different editors might just land you an assignment.

Sample introductory pitch email:

Dear Editor (person's name),

My name is _____ and I am an avid reader of _____.

I especially liked the piece you published last week on _____. I have an idea for a story that I hope you'll consider for _____. I am based in _____ and the band _____ is playing _____. I'm going to the show next week and wonder if you'd be interested in running a story about _____. Might this be something that _____ would be interested in publishing?

I would be happy to provide writing samples upon request and look forward to hearing from you soon.

All the best,

Your Name

EXPERT ADVICE FROM OUR WRITERS

We don't hear this often enough, but the written word and communications in general are in a period of seismic change unrivaled since Gutenberg built his printing press in the mid-1400's. Always hypercompetitive, the number of opportunities in dead-tree media continue to shrink, but this sad state of affairs (for people who'd like to get paid to write) arguably is offset by the ability to reach a larger audience than even the most prestigious print publication could offer in the past—to say something unique, in a colorful voice, which needed to be said, and to see it "go viral" with a reach far exceeding the front page of the *New York Times* or any other publication you could name. At the moment, that isn't necessarily paying. But the new media still are being invented, we have no idea what final form they will take, and we writers at least can hope for some profitable (as in sort of pay the rent) endeavor—or we can try to build it ourselves.—**Jim DeRogatis**, author, co-host of *Sound Opinions*, and lecturer at Columbia College Chicago

Social media has allowed writers to converse with each other—criticism has become more a dialogue than a monologue. But I wish more writers would resist the urge to make every thought public, and instead hole up with one record for a week, get obsessive, put every thought into one piece, and then come out with a richly detailed analysis of an album.—**Scott Tennent, 33⅓** author

The internet has provided incredible opportunities for music writers in that anybody can start a blog, and there's a certain meritocratic attitude about music writing on the internet that doesn't exist in a lot of other mediums. At the same time, there's so much noise that it's harder to get noticed.—**Kyle Anderson**, senior writer, *Entertainment Weekly*

One of the worst things about the pageview economy is that it creates a strong disincentive for editors to run anything about artists who don't already have a strong following.—**Matt LeMay**, senior contributor, Pitchfork

[It bothers me that] people are not taking risks, and I include my own website in that. I don't think anyone (apart from the likes of The Quietus) are really taking many risks with their analysis of what's going on around us, and that's a shame. Twenty websites all posting the same thing doesn't seem like a viable option anymore.—**Oliver Primus**, Site Editor, *The 405*

In the digital era the advertising firms run the entire show, there is complicity between them, the promotional agencies that represent artists, and the websites that promote both the artist and advertiser. That entire dynamic is a power brokerage supported by musicians' work, and its renown, and the musician is not remunerated by any of the players. This framework has to be destroyed, not changed.—**Chris Ott**, 33⅓ author

The possibilities are endless now. You can start a blog and become the most trusted music blog out there, if you're good at it. So I think a lot of the barriers have fallen and the tastemakers don't have access to a whole lot of music that you don't have access to. You can become an expert on Krautrock in like a week. I have met high school kids that know so much more than I do about entire genres of music, because they are sort of OCD and they have the internet. We are all music critics waiting to happen. (What a terrifying thought!) But making a living at this stuff has gotten to be near-impossible. And I don't think it has a ton of cachet anymore. Telling people that you wrote about music for a living used to be met with wide eyes and a lot of questions about who the most famous person you've ever interviewed was. Now it's met with eye-rolling, because nobody knows exactly what it means. Maybe you live in your parents' basement and write album reviews for your friend's blog. Which, incidentally, sounds like a pretty good gig to me, so if you're doing that you should just keep doing that.—**Casey Jarman**, Managing Editor, the *Believer*

The internet is a brand-new opportunity. I wouldn't say things are better or worse, they're just different. The main thing that has changed is that it's much tougher to do this full-time. But you can potentially get your work out to a readership all over the planet, instantly. That's pretty amazing.—**Michael Azerrad**, author, journalist and Editor-in-Chief of the *Talkhouse*

The internet provides unparalleled ways to get your work to a public. And cultivating a public—by writing reliably, relentlessly, even when the audience isn't there and seems like it will never come—is a great way to hone your craft. Writers who write well, often, and have a nascent following of their own are tremendously attractive to editors who are running their businesses on tight margins, and need every reader and writers who can file on time.—**R. J. Wheaton**, Publisher, *Hazlitt* magazine; author of **33⅓** *Portishead's Dummy*

Tiny Mix Tapes started in 2001, before online music writing was taken very seriously (wait, is it being taken seriously yet?). To me, it doesn't matter whether things are "better" or "worse"—things change, people adapt, and anyone with any grasp of how technology works could've predicted this increased shift to online music writing. What I find incredibly positive, though, whether or not it's to the detriment of "professional" music writers, is the increase in voices. Some people lament the ballooning number of so-called "amateur" writers (and, likewise, "amateur" musicians), but I personally welcome all the new voices and think that the spread of authority to non-paid music writers is something to celebrate. That doesn't mean that I personally like everything that's out there, of course, but I've read some incredibly thoughtful pieces published on a blog while reading incredibly terrible stuff published in the mainstream press.—**Marvin Lin**, Editor-in-Chief, Tiny Mix Tapes

As someone who is a co-founder of a successful website, I probably have a more positive view on all these changes than most. I do feel that the internet has made writing more accessible—you don't have to be part of some indie rock boys club to get in. I wrote for free for years before I ever got paid, and still write for free alongside my paid freelance work and day job at The Quietus. I don't especially see anything wrong with writing for free—it's a great way to learn the ropes and get some chops as a writer. I feel that the web allows for more varied writing, the ability to write about niche forms that the mainstream music press would never have covered, and the ability to do that on one website. At The Quietus we don't have to worry about a cover star, or covering big names to keep our readers happy. We cover what we think is interesting and want to share with the world, which means that in any one week we might have articles on Electro Chaabi music from Egypt, a hip-hop mixtape column, a feature on a sound artist like Chris Watson, retrospectives on 80s synth pop, new music and videos from new artists, opinion pieces on the music, politics, gender and sexuality . . . To be able to be so broad in outlook is the great joy and strength of the internet.— **Luke Turner**, Associate Editor, The Quietus

CHRIS DEVILLE ON MUMFORD & SONS

Deconstructing: Phillip Phillips, The Lumineers, And The Mumford-ization Of Pop*

The incessant shopping trips start to make your life feel like a single, unbroken stream of home-furnishings-related commerce when you reach a certain age and all your friends get married. So I'm not sure when or why I was in a mall parking lot with my wife when I first heard "Home" on the radio this year. What I do remember is that the song struck me as slightly unusual for WNCI, the local top-40 station we were bumping on that particular Macy's trip. The chorus reached to the heavens on the strength of acoustic guitars, arching choral harmonies and a relentless 4/4 thud maintained by kick drum and stomping feet. The earnest lead vocal was a robust tenor accented with folksy tremble and weathered beyond its years like distressed denim. The chorus went like this: "Settle down, it'll all be clear/Don't pay no mind to the demons that fill you with fear/The trouble it might drag you down/If you get lost, you can always be found/Just know you're not alone/Because I'm gonna make this place your home." This had to be Mumford & Sons, right?

My brain probably generated a few alternate origin stories for "Home," but none of them involved American Idol. Upon encountering the song again when it was smeared all over NBC's Olympics coverage, I was dumbstruck to discover this was the first single from Idol winner Phillip Phillips, and not just the kind of dumbstruck you feel when you realize somebody really named his or her child Phillip Phillips. Idol winners have a checkered history where actual pop stardom is concerned, but it wasn't surprising to hear this year's champ on the radio. The surprise was just that a fresh-faced Georgia boy like Phillips would be on the radio sounding like a bunch of fervid Englishmen who dress up like Jack White in *Cold Mountain*. "Home," written as Idol's Season 11 coronation song by Drew Pearson and Greg Holden, seems scientifically engineered to replicate the Mumford & Sons formula. Folk-rock—even inspirational folk-rock of the Mumford variety—is not a sound I expect to hear from an institution founded on wind-beneath-my-wings diva bluster.

Then again, why wouldn't a fame factory like Idol try to copy an approach that made Mumford & Sons the biggest band in the world? Just listen to these absurd statistics: Mumford's debut album *Sigh No More* climbed all the way to No. 2 on the

---

*DeVille, Chris. "Deconstructing: Phillip Phillips, The Lumineers, And The Mumford-ization Of Pop." *Stereogum*, November 12, 2012. Reprinted with permission.

Billboard 200 two years after its 2009 release, and it was still near the top of the chart when follow-up *Babel* dropped this September. *Babel* moved 600,000 copies in its first week, the best sales debut of the year until Taylor Swift came along. It was the biggest debut for a rock band since AC/DC sold 784,000 copies of *Black Ice* in 2008. (Yes, that happened.) *Babel*'s success extended to the Hot 100 singles chart, where Mumford became the first band to log six songs simultaneously since the Beatles. Mumford-mania translated to live shows too; when the band came to my native Columbus back in August, it was initially booked for the 5,000-capacity outdoor amphitheater LC Pavilion, but tickets were on pace to sell out during the presale, so the promoter moved the show to the parking lot behind the venue and doubled the capacity. Judging from the buzz in town that day and the number of people who lined up along the fence to hear the show, they could have easily filled an arena or two.

Imitating a band that's incurring that level of adulation is obviously a lucrative career move, so of course Phillips isn't the only one doing it; it seems to be working out for Denver folk trio the Lumineers. The group shares Mumford's aesthetic in both sight (a fondness for olde-timey instruments and attire) and sound (acoustic anthems with mega sing-along potential), and they recently pulled off a similar leap from budding underground sensation to legitimate chart power. The Lumineers' self-titled album made it up to No. 11, and clap-and-stomp-powered single "Ho Hey" is at No. 13 and climbing. A few months ago this band was part of the undercard at an independent radio fest here in Columbus. Now they're set to tour arenas with Dave Matthews Band, which—well, more on that in a second. First, let's talk about context.

What initially took me aback when I heard "Home," and what's so astonishing about this whole folk-rock-on-the-pop-charts movement, is how it's happening in an environment almost entirely geared around club music. The EDM explosion has been well-documented, so no need to belabor the point, but just consider for a moment how dance-oriented the singles chart is right now. The Top 20 almost exclusively comprises R&B (Rihanna, Chris Brown, Miguel), rap (Kanye West, Flo-Rida), alternative bands gunning for the dance floor (Maroon 5, fun., Alex Clare's polarizing Internet Explorer jingle "Too Close") and outright dance-pop (Ke$ha, "Gangnam Style"). Taylor Swift has all but abandoned her bedazzled guitar collection to fit in there. It's a wonder that a band in the Mumford mold could survive in this climate, let alone thrive.

How did it happen? Did Mumford and the Lumineers really just barnstorm the charts out of nowhere, or did they benefit from some trailblazing? One event that springs to mind is Arcade Fire's Album Of The Year win at the Grammys last year. After all, those guys were donning olde-timey costumes and singing their compassionate Canadian hearts out long before Marcus Mumford was a blip on the pop-culture radar. But Mumford & Sons were already well into their ascent by the time the 2011 Grammys rolled around—remember, they and the Avett Brothers performed with Bob Dylan during the ceremony that night. Speaking of the Avetts, they surely had a hand in establishing the lung-busting dress-up folk demographic. So did their bookish counterparts the Decemberists. Those two groups might as well have sired Mumford & Sons during a one-night stand at Bonnaroo, and I have to believe they both would have a shot at crossover success if they released the right single right now. Whoever manages Edward Sharpe And The Magnetic Zeros should be leaning hard on radio programmers right now, too.

So we can choose to see the success of Mumford and his progeny as a long-gestating underground movement that's finally spilling over into the mainstream, and there may be some truth to that. But I can't help thinking these acts are carrying a torch that dates back to long before indie rock got in touch with its inner Renaissance Faire—a torch that burns kind of like chlamydia burns. Dating back to my first dabblings with top-40 radio at the height of Blues Traveler's "Run Around," the format has always had room for that bro-friendly H.O.R.D.E. Tour sound. Sometimes it veers toward jam-band status (DMB), sometimes teeny bopper guitar-slinging (Jason Mraz), sometimes goofy gimmick pop (Barenaked Ladies), but it always seems to persist on the pop charts. Now bands like Mumford and the Lumineers are fulfilling that role, but they're also becoming the latest installment of the whole "indie goes mainstream"/"mainstream co-opts indie" thing that's been happening since Seth Cohen's heyday—or, you know, since Don Draper married Megan.

It's an unexpected intersection of galaxies, but it's happening. Really, what separates Mumford and Lumineers from the likes of Train and Howie Day? If we're honest, most of it comes down to marketing more than music. These bands dress like Wes Anderson characters. They're signed to indie labels—Lumineers with Dualtone, the home to Brett Dennen and Bobby Bare, and Mumford with Glassnote, which makes them colleagues with Stereogum favorites like Phoenix, Oberhofer, and Bloc Party's Kele Okereke. They're both bound to pop up if you listen to the Bon Iver Pandora station for a couple hours. But they also appeal directly to a segment of the population that probably makes a sizable swath of indie music fans squirm. Lumineers are about to hit the road with Dave Matthews, after all, and the number of DMB T-shirts at that Mumford concert over the summer was telling.

Phillips exposes the common threads by embodying them. On Idol, when he got the chance to choose which song to perform, he opted for Dave Matthews Band's "The Stone" and "Volcano" by Damien Rice, the Irish singer whose bleeding-heart folk is a clear precursor to Marcus Mumford's anthems. His debut album, *The World From The Side Of The Moon*, out this week on Interscope, affirms his status as a living, breathing Venn diagram overlap. (Listening to it feels very much like a trip to the mall. Not so much the Olympics.) Every detail vacillates between sounding like a Mumford production and a Matthews production depending on how you crane your ear. Every weathered vocal run is a pivot point, every acoustic strum a litmus test. It reminds me of that episode of Seinfeld where the girl Jerry's dating veers from gorgeous to grotesque depending on the lighting. But it's still the same girl.

The Trouble with Contemporary Music Criticism: Retromania, Retro-historicism, and History*

1

Two hundred years before the release of Daft Punk's *Random Access Memories*, people were losing their shit over a different sort of robot entirely. This one was known as the Mechanical Turk, and it was built at the end of the 18th century by a guy named Wolfgang von Kempelen. The Mechanical Turk comprised a puppet dressed in Turkish robes, sitting on top of a box containing an apparently complex set of mechanics. And it played chess. The Turk was so good at chess, in fact, that it toured the world for the best part of a century before it was finally destroyed in a fire in 1854. It played for Emperor Joseph II, Frederick the Great, Charles Carroll, and Edgar Allen Poe, and it actually beat Napoleon Bonaparte, Benjamin Franklin, and Catherine the Great. On one tour of the UK, it won 45 out of 50 matches, and it played them all with a one-pawn handicap.

The amazing Mechanical Turk turned out to be an elaborate hoax of course. The machine's interior was an ingenious system of smoke and mirrors, expertly designed by Von Kempelen to conceal the chess master, a small hunchback nestled snugly inside.[1]

2

In the realm of contemporary music criticism, there is an equivalent of Von Kempelen's Turk, a criticism machine that is making the rounds of contemporary music circuits, leaving an amazed, but largely unquestioning, audience in its wake.

The contemporary music criticism machine plays its game by confronting and demystifying any and all contemporary music as nothing but a series of historical references—well-known dance outfits from the 1990s, not so well-known German

---

*Croggon, Nicholas, and James Parker. "The Trouble with Contemporary Music Criticism." Tiny Mix Tapes, January 1, 2014. Used with permission.

[1] This piece takes its inspiration from Walter Benjamin's famous unfinished essay from 1940, *Theses on The Philosophy of History*. In this essay, Benjamin uses the Mechanical Turk to introduce a complex and cryptic critique of a particular type of writing history: that is, one underpinned by the concept of progress. Although we have adopted Benjamin's negative attitude towards history as progress, we have used the analogy of the Mechanical Turk in a different way and for a different purpose to Benjamin.

synthesizer duos from the 1970s, and totally obscure British sound recordings from the 1960s. We read this criticism and are impressed at its apparent rigor and erudition—never realizing that, concealed within the box, something else is pulling the strings.

3

In 2011, Simon Reynolds introduced the world of music criticism to the notion of "retromania."[2] The idea was that, more than ever before, contemporary music is concerned with being "retro," with repeating its own very recent past. In justifying this claim, Reynolds gave numerous examples of contemporary music, both pop and experimental, that referred either explicitly or implicitly to music of bygone eras: the eternal return of 60s- and 70s-era garage rock, Amy Winehouse and Adele's ludicrously successful neo-soul, and the onslaught of 90s Eurodance recently unleashed by David Guetta *et al.* on the world's charts. And in the global underground: chillwave, hypnagogic pop, hauntology, hipster house. In each case, Reynolds' diagnosis was almost entirely negative. For Reynolds, retromania is a sickness, a form of cultural malaise. With each passing year, he worried, the pulse of the present is growing increasingly faint.

Reynolds' book struck such a chord both with the public and in critical circles because his account married perfectly with a way of thinking that has dominated critical discourse about music since at least the 1960s. This approach is premised on the twin ideas of "novelty," on the one hand, and "historical progress," on the other.

In *Retromania*, as in so much of the music critical tradition, including Reynolds' own previous work, music is at its best—indeed, achieves its core social function—when it confronts the listener with the shock of the "new." By this, Reynolds means the exhilaration of experiencing a soundworld totally unlike anything heard before: the thrill of having "been there" at the birth of rock 'n' roll, hip-hop, techno, or rave. Importantly, this shock, this experience of radical novelty, is not only a *historical* experience, but also an experience of *what history really is*, of history *as such*. In Reynolds' terms, the excitement of new music is the experience of being on the very edge of the present as it hurtles into the future: it is the experience of what Reynolds considers to be the essential truth of human historical existence as constant progress and change.

The retromania of contemporary music, characterized so astutely by Reynolds, goes fundamentally against this way of relating to music. Its contemporaneity consists precisely in its *repudiation* of progress, its *refusal* to create new sounds: in some cases by shamelessly or irreverently copying or reframing, and in other cases by carefully

---

[2]Simon Reynolds, *Retromania: Pop Culture's Addiction to its Own Past*, New York: Faber & Faber, 2011.

paying tribute to or unarchiving the music of the past. Either way, a denial of the inevitability or desirability of change. And this is why Reynolds condemns it.

4

In the wake of *Retromania*, the world of music criticism has undeniably become increasingly "retro-sensitive." The contemporary music critic hears retro everywhere.

Of course, with the likes of YouTube, Wikipedia, Spotify, The Pirate Bay, Discogs, and a vast data-sea of blogs at their disposal, it is increasingly easy for them to do so. Struggling for a reference? Google it! Wondering which precise Ash Ra Tempel record the new Emeralds record sounds like? Spend just a few minutes surfing YouTube!

The result is a now almost ubiquitous form of music criticism that we call "retro-historicism." It can be found in the printed music press of the *Wire*, *NME*, and *Rolling Stone*, and most predominantly, of course, on the web. In essence, its critical project is the reduction of music criticism to a form of historical list-making: a mechanical exercise in influence fishing, the mere identification and cataloguing of historical reference points before moving on to pass judgment, as if that were in any way sufficient.

This is neither a tribute to nor a continuance of Reynolds' project, of course, but a depressing performance of precisely the approach to music he condemned. Contemporary music criticism has become infected by its *own* version of retromania, in other words, its own obsession with the past. Although, rhetorically, such criticism's appeal to history projects a certain kind of critical rigor, it is our belief that retro-historicism involves nothing less than the abandonment of the critical task.

5

Consider, for instance, the critical reception of Planet Mu founder Mike Paradinas' latest record, released midway through 2013. Titled *Chewed Corners* and released under the µ-Ziq moniker, everyone rushed to agree that it was "retro," and the mechanical retro-historical gears started turning. *The Guardian* placed the album alongside the year's other prestige act retro-releases, Daft Punk and Boards of Canada.[3] Boomkat touted it as a "recalibration," a form of "reconnection" with rave tradition.[4] PopMatters called it "revelatory rave, the sort of nuanced nostalgia that only someone who was there 'back in the day' could conceive of."[5] And for Allmusic,

---

[3]Kitty Empire, 'µ-ziq: Chewed Corners—review', *The Guardian*, Saturday 22 June 2013, http://www. theguardian.com/music/2013/jun/23/u-ziq-chewed-corners-review, accessed 2 July 2014.

[4]'Mu-ziq—Chewed Corners', Boomkat, no date, http://boomkat.com/cds/734844-mu-ziq-chewed-corners, accessed 2 July 2014.

[5]Gary Suarez, 'µ-ziq: Chewed Corners: Rave On and On and On', PopMatters, 25 June 2013, http://www. popmatters.com/review/172857—ziq-chewed-corners/, accessed 2 July 2014.

the record "reflected Paradinas' knowledge of, and pleasure in, over three decades' worth of electronic music."[6] *How* exactly, or *why* this would make the record worth listening to, nobody cared to say. In each case, it was sufficient to name the historical period being engaged and move on.

But the piece of writing that perhaps best exemplifies the retro-historicist tendency we are diagnosing was found on Pitchfork.[7] After pointing out that Paradinas' last EP *XTEP* apparently bore the influences of "chillwave, italo disco, piano house and plenty else besides . . ." the reviewer notes that "[the tracks] 'Taikon' and 'Twangle Melkas' draw on Kuedo's Vangelis-via-Southern-hip-hop schtick; 'Tickly Flanks' owes a debt to the sugar-rush hardcore-footwork hybrids of Machinedrum, though it's a little torpid in comparison to its forebear. 'Wipe's' syncopated rhythms nod to UK funky, while 'Houzz 10' could be a symptom of the recent house revival."

Of course, many of these references from the recent past may indeed by embedded in Paradinas' records, whether intentionally or otherwise. But surely the compilation of these historical references should not be a critical end in itself. Surely the critical questions are these: Why? And with what effect? That is, *if* Paradinas' music is so overtly referential, what are we to make of this? And if the album is indeed a series of empty musical reference-points, then surely *this* bears a certain amount of critical scrutiny and engagement.

6

The sort of retro-historicist criticism we are describing here is more than just bland and uninteresting writing. It is an approach that has its roots in, but also *conceals*, an ideological commitment that blinds us to what is most interesting about so much of the best music being released today. The fact that by and large we fail to notice this ideology is simply evidence of the extent to which it is entrenched. This is how ideology *always* works, of course. It is at its most effective precisely at the moment it disappears from view. Ideology always takes the form of the chess master inside the box; it's always what's inside pulling the strings.

Retro-historicism is driven by the same basic ideological commitment that we described above as underpinning both Reynolds' recent account and so much of the music criticism of the past 50 years: the idea of historical progress.

For the retro-historicist, as for Reynolds, music is all about progress. Once upon a time, this was more obvious—musical history unfurled itself like a ribbon, genres begetting genres, innovation stacking on innovation, each new generation constantly repudiating and then supplanting the one that came before. In more recent times,

---

[6]Heather Phares, 'μ-ziq: Chewed Corners', AllMusic, no date, http://www.allmusic.com/album/chewed-corners-mw0002549365, accessed 2 July 2014.
[7]Angus Finlayson, 'μ-ziq: Chewed Corners', 22 July 2013, http://pitchfork.com/reviews/albums/18207—ziq-chewed-corners/, Pitchfork, accessed 2 July 2014.

however, music has started to abandon its commitment to this historical procession. Over the course of the last 20 years or so—which is to say more or less contemporaneously with the explosion of the world wide web—the musical ribbon of history has started folding back on itself, forming interminable cycles of recursion and self-reference. Music criticism's commitment to progress, however, has never flagged. And so there's no real alternative but to keep pointing out—either with Reynoldsian despair or retro-historicist blandness—that we've "been there," "done that," and "heard this before", while grimly clinging on to the hope that one day the ribbon will begin to unfurl again.

There are alternatives.

7

Of course, a confrontation with the ideology of progress is not something new.

In an essay published in *e-flux* journal in 2010, the philosopher and art critic Boris Groys reminds us that the modern era, and particularly modern technology, constantly confronts us with the "inevitable" movement of progress: iPhone, iPhone 2, iPhone 3, iPhone 4, iPhone 4S.[8] The obvious problem with such movement is that it quickly becomes self-defeating. The iPhone 5 was always already superseded, obsolete. The real truth of its existence is the anticipation of the newer and better iPhone 6. What is new today will be old tomorrow, just as what is old today was new the day before. And the logic of progress suddenly starts to seem less exhilarating, more interminable.

As Groys explains, in the early 20th century the artistic avant-garde attempted to address this problem of the destructive progress of history. How to make the art of the future when that art is always, *necessarily*, rendered old? The answer was to stop creating the art of the future altogether. Only then would it be possible to produce something lasting, art that truly resisted the destructive forces of progress.

What we see with works like Kazimir Malevich's *Black Square* and Marcel Duchamp's *Fountain* is a shift from a logic of "invention" to one of "discovery"—a total repudiation, in other words, of progress and originality *as such*. These are works that no longer attempt to be "new," but rather to discern and to manifest something about the "conditions for the emergence and contemplation of any other image," any other work, in general.

So, in Malevich's case, what is being demonstrated is the necessity of the relation between image and frame. In Duchamp's, the act of exhibition itself. And in both instances, these fundamental gestures immediately become inescapable. After Malevich, whenever we see an image, we now also see the black square, because all images are, in one sense, nothing more than Malevich's simple relationship between image and frame. Likewise, after Duchamp, whenever we attend a museum, we now know that it is the

---

[8]Boris Groys, "The Weak Universalism," *e-flux* journal, 15, april 2010, http://worker01.e-flux.com/pdf/article_130.pdf, accessed 2 July 2014.

institutional conditions that produce the "artwork" at least as much as the artist. It is precisely the act of *placing* the urinal in the gallery and naming it art that makes it so. And in both cases, Groys shows us that it is the very "weakness" of the work—its refusal to manifest the *will* of the artist, precisely its refusal to be inventive or original, the fact that literally *anyone* could have done it—that guarantees its timelessness.

For Groys, the avant-garde attempted to overcome the tyranny of time's progress by making not "strong" masterpieces of art (Caravaggio's *David with the Head of Goliath*, Van Gogh's *Wheatfield With Crows*), but works (a urinal signed and dated, a black square) whose transcendence consisted precisely in their weakness.

8

It is not hard to see how one might run a similar argument in relation to music.

Think of Cage's *4′3″* or Eno's *Music for Airports*. Here are two pieces of music that reproduce Groys' logic almost exactly. *4′33″* is just about the "weakest" work imaginable. Even less than a black square on canvas, it consists of precisely nothing. The predetermined "art-content" of the work is zero, an absence of innovation. But, as we all know, this is exactly what makes it unique, what guarantees its position as one of the most significant musical works of the 20th century. With *4′33″* Cage is pointing, first, to the impossibility of silence and, second, to the act of listening itself: which is to say to the very conditions that make *all* music possible.

Brian Eno's *Music for Airports* is also an incredibly "weak" work—so weak, in fact, that it is hardly there. Musically, *Music for Airports* is totally uninteresting, which is precisely why it is interesting and even important. Whereas the effect of *4′33″* is to draw one's attention to the presence *in* "absence," the effect of *Music for Airports* is just the opposite: to transform "presence" *into* absence, to tend to disappear. Eno's "discovery" of ambience (and it is worth noting that, for both Cage and Eno, the artist's "discovery" is in actuality a kind of appropriation: from acoustic engineers at Harvard in the former case, and from Erik Satie and Buddhism, in the latter) alerts us to the question of attention, and in doing so points once again to one of the primary conditions of musical experience per se.

So both Cage and Eno can be read as having refused the progressivism of their respective traditions. In both cases, the strength of their works consists precisely in their weakness. They are important because they *refused* to "advance," choosing to alert us to the conditions of any such advancement instead.

9

As Groys notes, for the general public today, avant-garde art (from Malevich to Cage) is seen as non-democratic and elitist: we've all heard ourselves, our parents, or our friends stand in front of an allegedly important work of modern art and cry disdainfully, "I could do that!"

For Groys, however, this is precisely the point. Because avant-garde art is comprised of weak gestures, anyone *can* do it, which makes it fundamentally democratic. Popular art today is made for a population consisting of spectators, whereas avant-garde art is made for a population consisting of artists, who could be anyone.

10

Again, Groys' argument maps neatly onto contemporary music's underground.

Take, for instance, the 2012/13 experimental micro-genre vaporwave.[9] Here is a genre that is democratic in exactly the sense envisaged by Groys. Vaporwave is democratic because, in principle, anyone could do it. At its most basic—which is also to say at its most radical—vaporwave consists of nothing more than an act of reframing, normally of some chintzy piece of forgotten muzak dredged up from the depths of the web. Sometimes, admittedly, this is accompanied by a bit of artful chopping and screwing, but such techniques are also (relatively) democratic in the sense that they are available to anyone with Ableton and a computer.

Vaporwave is a particularly "weak" genre, in other words, because "by dramatically foregrounding the act of appropriation, precisely by *refusing* to be 'original,'" what vaporwave does is make "the listening experience all about that original; maybe even about the discourse of originality itself."[10] Vaporwave is not *itself* muzak, in other words, it is *about* muzak. And as a result, it forces us to reconsider the extent of our commitment to a whole series of apparent distinctions: between "-sic" and "-zak," high and low, art and commerce, culture and trash. It forces us to consider the conditions of contemporary musical listening and production per se.

Here's the rub. Because vaporwave is so weak, because it is democratic, it will never be genuinely popular: at least not to the general public. Its audience has been and will no doubt continue to be primarily other producers of vaporwave, on the one hand, and critics, on the other. This is why both groups are accused of being elitist: for being democratic at the level of production, not reception.

11

But vaporwave's weak gesturers are not the only contemporary musicians challenging the notion of a history as the endless progression of one damn thing after another.

---

[9]Vaporwave became well-known primarily through two articles by the music critic Adam Harper on the website Dummy: "Vaporwave and the Pop-Art of the Virtual Plaza," published on 12 July 2012 and "'Distroid'—the Muscular Music of Hi-DEF Doom," published on 13 July 2012, but also by virtue of a series of more regular engagements (reviews, video premiers etc) in the pages of Tiny Mix Tapes. See http://www.tinymixtapes.com/?search=vaporwave

[10]James Parker, "Emeralds: Just To Feel Anything" accessed 2 July 2014, www.tinymixtapes.com/music-review/emeralds-just-to-feel-anything

Jim Jupp, the man behind the UK musical entity Belbury Poly and co-founder of Ghost Box Records, is all about crafting new and weird historical narratives. As the retro-historicist would duly note, Belbury Poly's music contains samples from and references to library music, psychedelia, prog, and of course the creation, in the 1950s, of the BBC Radiophonic Workshop. Like the Mike Paradinas album, all these references feel nostalgic in an indeterminate sort of a way.

Of course, Jupp is acutely aware of all of this. Belbury Poly's deliberate blending of samples with evocative and referential newly recorded materials deliberately makes us question our sense of nostalgia. How, after all, can we feel nostalgic for a past that we never experienced, or indeed that is not even a past? The array of historical references further disrupts our sense that this music emanates from a coherent musical narrative: as he noted in an interview for the *Wire* in 2009, "Not just for Belbury Poly but for the whole of Ghost Box, it's 1958–1978 and it's all at once, we take little slices through that continuum."[11]

Belbury Poly's real material is history itself: it is the sound of history being chopped, screwed, sampled, and re-enacted to form a complex miasma, in which odd moments of the past leap into and disrupt the present, at the same moment as the present stumbles blindly into a previously unknown past.

12

Of course, not all contemporary music engaged with history is so interesting.

Daft Punk's *Random Access Memories* is, very obviously, attempting to establish a specific kind of relationship with the past. Its tracks refer back to a bygone era of music, both at the level of style ("Get Lucky's" disco groove) and, even more explicitly, at the level of content (Giorgio Moroder's almost documentary-style reminiscences about the birth of synthesizer disco in "Giorgio by Moroder").

Already it is clear that Daft Punk are taking a more theoretical approach to history than the simple historical list-making of the retro-historicist: the function of this album is not merely to *reference* the past, but to adopt an attitude towards it, to couch its references in a value system that preferences the birth of disco as an era of newness that we have lost. The album was also an *argument*: to "give life back to music" and "do it right," but to do so by going back in time.

As with Reynolds' argument, encoded in this injunctive is the idea that music *should* sound new and progressive. But paradoxically, for Daft Punk, this can only be achieved at one remove, by self-defeatingly re-enacting the period of music history when this was apparently best embodied.

Daft Punk is, in a way, the musical counterpart to Reynolds' retromania, accidentally exposing how old both their conceptions of the "new" really are.

---

[11] Mark Fisher, The *Wire* (May 2009), 12.

13

So, the lesson of Cage, Eno, and now vaporwave, Belbury Poly, and even Daft Punk is that history need not be conceived of as an endless hurtling into the future. Indeed, the important thing about these musics is that they not only concern history, but assume a critical position in relation to it—they both critique certain conceptions of history and offer new ones.

When Reynolds looks to contemporary music, he does so from the perspective of a narrative of progress. He is searching for the moment of the new that confirms—again and again and again—history's exhilarating sense of directionality. But in doing so, he misses what is most interesting about so much contemporary music: the fact that so many of these musicians are concerned precisely with undoing such conceptions of history. They are engaged, in other words, in a conceptually different task: not moving history forward, but formulating new forms of history entirely.

Unlike Reynolds' positive attempts to continue a critical project, however, the retro-historicist conceals its progressivism—tucks it neatly away inside the box—and then seeks to profit from its concealment. What looks like harmless list-making is actually a silent commitment to the progressive view of history—a music critical treading of water until music's ribbon of history begins to unfurl again. As such, not only is it fooling itself and *us*, but it is also missing the best of contemporary music because it simply doesn't have the critical tools to articulate what is good and interesting about it.

Ultimately, one of the interesting aspects of contemporary music is that, at this crossroads of retromania, retro-historicism, and historically concerned music, it is actually the music that is largely beating criticism to the critical punch.

The best in contemporary music *already* calls on us to see the trick of the retro-historicist machine and thus to understand its contingency as a method of encountering the history of music. We need to listen.

No, Ian Curtis Doesn't Come With the Kitchen Table: A Lesson in Fandom*

There are more, and stranger, ways than ever to try and feel close to the music we love. Look no further than recent headlines. For the same price as a liberal arts degree from a state university, the drum kit that ex-Guided by Voices drummer Kevin Fennell used on *Bee Thousand* can gather dust in your garage. Or, if your breakfast nook décor lacks a certain post-punk quality, you can pony up for a kitchen table that Joy Division's Ian Curtis allegedly once owned. The latter would be worth it alone for the Facebook statuses and tweets: Eating tuna fish tacos and paying cable bill at Ian Curtis's kitchen table. Tempting.

But there's no need to delve into the lifestyles of rich spendthrifts to find fans thinking the corporeal (e.g., a dead singer's kitchen table) can somehow connect them to the numinous (e.g., whatever you may feel when, say, "Love Will Tear Us Apart" spins). We all have our own examples. Steve, whom I attended high school with, keeps a framed Nine Inch Nails t-shirt on a hallway wall in his home. The significance? It was the shirt he was wearing when Trent Reznor spit water all over him during a *The Fragile*-era show. Naturally, it hasn't been laundered since. Another friend, Andy, returned from a No Doubt show with a piece of yellow fabric that Gwen Stefani had torn from her tank top and tossed into the crowd ("to me!" he insisted). He pulled up to my house two weeks later with murder in his eyes and accused me of having stolen his precious. For the record, not guilty.

In fairness, I'm not without my own relics, but they're far less creepy and possess no ostensible hold over me. One is a John Hiatt guitar pick, the other an autographed Jules Shear setlist. When Hiatt tossed the purple pick to me some years ago, I remember naively thinking, "This pick could've written 'Slow Turning' or 'Cry Love.'" On the way home that night, I noticed the back of my souvenir had "www.Johnhiatt.com" printed on it. A word to the wise: no artist ever wrote a song that you love with a guitar pick that has his or her website address on it. The Hiatt pick currently resides at the bottom of a jar of pennies. The framed Shear setlist—scrawled in black Sharpie on the back of a MapQuest—probably sits in an unpacked box from my move to Chicago three years ago.

I can't speak for top-dollar drum kits, or even Aquafina- and saliva-doused shirts, but my music-related keepsakes do little more than conjure fading memories of

---

*Melis, Matt. "No, Ian Curtis Doesn't Come with the Kitchen Table: A Lesson in Fandom." *Consequence of Sound*, November 22, 2013.

nights that hold little significance to me now. "Remember when…" rightly gets categorized as a poor brand of conversation, and memory falls within the same humble echelon when we're trying to connect to precisely what floors us about the music we love. Shear puts it well enough in his song "If We Never Meet Again," lamenting that "memories get old and flat like photographs." And he's right. Memories alone cannot sustain us, soon fade around the edges, and certainly don't get us any closer to a song that, if only for a chord change or chorus, understands exactly what it feels like to be us.

Nor, I'm afraid, does actually meeting the artist—an avenue many of us head down even before we've exhausted all the peculiar, high-end possibilities on eBay. Songwriters, after all, can usually tell you (if they're willing) their song's origin and intention, but they'll have no clue why some chords and words they happened to cobble together in their bedroom or touring van can drive you to despair or euphoria or sometimes both. At best these encounters are like speed dating (without the crutch of asking, "So, what do you do?"): you eye each other a bit, exchange banal pleasantries, notice imperfections (like moles or sweaty hands), and leave fairly certain you didn't impress. At worst—and we've all done it—you fumble through an incoherent, borderline psychotic explanation of what the artist's music means to you (tears optional), only to receive a polite, embarrassed shrug and "thanks." Ennui or mortification are the only regular outcomes. Talk about being spoiled for choice, and you're still no closer to the actual music.

Here's a for instance. Mark Mulcahy, a singer whose songs have soundtracked both my adolescence and adulthood, played a show at the Hideout in Chicago this past July. Finally, I thought, a chance to get to the bottom of why a simple song like "Love's the Only Thing That Shuts Me Up" leaves me speechless or how ambivalent lover's portrait "The Rabbit" (incidentally, one of the best songs of 2013) seems to know something about me that it shouldn't—like an eavesdropper. That was the agenda going in. What I actually came away with after meeting him was confirmation that he's an affable New England chap and the scintillating observation, "I always thought he was taller than that." Had the answers to all my questions leapt off Mulcahy in those 50 feet between the stage and the merchandise booth? Probably not. More likely they evaporated, as they normally do, with the final notes of an encore.

It's understandable that we want to feel closer to our music. It's so often what inspires us, consoles us, makes us appreciative, and, on a good many days, makes life tolerable. Nothing has ever been made worse by a good song, and how many things can you say that about? Late author and devout Humanist Kurt Vonnegut once wrote, "If I should die, God forbid, let this be my epitaph: The only proof he ever needed for the existence of God was music." It's a perfect note to go out on.

So, somebody may drop a year's salary on Kevin Fennell's drum kit, and, to a degree, I can understand the silliness. Macabre as the prospect seems, I can even imagine Ian Curtis's kitchen table sitting in my own kitchen. Of course, I'd be no closer to what really matters to me about Joy Division. Even if Curtis could actually join me for breakfast at that table, I know I would only babble on about the many known pleasures of *Unknown Pleasures*; then we'd probably just stare at our eggs in silence. No matter how much money we shell out for items like these, a much more intimate and meaningful relationship with the music we love can always be had through a 99-cent download and a $5 pair of earbuds. It's nothing you can show off to your bros or eat breakfast at, but it's the best bargain going.

WRITING PROMPT: THE BLOG PIECE

Music blogs are some of the most highly trafficked and successful sites on the internet. There are thousands of music blogs with varying degrees of popularity, tone and stature. Think about what blogs you frequent. Do you check Pitchfork every day? Maybe you find yourself on My Old Kentucky Blog or Tiny Mix Tapes for hours at a time. NPR has a fantastic music blog as well.

Select a music blog that you LIKE and read 3–4 recent pieces to get a feel for the tone of the blog. Some blogs rely on an austere tone to communicate the facts and others take a more colloquial tone, even using profanity for emphasis. When writing a blog piece you have the freedom to react quickly to news events or tackle complex histories and criticism without space limitations or layout considerations. Writing for a music blog affords you the opportunity to include sound and video to support your story. Sites like YouTube, Vimeo and SoundCloud allow you to easily copy and embed videos and sound clips into a blog post.

Twitter is an excellent source for breaking news. Set aside an hour of two and browse through the twitter feed of a major music publication (I'd suggest: @RollingStone, @SPINmagazine or @nprmusic) to find a breaking news story related to an artist. Do some quick research and start to formulate a story. Write a 500–1000-word blog piece that discusses at least two specific videos or sound clips. Remember that you are not breaking the story but you are trying to offer something new to the conversation.

If you're feeling brave contact the editors of the blog and submit your piece.

THE GO-BETWEENS

YOUR BIGGEST MISTAKE

I once changed a phrase in a black metal piece, at the urging of an editor, from "one of the earliest iterations" to "first wave" that then changed how people understood the piece; it made it sound like I didn't understand what I was referencing historically.—**Jessica Hopper**, Music Editor at *Rookie Magazine*, and Senior Editor, the *Pitchfork Review*

I was the news editor on *Rolling Stone*'s website, and I was often super lazy about actually editing copy on the stories that went up on the site. My attitude was, "Since the headline is the only important aspect of any given blog post 98 percent of the time, who gives a shit if anybody can actually understand what we were saying?" That was short-changing the narrative, the reader, and the product, so after a heart-to-heart with my managing editor, I probably over-corrected myself, placing craft over other important internet things like timeliness and efficiency. (I actually used to send blog posts back with edits, which is a fucking crazy thing to do on the internet.)—**Kyle Anderson**, senior writer, *Entertainment Weekly*

When I was the editor of an alt-weekly in a campus town, I wrote the weekly music news column. The week the local folk festival announced its preliminary lineup, I mentioned the names in the press release, and then meant to provide the folk festival's phone number (this was before websites)—which I didn't have on hand at the time. So I wrote something that surely would trigger me to fill in the correct info later: "For more information, call A BUNCH OF HIPPIE FUCKS." No one, including me, copy edited or proofread the column. It went to press. That led to some very awkward conversations with the festival, which my magazine was helping to sponsor—and on top of that, my own band was playing that year. That last fact helped smooth things over. The festival was run by extremely politically correct granola types, many of whom were upset, but some staffers made up T-shirts with the phrase on it and presented me with one at the festival.—**Michael Barclay**, freelance writer/broadcaster, co-author, *Have Not Been the Same: The CanRock Renaissance 1985–1995*

I didn't stand up for a subject who was wronged. I had interviewed the singer of The Little Kingz, a rad rock band comprised entirely of little people. (They played the dudes in *Zoolander* who Hansel met when he was ice-sailing in Finland!) The singer's single request was that we didn't use the m-word in the article, and I say "m-word" here because he compared the actual word to derogatory racial epithets that carry an equally hurtful impact. I made absolutely sure to convey this to my editor when I submitted the article, but when I opened the magazine, it was the first fucking word in the headline. It gutted me, and I sent off an immediate apology to the singer. It didn't matter. They tore me apart on the band's website. I emailed my editor about the situation as well, but he never responded. And it's there where I made a mistake, because I didn't do more to convey just how shitty this situation (and his action) was. And it wasn't long before I took another assignment from him, never to bring up the incident again. I failed to stand up for my subject—for another human being—because I feared it would burn some professional bridge, and that guilt still hurts. There's plenty of room for critical and humorous music writing in the world without personal attacks, and I'd like to think I can draw those lines even better now. And not that it's made any difference to that particular situation, but I have since crusaded for the cause whenever I hear the m-word now.—**Phillip Crandall**, author of the **33⅓** book on Andrew W.K.'s *I Get Wet*

I totally trashed an album (*Thick As A Brick*) in my college newspaper that later became one of my favorites. I couldn't fix that mistake but I've never made it again. First impressions aren't always lasting impressions. Before hauling off on a record or concert, I make myself take a step back and reconsider my opinion before proceeding. Even when you can't see how you might change your opinion about something, you can get the sense that a path is there (if indeed it is).— **Bruce Eaton**, Author, *Radio City* (**33⅓**)

When I got out of college my listening up to that point had been way too stringently confined to the "alternative/college rock" sphere, which quickly revealed itself to be a huge mistake both as a writer and a listener. From there on I've tried to keep an open mind and cast as wide a net as possible, listening-wise.—**Rob Harvilla**, Deputy/Culture Editor, Deadspin

I referred to someone as "the late ___ ___," when reviewing their record. I'd interviewed someone else involved with the record's making, and they spoke of the musician as though that person had recently died. I didn't fact-check this and the magazine where my article appeared, while having an industry-wide readership and reputation, didn't employ fact-checkers either, a curious thing. An apology appeared in the next issue. I'm told the musician in question, the guy I'd killed in effect, was amused by this at the time. He died, in the truly permanent and verifiable sense of the term, five years later. I shrivel inside even now when remembering this.—**Richard Henderson**, music writer and **33⅓** author

The biggest mistake I've made as a writer is assuming that I know an artist's motives. It's gross, and it's something I've done too many times. "This artist is *trying* to do this," etc. I fixed it by (hopefully) not doing that any more.—**Matt LeMay**, senior contributor, Pitchfork

The original arrogance of the rock writer demands that the answer is—no mistakes, nothing to fix. Some might say my greatest mistake is the constant urge to resist a conclusion, but I do not agree.—**Paul Morley**, writer and critic

When I edited *Ministry in Ibiza* we had a front-of-book section for "good" and "bad" things happening on the island, called "Dog's Bollocks" and "Cat's Arse", respectively (or perhaps not so respectively ... it's very much a colloquial English thing). Then the lovely, elderly owner of the nightclub Es Paradis invited us to his birthday party, which he had every year to thank his workers and friends. Free bar, free BBQ ... the full monty. So we wanted to say thanks by putting it in the "Dog's Bollocks" column ... only it somehow ended up in "Cat's Arse". As editor I should have been on top of that, but it was the last issue and we were totally drained by a summer spent in nightclubs, and counted out in discarded flyers. Ministry of Sound made me apologise to this chap, which I willingly did, in person, but he never believed me that it was a mistake. Crumbs, I still cringe thinking about it. The devil really is in the detail. I now use that story in classes I give about page layout, entitled: When Layouts Attack!— **Simon A. Morrison**, music journalist and Programme Leader for Music Journalism at the University of Chester

Just try and be honest about where I went wrong and do my best to make it right, even if it means subjecting myself to embarrassment.—**Mark Richardson**, Editor-in-Chief, Pitchfork

When I was very young, I psyched myself out when I got an assignment from a big-time publication, and I didn't complete it. That's no longer a problem. I don't know how specifically I fixed it except that over time I gained confidence in what I was doing, and perhaps more importantly I lost the romantic hero worship I'd had of institutions for whom I wanted to write.—**Marc Weidenbaum**, author of *Selected Ambient Works Volume II* (**33⅓**, 2014)

Going into music journalism instead of technology in the early '90s. I did not fix it.—**Douglas Wolk**, freelance arts journalist

CHAPTER 8
THE ARTIST PROFILE

INTRODUCTION

As a teenager, I read a lot about bands in profiles that weren't written in anyone's idea of deathless prose—not that I would have been able to discern much of a difference between literary greatness and run of the mill copy at that point (and it probably wouldn't have mattered much to me if I could have): I wanted to know about a band I loved, a guitarist I idolized, a frontman who was a certified rock star. The writing itself didn't have to compose itself in stylish sentences or provide insight beyond the basic facts to satisfy me.

I still have some of the mags I bought in those days to fill that fundamental need: *Circus* with Elton John on the cover in spangled platforms; *Creem* with a feature on the Runaways, Joan Jett's chilly stare competing with Cherrie Currie's teen-dream face impassive within the frame of her perfectly parted hair. I don't recall a single sentence or critical position from those pored over pages, but I know they meant something to me at the time. Did I think about the writer? Did he—or, only occasionally in the mid-70s, she—have a style that impressed itself upon me? For every Lester Bangs effusion in *Creem* there were pages of not-particularly-memorable quotation-driven profiles whose only distinguishing feature was their standard ironic stance, an attitude completely at odds with the reasons I bought the magazines in the first place.

I can't remember now if the promo copy came in an Aerosmith fan club publication (when you signed up you really did "get your wings" in the mail, plastic with a pin) or as part of an album insert, but some band flack wrote that any true Aerosmith fan could instantly distinguish a Joe Perry solo from one by his band mate, Brad Whitford. I blanched to read this: I counted myself a true fan, but I couldn't hear the difference. I may have been fan enough to convince the authorities at Carlisle Junior High to allow me, grudgingly, to paint a ten-foot long rendering of the band's name complete with asteroid on the wall between sets of lockers, but that anonymous publicist had me questioning what I knew, even who I was. I'd have to listen harder, rise to another level of fandom if I wanted to consider myself worthy. I'm not sure I kicked it up the requisite notch, but at that moment I confronted the fact that the writer knew more than I did.

One of the baseline reasons we read profiles of artists we care about—or even those we don't—is implicit even in that boilerplate fan club copy (if that's what it was): the writers who produce them know more than we do. They have access we don't have and therefore can tell us more about the musicians we listen to than we can find out on our own. What they do with that access depends on their ambition and skill-set, their temperament and moral sensibility. Lindsay Zoladz's profile of Pussy Riot is not only absorbing because I didn't have the chance to spend time with two of the Russian political collective's members when they visited New York and Zoladz did, but because she uses the occasion to consider the lack of relevance, of political bite, in contemporary American popular music. Zoladz also situates the profile perfectly by opening with the pitch-perfect set piece of visiting Judy Chicago's iconic installation *The Dinner Party* at the Elizabeth E. Sackler Center for Feminist Art with her subjects, "Puck" and "Headlight" (the pseudonyms the activist/musicians adopted for the purposes of the piece). The writer offers a frame that's a rich and complex version of third-wave feminism, both funny ("I feel like I'm looking at a radical feminist Starship Enterprise") and telling (at one point, Puck says, "In Russia, they're much more afraid of the word 'riot,'" ... adding with a laugh, "In America, they seem to be more afraid of the other word."). Zoladz not only uses her access to provide a way to bring her subjects and what they stand for into keen relief, but to make telling, coherent use of the facts and details she's gathered. The most lasting and affecting profiles do more than offer a simple portrait of the artist, they provide a context that makes a reader think and—more—understand.—MW

EXPERT ADVICE FROM OUR WRITERS

Features about specific artists require some research. Usually, I write about people whose work I already know and love. Having read extensively about an artist usually has me taking too much for granted—I've long ago formulated my own version of their story with fun facts to match, all of which by the time of writing may be inaccurate by a little or a lot. And so I return to the available literature on my subject, re-reading to verify or correct existing impressions.—**Richard Henderson**, music writer and **33⅓** author

My most recent piece was a *Rolling Stone* profile of the great Brian Eno, so the main challenge was trying to capture his brilliant words in just a page and a half of a magazine. But I try to immerse myself in the assignment and tune out everything else for a while—I like to concentrate on one thing at a time until it's finished, then move on to the next thing. My ideal work routine would be writing about a song all day, then writing about a different song all the next day.—**Rob Sheffield**, writer, *Rolling Stone*

For a feature called "The Unsung Melodies of Kurt Cobain" I sought to answer the question, "On the twentieth anniversary of his passing, what might Kurt Cobain's music have sounded like had he not left us?" It began as most stories do, with a conversation with my editor about how to approach the topic (sometimes it's in the news, but in this case it was a milestone from the past). We hammered out the goals, eliminated the types of things we knew we didn't want to do (no obits, no "final days" timelines, no oral histories), and plotted out who our primary sources would be (this was a list of about 30 people, of which 7 were available and game for interviews). Then we plotted a schedule for travel and reporting, and set a deadline for a draft. I was on the road for most of March, so the draft was crafted in between other projects and sent out about two and a half weeks before closing. It went through one batch of edits, then a second before it was passed along to a top editor, where it got an entirely new draft that we then had to trim by about 2,000 words. Then I took a nap.—**Kyle Anderson**, senior writer, *Entertainment Weekly*

I wrote a 5,000-word *SPIN* cover feature on Eric Church, a full-on country guy, which in terms of process involved about two years of my inexplicably getting into country music, several months to convince my normally country-averse *SPIN* editors to go for it, two days out in Nashville making awkward small talk with EC himself (I also watched him smear deer musk on trees), and a couple weeks to write the thing. (Took longer than usual, but it was the holidays.)—**Rob Harvilla**, Deputy/Culture Editor, Deadspin

Mine is such a hectic and haphazard process. My last piece was a profile of a singing lumberjack named Buzz Martin, who died in the 1980s. This made writing the story a challenge, as I couldn't rely on firsthand quotes as I normally would.

I guess the process worked as such. First I fell in love with a scratchy old country music record. That's where things almost always start with me: There is an artifact that I live with for awhile. I fall in love with it, and I like to imagine that I'm the only person in the world who has ever fallen in love with it. I like to define for myself what is special about it before I really go looking for anyone else's take. So I did that. Then, when I decided I liked it enough to write about it, I looked for all Martin's other records and I started to research and Google him every possible way I could. I looked for old articles, gathered contact information for people I thought might be helpful, and generally learned all I could. Unfortunately, the subject of this article had died in the '80s, so that was a challenge. I started cold-calling people I thought might know him. A lot of them had died within the last year or two, which was really depressing. But I found a few great sources, including the singer's son, who wound up really being the backbone of the piece. So I talked to him and other sources about Buzz. I can't really write from research alone. That feels like schoolwork to me, so I get bored. I need to talk to people. It can be harder to piece a story together from interviews, but it holds my interest more, and most of the time I think it makes for a more emotionally accurate story. So, anyway, I started interviewing people.

My process is a little funny, but for me the next step (after the bulk of my research has been done and my interview notes have been transcribed) is always to just sit down and write a story without looking at my notes. When you're neck-deep in a story, I think you can work really instinctively like that and you'll cover almost all of the important pieces. You've been turning it over in your head, so it's already forming there, and I think you can write a story that is about 90 percent finished without even looking back on your notes. Once that's all committed to the page, I read it over and I think about what's missing and what's there, and I try to make some placeholder text for the missing parts. Then I fill in all the dummy quotes that I recalled from memory with the real quotes from my notes. I fill in the dummy dates with real dates. And I see what I'm still missing. Usually I have to follow-up with subjects at this stage to get more information, because there are parts of the narrative that I realize I don't fully understand. So I fill in all the blanks, look back over my notes to make sure I haven't left out any truly golden quotes or pieces of information, and then I call it a first draft.

After that, I am pretty much sick of the story and I never want to look at it again. Which is why editors are the greatest. So at this stage I let an editor tell me what my story is missing (in the case of the Buzz story, that was the great Andrew Leland, who actually got me excited about my story again!) and I let that editor drag me through all the tweaks and challenges. I think the most important work happens right at the end, but unfortunately, I'm usually ready to just let someone else rewrite the whole thing by the time I get there. Because I've learned what I wanted to learn by this point. That's more exciting to me than deciding how to best tell another person about this thing that I love. So that's why I need a great editor. So he or she can tell me that the piece is worth refocusing on and improving and not just totally abandoning. Also, when you're really burned out, the best thing is always to turn off all the lights and just put on the record that got you so excited in the first place.—**Casey Jarman**, Managing Editor, The *Believer*

ALEX ROSS ON RADIOHEAD

The Searchers: Radiohead's Unquiet Revolution*

On a hot day in May, the city of Bilbao was shaken by a velvety roar, not unlike the sound of a jet plane waiting on a tarmac. At one end of Calle de Iparraguirre, which cuts across the town, the silver shell of the Guggenheim Museum was glistening in the sun. For a moment, it seemed as if the noise were coming from there—as if the building were about to lift off and rocket elsewhere. In fact, the source of the disturbance was a local bullring, the Vista Alegre, where a German experimental d.j. named Christoph de Babalon was testing his gear. He was the opening act for Radiohead, a five-man rock band from Oxford, England. Radiohead fans were gathered at the entrance, staring up at the sound and asking what it meant. One had on a Kafka T-shirt, and others wore shirts with a Radiohead logo, which can only be described as a demon in tears.

A side door led to a concrete corridor, where the bulls run on an ordinary day. From there, planks reached out to a temporary stage. Christoph was in the center, eyeing his mixer and his CD players. With ice-blond hair and black sunglasses, he looked like a young Bond villain, but he turned out to be a friendly, chatty sort of sonic terrorist. "I am familiar with dark, small clubs," he said after the sound check. "Now it is like I am in a gladiator film." He mentioned some of his musical influences, which included avant-garde figures like Merzbow and the composer Morton Feldman. "Sometimes I work with beats, sometimes with layers," he said. "Tonight I do layers."

Popular music in the year 2001 is in a state of suspense. No one can say where the mystery train is going. On the one hand, the Top Forty chart is overrun with dancers, models, actors, and the like; on the other hand, there are signs that pop music is once again becoming a safe place for creative musicians. The world fame of Radiohead is a case in point. Having established themselves with tuneful guitar rock in the nineties, the members of this band took the risk of doing as they liked, and they discovered things about the marketplace which others had missed. Last year, they released an album titled *Kid A*, an eerily comforting blend of rock riffs, jazz chords, classical textures, and electronic noise, which, in a demolition of conventional wisdom, went to No. 1 on the Billboard chart. *Amnesiac*, its like-minded successor, came out in June and is doing just as well. Radiohead's selling point is not their identification with any one genre but their way of ranging over music as a whole. They have intensity, intelligence, a personality in sound. In Bilbao, they were present in spirit before they

---

*Ross, Alex. "The Searchers." *The New Yorker*, August 20, 2001. Reprinted with permission.

played. The idea of placing a German d.j. in a Spanish bullring was Radiohead to the core—a tricky, eclectic song waiting to happen.

Christoph went to his dressing room, and the stage was empty for a while. Two shirtless old men sat on stone steps, looking as though they had not moved since Franco died. Radiohead's gear basked in the sun. On the left-hand side was a rack of guitars—twenty-three in all. Up front, in an area set aside for Ed O'Brien, one of three guitarists in the band, was a tangle of pedals, samplers, and inch-thick cords. In the center of the stage, to be shared by Colin Greenwood, the bass player, and Thom Yorke, the singer, were various keyboards, a piano, and an upright bass. Equipment for Colin's younger brother, Jonny Greenwood, stood on the right: more guitars, more keyboards, a xylophone, a transistor radio, a sci-fi stack of analog synthesizers, and a modified ondes martenot, one of the earliest electronic instruments. The ondes martenot is controlled by a ring that slides along a wire; fewer than a hundred people have mastered it, and Jonny is one. The only really conventional-looking apparatus was the drum set, although you could tell by some distress on the edges of the drums that the player, Phil Selway, had attacked the sides as well as the skins.

Backstage, the members of Radiohead were eating dinner. Colin Greenwood hovered over the catering table, inspecting an array of Basque dishes. He is typical of the group in that he looks nothing like a celebrity who has sold fifteen million records. He is thirty-two years old, with jet-black hair and large, kindly eyes. He is easily distracted and delighted by the world around him, favoring the words "mad," "brilliant," and "amazing"—the last spoken with a long, liquid stress on the second syllable. He has a habit of suddenly burying his face in his hands, as if he were sinking into despair, or falling asleep; after a moment, his face lights up again. Lavishly well-read, he can talk at length about almost any topic under the sun—Belgian fashion; the stories of John Cheever; the effect of different types of charcoal on barbecued meat—but he gets embarrassed by his erudition and cuts himself off by saying, "I'm rambling." He is not above wearing a T-shirt that says "Life's a beach and then you shag." You might peg him as a cultish young neo-Marxist professor, or as the editor of a hip quarterly. But he is a rock star, with several Web pages devoted to him.

"It's full on out there, isn't it?" Greenwood said, looking toward the bullring, which was filling up with fans. "I'm scared." He occupied himself by talking about "Faust's Metropolis," Alexandra Richie's thousand-page history of Berlin. Outside, Christoph began to play for real, and was received in bemused silence.

An hour later, Radiohead hit the stage with a confidence that had been invisible before the show. The sound was huge, but it was awash in colors, contrasts, and detail. It was grand in effect, cool in tone, dark in mood. The set was a mixture of older tunes, from the band's breakthrough albums of the mid-nineties—*The Bends* and *OK Computer*—and newer ones, from *Kid A* and *Amnesiac*. The old songs had choruses that the fans knew by heart, but the new ones, which have been described as "anti-commercial" in the rock press, made the crowd dance harder. "Idioteque" set off fierce rhythmic clapping, even though it was dominated by jagged beats, computer-music samples, and squawks from the old-school synths. It must have helped that the singer, when he was done singing, launched into a demonically silly dance, kicking his legs as if someone were firing a gun at his feet. It may also have helped, on an unconscious level, that love-drunk chords from "Tristan und Isolde" lurked at the heart of the song, courtesy of a Paul Lansky composition called "Mild und Leise."

In the middle of the set, Radiohead played a song called "Airbag," which showed why this band is taken as seriously as any since the Beatles. It was a rugged ritual, full of cabalistic exchanges, with each player taking a decisive role. Jonny started off with a melody that snaked along in uneven time—one-two-three-one-two-three-one-two—and swayed between A major and F major. O'Brien added leaner, brighter curlicues on guitar. Selway came in with a precise but heavily syncopated beat. Then Yorke began to sing, in a well-schooled, plaintive voice, an oblique account of a near-fatal collision: "In the next world war/In a jackknifed juggernaut/I am born again." At the mention of war, Colin let loose a jumpy bass line, giving a funky spin to the hymns in the treble. The music cut through a jumble of verses and choruses, then held fast to a single chord, as Yorke fell into synch with O'Brien's chiming lines. Just before the end, Colin grinned, leaped in the air a couple of times, and seized hold of his brother's tune, the one that had set the song in motion. The doubling of the theme had a kind of thunderous logic, as if an equation had been solved. The interplay was as engaging to the mind as anything that has been done in classical music recently, but you could jump up and down to it.

In the old days, rock bands had a haircut, a lingo, a house style. The disconcerting thing about Radiohead is that its members do not really look or act alike. They are basically a group of smart English guys in their late twenties and early thirties. They read books, but they also check the football scores. Three are married; two have kids; all live in Oxford, where they grew up. Thom Yorke, who writes most of the songs, is compact, boyish, and impish; he has a lethally quick mind and a subtly powerful charisma. Ed O'Brien, almost a foot taller than Yorke, has the jutting jaw and floppy bangs of an actor in a period war movie; he is suave and direct and seems to have rolled in from a different posse. Jonny Greenwood, a lanky figure with unruly black hair, is more cautious than his brother Colin, but when he starts talking he excitedly involves himself in dense, Victorian sentences, biting clauses out of the air. Phil Selway is bald and sweet-faced, and talks in a gentle voice. He looks like the nice, ordinary one, but he often has a trace of a wicked smile.

How these five mildly eccentric young Englishmen became the Knights Templar of rock and roll is anyone's guess. They are not too sure themselves. "Everyone comes to us with their heads bowed, expecting to be inducted into the mystery of Radiohead," Selway said. He made a King Tut gesture with his arms. "We were hoist on our own petard with that. At a certain point, around 1997, we were simply overwhelmed and had to vanish for a bit. This was our honest reaction to the situation we were in. But some people thought we were playing a game, or had started taking ourselves too seriously. Really, we don't want people twiddling their goatees over our stuff. What we do is pure escapism."

What happened to Radiohead in 1997 was that they caught a wave of generational anxiety. The album *OK Computer*, with titles like "Paranoid Android," "Karma Police," and "Climbing Up the Walls," pictured the onslaught of the information age and a young person's panicky embrace of it. Yorke's lyrics seem a mixture of overheard conversations, techno-speak, and fragments of a harsh diary: "I trust I can rely on your vote"; "An airbag saved my life"; "Ambition makes you look pretty ugly." The songs offered images of riot police at political rallies, anguished lives in pretty suburbs, yuppies freaking out, sympathetic aliens hovering overhead. Yorke even dared to describe the feeling of letdown that follows a blast of hype, such as the one his band was producing. "When it comes, it's so-so," he sang. "It always ends up drivel." The album sold more than four million copies worldwide, enabling the group to become, by 1999, an independent operation. Radiohead were the poster boys for a certain kind of knowing alienation—as the Talking Heads and R.E.M. had been before.

Radiohead remain a magnet for misfits everywhere, but their outsider status is only a part of their appeal. What fans seem to like, even more than the content of the songs, is the sense that the band members have labored over every aspect of the product. They are skilled, first of all, at inventing the kinds of riddles that teen-agers enjoy unravelling. The records, the videos, the official Web site, even the T-shirts all cry out for interpretation. Why are words spelled funny? What are all these charts and diagrams? What about the grinning bears and crying Minotaurs? "We liked worrying over that kind of thing when we were kids, and we're still in the same mind-set a lot of the time," Selway said. "But it's a bit incidental. We're dead set on the music. That's the thread running through this whole thing. We met at school playing music together, and we still get together over music now. We like solving musical puzzles. That's what Thom gives us."

A Radiohead song is usually written in three stages. First, Yorke comes up with a rough sketch; then Jonny, who studied classical composition in school, fleshes out the harmony; finally, the others digest it for a while, working out their parts on their own. It can be months, even years, before a song comes together in a way that satisfies all of them. Take away any one element—Selway's flickering rhythmic grid, for example, fierce in execution and trippy in effect—and Radiohead are a different band. The five together form a single mind, with its own habits and tics—the Radiohead Composer. This personality can be glimpsed in the daily bustle of the group, but you can never meet it face to face, because it lives in the music. A lot of what has been written about Radiohead—there are six books, hundreds of magazine articles, and millions of words on the Internet—circles around an absent center.

During Radiohead's recent tours, the best picture of the band at work came during the sound checks. Yorke led these pre-show rituals with the assurance of a seasoned conductor with limited rehearsal time. He'd shout "Next!" just as a song was building to its climax. All problems had to be addressed on the spot. At one point, Colin said, "That's something we can work on later," whereupon Yorke muttered to himself, and Colin added, a little wearily, "It is also something we can work on now." There were moments, though, when Yorke was at a loss. Once, during a run-through of "The Tourist," he forgot the final chord, and so did everyone else—including Jonny, who had written the song. "Does anyone have a copy of *OK Computer*?" Yorke called out. No one did. The Composer was taking a nap. A couple of weeks later, the problem still hadn't been solved. "Shall we nominate an ending and play through it to see what it sounds like?" O'Brien said, impatiently. "What do you have in mind?" Yorke said. "D7, perhaps?" "O.K., let's try it."

On their days off, Radiohead dissolve into literate anarchy. They buzz with curiosity, pepper strangers with questions, digest the answers, and wander off on their own. On the day after the Bilbao show, they took a ramble around the city, and the city was caught off guard. One stop was the Guggenheim, where they had an unsuspecting tour guide named Maria. While Maria was still trying to muster everyone in one place, Colin began reciting facts about the structure: "The limestone had to be cut by a computer. Each curve has its own algorithm. I read an article somewhere. The A/C is fucking brilliant, man. Air pumps out of that vent way up there and goes all the way down here." When Colin arrived in front of Richard Serra's massive steel sculptures, he declared that one of the pieces had gone missing from its usual place. "This is wrong," he said. "There should be a second plate bisecting the first." Selway and O'Brien started making fun of him—"Can't have gone far"; "Call lost and found"—but Maria confirmed that, in fact, the sculptures had been rearranged. As Radiohead fanned out through the museum, clumps of fans in *Kid A* T-shirts followed at a respectful distance. The group slowly disintegrated, and Maria gave up. At the exit, she said sternly, "Not once this entire time have you all been together." Yorke smiled sympathetically and replied, "Not the first time, won't be the last."

The same day, the band had a meal at a restaurant called Etxebarri, in the hills above Bilbao. The conversation was an intelligent blur, jumping from high to low and back again. On one side of the table, Jonny was talking about twentieth-century classical music. "I've been listening to a CD of Berg's 'Lulu' Suite," he said, picking at a plate of lettuce. "I'm killing myself because I forgot to bring my Messiaen." Jonny is fascinated by Olivier Messiaen, the late French composer; it is because of Messiaen that he became interested in the ondes martenot, which is featured in many of the composer's works. "I heard the 'Turangalîla Symphony' when I was fifteen," Jonny went on, "and I became round-the-bend obsessed with it. I wish I could have met him or shaken his hand. I did get to meet his sister-in-law, the ondeiste Jeanne Loriod. I'm learning Messiaen's 'Trois Petites Liturgies' for a performance in London." Jonny also mentioned a meeting with Esa-Pekka Salonen, the music director of the Los Angeles Philharmonic, who wants Radiohead to write a work for him.

On the other side of the table, Yorke, whose meal consisted of a bowl of bean soup, started complaining about pop-music conglomerates. He and the rest of the band have become politically outspoken, protesting globalization and corporate capitalism. The previous night, he had dedicated "No Surprises"—which contains the lines "Bring down the government/They don't speak for us"—to George W. Bush. This summer, Radiohead have chosen to play a number of open-air venues—such as Liberty State Park, in Jersey City, where they are appearing on August 16th and 17th—because these sites have so far escaped the tentacles of an aggressive promotion company called S.F.X., whose parent corporation, Clear Channel, also operates more than a thousand radio stations.

"S.F.X. is a parasite that needs a host to feed on," Yorke said.

"It's effective only as long as it keeps growing," O'Brien added. "At some point, it will cease growing, and then its reason to exist will disappear."

"No," Yorke said, "it's a virus that's just going to keep spreading forever."

Chris Hufford, one of the band's managers, who has to negotiate with viruses on the phone, grew impatient. "This is reality, Thom," he said. "This is the marketplace we're in."

"No," Yorke replied, "the marketplace is where we sell records. This isn't the marketplace. It's an area of, I don't know, oversight."

"Come on," Hufford said, "it's capitalism, it's what we have to work with."

"Bollocks!"

"Capitalism!"

"Bollocks!" Yorke yelled. He got up in a mock huff to go to the bathroom. Colin looked up from his steak and gestured toward the wine in the middle of the table. "Brilliant!" he exclaimed. "Booze in the afternoon!"

That night, Radiohead got on a bus to go to their next gig, in the French village of Vaison-la-Romaine. They played a show at a magnificent Roman amphitheatre there, and then went to Verona, in Italy, where they performed for a crowd of fifteen thousand in the legendary Arena, displacing scenery for "Aida" onto the piazza. Along the way, they made on-the-fly recordings with Nigel Godrich, their young, wizardly producer, on assorted Apple PowerBooks; appeared on a popular BBC radio show called "Mark & Lard," where they were required to shout the phrase "Biggity-biggity-bong!"; greeted a radio-contest winner who hailed Yorke as "a genius" and "sincere"; and avoided some overzealous fans who hollered, "We have come all the way from Venezuela, give us your autograph!" even though they had French accents and were not from Venezuela. There were also quiet moments here and there, as when they sat in a hotel lobby reading the English papers, sun streaming on the marble, and seemed to be fulfilling Colin's notion of the band as "the E. M. Forster of rock."

Radiohead began at Abingdon School, a boys' school outside Oxford. Abingdon has a history dating back to the twelfth century, but it is not an élite bastion on the order of Eton or Winchester. Its students tend to come from the Thames Valley region, rather than from all over England, and many rely on scholarships. The members of Radiohead were born into ordinary middle-class families: Yorke's father was a chemical-equipment supplier; Jonny and Colin's father served in the Army. They were, basically, townies—the kids on the other side of the ancient walls. Even at Abingdon, they felt out of place. The headmaster of the school, Michael St. John Parker, cultivated a pompous manner that many alumni—not just Radiohead—remember less than fondly. Parker is still in charge, and has described the school spirit in these terms: "Competition is promoted, achievement is applauded, and individual dynamism is encouraged."

In schools of this kind, many students gravitate to the art, music, and drama departments, where the sense of discipline is looser. For Radiohead, the saving grace of Abingdon was an exceptional teacher named Terence Gilmore-James, who headed the music program. "I was a sort of leper at the time," Yorke recalled, "and he was the only one who was nice to me." Yorke was born with his left eye paralyzed; in his childhood, he endured a series of not entirely successful operations to correct it, and the oddity of his half-open eye made him a target for bullies. Tougher than he looked, he often fought back, but he preferred to disappear. "School was bearable for me because the music department was separate from the rest of the school," he said. "It had pianos in tiny booths, and I used to spend a lot of time hanging around there after school, waiting for my dad to come home from work." Other members of the band also studied with Gilmore-James and were encouraged by him. "When we started, it was very important that we got support from him," Colin said, "because we weren't getting any from the headmaster. You know, the man once sent us a bill, charging us for the use of school property, because we practiced in one of the music rooms on a Sunday."

The yen for freedom in Radiohead's sound owes a lot to Gilmore-James, who immersed his students in twentieth-century classical music, avant-garde music of the postwar era, classic jazz, and film scores. Once, he had the school orchestra perform Richard Rodney Bennett's score for *Murder on the Orient Express* while the film was playing. He left Abingdon in 1987 to devote himself to the legacy of his father-in-law, the Welsh composer Mansel Thomas, whose music he is editing for publication. "I watch over Radiohead much as I watch over my children," he said in a phone call. He spoke with the fastidiousness of a lifelong teacher, and yet his tone was enthusiastic rather than dogmatic. "They were all of them talented boys, in the sense that they had more than average abilities to think for themselves. I was of a different generation, and I did not always grasp what they were after, but I knew that they were serious. And they were delightful to be around, always getting carried away by their latest discoveries. Whenever I see them"—his voice became firm—"I tell them that they must continue to pursue their own original line."

In the schoolboy cadre of Radiohead, Yorke was the bossy one from the start. His very first words to Selway at rehearsal were "Can't you play any fucking faster?" The band's early songs were all over the map, sounding variously like the Smiths, R. E. M., Sonic Youth, and the Talking Heads, whose song "Radio Head" gave the group its name. (At first, they performed under the name On a Friday, but they wisely changed

223

their minds.) The strongest influence came from the Pixies, the incontestably great but never world-famous Boston band whose gritty, brainy songs, shaded soft and loud, also inspired Nirvana. Even as the boys wandered off to university, they got together over weekends, practicing, arguing, and searching for a style. In 1991, Hufford, the co-owner of an Oxford sound studio, came to hear them play, at a place called the Jericho Tavern, and was mesmerized by Yorke's dire energy onstage. He and his partner Bryce Edge produced a demo tape and signed on as managers. Colin, who was working at a record store, gave the tape to Keith Wozencroft, a sales rep for EMI, who moved to A. & R. shortly afterward and began to tout the band. They signed with EMI later that year.

"I was getting ready to quit EMI when these lads appeared," Carol Baxter, Radiohead's international record-company representative, recalled. "Bunch of disturbed consumptives, I thought. But they were ambitious and smart. At first, I had to hide my Radiohead paperwork behind the Tina Turner and Queensrÿche files, because my boss thought I was wasting my time. Then the call came in, from Israel, actually, saying that the band had a hit." Tim Greaves, Radiohead's longtime tour manager, commented on the band's overnight success. "The funny thing about Radiohead early on was that they were more famous abroad than in England," he said. "They'd go around in a van, playing in sweaty little clubs. Then they'd go to Israel and they were rock stars. Same in America. Then it was back to England, back to the van, back to the clubs. They had a good early introduction to the relativity of fame. Fame for this band is a holiday that lasts a few weeks."

Radiohead's ticket to fame was a song called "Creep." It became a worldwide hit in 1993, when grunge rock was at its height. The lyrics spelled out the self-lacerating rage of an unsuccessful crush: "You're so fucking special/I wish I was special/But I'm a creep." The music was modelled on Pixies songs like "Where Is My Mind?": stately arpeggios, then an electric squall. What set "Creep" apart from the grunge of the early nineties was the grandeur of its chords—in particular, its regal turn from G major to B major. No matter how many times you hear the song, the second chord still sails beautifully out of the blue. The lyrics may be saying, "I'm a creep," but the music is saying, "I am majestic." The sense of coiled power is increased by several horrible stabs of noise on Jonny Greenwood's guitar. Radiohead have stopped playing "Creep," more or less, but it still hits home when it comes on the radio. When Beavis of "Beavis and Butt-head" heard the noisy part, he said, "Rock!" But why, he wondered, didn't the song rock from beginning to end? "If they didn't have, like, a part of the song that sucked, then, it's like, the other part wouldn't be as cool," Butt-head explained.

"Creep," as Butt-head must have noticed, was the first of many Radiohead songs that used pivot tones, in which one note of a chord is held until a new chord is formed around it. (In the turn from G to B, the note B is the pivot point.) "Yeah, that's my only trick," Yorke said, when this was pointed out to him. "I've got one trick and that's it, and I'm really going to have to learn a new one. Pedals, banging away through everything." But a reliance on pedal tones and pivot tones isn't necessarily a limitation: the Romantic composers worked to death the idea that any chord could turn on a dime toward another. Yorke's "pedals" help give Radiohead songs a bittersweet, doomy taste. ("Airbag," for example, being in A major, ought to be a bright thing, but the intrusion of F and C tones tilts the music toward the minor mode. "Morning Bell" sways darkly between A minor and C-sharp minor.) It's a looser, roomier kind of harmony than the standard I-IV-V-I, and it gives the songs a distinct personality. It also helps sell records: whether playing guitar rock or sampling spaced-out electronica, Radiohead affix their signature.

Through the years, many bands have thrown bits and pieces of jazz and classical into their mix. The Beatles were by far the best at this kind of genre assimilation. Lesser psychedelic and prog-rock bands turned orchestral crescendos and jazz freak-outs into another brand of kitsch. But Radiohead's classical complexity isn't pasted on the surface; it's planted at the core. If you did a breakdown of the music, you'd find the same harmonic DNA everywhere. Another trademark is the band's use of musical space. Riffs are always switching registers, bouncing from treble to bass, breaking through the ceiling or falling through the floor. In "Just," from *The Bends*, the Greenwood brothers play octatonic scales that sprawl over four octaves; the effect is of music looming miles above you.

There are times when Radiohead seem to be practicing a new kind of classical music for the masses. In the sessions for *Kid A* and *Amnesiac*, which began in 1999 and dragged on for a year and a half, their sound became bewitchingly intricate. On "Pyramid Song," for example, a string section played glissando harmonics, a texture that Stravinsky's "Firebird" made famous, while Selway laid on a shuffling rhythm that defies description, because, as he said, "there is no time signature." On "Dollars & Cents," O'Brien used a pedal to bend a chord from major to minor and back again. For "Like Spinning Plates," Yorke learned the vocal line of an unused song backward and made up new words while driving around in his car. The guitarists set aside their instruments for a while and taught themselves to use heaps of electronic equipment. In "Treefingers," on *Kid A*, O'Brien generated something that sounded a lot like Jonny's beloved Messiaen. Both albums were also heavily influenced by jazz, especially by Mingus, Alice Coltrane, and Miles Davis in his fusion phase.

Behind this creative frenzy, however, was an ongoing debate about the direction of the band. The five of them often have to thrash out issues among themselves: how to balance tours with family life; how to keep the media at bay; how, simply, to get along. In this case, Yorke was fed up with the kind of verse-and-chorus music Radiohead had made throughout the nineties, and not everyone else agreed. O'Brien, in particular, thought that the band should return to the kind of classic guitar rock that by the end of the decade had become an endangered species. "There was a lot of arguing," Nigel Godrich recalled. "People stopped talking to one another. 'Insanity' is the word. In the end, I think the debate was redundant, because the band ultimately kept doing what it has always done—zigzagging between extremes. Whenever we really did try to impose an aesthetic from the outside—the aesthetic being, say, electronic—it would fail. All the drama was just a form of procrastination. Next time, three weeks, and we're out."

Radiohead may change direction once again. Several songs on *Amnesiac* stand out for their straight-ahead pop appeal. "I Might Be Wrong" is all snarling guitars; "Knives Out" goes back to the clean-cut heartbreak of the Smiths. The ominously beautiful "Pyramid Song" could almost be a variation on "Swing Low, Sweet Chariot":

> I jumped in the river, what did I see?
> Black-eyed angels swam with me. . . .
> We all went to heaven in a little rowboat
> There was nothing to fear and nothing to doubt.

This is very much Yorke's song, and it sounds best when he performs it alone, on an upright piano. You notice that he sings from the chest, breathing through his phrases. You also notice the plain mystery of his piano chords. Laced with suspended tones, they hang mysteriously in the air, somewhere between serenity and sadness. "I bought a piano after *OK Computer*, at a time when picking up a guitar just didn't do anything for me at all," he says. "I bought a really flashy piano that I couldn't play at all. In true rock-star style." In fact, he gets a warm, mellow tone out of the piano, caressing rather than pounding the keys. He keeps his wrists high, as if Terence Gilmore-James were looking over his shoulder.

Yorke is the essential spark of the Radiohead phenomenon. Like all greatly gifted people, he is not always easy to be around. When a stranger approaches him, wanting unscheduled attention, he can be unsettlingly mute. He is, by his own admission, temperamental and chronically dissatisfied. But his fault-finding circles back to the music, which is why the other band members go along with it. When he is happy, it feels like history in the making. Curled up on a dressing-room sofa after a show, he comes across as warm, alert, and faintly mischievous. "It's nice when people talk to you as if you're a human being, rather than as if you'd just landed from another planet," he said. "We're fallible, this is fallible, sometimes we're shit, sometimes we're not. We want to kind of mellow it all out a bit. Just chill the fuck out." He grinned quickly, perhaps realizing that the last phrase was a contradiction in terms.

At the beginning of June, *Amnesiac* went on sale in the United States. There was mild Radiohead mania all over New York. The core audience was represented by Helen Weng, an eighteen-year-old from Long Island, who waited at the Virgin Megastore with her friend Melissa Torres to buy *Amnesiac* at a midnight sale. In her bag, she carried a letter from Thom Yorke, written in his own hand, with advice on how to make yourself happy. "It's good to know someone else has had the same feelings," she said, clutching the paper. Over at Fez, Justin Bond, the cross-dressing star of the scathingly brilliant cabaret duo Kiki & Herb, sang "Life in a Glasshouse," from *Amnesiac*, even though the record was not yet in the stores. He attributed it to "Rodeohead, a very exciting young English rock ensemble," and rendered it as a demented torch song, which it already mostly was.

Radiohead's appeal to a cross-section of the American public defies the untranslatability of English pop. Steve Martin, a publicist for the band, explained it this way: "Americans don't go for 'cheeky.' We like earnest." Radiohead may be cagey, but they are never cheeky, and they are massively earnest. They have worked hard in America, logging time in the middle of the country as well as on the coasts. They are noted in the music business for being polite and unproblematic. A French hotel reservation of theirs extravagantly requested, "Extra towels." One hotel doorman described them as "nice, sharp-witted, entertaining young men. Not trash-headed and stupored, as you might expect." Despite the fatigue of their last big tours, in 1997 and 1998, they were game for America this summer.

"Sure, the last tour was bloody awful," Ed O'Brien said, "but that was where we were at mentally, not a reaction to America. This place is just too huge to generalize about. When I was in college, I took six months off to ride around in Greyhound buses, and I got a sense of it." He was excited about playing at Red Rocks Amphitheatre, in the foothills of the Rockies. "Basically, we've had a fantasy scenario of reenacting U2 live at Red Rocks," he said. "We watched the video a million times when we were kids and know every frame. 'This song is not a rebel song!'" He lifted his fist and let out a soft roar. Fans who worry that Radiohead are losing touch with rock and roll can always look to this man, who enjoys the role of the guitar hero, even if he also sometimes kneels down in front of his samplers and molds the music into a smear of color.

Radiohead checked into a Denver hotel on June 19th. Fans descended on Red Rocks the following morning, squatting on a half-mile flight of steps that leads to the arena. Down at the bottom was a group of college students, from Pepperdine and the University of Colorado at Boulder. Their names were Elke Goldstein, Amber Hollingsworth, Matt Duffy, and Kendall Lux. "Radiohead is music for miserable people who were dropped on the floor when they were little," Amber explained. "I don't know about that," Elke said. "I mean, that's the reputation, but are we miserable?" Munching on carrots, they did not look miserable.

Matt delivered a critique of the band, speaking rapidly, as if from memory. "Thom is suffering from Bono syndrome," he said. "Getting political. What's he doing hanging out with Bono? What's Bono doing hanging out with presidents and the Pope? He's a rock singer, damn it! Here's the difference between U2 and Radiohead: U2 says, 'The world sucks, and we have to change it,' whereas Radiohead says, 'The world sucks and not much can be done about it. The world is lame, ridiculous.'" Elke rolled her eyes. "May-be," she said. Matt barreled on: "Their records are put out by EMI, a multinational conglomerate, so it's hard to see how they can attack capitalism from that position. *Kid A* and *Amnesiac*? Ambient blueprints for music we haven't quite heard yet. Thom listens to Brian Eno, Aphex Twin, the whole Warp Records back catalogue. 'Packt Like

Sardines'—what's that, one pattern stuck in a groove? But when they play it we're all going to go, 'Yeah!' No one can really say why they like them. Yet here we are."

In a matter of minutes, Matt had summed up everything that has been written about Radiohead in the past few years. Rock critics, like adolescent fans, have feisty friendships with the bands they admire, lacing hero worship with contempt. It's one thing to hear this from a college student; it's another to read it in cold print, in all its meandering incoherence. If some magazines didn't use rating systems, you would have no idea what the reviewers thought. The magazine Q, for example, gave *Amnesiac* four stars and then called it "numb, petty, desolate." *SPIN* wrote, "They're just trying to get home in one piece, life is but a dream. Fa fa fa. Blip blip." Rating: 7 out of 10. Some of the criticism has been peculiarly personal, especially in England. *Melody Maker* once said that Yorke was "marked for destruction" and suggested that he might end up killing himself, like Kurt Cobain. As a result, the singer has developed an aversion to English rock writers, and they, in turn, have goaded him at every turn. Ill feelings all around have led to unrecognizable profiles in which the band seems to be composed of curmudgeons.

At Red Rocks, Radiohead agreed to sit down for a rare collective interview with a journalist. A brave young MTV correspondent named Gideon Yago showed up to interrogate them. A Queens native who started working at MTV at the age of twenty-one, Yago has loved Radiohead since his teens. He had a sheaf of notes on his clipboard, including a chart of the band members' personalities. O'Brien and Selway struck him as "the sensible ones"; the Greenwood brothers he pegged as "will eat you alive." He wasn't sure what to make of Yorke. His impressions were based largely on a Radiohead tour documentary, "Meeting People Is Easy," which came out in 1998. This unpleasant film was a kind of counterstrike against the music press, recording scores of pointless interviews with dead-tired members of the band. During one of them, Colin seemed ready to lapse into a coma. "I don't want to be just another dolt with a microphone," Yago said. "Like the guy in the movie who asks Thom if he got to talk to Calvin Klein."

Yago knew a lot about music and a lot about Radiohead, but when the cameras rolled he elected to keep much of his knowledge hidden. "Remember," his producer, Liane Su, told him, "you're not an expert, you're just a fan." The fans wanted to know whether the band thought it was experimenting too much, why *Kid A* and *Amnesiac* hadn't been released as a double album, what all the songs on *Amnesiac* meant. Radiohead did snap at Yago once or twice, as when he characterized *Amnesiac* as "a collection of outtakes from the *Kid A* sessions," and Selway shot back, "Try again!" But the mood was relaxed, for the most part. Yago got them all to laugh when he introduced a question from a so-called "Stanley from Coney Island," which read, "How do you guys feel about the fact that bands like Travis, Coldplay, and Muse are making a career sounding exactly like your records did in 1997?" Yorke cupped his hand around his mouth and called out, "Good luck with *Kid A*!" When the interview was over, Yago looked shell-shocked but relieved. "That was relatively painless," the journalist said, gulping down a Molson.

Last month, Radiohead returned home to play in South Park, a broad meadow outside the center of Oxford. It was a drizzly day, and the towers of the university were gray lumps in the distance. The event was a kind of mini-festival, mostly given over to performances by bands that Radiohead admired. Like other summer festivals, it had kebab stands, beer huts, and T-shirt booths. Forty-four thousand fans, mostly in their teens and twenties, sat on the lawn. After a few hours, the grass was carpeted with plastic-foam cups, each one displaying the *Amnesiac* logo. To an outsider, it might have seemed like just another messy rock show.

It wasn't. At about four o' clock, Humphrey Lyttelton, the eighty-year-old jazz trumpeter, appeared onstage. After a few words of introduction, he and his band launched into a deft set of Armstrong and Ellington numbers. A guy in a "Blur: Are Shite" T-shirt shouted, "You're great!" Next up was Sigur Rós, a group of Icelandic musicians, who play a kind of mystic-minimalist rock that builds to climaxes over five- and ten-minute spans. In the half-mile-long line of people who were shuffling toward the "Alcoholic Fresh Juices" stand, every other face was lost in wonder at the gentle power of the chords. South Park had been overtaken by the Radiohead ethic—a love of far-flung sounds, a knack for sinuous juxtapositions, a faith in the audience's ability to take it all in.

Something about Radiohead inspires a disorienting kind of hope. Unlike so many professional cynics in the business, these musicians believe that their art can go still higher. They have promoted dozens of lesser-known, musically inventive acts, including Autechre, the Beta Band, Clinic, Kid Koala, Lali Puna, Low, Sparklehorse, and, of course, Christoph de Babalon. They have also boosted favorite authors, helping to sell thousands of copies of Naomi Klein's anti-globalization screed *No Logo*. The artists who appear on this roster have little or nothing in common, and that is what they have in common: they are a funky clamor of voices, not a line of products. Such guerrilla marketing is, in the end, a form of politics—a protest against the growing sameness of the cultural landscape. The sheer cussedness of the enterprise is amazing to behold. The loudest protest comes in Radiohead's own songs, which, next to the white noise of prefab pop, sound like the music of a hidden world, hymns from a sunken cathedral.

"Lots of really talented artists are being thrown by the wayside," Yorke had said during the American tour. "They are not being given the time of day, because they're not doing things that fit the moment. Madmen with machetes are chopping away at the wood—any wood, deadwood, doesn't matter. You want to slap people and say, 'Why don't you go back and look at all the beautiful things that have been made in the music business and realize that you have to have faith in people?' In the long run, the industry wants to make money, but if a company wants to make money then it has to take a risk. These people don't take risks. They make quick money and then that's it. And the world isn't a nicer place for it. What really makes me fucking spit blood is when people in the industry start complaining about how there's no talent around. I know it's there and you know it's there. But you are too shit scared to do anything about it."

229

Radiohead came onto the South Park stage at eight-thirty. It was not the most flawless show of the past few weeks, but it may have been the most intense. Yorke's voice glowed with emotion. If Terence Gilmore-James had been there, he would have been happy; you could hear how Radiohead's storm of sound was centered on a singing line. During "How to Disappear Completely," a drenching rain began to fall. The crowd, religiously attentive, stayed in place. Yorke appeared alone for the last number, and hit a few plangent chords. His instrument went dead. "Es ist kaputt, ja?" he said. "I have another idea." The others came back onstage, and together they launched into the familiar strains of "Creep," which had gone unplayed since 1998. G major wheeled majestically into B. Jonny made his Beavis-and-Butt-head noise. Yorke sang, "What the hell am I doing here?"

Afterward, in the dressing room, Yorke looked happy. "Don't know if you could tell," he said to Colin's wife, Molly, "but I was in tears for the last part of it." Then the perfectionist in him reawakened. "Horrible diesel smell coming from somewhere," he said.

The next day, Colin invited some friends over for brunch. He and Molly live in a semidetached house on an Oxford side street. This was the beginning of a three-week holiday for the band, and Colin faced the prospect of having nothing to do. "We might go to a movie," he said, as if he were going to the moon. He picked through some LPs and CDs, putting on Brad Mehldau. When someone asked him if he had got a sense of the crowd at South Park—it may have been the largest public gathering in the thousand-year history of Oxford—he rubbed his eyes and smiled. "'Fraid not," he replied. "I was too busy looking at Phil's calves. That's where the beats are."

JOHN JEREMIAH SULLIVAN ON AXL ROSE

The Final Comeback of Axl Rose*

(I)

He is from nowhere. I realize that sounds coyly rhetorical—in this day and age, it's even a boast, right? Socioeconomic code for *I went to a second-tier school and had no connections and made all this money myself.*

Yeah, I don't mean it that way. I mean he is from nowhere. Given the relevant maps and a pointer, I think I could convince even the most exacting minds that when the vast and blood-soaked jigsaw puzzle that is this country's regional scheme coalesced into more or less its present configuration after the Civil War, somebody dropped a piece, which left a void, and they called the void Central Indiana. I'm not trying to say there's no there there. I'm trying to say there's no there. Think about it; let's get systematic on it. What's the most nowhere part of America? The Midwest, right? But once you get into the Midwest, you find that each of the different nowherenesses has laid claim to its own somewhereness. There are the lonely plains in Iowa. In Michigan there is a Gordon Lightfoot song. And Ohio has its very blandness and averageness, faintly comical, to cling to. All of them have something. And now I invite you to close your eyes, and when I say "Indiana" . . . blue screen, no? And we are speaking only of Indiana generally, which includes Southern Indiana, where I grew up, and Northern Indiana, which touches a Great Lake. We have not even narrowed it down to Central Indiana. *Central* Indiana? That's like, "Where are you?" "I'm nowhere." "Go there." And when I asked Jeff Strange, a morning-rock deejay in Lafayette, how he thought about this part of the world—for instance, did he think of it as the South? after all, it's a Klan hot spot (which I am inclined to read as a somewhat desperate affectation); or did he think of it as the Midwest or what—you know what he told me? He goes, "Some people here would call it 'the region.'"

That's where he's from.

William Bruce Rose Jr.; William Bruce Bailey; Bill Bailey; William Rose; Axl Rose; W. Axl Rose.

That's where he's from. Bear that in mind.

(II)

On May 15, he came out in jeans and a black leather jacket and giant black sunglasses, all lens, that made him look like a wasp-man. We had been waiting—I don't really

---

*Sullivan, John Jeremiah. *Pulphead*, New York: Farrar, Straus and Giroux, 2011. Reprinted with permission.

know how to calculate how long we'd been waiting. It was the third of the four comeback shows in New York, at the Hammerstein Ballroom. The doors had opened at seven o'clock. The opening act had been off by eight thirty. It was now after eleven o'clock. There'd already been fights on the floor, and it didn't feel like the room could get any tenser without some type of event. I was next to a really nice woman from New Jersey, a hairdresser, who told me her husband "did pyro" for Bon Jovi. She kept text-messaging one of her husband's friends, who was "doing pyro" for this show, and asking him, "When's it gonna start?" And he'd text-message back, "We haven't even gone inside." I said to her at one point, "Have you ever seen a crowd this pumped up before a show?" She goes, "Yeah, they get this pumped up every night before Bon Jovi." I didn't want to report that last part, but in the post-James Frey era, you have to watch your topknot.

Then he was there. And apologies to the nice woman, but people do not go that nuts when Bon Jovi appears. People were: Going. Nuts. He is not a tall man—I doubt even the heels of his boots (red leather) put him at over five feet ten. He walked toward us with stalking, cartoonish pugnaciousness. I feel like all anybody talks about with Axl anymore is his strange new appearance, but it is hard to get past the unusual impression he makes. To me he looks like he's wearing an Axl Rose mask. He looks like a man I saw eating by himself at a truck stop in Monteagle, Tennessee, at two o'clock in the morning about twelve years ago. He looks increasingly like the albino reggae legend Yellowman. His mane evokes a gathering of strawberry red intricately braided hempen fibers, the sharply twisted ends of which have been punched, individually, a half inch into his scalp. His chest hair is the color of a new penny. With the wasp-man sunglasses and the braids and the goatee, he reminds one of the monster in *Predator*, or of that monster's wife on its home planet. When he first came onto the scene, he often looked, in photographs, like a beautiful, slender, redheaded 20-year-old girl. I hope the magazine will run a picture of him from about 1988 so the foregoing will seem a slightly less creepy observation and the fundamental spade-called-spade exactitude of it will be laid bare. But if not, I stand by it. Now he has thickened through the middle—muscly thickness, not the lard-ass thickness of some years back. He grabs his package tightly, and his package is huge. Only reporting. Now he plants his feet apart. "You know where you are?" he asks, and we bellow that we do, we do know, but he tells us anyway. "You're in the jungle, baby," he says, and then he tells us that we are going to die.

He should be pleased, I think, not only at the extreme way that we are truly freaking out to see him but also at the age range on view: There are hipsters who were probably born around the time *Appetite* got released, all the way up to aging heads who've handed in their giant rock hair for grizzled rattails, with plenty of microgenerations in between. But why should I even find this worth remarking? The readers of *Teen* magazine, less than one year ago, put him at number two (behind "Grandparents") on the list of the 100 Coolest Old People ... Axl Rose, who hasn't released a legitimate recording in thirteen years and who, during that time, turned into an almost Howard

Hughes-like character—ordering in, transmitting sporadic promises that a new album, inexplicably titled *Chinese Democracy*, was about to drop, making occasional, startling appearances at sporting events and fashion shows, things like that—looking a little feral, looking a little lost, looking a little like a man who's been given his first day's unsupervised leave from a state facility. Now he has returned. The guitarists dig in, the drummer starts his I-Am-BUil-DINg-UP-*TO-THE!*-**VERSE!** pounding section, and although it may give away certain deficiencies of taste on my part, I must say: The sinister perfection of that opening riff has aged not a day.

There's only one thing to do, and you can feel everybody doing it: comparing this with the MTV thing in 2002. If you've seen that, you may find a recounting here of its grotesqueries de trop, but I say, never forget. About the guitar player Buckethead. About the other guitar player. About Axl's billowing tentlike football jersey or the heartbreaking way he aborted his snaky slide-foot dance after only a few seconds on the stage projection, like, "You wanna see my snaky dance? Here, I'll do my snaky dance. Oh shit, I think I just had a small stroke. Run away." Or the audible gasp for oxygen on the second "knees" in *Sh-na-na-na-na-na-na-nana-na-na-na knees, kn*[gasp!]*ees.* The running and singing that came more and more to resemble stumbling and squawking as the interminable minutes groaned by. The constant, geriatric-seeming messing with the earpiece monitor. I'll stop. My point is, it's different tonight. For one thing, these guys can handle or choose to handle Slash's parts. Buckethead has been replaced by a guy called Bumblefoot (again, reporting), and Bumblefoot can shred. So can Robin Finck, formerly of Nine Inch Nails. Remember those experiments where they shot up spiders with acid? If they'd shot up storks instead, and one of the storks had broken loose and dressed in womany wizard's clothing and learned how to play guitar, that'd be Robin Finck (but then, all extremely tall people are inherently misshapen). Listen, these guys aren't fake-booking, like happened on MTV. Everything's note for note. And although we could get into the whole problem of virtuosity as it applies to popular music—namely, that for some reason people who can play *anything* will, nine times out of ten, when asked to make something up, play something terrible—still, if you mean to replace your entire band one instrument at a time and tell them, "Do it like this," you'll be wanting to find some monster players.

The whole arc of the show has this very straightforward plot, and I hope my crudity is in the service of truth-telling here: It's a battle between the dissonance of seeing all these guys who were not in Guns N' Roses jumping around with Axl and playing Guns N' Roses songs—between the off-putting and even disturbing dissonance of that—and the enduring qualities of the songs themselves. The outcome will determine whether tonight was badass or "Sort of sad, but it's Axl, y'all." What happened? Well, call me a twisted fanboy, but I thought he won. His voice is back, for starters. He was inhabiting the notes. And his dancing—I don't quite know how to say this. It has matured. From the beginning, he's been the only indispensable white male rock dancer of his generation, the only one worth imitating in mockery. I consider the moment in the "Patience" video when he does slow-motion snaky slide-foot dance while letting his hands float down as if they were feathers in an airless room—one fleeting near-pause in their descent for each note that Slash emphasizes in his transition to the coda—the greatest white male rock dance moment of the video age. What Axl does is lovely, I'm sorry. If I could, I would be doing that as I walk to the store. I would wake up and dance every morning like William Byrd of Westover, and that would be my dance. And while I cannot say he is dancing as well tonight as he used to, that so fluidly are his heels gliding out and away from his center they look each to have been tapped with a wand that absolved them of resistance and weight, and although he does at particular moments remind one of one's wasted uncle trying to "do his Axl Rose" after a Super Bowl party, he is nevertheless acquitting himself honorably. He is doing *dammit just dropped a bowling ball on my foot* spin-with-mike-stand dance; he is doing *prance sideways with mike stand like an attacking staff-wielding ritual warrior* between-verses dance. And after each line he is gazing at the crowd with those strangely startled yet fearless eyes, as though we had just surprised him in his den, tearing into some carrion.

(III)

VERY-NEAR-VERBATIM exchange with my wife, Mariana, June 27, 2006:

HER: What?

ME: Oh, my God. Axl just bit a security guard's leg in Sweden. He's in jail.

HER: Is that gonna affect your interview with him?

ME: No, I don't think they ever really considered letting me talk to him . . . Biting somebody on the leg, though—it forces you to picture him in such a, like a, disgraced position.

HER: Does anybody help Axl when that happens?

(IV)

I'd been shuffling around a surprisingly pretty, sunny, newly renovated downtown Lafayette for a couple of days, scraping at whatever I could find. I saw the house where he grew up. I looked at his old yearbook pictures in the public library. Everyone had his or her Axl story. He stole a TV from that house there. Here's where he tried to ride his skateboard on the back of a car and fell and got road rash all up his arm. He came out of this motel with a half-naked woman and some older guys were looking at her and one of 'em threw down a cigarette, not meaning anything by it, but Axl freaked out and flipped 'em off and they beat the crap out of him. Hard to document any of this stuff. Still, enough Wanted On Warrant reports exist for Axl's Indiana years to lend credence to the claim that the city cops and county troopers pretty much felt justified, and technically speaking were justified, in picking him up and hassling him whenever they spotted him out. One doubts he left the house much that they didn't spot him, what with the long, fine, flowing red hair. Must have been sweet to be Axl.

I went to the city cops. They've mellowed along with the town. In fact, they were friendly. They found and processed the negatives of some heretofore unknown mug shots for me, from '80 and '82, the latter of which (the one where he's shirtless) is an anonymous American masterpiece. Then the ladies in the records department rummaged some and came back with this report, which I've never seen mentioned in any of the bios or online or anything. It's written by an officer signing himself "1—4." I took it back to the Holiday Inn and spent the rest of the afternoon reading. Let's call it The Sheidler Incident. It begins:

FULL NAME: BAILEY, WILLIAM BRUCE . . .
ALIASES: BILL BAILEY . . .
CURRENT PLACE OF EMPLOYMENT: SELF EMPLOYED—BAND
CHARGE: W[ANTED]O[N]W[ARRANT]BATTERY . . .
AGE: 18; **HEIGHT:** 5'9"; **WEIGHT:** 149
HAIR: RED; **EYES:** GRN; **BUILD:** SLENDER; **COMPLEXION:** FAIR . . .

Here's how it all went down that day—allegedly. I'm about to cherry-pick the pivotal bits. A little kid named Scott Sheidler was riding his bike in front of an older kid named Dana Gregory's house. He made skid marks on the sidewalk. Dana Gregory ran out, picked Scott up under the armpits, kicked over his bike, and ordered the boy TO GET ON HIS HANDS AND KNEES AND SCRUB THE SKID MARKS OFF THE SIDEWALK. The kid went squealing to his old man, Tom Sheidler. Tom Sheidler went to Gregory and asked if it was true, what Scotty had said. Dana Gregory said, "YES AND I'M GOING TO BEAT THE FUCK OUT OF YOU." The mom, Marleen, ran up to the scene and began to shout. Around the same time, BILL BAILEY appeared, red, green, slender, and fair. And here I need to let the report take over, if only temporarily, as I can't begin to simulate its succinctness or authority:

M. Sheidler stated that BAILEY was also arguing with SHEIDLER and that he was using the "F" WORD in front of her kids. M. SHEIDLER stated that she went up to BAILEY and pointed her finger at BAILEY and told him not to use the "F" WORD in front of her kids. M. SHEIDLER stated that BAILEY, who has a SPLINT ON HIS ARM, then struck her on the arm and neck with the splint. I looked at M. SHEIDLER and could see some RED MARKS on her ARM and NECK which could have been made by being struck.

This matter of which hand it was subsumes the narrative for a stretch. Marleen Sheidler says "with the SPLINT," and little Scott says "with a SPLINT," but Dana Gregory's younger brother CHRIS 15 says "with the opposite hand that his SPLINT is on" (adding that Bailey struck Sheidler in response to "SHEIDLER STRIKEING *[sic]*" him). Bill Bailey himself then goes on to say that he "struck M. SHEIDLER in the FACE with his LEFT HAND the hand with out the SPLINT." Once again, this only after "MARLEEN SHEIDLER struck him in the face" (though seconds earlier, by his own admission, he'd told her "to keep her fucking brats at home"). The story ends with a strangely affecting suddenness: "BAILEY stated SHEIDLER THEN JUMPED AT him and fell on his face, he then left and went home ..."

The thing I couldn't stop wondering as I read it over was: Why were they so freaked out about the skid marks? Is making skid marks on the sidewalk a bad thing to do? It makes me think I spent half my childhood inadvertently infuriating my entire neighborhood.

(V)

Local Lafayette morning rock deejay Jeff Strange, on Axl's extremely brief but long-reported fisticuffs with the diminutive and seemingly gentle designer of mall clothes Tommy Hilfiger; actually, "fisticuffs" is strong—accounts suggest that the fight consisted mostly of Hilfiger slapping Axl on the arm many times, and photos show Axl staring at Hilfiger with an improbable fifty-fifty mixture of rage and amused disbelief, like, 'Should I hurt it?':

"Man, I saw that, and I thought, That is *straight* Lafayette."

(VI)

I found Dana Gregory. I called his stepmom. He's Axl's oldest friend and worked for him at one time in L.A., after Guns had gotten big. When I sat down at the table in the back-patio area of a pub-type place called Sgt. Preston's, he had sunglasses on. When he pushed them up into his bushy gray hair, he had unnervingly pale mineral-blue eyes that had seen plenty of sunrises. Sunrises surrounded by laughing dolphins and swirly, twirly pinwheels. He'd been there. You knew it before he even spoke. He'd done a spectacular amount of crazy shit in his life, and the rest of his life would be spent remembering and reflecting on that shit and focusing on taking it day by day. The metamorphosis of Bill, the friend of his youth, in whose mother's kitchen he ate breakfast every morning, his Cub Scouts buddy (a coin was tossed: Bill would be Raggedy Ann in the parade; Dana, Raggedy Andy), into—for a while—the biggest rock star on the planet, a man who started riots in more than one country and dumped a supermodel and duetted with Mick Jagger and told *Rolling Stone* he'd recovered memories of being sodomized by his stepfather at the age of 2, a man who took as his legal name and made into a household word the name of a band—Axl—that Gregory was once in, on bass, and that Bill was never even in ... This event had appeared in Gregory's life like a supernova to a prescientific culture. What was he supposed to do with it? I found him intensely compelling.

I said, "Do you call him Bill or Axl?"

He smiled: "I call him Ax."

"Still talk to him much?"

"Haven't talked to him since *1992*. We had sort of a falling-out."

"Over what?"

He looked away. "Bullshit." Then, after a few pulls and drags, "It might have been over a woman."

He was nervous, but nervous in the way that any decent person is when you sit down in front of him with a notebook and are like, "I have to make a two-thirty flight. Can you tell me about the heaviest things in your life? And order more spinach-'n'-artichoke dip. I can expense it."

He finished beers quickly. He used, repeatedly, without the slightest selfconsciousness, one of my favorite American idioms—"*Right* on," spoken quickly and with the intonation a half octave higher on "Right," to mean not "That's correct" or "Exactly" but simply "Yes," as in "Hey, you like to party?" "*Right* on."

"Tell me about L.A.," I said. "You said you were working for him out there. What kind of stuff?"

"Fixing shit that he broke," Gregory said.

"Did he break a lot of shit?" I said.

"His condo had these giant mirrors going all around it. And every now and then, he'd take that spaceman statue they give you when you win an award on MTV and smash up the mirrors with it. Well, he slept till four o'clock in the afternoon every day. Somebody had to let the guy in when he came to fix the mirrors. Shit like that."

He told me another L.A. story, about the time Axl picked up Slash's beloved albino boa constrictor and it shat all over Axl. And Axl had on some expensive clothes. He got so mad he wanted to hurt the snake. He was cussing at it. But Slash picked up his guitar—here Gregory imitated a tree-chopping backswing pose—and said, "Don't. Hurt. My. Snake." Axl backed off.

I guess we sat there a pretty long time. He has four children and four grandchildren. When I said he seemed young for that (can you imagine Axl with four grandchildren?), he said, "Started young. Like I was saying, there was a lot of *experimentation*." His ex-wife, Monica Gregory, also knew Axl. She gave him his first P.A. Gregory said he talks to her only once a year, "when I have to." He said what he wants is to lower the level of dysfunction for the next generation. He told me about how he and Axl and Monica and their group of friends used to go to a park in Lafayette after dark, Columbian Park—"We ruled that place at night"—and pick the lock on the piano case that was built into the outdoor stage and play for themselves till the small hours. I'd wandered around Columbian Park. It's more or less across the street from where those boys grew up. Not twenty feet from the stage, there's a memorial to the sons of Lafayette who "made the supreme sacrifice in defense of our country," and it includes the name of William Rose, probably Axl's great-great-great-grandpa, killed in the Civil War, which I suppose was fought in defense of our country in some not quite precise, rather abstract way. And now, as Gregory talked, I thought about how weird it was, all those years of Axl probably reading that name a hundred times, not making anything of it, not knowing that it was his own name—he who one day, having discovered his original name while going through some of his mother's papers, would sing, *I don't need your Civil War* and ask the question *What's so civil about war, anyway?*

Back then, Gregory said, Axl played all kinds of stuff. He mentioned Thin Lizzy, which you don't hear done much anymore. "But the only time I ever really heard him sing was in the bathroom. He'd be in there for an hour doing God knows what. Prancing around like a woman, for all I know."

"So, what is there of Lafayette in his music, do you think?"

"The anger, man. I'd say he got that here."

"He used to get beat up a lot, right?" (More than one person had told me this since I'd come to town.)

"*I* beat him up a lot," Gregory said. "Well, I'd win one year, he'd win the next. One time we was fighting in his backyard, and I was winning. My dad saw what was going on and tried to stop it, but his mom said, 'No, let 'em fight it out.' We always hashed it out, though. When you get older, it takes longer to heal."

It was awkward for me, trying incessantly to steer the conversation back toward the Sheidler business without being too obvious about it. Did he honestly have no memory of the fracas? He kept answering elliptically. "I remember the cops wanted to know who'd spray-painted all over the street," he said, smiling again. "The night he left for L.A., he wrote, 'Kiss my ass, Lafayette. I'm out of here.' I wish I'd taken a picture of that."

Finally, I just grew sort of exasperated and said, "Mr. Gregory, you can't possibly not remember this. Listen: You. A kid with a bike. Axl and a woman got into a fight. He had a splint on his arm."

"I can tell you how he got the splint," he said. "It was from holding on to an M-80 too long. We thought they were pretty harmless, but I guess they weren't, 'cause it 'bout blew his fucking hand off."

"But why were you so mad about the skid marks in the first place?" I asked.

"My dad was in construction. Still is. That's what I do. It's Gregory and Sons—me and my brother are the sons. Mostly residential concrete. My brother, Chris" (this was little CHRIS GREGORY 15, I realized, from the report, the one who probably spared Axl a battery charge by corroborating the assertion that M. SHEIDLER had struck first), "he's dead now. He was 39. A heart thing. My dad still can't bring himself to get rid of the 'Sons.' Anyway, see, we poured that sidewalk. He'd get so pissed if he saw it was scuffed up—'Goddammit, you know how hard it is to get that off?' He'd think we done it and beat our ass. So, I saw [little Scott Sheidler's handiwork], and I said, 'No, I don't think that's gonna do.'"

That was all. I couldn't get too many beats into any particular topic with Gregory before his gaze would drift off, before he'd get pensive. I started to get the feeling that this—his being here, his decision to meet with me—was *about* something, that we had not yet gotten around to the subject he was here to discuss.

"You know," he said, "I've never talked to a reporter before. I've always turned down requests."

"Why'd you agree to this one?" I asked.

"I wasn't going to call you back, but my dad said I should. You oughta thank my dad. My son said, 'Tell him what an asshole that guy was, Dad.' I said, 'Ah, he knows all that shit, son.'"

"Is it that you feel it's been long enough, and now you can talk about all that stuff?"

"Shit, I don't know. I figure maybe he'll see the article and give me a call. It's been a long time. I'd really love just to talk to him and find out what he's really been into."

"Do you still consider him a friend?" I said.

"I don't know. I miss the guy. I love him."

We were quiet for a minute, and then Gregory leaned to the side and pulled out his wallet. He opened it and withdrew a folded piece of white notepaper. He placed it into my hand, still folded. "Put that in your story," he said. "He'll know what it means." I went straight to the car after the interview and remembered about the note only when I was already on the plane. Written on it in pencil were a couple of lines from "Estranged," off *Use Your Illusion II*:

BUT EVERYTHING WE'VE EVER KNOWN'S HERE.

I NEVER WANTED IT TO DIE.

(VII)

Axl has said, "I sing in five or six different voices that are all part of me. It's not contrived." I agree. One of them is an unexpectedly competent baritone. The most important of the voices, though, is Devil Woman. Devil Woman comes from a deeper part of Axl than do any of the other voices. Often she will not enter until nearer the end of a song. In fact, the dramatic conflict between Devil Woman and her sweet, melodic yang—the Axl who sings such lines as *Her hair reminds me of a warm, safe place* and *If you want to love me, then darling, don't refrain* and *Sometimes I get so tense*—is precisely what resulted in Guns N' Roses' greatest songs. A lot of people will try to convince you that the band's street-tough image and attitude are what made them so massive. Of course, that's foolish. The "media" adore street-tough image and attitude and, via a curious circular maneuver, will frequently work to convince you that street-tough image and attitude are the reason you love some band, but you, the people of the world, tend to buy 15 million copies of a debut album because it's chockablock with hits. G N' R wrote four or five untouchable pop songs, and that's why we're still talking about them—that's why the mere fact of Axl's mounting a comeback is newsworthy. You go, "Dude, speaking of *circular!* You're a widget in the whole tremendous machine that's trying to make it *seem* newsworthy!" YES AND I'M GOING TO BEAT THE FUCK OUT OF YOU.

Take "Sweet Child o' Mine," which, in my unassuming view, shares with the Wrens' "I've Made Enough Friends" the distinction of being the most perfectly achieved rock 'n' roll song of the past twenty years. It's not that you don't love it from the beginning, what with the killer riffs and the oddly antiquated-sounding chorus, yet a sword hangs over it. You think: This can't be everything. Come on—I mean, *Now and then when I see her face/It takes me away to that special place*? Then, around 5:04, she arrives. The song has veered minor-key by then, the clouds have begun to gather, and I never hear that awesome, intelligent solo that I don't imagine Axl's gone off somewhere at the start of it, to be by himself while his body undergoes certain changes. What I love is how when he comes back in, he comes in on top of himself ("five or six different voices that are all part of me"); he's not yet all the way finished with *I, I, I, I, I, I, I, I* when that fearsome timbre tears itself open. And what does she say, this Devil Woman? What does she always say, for that matter? Have you ever thought about it? I hadn't. "Sweet Child," "Paradise City," "November Rain," "Patience," they all come down to codas—Axl was a poet of the dark, unresolved coda—and to what do these codas themselves come down? *Everybody needs somebody. Don't you think that you need someone? I need you. Oh, I need you. Where do we go? Where do we go now? Where do we go? I wanna go. Oh, won't you please take me home?*

(VIII)

I know the collage number gets cute fast, but I beg you to indulge me in a personal-experience thing. It's about when I drove back to Indiana with my oldest friend, Trent. We'd grown up in the same small river town and both went off to school elsewhere at about the same time, so we romanticized our childhood haunts and playmates a little, the way you do. The summer before our senior year of high school, we made a sentimental journey home to drop in on everybody and see how each had fared. This is 1991, when *Use Your Illusion* came out. "Don't Cry" was on the radio all the time. It turned out to be one of the more colossally bleak afternoons of my life. To a man, we'd divided along class lines. Those of us who'd grown up in Silver Hills, where kids were raised to finish high school and go to college, were finishing high school and applying to colleges. Those who hadn't, weren't. And there were these two guys from our old gang, Brad Hope and Rick Sissy. Those aren't their real names, though their real names were just as strange. Their fathers were working-class—one drove a bus and the other a concrete truck; the latter couldn't read or write. But the public elementary where we met them was mixed in every sense. And there's something about that age, from 9 to 11—your personality has appeared, but if you're lucky you haven't internalized yet the idea that you're any different from anyone else, that there's a ladder in life.

We stopped by Ricky's house first. Ricky had been a kind of redneck genius, into everything. You know those ads in the back of comics that say you can make a hovercraft out of vacuum-cleaner parts? Ricky was the kid who made the hovercraft. And souped it up. He was taller and chubbier than the rest of us and had a high-pitched voice and used some kind of oil in his hair. Trent got into the University of

Chicago and wound up writing a 200-page thesis on the Munich Conference, and even he would tell you: Ricky was the smartest. One time Ricky and I were shooting pellet guns at cars in the small junkyard his father maintained as a sort of sideline. We were spiderwebbing the glass. All of a sudden, Ricky's dad, who had just been woken up from one of his epic diurnal naps, hollered from the window of his bedroom, "Ricky, you'd better not be shooting at that orange truck! I done sold the windshield on that." I'll never forget; Ricky didn't even look at me first. He just ran. Dropping the pistol at his feet, he ran into the forest. I followed. We spent the whole rest of the day up there. We found an old grave in the middle of a field. We climbed to the top of Slate Hill, the highest knob in our town, and Ricky gave me a whole talk on how slate formed, how it was and was not shale.

I remember the scared, ecstatic freedom of those hours in the woods. When Trent and I found Ricky, he was sitting alone in a darkened room watching a porn movie of a woman doing herself with a peeled banana. He said, "What the fuck is that thing on your head?" I was in a bandanna-wearing phase. This one was yellow. He said, "When I saw you get out of the car, I thought, Who the fuck is that? I 'bout shot you for a faggot." We asked him what was going on. He said he'd just been expelled from school, for trying to destroy one of the boys' restrooms by flushing lit waterproof M-80s down the toilets. Also, he'd just been in a bad jeep accident; his shoulder was messed up somehow. All scabbed over, maybe? This entire conversation unfolded as the woman with the banana worked away. Ricky's dad was asleep in the next room. Retired now. We told him we were headed over to Brad's next. He said, "I haven't seen Brad in a while. Did you hear he dorked a spook?" That's what he said: "dorked a spook."

Brad had a real mustache already. He'd always been an early bloomer. When we knew him well, he was constantly exposing himself. Once I watched him run around the perimeter of a campsite with his underpants at his ankles going, "Does this look like the penis of an 11-year-old?" And it did not. Brad used to plead with his mom to sing "Birmingham Sunday" for us, which she'd do, a cappella, in the kitchen. Now he was all nigger this, nigger that. Trent was dating a black girl in Louisville at the time. Neither of us knew how to behave. Brad must have noticed us squirming, because he looked at me at one point and said, "Ah, y'all probably got some good niggers in Ohio." That's where I was living. "We're fixin' to have a race war with the ones we got here," he said. He had dropped out of high school before they had a chance to expel him. It had been only four years since we'd been sleeping over at his house, doing séances and shit, and now we had no way to reach one another. A gulf had appeared. It opened the first day of seventh grade when some of us went into the "accelerated" program and others went into the "standard" program. By sheerest coincidence, I'm sure, this division ran perfectly parallel to the one between our respective parents' income brackets. God, if I could I'd drop lit waterproof M-80s down every "tracking" program in the country. I remember Ricky and I running into each other in the hallway the first day of seventh grade and with an awkwardness that we were far too young to handle, both being like, "Why aren't you in any of my classes?" When I think about it, I never saw those boys again, not after that day.

Axl got away. That's what I wanted to tell you.

(IX)

And then about three hours after I wrote that last sentence, I was sitting there thinking, Did he?

(X)

There were hundreds of blue flags draped along the south bank of the Nervión in Bilbao, and across the top of each it said GUNS N' ROSES. The flags were of Moorish blue, and they shook against a spotless sky that was only barely paler. Late that night, in the hills over the city, the band headlined a three-day festival, and the river valley echoed the sound so clearly, so helplessly, people in the old part of town could, if they understood English, make out the individual words, but for now Bilbao retained its slightly buttoned-up tranquillity and charm. There's a fountain next to the Guggenheim that fires bursts of water every four or five seconds, and the olive-skinned kids jump up and down in it. They just strip to their underpants and go wild, male and female, and to watch them at it was lovely. Can you imagine, in the center of some major American city, a bunch of 12-year-old girls in their panties capering in the water, their lank hair flinging arcs of droplets? Hard to say which would be greater, the level of parental paranoia or the actual volume of loitering creepy creepos. Here things seemed so sane. Axl and the boys hadn't landed yet. They were still in the air.

The district where they played is called Kobetamendi. It's high up, and from there you could see the city, the river, the spires, the flashing titanium scales of the museum. When it got dark, you could see the lights. When there aren't stages set up at Kobetamendi, it's just a large empty field with a road and, across the road, some modest farmhouses. As I reached the crest of the hill, a rap-rock band was playing. I don't "get," as they say, rap-rock, and I'm a person who's cultivated a taste for some fairly awful music. The justification for rap-rock seems to be that if you take really bad rock and put really bad rap over it, the result is somehow good, provided the raps are being barked by an overweight white guy with short hair and forearm tattoos. The women from those few little farmhouses had gathered at their fence; they leaned and mumbled and dangled their canes. One of them was one of the oldest-looking old people I have ever seen, with stiff white hair and that face, like the inside of a walnut shell, that only truly ancient women get. She and her friends were actually listening to the rap-rock, and part of me wanted to run over to them and assure them that after they died, there would still be people left in the world who knew how horrifying this music was, and that these people would transmit their knowledge to carefully chosen members of future generations, but the ladies did not appear worried. They were even laughing. I'm sure they remembered Gypsy circuses in that field in eighteen ninety something, and what was the difference, really?

Want to know how to get backstage at shows, peckerheads? Okay, I'm 'a tell you. First, find a Portuguese model. And we're not talking the kind of model who hiphop dances in halftime shows; we're talking the kind who gets flown to Tokyo for the day. She will have brought along two friends from Lisbon, but there will be a pass waiting for only one of them. Somebody forgot to forward *un correo electrónico*. Now, there will be two passes waiting for you, because when you first requested the passes, you thought you were bringing a photographer, but in the event, you've come alone. Stand and listen to her and her two friends be like, "What'll we doooo?" for a while. Choose your moment. Go up to her and say, "I couldn't help overhearing that you need another pass. I happen to have an extra. I even have an extra special-access badge I can give to your friend." At this point, the model will say, in the Spanish she turns out not to speak all that much better than you, "It's a miracle!" Next, she will get you stoned. This really happens! Her friend to whom you gave the pass will boast of being the owner of the third-largest collection of Axl Rose paraphernalia in the world, and the revelation that he intends to include your spare, mint-condition media badge in this collection will lead to levels of bonhomie and group fealty beyond your prior imagination, until finally, when the security guard on the back ramp leading up to the stage, who does not even make eye contact with the Portuguese model as she floats past him, puts his palm against your chest, as if to say, "Whoa—*that's* a little much," she will turn around briefly and say, "*Está conmigo.*" She will say this with about the level of nervousness and uncertainty with which she might say, to a maître d', "Smoking." Before you can thank her, you'll be watching Axl dance from such an inconceivable propinquity that if you were to bend your knees, thrust your hands forward, and leap, you would be on the front page of the entertainment section of *El País* the next day for having assaulted him in front of 25,000 people.

Jesus. I've been a *part* of plenty of virtual seas of screaming sweaty kids before, but to see one from the stage, from just above, to see *that* many thousand people shaping with their mouths some words you made up in your head one time while you were brushing your teeth (needless to say, I was trying to imagine I wrote them) ... it's heady. Two half notes followed by two quarter notes in immediate succession, followed by a beat of silence, that's the staccato rhythm of the chant: "Guns and RO-SES, Guns and RO-SES" ... Axl's pounding with the base of his mike stand on the stage in time to it. There's a kid with a beard who looks at you every ten minutes or so, puts his hands on his ears, and mouths the word "pyro." Then you're supposed to put your hands on your ears, because the explosion is about to take place ten feet away. Sometimes the kid forgets—he's busy—and then everyone goes "Aaaarrrgh!" and clutches rather than cups their ears.

There's a sort of shambling older dude next to me in a newsboy cap, with a guitar in his hands—a tech, I figure, or else someone who already knew about the Portuguese-model trick. Then he runs out onto the stage, and I'm like, "That's Izzy Stradlin."

Izzy, I'm convinced, is the reason the band sounds so much better than they did two months ago in New York. He started joining them for three or four songs the very next night and has been showing up periodically ever since. His presence—or to put it more accurately, the presence of another original member of the band—seems to have made the other guys feel more like they are Guns N' Roses and less like, as *El Diario Vasco* will put it tomorrow, "*una bullanguera formación de mercenarios al servicio del ego del vocalista*," which I'm pretty sure means something like "a noisy bunch of mercenaries in the service of the vocalist's ego."

(Cognates, you know.)

The Spanish press—man, they weren't kind. They said Axl was a "grotesque spectacle"; they called him "*el divo*" (I intend to steal that); they talked about the endless, Nigel Tufnel-esque "*solos absurdos*" that he makes each of the band members play, in an effort to get the audience to emotionally invest in the new lineup (it's true that these are fairly ill-advised, as has been the rock solo generally since Jimi died). One article says that "*Las fotos de Axl dan miedo*," which translates literally and, I think, evocatively as "The pictures of Axl give fear," "with his goatee that gives him the look of a Texas millionaire." In a crowning moment, they say that he has "the voice of a priapismic rooster." They say he demands his room be covered in Oriental carpets and that he not be required to interact with the other band members. That he arrived on a separate plane. They say security guards have been ordered never to look him in the eye. They say the other band members also hate one another and demand to be placed on different floors of the hotel. They say he's traveling with a tiny Asian guru named Sharon Maynard, "*alias Yoda*," and that he does nothing without her guidance, that she chooses the people he should hire by examining their faces. But mostly the Spaniards are fixated, as have been all the European media gangs on this tour, with the secret oxygen chamber into which he supposedly disappears during the shows and from which he emerges "*más fresco que una lechuga*"—fresher than a head of lettuce.

I cannot confirm or deny the oxygen thing, and it's hard to say whether the constant mentions of it in the press are evidence of its being real or just a sign that people are recycling the same rumor. The manager of a Hungarian band called Sex Action, which opened for G N' R, claims to have seen the device itself, but Hungarians make up tales like that for entertainment, and anyway, I heard people in the men's room at the Hammerstein being like, "Maybe he keeps an oxygen tank back there or something—ha ha!" trying to account for the way he kept bolting from the stage—*fleeing*, that's how it looked—not just between songs but during them as well.

What I can tell you, based on my privileged vantage point, is that there is a square cell entirely covered in black curtains just to the rear of stage left. You cannot see as much as a crack of light through the curtains, and I kept trying. Axl runs into this thing about fifteen times during the course of a show. Sometimes he emerges with a new costume on—makes sense—but sometimes he doesn't. Sometimes he goes in there when one of the guys is soloing or something—makes sense—but sometimes he goes in there at a moment when it's really weird and distracting *not* to have him onstage. I do not know whether Sharon Maynard is in this cell. I do not know what he does in there. If he's huffing reconstituted gas, I don't know whether it's in a Michael Jackson "This is good for me" sort of way or if he has a legitimate lung problem. I don't know anything about what goes on in the cell, only that it exists and that being in there is important to him. Past that, let's give the man some privacy. Crissakes, you people are Nosey Parkers.

I'm afraid that, overall, I can't agree with my fellow ink-stained wretches in the Old World. This show kicks much ass. He is sounding fuller and fuller. Every now and then the sound guy, just to make sure the board is calibrated, pushes his mike way up in the mix, and we hear nothing but Axl, and the notes are on. Nor is he fat. In fact, he looks pretty lithe. At one point, he puts on a rather skimpy T-shirt and sprints from one end of the stage to the other, and it is not a fat boy's sprint, with quivering man dugs, a sight from which one must turn away; it is the sprint of the cross-country runner he used to be. Dana Gregory told me Axl used to run everywhere. Just run and run. Dana Gregory said there was one time out west when G N' R played in a stadium that had a track around it, and Axl just started sprinting around the track during a song. When a security guard, believing him to be a crazed fan, tried to tackle him, Axl kicked the guy in the face. "That happened ten feet in front of me," Gregory said. And now here the bastard was, ten feet in front of *me*. The moon looked like she was yelling for help because some dark power was erasing her side. They brought out a piano so that he could do "November Rain," and the way they positioned the piano, he was facing me directly. Like we were sitting across a table from each other. This is as close as I ever got to him and as close as I ever wanted to get, truth be told. And what I noticed at this almost nonexistent remove was the peace in his features as he tinkled out the intro. Absolute peace. A warm slackness to the facial muscles way beyond what Botox can do, though I'm not saying it didn't contribute. His face was for now beyond the reach of whatever it is that makes him crazy.

After the final encore, he and the rest of the band ran down a ramp into the open door of a waiting van. Big, heavy men in black ran alongside them, like drill instructors. The van squealed away. Big, heavy black cars pulled out alongside the van. And then there was quiet. The Basque country.

(XI)

They were the last great rock band that didn't think there was something a tiny bit embarrassing or at least funny about being in a rock band. There are thousands of bands around at any given time that don't think rock is funny, but rarely is one of them good. With G N' R, no matter how sophisticated you felt yourself to be about pop music (and let's leave aside for now the paradoxical nature of that very cultural category), you couldn't entirely deny them. They were the first band I got to be *right* about with my elder brother. You know what I mean? I think it was that way for a lot of people in my generation. All my life, my brother had been forcefeeding me my musical taste—"Def Leppard sucks; listen to the Jam"—and now there was finally one band I wouldn't have to live down; and I recall the tiny glow of triumph, blended with fraternity, that I felt when one day he said, "Dude, you were right about Guns N' Roses. That's a good record." That was *Appetite*, of course. Things got strange after that. Now, I've read all this stuff that said Nirvana made Guns N' Roses obsolete. But Guns N' Roses were never made obsolete. They just sort of dimmed. What, you think if they got back together, with something even approximating the original lineup, and put out a record with, let's say, one good radio song on it, the record wouldn't sell a jillion copies? I saw that show in New York City; I saw the crowd. It would.

Closer to the case is that G N' R made Nirvana *possible*. When you think about the niche that Nirvana supposedly created and perfected—a megaband that indie snobs couldn't entirely disavow, no matter how badly they wanted to—G N' R got there first. They didn't get all the way there, I realize. They dressed silly. They didn't seem to know the difference between their good songs and their crap songs. But we have to remember, too, how they came along at a time when bands with singers who looked like Axl and thrust their hips unironically, and lead players who spread their legs and reeled off guitar-god noodling weren't supposed to be interesting, melodically or culturally or in any other way. G N' R were. They were also grotesque and crass and stupid sometimes, even most of the time. Even almost all of the time. But you always knew you were seeing something when you saw them.

I don't know where this new situation is headed. Velvet Revolver? Are they any good? Seriously, I'm asking. Everybody I know who's heard the leaked *Chinese Democracy* tracks says the album sounds like a bummer. Shouldn't the band just get back together? Don't they know how huge that'd be? But Dana Gregory told me Slash and Izzy will never play full-time with Axl again: "They know him too well."

I don't know him at all. Maybe if his people had let me talk to him, he'd have bitten and struck me and told me to leave my fucking brats at home, and I could transcend these feelings. As it is, I'm left listening to "Patience" again. I don't know how it is where you are, but down south where I live, they still play it all the time. And I whistle along and wait for that voice, toward the end, when he goes, *Ooooooo, I need you. OOOOOOO, I need you.* And on the first *Ooooooo*, he finds a note so tissue-shredding it conjures the image of someone peeling his own scalp back, like the skin of a grape. I have to be careful not to attempt to sing along with this part, because it makes me, like, sort of throw up a little bit. And on the second *OOOOOOO*, you picture just a naked glowing green skull that hangs there vibrating gape-mouthed in a hyperbaric chamber.

Or whatever it is you picture.

LINDSAY ZOLADZ ON PUSSY RIOT

Fear of Music: Pussy Riot in New York*

It's 10:30 a.m. on a sunny Wednesday morning in June, and I'm in a dim room on the fourth floor of the Brooklyn Museum with two members of the Russian feminist punk group Pussy Riot, staring down a porcelain sculpture of Georgia O'Keeffe's vagina. Curator Catherine Morris is giving us a private tour of the museum's Elizabeth A. Sackler Center for Feminist Art, the only permanent collection of its kind in any major American museum. We eventually arrive at its centerpiece: American artist Judy Chicago's seminal and wildly controversial 1979 installation *The Dinner Party*. The visually imposing work is comprised of a giant, triangular table for 39, each place set for an important woman in (or, in most cases, written out of) history: unnamed Amazon goddesses, Sacajawea, Sojourner Truth. Except for a few overhead lights that dot the ceiling like distant stars, the room is reverently dark. Morris explains it's so the hand-embroidered runners on each place setting don't fade over time, but it also gives the room an uncanny arts-and-crafts-in-outer-space vibe. Taking in *The Dinner Party* from afar, I feel like I'm looking at a radical feminist Starship Enterprise.

As we get closer, the most controversial part of the piece becomes clear: the design on each plate is abstractly yet unmistakably vaginal. "It might be hard to believe now," Morris says, gesturing towards O'Keeffe's plate, an impressionistic swirl of sky-blues and lilacs that looks a little bit like one of her paintings, "but 40 years ago, this was deemed obscene." The taller of the two members of Pussy Riot, who goes by the name Headlight, lifts her teal digital camera and snaps a picture.

They've chosen seemingly random nicknames for their trip to America (the other one is Puck), and when we meet outside the museum half an hour earlier, they tell me, with the help of a translator, that it doesn't matter who's who or who's saying what. In Pussy Riot, individuals are subsumed by the goals and identity of the collective as a whole.

In small talk, Puck and Headlight are friendly but guarded. As we walk up to the fourth floor, I ask how long they've been in New York, and they politely decline to answer. They've come to the U.S.—on the heels of a similar whirlwind tour in Europe—to make connections with musicians, human rights groups, and like-minded activists, but they're also constantly aware of the potential danger they'll face when they go back to Russia. Before we enter the Sackler Center, they remind me one last time of the ground rules we've agreed upon for this article: no real names, no physical descriptions, and absolutely no photographs.

---

*Zoladz, Lindsay. "Articles: Fear of Music: Pussy Riot in New York," Pitchfork, June 14, 2013. Reprinted with permission.

But after we spend some time taking in *The Dinner Party* (which they both love), they're faced with a predicament. Judy Chicago is apparently ecstatic that the girls have come to see her piece, but bummed that she couldn't be there to meet them in person. A museum photographer and his assistant have shown up, gear in hand, to ask for a photo of the girls to give to the artist. Puck and Headlight are hesitant at first, but after chatting among themselves, they reach a compromise. "Only if we can change first."

The museum opens in 10 minutes, and just to be safe, Rob Lieber, an American who helps run the website freepussyriot.org and is acting as Puck and Headlight's de facto press liaison, wants to make sure we leave before the general public starts filing in. There's no time to make it down to the restroom a couple of floors below, so Morris apologetically ushers the pair—who are wearing a variation on the standard New York summer-tourist uniform—into a nearby closet to change. Two minutes later, the unassuming girls I've been talking to for the past hour dart out in a blur of bold colors—those already-iconic tights, dresses, and balaclavas. I can tell from their body language that the uniform, or perhaps the familiar comfort of anonymity, gives them a jolt of almost-superhuman confidence. I get chills as they breeze past me to take their place before *The Dinner Party*. It's like seeing Superman bust out of a phone booth.

Pussy Riot formed on September 24, 2011, the same day Vladimir Putin made the controversial announcement that he'd seek a third term as President of Russia. "At that point," a member of the group recalled in a 2012 interview with *Vice*, "We realized that this country needs a militant, punk-feminist street band that will rip through Moscow's streets and squares, mobilize public energy against the evil crooks of the Putinist junta and enrich the Russian cultural and political opposition." Citing oi!-punk and the riot grrrl movement as inspiration, they wrote fast, furious protest songs with titles like "Putin Has Pissed Himself" and staged guerilla-style performances in increasingly daring locations: outside a subway station, in a boutique, and later in the heart of Red Square. On February 21, 2012, intending to protest the entanglement of church and state in Putin's Russia, five members participated in the group's most audacious performance yet. They entered Moscow's Cathedral of Christ the Saviour, stormed the altar, and began to perform to a recording of a new song, "Virgin Mary, Put Putin Away". They were detained after about 40 seconds, and a few days later three members—Nadezhda "Nadia" Tolokonnikova, Maria "Masha" Alyokhina and Yekaterina "Katya" Samutsevich—were taken into custody.

Last summer, people all over the world were captivated by Pussy Riot's chillingly theatrical trial. As Nadia, Masha, and Katya sat in a glass box and shot looks of defiance and eye-rolling disbelief to the assembled media circus (Nadia: "I still can't shake the feeling that I've spent the last six months acting in a big-budget movie"), Western artists and activists voiced solidarity and demanded their release. Videos of their performances went viral. People donned balaclavas and organized rallies all over the world, Amnesty International declared them "prisoners of conscience," and a long list of musicians including Madonna, Björk, Paul McCartney, Green Day, and Patti Smith spoke out in support. The overwhelming global attention surprised people in Russia (where the public opinion of them wasn't terribly high), but even in America, it felt like an oddity: at a time when every other week seems to bring an article pronouncing the death of either feminism or punk rock, to see a madcap, menacingly articulate all-female punk group making headline news was nothing short of a revelation. Still, pressure from the rest of the world didn't affect the verdict. All three were found guilty of the vague charge of "hooliganism motivated by religious hatred." After the appeal, Katya was set free (her lawyer pointed out that she hadn't had time to plug in her guitar and reach the altar before she was detained), but Nadia and Masha were sent to serve two-year sentences in penal colonies, where they remain today. At the time of Puck and Headlight's visit, Masha had just ended an 11-day hunger strike, protesting the prison's conditions.

Puck and Headlight—who, for their own safety, won't reveal whether or not they played a part in the Christ the Saviour performance—have come to the U.S. ostensibly to promote *Pussy Riot: A Punk Prayer*, Maxim Pozdorovkin and Mike Lerner's festival-favorite documentary that premiered this week on HBO. But judging by their New York itinerary (which includes meetings with activists from Occupy Wall Street, the Willie Mae Rock Camp for Girls, and culture jammers the Yes Men), they're not interested in the PR cycle so much as having intimate conversations with like-minded people.

On Monday night, two days before our museum tour, they're at Bluestockings, a radical bookstore on the Lower East Side, for an unannounced Q&A. "We're very excited, and a little bit nervous," the moderator says to the assembled group of about 50. The girls have agreed to appear before us without their masks (wisely: the balmy June air feels extra thick in the un-air conditioned space), but before they speak, the moderator makes us raise our hands and take an oath that we won't record, take pictures, or tweet about the event for at least two days.

The reason for all the secrecy and nervousness soon becomes clear. Puck tells the crowd that, in the past month, Russian legislators have passed a series of laws informally known as "Pussy Riot laws"—basically because they preemptively make any behavior the group might engage in illegal. It's now a crime to cover your face in Russia (whether it's a balaclava or an herbal face mask, Puck quips) or offend a believer of the Russian Orthodox Church. But perhaps most disturbingly, it's now against the law for a Russian citizen to speak ill of the government to the foreign press. Which is what Puck and Headlight are doing at that very moment.

When the floor opens up for questions, attendees are curious to know if this is the girls' first time in America (it is), what sort of contact they've had with Nadia and Masha (minimal, though the free members are able to write them letters), and if Pussy Riot are planning any upcoming performances (it's too risky in Russia at the moment).

"In Russia, they're much more afraid of the word 'riot,'" Puck says, adding with a laugh, "In America, they seem to be more afraid of the other word." For the most part,

Headlight is quiet, but—like almost every other time I'll see her that week—her camera is pointed unwaveringly at us, with the red light on.

Puck and Headlight are a little more laid back on Wednesday afternoon, when we sit down to talk at a corner table at the Brooklyn Museum's cafe. Puck leisurely spoons the foam off the top of her cappuccino; Headlight offers me a bite of her Hershey bar—she's been dying to try one since they've arrived. "In Russia," she says, in an uncharacteristic moment of levity, "We don't have such a variety of chocolate."

They say their trip to America has been "unforgettable," but you can tell they're a little fatigued. They're scheduled to make a surprise appearance at the HBO-hosted *Punk Prayer* premiere later that night (this time with balaclavas on), and midway through our conversation, Rob cuts in to let them know that the few hours of downtime they've built into their day are now on the chopping block; more journalists keep calling. They're good sports about it, though. Speaking freely to the press is a luxury they don't have right now in Russia, where most media is state-sponsored. Four of Pussy Riot's five videos have now been banned as "extremist" in their home country, which means that Russian journalists who so much as quote their lyrics or link to one of their songs can be sued.

Even so, when I ask what's surprised them most about America so far, Puck quickly answers, "How many problems we have in common—there's still a very negative portrayal of feminists [in America], too." She's been inspired by the other young women she's met here, but a little dismayed to find that, as in Russia, the movement's essential message of equality has been bogged down by misconceptions. As our translator relays Puck's next observation, she shakes her head and laughs in consensus. "It seems like most Americans believe some stereotypical notion that feminism was just a fight for women to be worse-looking."

The girls both agree that Pussy Riot couldn't have formed or had global influence without the internet. Embracing the viral music video as a form of protest has helped them break barriers like ticket prices and geography, letting an unprecedentedly large audience be "present" for Pussy Riot's performances. But what they call the "open source" goal of the leaderless, horizontally-structured group presents its own challenges, too.

In November, Samutsevich spoke out against her former lawyer, Mark Feygin, who allegedly tried to trademark the Pussy Riot name without the group's consent. (They're strictly against making a profit off of anything Pussy Riot-related and make an effort to "distance themselves from any attempts to exploit [their] brand.") There was also a controversial, decidedly Pussy Riot-esque photo in an online Russian IKEA ad (later removed).

And let's not forget that other group of girls who gained recent notoriety for crimes they committed while wearing neon balaclavas: at Bluestockings, amidst questions about Putin, Chechnya, and Ukrainian protest group FEMEN, someone asks Pussy Riot if they've seen *Spring Breakers*. Headlight has. She calls it a "horrible film" that "exploits" Pussy Riot's imagery to spread a message that goes against everything that the group stands for. (Many viewers have pointed out the resemblance, but director Harmony Korine claims it's just "an awesome coincidence.") Interestingly enough, it's not the film's sex and violence that bothers her; the particular scene she lashes out against is the one in which the girls aren't paying attention in history class. As Nadia, Masha, and Katya's literate and well-informed closing statements (which also went viral) attest, Pussy Riot advocate an in-depth knowledge of history, if only to know how to fight against it in a meaningful way.

Still, they understand that when your image is so iconic, reappropriation is the nature of the beast—or maybe even the whole point. "The way we do our activism is open-source," Puck says. "So we understand that other artists will come and make their own take on it. That's OK—that's actually a crucial part of it ... even with the image of the balaclava, it's not about us per se, but it's about the ideology, spreading that idea along."

Headlight jumps in and suggests a metaphor that the translator doesn't understand. Instead she turns to me, and the universal language of punk: "Like ... straight edge?" I nod in recognition, and she goes on. "Straight edge is no longer about who started it, it's about everyone's individual interpretation, and the people who uphold it [as a lifestyle.]"

Pussy Riot are not a band. They make a point of clearing up that popular misconception at almost every stop on their trip: They're an arts collective that "chose the language of music" (and of punk in particular) to express themselves. But the more time I spend with them, the less I think the semantics matter. Band or not, Pussy Riot have reminded people of something essential—so simple that it's all to easy to dismiss it as cheesy, or take it for granted—about music's primacy, its power to provoke, its potential to facilitate change. "It's one of your competitive advantages," says Hunter Heaney, founder of the nonprofit The Voice Project, who has also helped set up a Pussy Riot Support Fund. "When you're going up against whatever you're going against—whether it's corporations or authoritarianism, it's the protester, the individual, the artist who can always make better music than the other side."

As I watch them make their way around New York, it's impossible not to feel grateful to live in a country where (in theory, at least) free expression is not feared, and where I won't be sued for simply linking to one of the band's videos. But most of the Americans I talk with throughout the week agree that their presence here (not to mention the unblinking gaze of Headlight's camera) brings into focus something lacking in American music right now. For all the good that the Occupy movement did, plenty of people rightly wondered why—unlike the countercultural movements of the 60s—music hadn't played a more central role. "Where's Occupy's Woody Guthrie?" one website wondered. Has music in the 21st century outlived its revolutionary potential? What Pussy Riot give us is a new, viral-ready model for the digital age—proof that, like feminism and punk rock, the protest song is alive and high-kicking.

Headlight and Puck exit New York in the same haze of mystery and privacy in which they arrived: No one will say exactly when they're leaving, how they're getting there, where they'll go. Before their secret departure, I follow them to a few more events around the city that suggest something about the impossibly wide appeal of the group. At the HBO premiere, they inform a celeb-studded audience about the Russian government's latest violation of their rights: "We do not have freedom of speech. We do not feel safe now anywhere." At the decidedly less glitzy academic conference Left Forum, they play videos of their punk songs to an assembled crowd of progressive scholars and intellectuals. Something about it all feels elusive, powerfully contradictory, hard to pin down—which, I'm guessing, is exactly what they want. By the end of the week, I can't decide if I've been in the presence of a group of real-life superheroes, or just getting to know a couple of down-to-earth Clark Kents.

SASHA FRERE-JONES ON BEYONCÉ

The Queen: Beyoncé, At Last*

Bruce Springsteen is the de-facto governor of New Jersey, and if America were Europe Aretha Franklin would have a duchy, so both obviously belonged at the joyous Obamathon. But what about Beyoncé Knowles, the twenty-seven-year-old who was chosen to sing for Obama at two inaugural events?

The world met Beyoncé in 1998 as the leader of Destiny's Child, a girl group conceived in part and managed by Matthew Knowles, her father. Destiny's Child was high-tech declarations of autonomy and flair: "No, No, No," "Bills, Bills, Bills," "Independent Women, Pt. 1," and "Survivor." To underestimate Knowles and her rotating cast of backup singers is to find yourself on the business end of a No. 1 song. (Destiny's Child is the most successful female R. & B. group in history.) Yet none of this involved Beyoncé cursing, committing infidelity, or breaking any laws, even in character. The Knowles empire is delicately balanced on one of the thinnest-known edges in pop feminism: as unbiddable as Beyoncé gets, she never risks arrant aggression; and as much of hip-hop's confidence and sound as she borrows, she never drifts to the back of the classroom. She is pop's A student, and it has done her a world of commercial good.

She is also a strange and brilliant musician. Young black female singers rarely get past the red rope and into the Genius Lounge—the moody, the male, and the dead crowd that room. But with or without co-writers, Knowles does remarkable things with tone and harmony. The one time I met her, backstage at a Destiny's Child concert in Peoria in 2000, she talked about listening to Miles Davis and Fela Kuti—affinities I didn't know how to process until I heard "Apple Pie à la Mode," from the following year's Destiny's Child album, *Survivor*. It's a slinky song, something of a throwaway, except that Prince or D'Angelo could easily have done the throwing away. Who else in the stratosphere of R. & B. pop plays around with the conversational voice like Beyoncé? Who feels comfortable with adding so much unexpected, generous harmony to a trifle about a delicious crush? Anyone else with "Apple Pie à la Mode" in the bag would flip over backward, buy a retro-glam outfit, and construct an entire side project around it. Knowles simply kept moving.

Where she was heading, as she and her father must have always known, was toward a gigantic solo career. That meant that she would have to choose among unity of purpose (the way Céline Dion chose the power ballad as her sidearm of choice), full-

*Frere-Jones, Sasha. "The Queen: Beyoncé, At Last," *The New Yorker*, February 9, 2009. Reprinted with permission.

253

on idiosyncrasy (as Björk did, after leaving the Sugarcubes for a life of dedicated unpredictability), or some compromise between the two that could retain old fans while convincing tourists that she was worth following. Executed successfully, this move is called the Sting (who never matched the songwriting quality of his old band the Police but has provided himself with a robust living and a large, loyal following). Done wrong, it's called—well, many names, all of which involve repeated pleas for the old band to regroup.

Beyoncé has yet to come to a decision, though her success as a solo artist seems to be entirely secure. (She has made three solo albums, all of them yielding No. 1 songs.) This is a testament to something deeply appealing about Beyoncé, because her first album, *Dangerously in Love* (2003), has three good songs, at best; her second, *B'Day* (2006), is completely enjoyable; and her new one, *I Am . . . Sasha Fierce* (featuring a supposedly new, wilder alter ego), is something of a mess. Apparently, Knowles felt that it was high time to offer a different definition of Beyoncéness. But why?

I Am . . . Sasha Fierce stretches an hour's worth of material over two compact disks, the first supposedly by our old friend Beyoncé, the second by Ms. Fierce. The album began arriving on the Internet in November with "Single Ladies (Put a Ring on It)," whose video has eclipsed the song itself. (The choreography for Beyoncé and her two dancers is borrowed from some old Bob Fosse routines and has inspired dozens of imitations, including one by an almost-naked man dancing in the Alaskan snow and one with Justin Timberlake, doing his best drag routine for *Saturday Night Live*.) The song, produced by The-Dream and Tricky Stewart, is reminiscent of the best moments on *B'Day*. The rhythms are provided in part by handclaps, and the chanting vocal line is underscored by a swell of weird, dark synthesizers that don't seem to know about the party going on in the rest of the song. But, then, the whole thing is a bit off. The singer is out on the town, engaging her single lady friends and enjoying the attention of a new man. Why is she out on the town? Because her man didn't "put a ring on it." But this is Sasha Fierce we're talking about here. And what does Sasha want? Matrimony! When does she want it? Before "three good years" are up. "Single Ladies" is an infectious, crackling song and would be without fault if it weren't the bearer of such dull advice. The wild R. & B. vampire Sasha is advocating marriage? What's next, a sultry, R-rated defense of low-sodium soy sauce?

I Am . . . Sasha Fierce trips on this idea of redefinition, largely because Beyoncé has been relatively fierce since she started. The first disk's initial single, "If I Were a Boy," is a slow, almost rocklike ballad that ponders the gender differential. Boys get to wear what they want, chase girls, and enjoy normative privilege. Y'know—the patriarchy. But Destiny's Child handled all this on "Independent Women, Pt. 1," and with a lot more verve.

For all that, liking Beyoncé is still a wise bet. What Knowles fails to convey with Sasha Fierce she accomplishes in the movie *Cadillac Records*, with her portrayal of someone who headlines in the Genius Lounge—Etta James. When Beyoncé rolls her body and her voice into James's music, the results are not safe. Her version of James is a worthy tribute to the sexuality and craft of the woman we know from her Chess recordings. Why Knowles could not make her own record as spontaneous and magnetic probably has something to do with the Knowles vision of Beyoncé's fans and how much actual fierceness they can take.

When Beyoncé sang for the Obamas at the Neighborhood Ball on January 20th, the whole shebang revealed itself in a synergistic flash. The song of choice was Etta James's "At Last." Team Knowles was not going to waste one of the year's biggest broadcast events. As the exuberant First Couple slow-danced, Knowles did her part to turn basic romantic folderol into historic prophecy: our lonely nights are gone, the skies are blue, we've all found a dream. One slightly artless twirl-about was all that the crowd needed to cheer the President on. Knowles gave the song the right blend of smoothness and grit, watching the couple, and holding back what looked like bona-fide tears. It was pitch-perfect and seemed genuine. And maybe this is why Beyoncé's audience isn't much bothered by her need to futz about with unconvincing role-playing. She's really good at being good.

WRITING PROMPT: THE LOCAL ARTIST PROFILE

Write a 2500–3000-word profile of a local artist or band (whether on your campus, in your town, or in the garage next door). Choose as your subject an artist or band to whom you have or think you can gain access. Your profile should offer the following features:

- Make it a first-person account—you should "be there," observing, leading, and offering opinions and analysis of what you show us in a carefully constructed personal "voice." Your presence need not call attention away from the subject, but the first person perspective may allow you to account on the page for your proximity to the artist in a more natural way.

- A guiding focus or idea about the artist's work and life. (You're not only reporting facts neutrally but have the burden of offering your insights about what you've come to understand about your subject.)

- A description of the artist or band members in physical, psychological and emotional terms.

- Detailed description, discussion and analysis of the work of the artist.

- Development that leads from description, quotation, and fact to opinions and ideas.

Your goal is to find a perspective on your subject that provides a way to organize your material and create interest and focus.

The Process

Familiarize yourself exhaustively with your subject's music. First, you'll collect somewhat indiscriminately and omnivorously a great deal of information: facts, quotations, descriptions, ideas, details, criticism, and reviews. (If the artist isn't yet reviewed, you can ask other people who are familiar with the music about their opinions of and responses to it.)

Begin by writing in an exploratory way about at least two examples of the artist's music, describing what you hear and the nature of the lyrics.

Spend time with and observe the artist in the studio, on stage, rehearsing, and writing, Write freely about the experience and include lots of observations and details about the artist at work.

Spend time with the artist outside of any direct musical context: have a meal together; go out and socialize in a group; participate in an activity unrelated to music that the artist enjoys. Write about what you did together and what you observed.

Work up interview questions once you become familiar enough to know what you want to ask. Conduct an interview with your subject (see the Expert Advice from Our Writers in the Artist Interview section to help you prepare). You will most likely benefit by following up with the artist later in the process for a second conversation once you've identified your central focus.

Transcribe and edit with the interview answers, highlighting what's of particular interest to you and making connections between the answers, the music and the artist.

Organize your material into a shape that reflects your emerging perspective on the artist, omitting some information and expanding other points of interest, until you have a full first draft.

Revise and rework the draft to arrive at the final version of the profile.

THE GO-BETWEENS

WHAT SOURCES DO YOU USE?

Depends. Google for fact checking. Books if it something I don't know enough about. Most of my criticism is an articulation of what I think and I keep my own counsel. I use the *American Oxford Writers Thesaurus.*—**Jessica Hopper**, Music Editor at *Rookie Magazine*, and Senior Editor, the *Pitchfork Review*

Google Books is an astounding resource that is, ironically, difficult to search. But they have an immense archive of back catalogued books and magazines that I often turn to for research purposes. And I'm spoiled in that I have access to Time Inc.'s entire digital archive, which is most every issue of *EW*, *People*, *Time*, and—this is the most thrilling—*NME.*—**Kyle Anderson**, senior writer, *Entertainment Weekly*

Rock's Backpages is an amazing resource. The best.—**Pete Astor**, writer, academic, musician

For my 80s work, I love trawling things like this archive of *NME* and *Melody Maker* issues: archivedmusicpress.wordpress.com, and (less mainstream) sites devoted to hardcore punk like http://www.killfromtheheart.com/. I also like reading Pitchfork reviews, which are entertaining and often get at important ideas, and I like trying to find interviews with other artists in the same scene—who usually mislead and obfuscate in suggestive ways. And other **33⅓s**, of course, which display a range of approaches and are helpful to me in formulating my own.—**Nick Attfield**, music academic

Like so many writers I marvel at those who wrote good books before the internet. The web can be a good place to start, to get some ideas of where to go next, and whatever project I'm working on dictates where I burrow in. I keep up online with *PopMatters*, Pitchfork, *The Rumpus, Rolling Stone, No Depression*, etc., and I regularly read magazines like *Oxford American, Ugly Things, Uncut, The Big Takeover*, etc. Facebook has proven to be a terrific resource in the form of groups devoted to genres or artists or collecting or "rock and roll" in general, peopled by knowledgeable, enthusiastic, and generous members. I've learned plenty on Facebook, and in user comments on music sites.—**Joe Bonomo**, music columnist, *The Normal School*, and Associate Professor of English at Northern Illinois University

If it's been printed, I'll use it and attribute accordingly. The Wayback Machine digital archive has been a priceless tool for finding things that the growing and occasionally fickle Internet has left behind.—**Phillip Crandall**, author of the 33⅓ book on Andrew W.K.'s *I Get Wet*

Amazon is a reliable source for song titles and albums, but not release dates.

Wikipedia is not trustworthy, but it often links to primary sources. It's not a bad place to start, but never trust it as a solitary source for anything.—**D.X. Ferris**, Ohio Society of Professional Journalists Reporter of the Year, Professor, 33⅓ author

Oh, y'know, the standard Pitchfork/*Rolling Stone*/Gawker universe/Grantland/Vulture + *New York Magazine*/*New Yorker* universe, plus a host of writers' personal blogs and smaller sites. I also over-rely on Twitter, but I comfort myself with the suspicion that everyone is, to some degree.—**Rob Harvilla**, Deputy/Culture Editor, Deadspin

This is getting harder in the internet age, because so many sites just regurgitate information that sometimes you're reading third-hand information with third-hand errors in it. But I think any fact-checking resource is OK. I mean Wikipedia is not a reliable source, but if you use it in tandem with a few other sources, it can still be helpful. The holy grails for us are places like the *New York Times* or *LA Times* or the *Guardian*, but even those outlets are fallible, so at the end of the day I think you search for quality, but also quantity. I always stress to our fact-checkers that if something seems murky in the slightest, call that out and we can bring it to the attention of a writer or to the attention of a source. Often times they know a lot more than you do, and can explain the nuances of something that might seem really simple to a newcomer.—**Casey Jarman**, Managing Editor, the *Believer*

I almost always find myself checking allmusic.com, since it's super-comprehensive and usually includes pretty exhaustive album credits.—**Matt LeMay**, senior contributor, Pitchfork

The twenty-third page of a Google search.—**Paul Morley**, writer and critic

It depends on the kind of research. On the simple end of contact information, I find that more than anywhere else, bands will list contact info on their Facebook pages, where they might not have it on their websites. When other writers ask me for artist contact info, more times than not I'll find it tucked away on the artist's public Facebook page, where many people don't bother to check. For other kinds of research, especially about older bands with a longer press history, I use Lexis Nexis or Rock's Backpages. All Music Guide is great for complete discographies and go-to reviews. Wikipedia is good ONLY as a starting point to lead you to other links and resources—it is far too unreliable to use as a direct source, never ever do that.—**Evie Nagy**, *Fast Company* staff writer, former editor at *Billboard* and *Rolling Stone*

Liner notes are always an intriguing place to start because they give you a sense of the number of hands directly or indirectly involved in the finished recording … Spotify and YouTube can be tremendously useful for accessing obscure recordings and old television and film footage if you're unable to locate it anywhere else. Depending on the historical and cultural scope of your research, there's definitely something to be said for the dusty stacks and hidden archives at public and university libraries, which I dig through on a regular basis.—**Luis Sanchez, 33⅓** author

My most-used resource is my personal stash of rock magazines and fanzines—especially *Select* (my favorite Brit music mag of the nineties), the *Village Voice* music section during the 1980s and 1990s, and fanzines ranging from *Conflict* and *Forced Exposure* to *Radio On* and *Why Music Sucks*. Good luck finding any of this slop online—that's why I'm glad to have my hard copies.—**Rob Sheffield**, writer, *Rolling Stone*

For news stories, I follow various music sites on Twitter and subscribe to their RSS feeds using a reader. I also utilize sites such as Reddit. Other stories might come from press releases or original reporting. In terms of fact-checking, we try to always have another editor review the story before publishing.—**Alex Young**, founder and publisher, Consequence of Sound

CHAPTER 9
ALTERNATIVES

INTRODUCTION

It had been almost two years since I had thought about Black Flag. Sure, I'd listen to them occasionally and would see the iconic T-shirt with the misaligned black vertical rectangles on men and women all over Brooklyn but it had been a while since I really *thought* about the band. In fact the last time was probably in the spring of 2012 when David Barker (the **33⅓** series founder) and I ran an open call for **33⅓** proposals. There were over 470 submissions during that round but one proposal really stuck in my mind even though we didn't select it. It was a graphic novel about Black Flag's 1981 album *Damaged* by a talented comic book illustrator and author named Marty Davis. The proposal wasn't right for the series because the tiny format of **33⅓** wouldn't have done justice to Davis's artwork but those eight roughly sketched pages depicting the early distribution scheme for *Damaged* really stuck in my mind.

When Marc Woodworth and I started outlining the chapters in this book we knew that we wanted to have a section that wasn't just about writing but instead would show less familiar ways to represent music, ones that don't involve perfectly constructed sentences. Marty Davis's artwork immediately came to mind as a brilliant and beautiful *alternative* to straight music criticism, so I got back in touch with him two years after his submission to **33⅓** to ask if we could print the excerpt from his Black Flag graphic novel in these pages. It's not just that Davis is a skilled artist, but that these few frames illustrate a narrative of a band struggling to navigate the music industry in such a compelling manner. This story could of course be told over several pages with interviews and citations of sales figures, but here the story comes to life in a fresh way. When you just like to draw or are a talented graphic artist try experimenting with illustrating your album reviews.

Most **33⅓** proposal submissions are straight music criticism but many come in more creative forms like novellas, screen plays, poems, memoirs and yes, several graphic novels. One of the most interesting books in the series, as Rick Moody points out in his introduction to this book, is John Darnielle's on Black Sabbath's *Master of Reality*. It's a novella about a troubled teen who is completely obsessed with Black Sabbath. Though the plot is about a teen's stay in a mental hospital, his diary is an encyclopedic cataloging and unraveling of the album. Telling the story of an album through fiction is incredibly difficult to do and Darnielle's book sets the bar pretty high.

No one intertwines his personal experiences with music more engagingly and emotionally than Rob Sheffield. His 2007 book *Love is a Mixtape* is a harrowing and beautiful memoir of his first marriage that ended with the very sudden and tragic death of his wife. Each chapter begins with a mix-tape, a list of songs to guide the narrative. Sheffield presents and explores his eclectic musical taste in the context of love and tragedy.

Just as Sheffield's mix tapes serve as an unexpected and beguiling scaffolding for his memoir, Campbell McGrath uses Bob Dylan's own verbal rhythms in a free verse poem about the artist in 1965. The poem riffs on the language and rhythms of Bob Dylan's lyrics with an exuberance that is at once homage and satire. Even if you're not a poet, trying a fresh form and going out of your comfort zone might prove worthwhile. It's a clever and inventive format that might make you uncomfortable at first but trying to rhyme with a band name like . . . And You Will Know Us By the Trail of Dead might just be the thing you need to punch up that album review.—AJG

JOHN DARNIELLE ON BLACK SABBATH

33⅓ Volume #56 *Master of Reality**

October 20, 1985

It is before wakeups, I am writing in the dark again. Normally on a morning like this I would put on my headphones and just kick back, when I wake up I have music in my head and I like to start out the day that way. Guess not today you assholes!! That was when I got the idea to try to tell you about my favorite tape, which is also my favorite LP, I will explain that later. If you don't think this is a good way to use this journal then fuck you Gary!

OK so Black Sabbath is a rock band. They are from Birmingham, England. They have been popular since 1970. Although their first album, is not as popular as their other albums. It was a less hard album than what they did later. I do not own their first album, which is just called *Black Sabbath*. But my friend Mike loaned me his copy. I want to give it back to him, but now I am in here so he will have to wait to get it back. Right now it is just sitting at home not doing anybody any good. It is a UXB! I don't know if you saw this show they had on channel 28 but it was called *Danger UXB*. It is about soldiers in England who go around finding bombs that are sitting in people's basements or in subway tunnels. They are UXBs that means "unexploded bombs." To me the first Black Sabbath album sitting in my house is a UXB because it has not gotten the chance to explode inside my head yet! It's hard to explain but hey I tried.

The first time I listened to Black Sabbath, was on a rainy day after band practice. I was stoned. You will probably tell my family this, I don't care. When most of my friends get stoned they say it feels rad but I usually feel kind of weird afterwards. It was like that on that day, I smoked with every body after practice and then I just walked home. When I was getting to the tunnel under the freeway two blocks before my house it had started to rain. Well before I left practice I borrowed the first Black Sabbath album from Mike our drummer because I was looking at the front cover when I was all stoned and it gave me a certain feeling. It wasn't trying to feel all good and happy but it wasn't totally weird either. It was like, it was weird but it wasn't trying that hard. It was like a weird person made it, and showed it to other weird people and they all thought it was good, but if you were not as weird as them then it would look totally haggard to you. We say haggard to mean gnarly in my school.

So I got inside the house, my hair was wet and the rain was coming in through my shoes. My stepfather was asleep in his room because he works the NOC shift from

*Darnielle, John. *Master of Reality*, New York: Bloomsbury, 2008. 11–13, 34–42. Reprinted with permission.

eleven at night until seven in the morning. And I went back to my room, a lot of the pot had worn off because it takes me about an hour to walk home from Mike's house. And I was just feeling tired. So I put on the record and listened with headphones and it was totally depressing. Ozzy, he is the singer, he was singing about witches and devils and wizards and corpses. But there were barely any stories. Not like in Rush songs where if there is a wizard or whatever, there will be a whole story, like a Robert A. Heinlein book. I have read about three. Those books and Rush songs they all have big stories and lots of things happen and there is some big meaning. But on the first Black Sabbath album, the whole story in the song will be like "There is a wizard and he is going to kill you," or "There is a devil and you are the sacrifice." Song after song. Like stories you try to make up around the campfire only you didn't get enough time to think about your story before it was your turn to tell, so when it got to your turn alls you did was you said everything you had in your mind and hoped it was scary even though in your story nothing really happened.

So on this song called "Black Sabbath," first song on the album, Ozzy keeps saying "Oh No. No, No. Please God." That is the chorus of the song more or less. I think it's supposed to freak you out, but on that day when I was listening it just made me feel like the world was sad. Like, it's sad to be alive. And that is not normally how I feel when I listen to Blue Oyster Cult, AC/DC, Frank Marino and Mahogany Rush (different from Rush), or newer bands like Helix, Scorpions, Winger. Normally even the hard music is supposed to sort of take you higher but when I borrowed this album from Mike I knew it wasn't just the pot, it was like the whole point was "everything is a bummer, even your fantasies are a bummer."

I hate it when people talk all "la la la drugs changed my life" but when I listened to that song on that rainy stoned day everything changed. My hand is tired so I will write more soon. If you are reading still I will be surprised but if you are I hope you enjoy the Black Sabbath story because telling it is taking my mind off my totally fucked up situation.

October 26, 1985

Fuck you Gary you fucking asshole! Just when I think I can trust you, and that you maybe understand, it turns out you are the same as them all. I asked the Saturday staff today, "Did Gary say if I can have my tapes" and they said "There's nothing here about it." What do they even mean? At the same time I know everybody here is so stupid that they could have it wrong so I hope I see you Monday because staff always gets things wrong, for example when Saturday staff said "There's nothing here about it" they weren't even looking at anything except their clipboards. Even I know they should look at the chart if they want to know anything.

So I am confused and sad and VERY ANGRY because I thought after therapy yesterday you would give me back my stuff for sure. You can see that I am following the rules around here. I write in my journal probably a hundred times more than anybody else and I tell you the real story about what is going on in the unit. I don't assume you are all stupid, I try to tell you the real deal. I am nice to the other kids and I try to help people when they are having a hard time. There is no point in even talking to you about my feelings if you don't really care though so I will just torture you with some more Black Sabbath, check it out now. I know you have to read it because it is your job, I hope you choke on it!

This is my Black Sabbath collection which I know by heart!! About half of them are tapes but I have the albums of *Never Say Die* and *Paranoid* because I could get them used and they were cheaper than tapes.

*Black Sabbath**

Master of Reality

*Paranoid**

Sabbath Bloody Sabbath

Never Say Die

*Heaven and Hell***

*Born Again****

* like I told you before these actually belong to my friend Mike. If something happens to me in here please make sure that Mike gets his records back.

** this is after Ozzy left.

*** this is the newest one, when I had a girlfriend she got it for me for my birthday. She gave it to me when we met at the benches between second and third period. It made that the best birthday ever! Because my Walkman was in my locker, we can't carry our Walkmans around with us or they will take them away and you won't get them back for a month. So, she gave me the tape, it was wrapped with a ribbon, and I opened it and I was so excited, and I put it in my backpack and then I had to walk around the whole rest of the day until lunch thinking about how great my girlfriend was and how excited I was. It was like the tape was burning through my backpack. Like it was GLOWING. So when it was finally lunchtime after Spanish II, I went to my locker to get my Walkman and then booked ass across the football field to the benches and sat there listening. Now a lot of people say that Black Sabbath is completely over because Ozzy has a new band, the Blizzard of Ozz, and they have songs like "Crazy Train" and "Flying High Again" and some of the songs are really good and some are totally stupid ("Mr. Crowley," "I Don't Know," those are just two, some people might disagree about these). I think the Blizzard of Ozz is fine and I have the first two tapes but it doesn't seem as special as the old band to me. Blizzard has Ozzy, so it's awesome, but it's also confusing because you can't tell if it's maybe supposed to be a joke.

He is wearing these capes on the cover. If you ever see the cover of *Sabbath Bloody Sabbath* or *Technical Ecstasy* or really any of the Black Sabbath album covers, you know it's got to be cool! Even that one *Sabotage* gives off a vibe where you know whether you like it or not. They are in costumes on that one, even a cape I think, but it's very strange and cool. When I look at the solo Ozzy covers though, I'm not sure whether he's talking to me or to somebody else. Do you know what I mean? I don't know if you can understand this. But all the old Black Sabbath albums, I feel like they were made for me, or not for me but like they were always just waiting for a guy like me to come along and find them. It's weird! Not like that with Ozzy solo. Anyways, my exgirlfriend Karen knew this was how I felt, that Black Sabbath is special, so for my birthday present she bought me the new Black Sabbath and the cover is just like I was saying, it's like a secret code for people like me. It's a red infant baby with yellow horns and yellow fingernails and he is showing his fangs. He is Born Again! To me this is saying to all the people who hate Black Sabbath, fine, if this is how you are going to talk about us then how do you like this evil devil baby, why can't he be born again too like all of you! But if you listen to the music the picture you get is a lot bigger.

By the way a girl I know here named Starr says that the new singer from Black Sabbath is now some Christian guy named Jeff! But I want the world to know that I will never accept that band as Black Sabbath if this happens, and I will always call the new band Jeff Sabbath. Why does everything good have to not just stop being good but totally turn to shit?

Why why why! But before Christian Jeff, who Starr says was in *JESUS CHRIST SUPERSTAR*, the singer on *Born Again* was this guy named Ian Gillan. He replaced Ozzy. Of course we know that no one can ever replace Ozzy! But Ian Gillan was the singer from Deep Purple, who as everyone knows did that song "Smoke on the Water," which is the first song everybody learns to play on guitar. He is a very different singer from Ozzy and if you understand how he is different then you also can understand what makes Ozzy the "taster's choice!" Haha OK that is a totally stupid thing to say but I kind of mean it. Because Ian Gillan is a much MUCH better singer than Ozzy Osbourne. Ozzy Osbourne can only sing about 1/2 of the notes that Ian Gillan can sing, and also Ian Gillan can make his voice shake like an opera singer. He sounds like he took singing lessons, and also listened to all the important old bands like Eric Clapton. He is a professional.

Well I guess Ozzy is also a pro by now, he's been singing for as long as I've been alive! But no matter how many songs he sings, Ozzy always ALWAYS sounds like they just grabbed him off the street and stuck him in front of a microphone, and then either they handed him a piece of paper with some lyrics on it or he already had some written on his hand or something.

Or maybe like he was asleep or watching some cool movie in another room and then they ran in and said "Hey Ozzy it's almost time for you to sing," so he just started getting his thoughts together and then ran in and sang along with the band. No matter what he's singing, Ozzy sounds like he was going to sing that anyway, even if there was nobody listening, even if everybody hated it, even if nobody was even going to put his record in the stores. He isn't Mr. Rock Star. He is just the singer in a band called Black

Sabbath, and he sounds like he just loves listening to the band play, like he's super siked just to be doing it so he tries to fit in. Not to be the best. Just to be the guy who's doing his job.

I look up to Ozzy! You fuckers send these dumbasses to talk to us or make us go to therapy and try to make us think that we need to be like you but we don't want to be anything else besides what we already are! Some kids say that we are the losers but I don't like the way that feels. It's not about losing or winning, is what I want to say! It's just being who you want to be, even if you are a poor kid making loud music about being unhappy! Why can't you people understand this, are your brains broken or something? But then again in a way this doesn't even matter because Black Sabbath is not just Ozzy, it is also Bill Ward and Tony Iommi and Geezer Butler, anybody who says Sabbath without Ozzy can't rock needs to listen to *Born Again* and quit being a dick! Some of the guitar solos on it are *awesome*. And there is an instrumental song called "Stonehenge," which reminded me of the two instrumental songs on *Master of Reality*, which are "Embryo" and "Orchid," some people hate them but those people should die! I have to stop now.

October 27, 1985

They made me stop yesterday because I kicked a chair over while I was typing and I guess I was singing too loud. I don't know why they care how loud I sing when I am in that room all alone. But after I kicked the chair I knew they would just all come and say "What's going on in here," so I calmed down and tried to pretend I didn't know what the noise was, but they didn't believe me so they said "That's enough." It was more like just a leg twitch from excitement but one thing I have learned is that if you ever try to explain yourself to staff, you are going to lose. So I just said "Nothing sorry I'm done anyway." And I did not finish what I was going to say about *Born Again*, so I will continue the story of *Born Again* today because it is my second favorite. I can hear you saying if you are smart, "Wait how can you say that? *Master* is from when they still had Ozzy, but *Born Again* just came out six months ago! How can that even be true!" but just sit back while I blow your mind. Here is the story.

Everybody knows that *Paranoid* is the most famous Black Sabbath album. Even cheerleaders like *Paranoid*. If you do not like *Paranoid*, it is probably because you are worried about Satanism, or maybe you just don't like good music. But if you like good music you have to like *Paranoid*. Period. That is just how it is. However, that is also why *Paranoid* can never be my favorite Black Sabbath album! It's like, any day now I expect to hear it at Pizza Hut or something. But will I ever go to Pizza Hut and order a sausage, bell peppers and anchovies pizza (my favorite) and be sitting there kicking back and then suddenly hear "Children of the Grave"? Fat chance man! Mike says, it doesn't matter which one is the one everyone likes, it just matters which one is the best one. I feel like he is right in some ways. But when something is a secret, or half secret, or hidden in some way, it becomes cooler for me.

And that is why *Born Again* is totally special and awesome. Did you ever hear a saying, "hide in plain sight," it is from the world of ninjas. It means, you can be like the invisible man, only better and more powerful, because it's not that you are really invisible, it's just your power of siking everybody out. Hell yeah! The day my exgirlfriend bought me *Born Again* I went across the field at lunch with my Walkman and my new tape, and I sat there listening to this album I had never heard before and I knew nobody else even knew there was a new Black Sabbath album. Because hardly anybody at my school cares about Black Sabbath. So there I am listening to an album that is like a secret message from another world with a totally messed up cover and songs like "Zero the Hero," "Trashed," and "Disturbing the Priest." It made me want to disturb a priest, I don't really know any priests though. Too bad! Just kidding. My point is, the album is really good, the guitar playing is the best I have heard on a Black Sabbath album in a long time and the singing is weird because there is a lot of echo. And the drums echo too. Even the guitar solos echo. Maybe their new recording studio is a cave! Or maybe the point is, when you listen to *Born Again*, you are going into a cave for a while, because nobody else is listening with you. That is what I take from it. So it's like me and the band are in a hidden cave and they are telling me horror stories and if I even tried to tell someone about it there is no way they could understand, because they don't even know there is a cave.

This is very different from *Master of Reality*, which is partly why my #2 album is *Born Again*, because it shows that the band has so many different talents. *Master of Reality* is the opposite of the cave. It is the band on top of a mountain north of town, like Mt. Baldy is from my town only closer. Like imagine that there's a town that's only twenty houses with families, and then right there smashed up against it there's that mountain that's about three stories high and Black Sabbath is on top of it in black and purple robes. And they are saying, "We are the Masters of Reality! This is your reality!" And telling everybody the truth about smoking pot, and the afterlife, and war and loneliness. New Black Sabbath is more about stories that you can hear. But Ozzy on *Master* is like a preacher, a totally crazy preacher and nobody is listening so it just makes him more insane. Somebody has already disturbed that priest!

It gets me all excited, I wish I had somebody to talk to about it who could understand. I hope you know that I am telling you this stuff because it helps me! And it would help me even more, to hear my music! I just want you to know!

MARTY DAVIS ON BLACK FLAG

Black Flag in The Story of *Damaged*

The illustrations that follow are part of a graphic novel about Black Flag's 1981 album *Damaged*. This was part of a book proposal for the 33⅓ series made by comic book creator Marty Davis in 2012. The proposal wasn't right for the series because the tiny format of 33⅓ wouldn't do justice to Davis's artwork. There are myriad ways to discuss a piece of music beyond just writing about it: through art, dance, other music, and through poetry. Here is a prime example of how to write about music that doesn't exactly revolve around perfectly constructed prose.

ROLL AFTER ROLL OF STICKERS--APPLIED TO BOX AFTER BOX OF FRESHLY-MINTED ALBUM COVERS. IF YOU KNOW THE BAND, YOU'D THINK IT A SCENE OF CLASSIC D.I.Y., DO-IT-YOURSELF INDUSTRIOUS-NESS: INDY PIONEERS *BLACK FLAG*, SOLE OWNERS OF *THEIR* TRAIL-BLAZING RECORD LABEL *SST*, PREPPING THEIR FIRST FULL LENGTH L.P. FOR RELEASE....

ALL *TRUE*--ONLY, THIS WASN'T *THE PLAN*.

BLACK FLAG

THE LINE-UP, CIRCA DECEMBER, 1981

GREG GINN
FOUNDER
LEAD GUITAR
PRIMARY
SONG WRITER

CHUCK DUKOWSKI
(née GARY McDANIEL)
BASS
SOMETIME
SONG WRITER
TOUR BOOKING

ROBERTO VALVERDE
AKA
'ROBO'
DRUMS

DEZ CADENA
LEAD SINGER UNTIL
4 MONTHS AGO, NOW
RHYTHM GUITAR
AND BACKING VOCALS

... AND HENRY,
THE NEW SINGER

...TODAY IT'S ALL HANDS ON DECK. THE NEW L.P.'s CALLED 'DAMAGED,' AND IT'S SCHEDULED FOR A RELEASE DATE OF <u>NOW</u>. BUT THERE'S A PROBLEM — AND IT'S WITH THE ALBUM'S VISUALS, WHICH MEANS 'CORRECTING' SOME 25,000 RECORD SLEEVES...

...BY HAND.

DAMAGED

USING STICKERS.

ANY AND ALL AVAILABLE SST RECORDS PERSONNEL* AND A FEW TRUSTED SUPPORTERS** SHOW UP TO HELP....

NO, THE PROBLEM'S NOT SOME OFFENSIVE MESSAGE THAT MUST BE REMOVED FOR DECENCY'S SAKE, OR SOME OUTRAGEOUS RAYMOND PETTIBON ARTWORK.***

IT'S MORE SERIOUS THAN THAT.

* SST FOLK LIKE MUGGER AND NEW BOY JOE CARDUCCI, BROUGHT IN BY GINN AND DUKOWSKI AS A CO-OWNER WHO CAN HELP RUN THE LABEL — AND BRING SOME WELCOME CA$H.
** SUPPORTERS LIKE PHOTOGRAPHER GLEN E. FRIEDMAN
*** PETTIBON, BROTHER OF GINN AND ARTIST WHOSE PROVOCATIVE PEN-AND-INK DRAWINGS GRACED JUST ABOUT EVERY BLACK FLAG RELEASE <u>EXCEPT</u> 'DAMAGED.' ('PROVOCATIVE,' E.G., DEMONS W/RAGING ERECTIONS KILLING TERRIFIED COPS.)

SEE, GINN & DUKOWSKI WANT AS BIG AN AUDIENCE AS POSSIBLE FOR THEIR NEW DISC -- SO THEY OK A DEAL TO HAVE 'DAMAGED' DISTRIBUTED BY RECORD INDUSTRY HEAVYWEIGHTS MCA. AT THE TIME, IT SEEMS LIKE A COUP...

BUT DAYS THE RE- THE DEAL

Bass — Charles Dukows
Drums — ROBO
Recorded at Unicorn Studios Hollywood
Produced by SPOT and BLACK FLAG
Engineered by SPOT and Francis Buckley
assistant engineer Chuck Vogt
Cover Photo — Ed Colver

SST

T Records, P.O. Box 1, Lawndale, Calif.

TAKE A CLOSER LOOK AT THE CREDITS ON THIS HERE ALBUM...

WE SEE THE FAMOUS SST LOGO, AND THE LABEL'S **LAWNDALE** * P.O. BOX --BUT WHAT'S WITH THE PONY? **

*THIS TOWN -- "LAWNDALE" -- YOU HAD TO WONDER IF THEY WEREN'T PUTTING US ON... IT SOUNDED LIKE EVERYTHING BLACK FLAG STOOD AGAINST— THE PERFECT SPOT TO DROP THE BAND'S H.Q. AND PLANT ITS FLAG OF ANARCHY. IN FACT, IT'S AN ANONYMOUS, INDUSTRIAL SPLINTER OF A TOWN LODGED IN THE SOUTHBAY'S BACKSIDE.

** A UNICORN?! COULD THERE BE A LESS HARDCORE, LESS SST ANIMAL? HOWEVER, THE CLOVEN HOOFS ARE A NICE TOUCH.

ROB SHEFFIELD ON TOMMY JAMES AND THE SHONDELLS, PIXIES, THE CURE, ROLLING STONES AND OTHERS

FROM *LOVE IS A MIX TAPE**

via vespucci

DECEMBER 2002

A SIDE ONE DATE/TIME	**B** SIDE TWO DATE/TIME
Elton John: "Mellow"	• Stevie Wonder: "Golden Lady"
John Lennon: "Oh My Love"	• Tom T. Hall: "I Miss a Lot of Trains"
Fairport Convention: "Tale in Hard Time"	• Lonnie Donegan: "Does Your Chewing Gum Lose Its Flavor (On the
Gary Stewart: "Out of Hand"	• Bedpost Overnight)"
Lou Christie: "Two Faces Have I"	• The Monkees: "Daydream Believer"
The Dovells: "Bristol Stomp"	• The Chordettes: "Mr. Sandman"
Martha and the Vandellas: "No More Tearstained Make Up"	• Lou Christie: "The Gypsy Cried"
	• Swingin' Medallions: "Double Shot
Gary U.S. Bonds: "Quarter to Three"	• (Of My Baby's Love)"
Ron Wood: "Mystifies Me"	• Jive Five: "Hully Gully Calling Time"
Jerry Butler: "For Your Precious Love"	• Ray Barretto: "El Watusi"
Elton John: "Dirty Little Girl"	• Freddy Cannon: "Palisades Park"
Beach Boys: "Johnny Carson"	• Chubby Checker: "The Fly"
Jerry Lee Lewis: "Whole Lotta Shakin'"	• Joe Jones: "You Talk Too Much"

*Sheffield, Rob. *Love Is a Mix Tape: Life and Loss, One Song at a Time*. New York: Crown Publishing, 2007, 27–37. Used with permission.

Everly Brothers: "All I Have to Do Is Dream"	• Dion and the Belmonts: "Love Came to Me"
Five Americans: "Western Union"	• Brenda Lee: "Sweet Nothin's"
	• Tommy James & the Shondells: "Mirage"
	• Merrilee Rush and the Turnabouts: "Angel of the Morning"
	• Ohio Express: "Yummy Yummy Yummy"
	• Fats Domino: "I'm Walkin'"

I made this tape while moving into my new apartment in Brooklyn. The living room has a china cabinet, but I loaded it up with tapes instead of dishes, unpacking one box of cassettes after another. I still haven't finished unpacking—by the time I do, it'll be time to move again.

One of the things I love about my neighborhood is the junk shop on Manhattan Avenue that has a basement full of used vinyl. The store doesn't have a name, or a sign out front, but once you venture down the stairs, you're in a shrine. I have never seen so many records crammed into one room, ceiling to floor. They're not in any order, so it's a place to spend a winter day scavenging for buried treasure. After my first visit there, I look my armful of records home and made this tape. There are crackles and scratches everywhere. Some of the songs are old favorites, some are new to me. I had never even heard of Tommy James and the Shondells' "Mirage"—how did I possibly live so much of my life without that song? Martha and the Vandellas' *Watchout!*—how did I manage without that one?

I live in a new city, where I have found friends who never met Renée and only know her through me. My ears runneth over with new favorite songs, new favorite bands, new favorite people to share them with. I met a girl, an astrophysicist who moved here from Charlottesville, and fell in love. We met while I was visiting friends down there; I first heard her voice on the car radio, where she was doing a Pixies tribute show on WTJU as DJ Astrogrrrl. She made me a mix for my birthday, a real cassette, although I couldn't read the label because she wrote it in Japanese. So many great songs: The Normal's "Warm Leatherette," Siouxsie's "Happy House," The Pixies' "Cactus," The Cure's "A Night Like This." Well, clearly this was nothing but good.

Ally Astrogrrrl and I listened to the iPod I gave her for her birthday, which is pink to match the winter coat she wears over her fishnets. Last Christmas she used it to DJ the NASA holiday party, blasting the Stooges and David Bowie until one of the other scientists came over to turn the volume down. On Friday nights, we go eat sushi and play pinball, while she feeds quarters into the jukebox to play Bauhaus and Sisters of Mercy, bands I used to hate until I met her. Her specialty is galactic structure—and I can't even find my way around McGuinness Boulevard. She explains the movements of the galaxies to me; she digs through her shoebox of high school tapes and plays me Skinny Puppy, Revolting Cocks, My Life with the Thrill Kill Kult, and other bands I never gave a damn about. They took Love and Rockets' "Ball of Confusion" off the jukebox at The Library on Avenue A because she wouldn't stop playing it. Her karaoke anthem is Nirvana's "Lithium."

On weekend afternoons, Astrogrrrl and I can hear my upstairs neighbor sing along with her favorite Queen song, which is "Don't Stop Me Now." She likes that song *a lot*. She never plays it just once. I didn't notice before, but it has the exact same lyrics as Eric B. and Rakim's "Follow the Leader." I don't know my upstairs neighbor's name, or where she's from, but I know she loves to hit those Freddy Mercury high notes and blast off. She had a boyfriend for a while who used to listen to folk music, but now he doesn't seem to be around anymore. She still has "Don't Stop Me Now," though. The cars outside of my window blast Polish hip-hop, 24/7. I'm literally surrounded by music.

Sometimes I run into old friends I haven't seen in years, who ask how Renée is—that still happens. Now it happens maybe once a year or so. They usually tell me a Renée story I haven't yet heard. I am always happy to hear her name. I was once at a house party in Brooklyn, waiting in line for the bathroom with a friend I didn't meet until a couple of years ago, when he randomly asked, "Hey, what was Renée's favorite Hank Williams song?" That made my night. (It was "Setting the Woods on Fire.") I meet new songs, too, and the new songs will sometimes bring her up. Renée told me about Gary Stewart's "Out of Hand" once, said it could have been written about us. I recently heard it for the first time. She was right.

I make new friends and hear their stories. Last fall, I was sitting at the kitchen table of two friends who have been together since 1972. They tell me a story about how they got together. She couldn't decide between two suitors, so she left New York City to spend the summer in an ashram. (Did I mention it was 1972?) One of the suitors sent her postcards while she was gone, the famous postcards that came inside the sleeve of the Rolling Stone's *Exile on Main Street*. Needless to say, he was the suitor who won her hand. They tell me this story, laughing and interrupting each other, as their teenage daughter walks through the kitchen on her way out to a Halloween party. I've heard of these postcards—over the years, I've heard plenty of record-collector guys boast that they own the original vinyl *Exile on Main Street* with the original postcards, intact and pristine in the virgin sleeve. I've never heard of *anybody* getting rid of their prized *Exile* postcards, much less actually writing on them and sending them through the mail to a girl. I watch these two, laughing over this story at the same kitchen table they've shared for thirty years. I realize that I will never fully understand the millions of bizarre ways that music brings people together.

If I didn't want to have these experiences, didn't want to run into living things that reminded me of the past, I would have to hide under a rock—except that would remind me of the past, too, so I try not to hide. What shocks me is that the present is alive. It wouldn't have shocked Renée.

I depend on my friends to remind me that what started in the nineties isn't all dead, and the struggles of those years are not all lost, and the future is unwritten. Astrogrrrl and I go see our favorite local bar band, the Hold Steady, every time they play. They always end with our favorite song, "Killer Parties," and sometimes I think, man, all the people I get to hear this song with, we're going to miss each other when we die. When we die, we will turn into songs, and we will hear each other and remember each other.

JOSEPH DEUEL ON HÜSKER DÜ

Hüsker Dü in Philadelphia, 1984 by Joseph Deuel. Used with permission from the artist.

I took this 1984 photograph of Hüsker Dü in a Victorian row-house basement in Philadelphia dubbed the West Side Club, a play on the East Side Club, an established disco on the other side of town. There was a converted coal-burning asbestos-covered furnace in the middle of the floor and no stage, just a clip-on lamp over Bob Mould. Hüsker Dü couldn't get a gig anywhere else in town so they agreed to play there. They seemed disgruntled and played an abbreviated set. It's still the loudest, most kinetic show I've ever seen. A friend and I were standing right up at the front and ten beats into the first song we found ourselves pressed against the back wall. People were slamming into one another like atoms. I finally got brave enough to move toward the front again to take some pictures: I'd scuttle forward along the wall for a few feet before this mass of bodies would slam me into the wall while I protected my camera with both arms. The bodies would then bounce to the other side of the room for a few seconds and I'd move forward a few more feet before the bodies came back again. I finally got close enough to get this picture. I want a photograph to give the feel of what a show was like. In this shot, Bob Mould is a bit blurry which for me captures the frenetic feel of that performance.

I love music that is truly obscure and flourishes in small, dark corners of venues that hold less than a hundred people. Places like Caffè Lena tend to have very flat lighting so it's hard to coax good photographs out of such a space. You can't take successful photographs in a venue like that with an automatic because the camera tries to make the image look like you're shooting in daylight and you end up with a blurry, bright photo when you really want it to look like what it is, a dark, atmospheric place. If you need to take photographs of the shows you write about, consider buying a camera with a decent zoom lens—you need an optical zoom rather than a digital one. That alone will make your photographs a lot better than those you take with your phone.

Here are a few of Joseph Deuel's suggestions to help you take better live music photographs:

- Take whatever you can get. Before digital, I would shoot a roll or half a roll of film, but now with my digital camera I might shoot 200 photos at a show. That really does increase your chances of getting an image you like.

- Take pictures of people when they're not performing full tilt. Not every image should be a high drama shot. Photograph your subjects looking down or when an expression comes over their faces that tells you they're thinking about something.

- Make the light work for you. Find an angle on your subject rather than shooting it head-on—straight ahead flat light is the worst so you want to be off to the side rather than right in front of someone you're photographing.

- Shoot close more often rather than taking a picture of the whole room or the full stage. A close shot is not something your cellphone is going to do well because even if you zoom in you're just cropping rather than getting the benefit of a real optical zoom lens. Getting up close with a decent lens will combat the problem I see every week on Facebook: pictures from Lena's shot with phones that look like what they are—bad phone photos.

- Go down low or up high to shoot. A lot of people shoot from eye level all the time. One of the advantages of a good digital camera is the live view feature. I can hold the camera over my head to shoot like I've always done but now I can see what I'm shooting.

- Avoid conventional shots. You can get worthwhile images with any camera as long as you think about what you're doing and how you frame your subject. A lot of people place a subject's face right in the middle of the frame instead of thinking of the whole frame as a palette. Photograph someone off to one side or make the lighting, the stage, or the background part of the photo instead of just sticking your camera right in front of your subject and firing away.

Joseph Deuel has been an avid photographer since grade school. He discovered Caffè Lena, the country's oldest continuously operating folk coffeehouse, in his home town of Saratoga Springs, New York during high school in the early 1970s and has been taking photos there ever since of artists ranging from Dave van Ronk to Arlo Guthrie and Ani DiFranco to Rick Danko. Many of his photographs have appeared on album covers and in magazines. His work appears prominently in the recent book *Caffè Lena: Inside America's Legendary Coffeehouse* (Brooklyn, NY: powerHouse Books, 2013).

CAMPBELL MCGRATH ON BOB DYLAN

The Style for Dylan (1965)*

Adorable Bob, deplorable Bob, not yet mascara-and-fedora Bob, lean and hungry, all
    cheek bones, fawn and leopard skin,
ain't got nothing to lose Bob, adrenaline and benzedrine Bob, hungry and frugal,
    positively 4th and McDougall Street Bob,
wings of mercury Bob, hermetic and copacetic Bob, poetic Bob in his pointed shoes
    and bells, glibly Shakespearean,
high-toned and empyrean, rollicking, frolicsome Bob hitting only high notes,
    primetime Bob wraith-like in the limelight,
swanning, sneering, bejeweled in black shades, baby faced Bob with a headful of
    snakes, meal-scrounging changeling chasing the dragon,
O precious gifted snarling unrefusable Parnassian haughty habit-forming Bob,
    masterful and disaster prone, wicked and aquiline,
working stiff Bob, put you on the day shift Bob, swaggering and stomping in the back
    alley Bob, folkways Bob, payday Bob, next-in-line-for-the-big-time Bob,
strung out Bob, everybody-who-was-hanging-out Bob, cast down and resurrected,
    chooga-looga bluesman manqué,
rock and roll Bob lifting the riff from "La Bamba," stealing a march on Lennon &
    McCartney, revolutionary youth to the electrified barricades,
plugged in Bob, Stratocaster Bob kicking out the jams, fortune and fame Bob, bridge
    and chorus, verse and refrain Bob,
Bob the troubadour caught in a revolving door, crowned with laurels, crowned with
    thorns, amphetamine Bob cruising the skyline in a Buick 6,
handsome cab and Detroit chariot Bob, Triumph motorcycle and freight train Bob,
    bootstrap Bob, imposter Bob, Judas Iscariot Bob,
ear to the ground Bob and burn it down Bob, hey you get off of my cloud Bob,
    whatever you do, play it fuckin' loud, Bob.

---

*McGrath, Campbell. Printed with permission from the author.

WRITING PROMPT: THE ANNOTATED MIX TAPE

Make a mix tape or playlist of either five or ten songs for a friend or lover and write 200 words about each one, what it means to you and why you chose to include it on the "tape" for the intended recipient. Think beyond what you *like* about the songs and focus on how you discovered them, how they sound and what emotions they reveal in the context of your relationship with the person for whom you made the mix.

WRITING PROMPT: OTHER VOICES

Inserting personal experience into your music writing is just one of the ways to get intimate with the music. How about embodying a fictional character you encounter in a song?

What did Billie Jean have to say about the paternity battle? (Michael Jackson).

Offer a riposte from Maggie of "Maggie's Farm" to the song's narrator (Bob Dylan).

Use one of these characters or select one of your own and write a 1000-word story told from the perspective of a character in a popular song. Write about his or her life outside of the song. What is your character's daily life like? What did he or she do before or after the events of the song take place?

WRITING PROMPT: HEADLINES
FROM TITLES

Harry Smith wrote newspaper-like headlines for the songs he collected in the "Ballads" section of his *Anthology of American Folk Music*.* Read several of Smith's headlines after listening to the songs they describe. Here are a few examples:

For Coley Jones's "Drunkard's Special": Wife's Logic Fails to Explain Strange Bedfellow to Drunkard

For Chubby Parker's "King Kong Kitchie Kitchie Ki-Me-O": Zoological Miscegeny Achieved in Mouse Frog Nuptuals, Relatives Approve

For Uncle Eck Dunford's "Old Shoes and Leggings": Mother Hospitable, But Girls Find Shoddy Oldster Perverse

Find several more recent songs that have a strong narrative and write your own headlines for them.

Suggestions: Thin Lizzy's "The Boys Are Back In Town"; Elvis Costello's "Alison"; Richard Thompson's "Beeswing"

---

*Smith, Harry, editor. *Anthology of American Folk Music* (Smithsonian Folkways, 1952 [remastered and rereleased on CD 1997])

THE GO-BETWEENS

DESERT ISLAND DISCS

In 1942 the BBC first aired Desert Island Discs, a radio program in which invited guests are interviewed and asked to select the music that they would keep with them if stranded on a desert Island. The show is currently hosted by Kirsty Young and you can find recordings of the show through the BBC website's iPlayer. Each "castaway," as the guests are called, needs to select 8 songs, 1 book and 1 luxury item. We polled our 40 experts with a similar question: If you were stranded on a desert island for 1 year (assuming you have food and shelter) and could only bring 3 songs, 2 objects, and 1 novel, what would they be?

Songs: Metallica's "Welcome Home (Sanitarium)," Otis Redding's "Sittin' On The Dock of the Bay," and Rick Ross' "B.M.F." Objects: iPad and turntable. Novel: *The Great Gatsby.*—**Kyle Anderson**, senior writer, *Entertainment Weekly*

"Tomorrow Never Knows"—the Beatles, "Soon"—My Bloody Valentine, "On the Western Plains"—Leadbelly, a 3D printer, a laptop with internet, and *Ulysses.*—**Michael Azerrad**, author, journalist and Editor-in-Chief of the *Talkhouse*

"The Winner Takes It All," ABBA. "Let's Go Crazy," Prince. "Bizness," TuneYards. A record player (obviously), an accordion. "Candide," by Voltaire.—**Michael Barclay**, freelance writer/broadcaster, co-author, *Have Not Been the Same: The CanRock Renaissance 1985–1995*

Songs: Sam and Dave's "When Something Is Wrong With My Baby," The Flamin' Groovies' "Shake Some Action," and Skafish's "Wild Night Tonight." Objects: My iPod; a camera. Novel: Jeffrey Eugenides's *The Virgin Suicides* glued to William Faulkner's *The Sound and the Fury* (I cheated)—**Joe Bonomo**, music columnist, *The Normal School*, and Associate Professor of English at Northern Illinois University.

The songs (doing a First Thought, Best Thought thing here): Pavement's "Grounded," Elvis's "Tomorrow Is a Long Time," Santo and Johnny's "Sleep Walk"; the objects: a harpoon and a machete; the novel: Proust's *In Search of Lost Time.*—**Bryan Charles**, writer and **33⅓** author

The songs would all have to be for creature comfort, so I'm thinking: Andrew W.K.'s "We Want Fun," Weezer's "You Gave Your Love To Me Softly," and Queen's "Don't Stop Me Now." As for the rest, I'd look at the year as a woodshedding opportunity and bring a piano to finally practice, *Infinite Jest* to finally read, and a baseball to finally learn the knuckleball.—**Phillip Crandall**, author of the **33⅓** book on Andrew W.K.'s *I Get Wet*

"Moonage Daydream" from Bowie Live in Santa Monica 1972, "Can't Get Started" by Bunny Berigan and "Concerto for Orchestra" by Bartók. The objects would be pencils and plenty of paper (the better to sketch with), and the novel would be *War & Peace* (tho' I'd probably feel guilty that I didn't choose *Anna Karenin* . . . or the bible).—**Marty Davis**, comic book creator

Songs: "Layla," "Heard It Through the Grapevine," and "Gimme Shelter." Objects: MacBook Air (if I could keep it running w/o AC!); eyeglasses. Novel: *Ulysses*.— **Kevin J. H. Dettmar**, author, **33⅓** book, Gang of Four's *"Entertainment!"*

Songs: "Discreet Music" by Brian Eno, "He Loved Him Madly" by Miles Davis and "Desolation Row" by Bob Dylan. Objects: A good knife and a sturdy metal pot. Novel: *War and Peace*.—**Bruce Eaton**, author, *Radio City* (**33⅓**)

Songs: "Dreaming My Dreams With You" by Waylon Jennings, "I Just Wasn't Made for These Times" by the Beach Boys and "Throw It Away" by Abbey Lincoln (these three songs will be different tomorrow, by the way). Objects: My guitar and a rubber ball. Novel: *The Blue Flower* by Penelope Fitzgerald.—**Jim Fusilli**, rock and pop critic, *The Wall Street Journal*, Editor, ReNewMusic.net

I'd bring Otis Redding's "Sittin On The Dock of the Bay," Clipse's "Ride Around Shining," and The Beatles' "A Day in the Life." For objects, I'd bring a picture of my wife and kid and a bottle of Sazerac 18 rye. For a novel, I'd bring *Gravity's Rainbow* so I'd be forced to finish it.—**Matthew Gasteier**, **33⅓** author

Songs: 1. Desert Island? I think one song would have to be reggae: Steel Pulse's "Wild Goose Chase." I don't agree with the lines about contraception and abortion but if I could only choose one Steel Pulse song, "Wild Goose Chase" is the one ("Throne of Gold" would make me too love sick). 2. I think a second song would be Odd Future's "Oldie." This is basically the more bang for your buck principle. Ten minutes of music and a whole crew of innovative emcees. 3. Carol King's "Far Away." She's the best, and if I was stuck in one place missing people at certain moments, this song would do me good. Objects: A thick notebook for writing and an endless ink pen (I'd have to research the best one).

Book: It would have to be a long novel that I've never read before. Perhaps the bible.—**Anthony Kwame Harrison**, popular music scholar, Virginia Tech

Songs: Pamelo Mounk'a—"L'Argent Appelle L'Argent," Rolling Stones—"You Better Move On" and Nick Drake—"Northern Sky." Objects: A Crocodile machete (I collect machetes. Crocodile is the Rolls-Royce of machete makers.) A bowl from Heath Ceramics (the interior glaze is a different yet complimentary color to the outer finish, like Japanese ceramics but a lot sturdier). Novel: Denis Johnson—*Jesus' Son.*—**Richard Henderson**, music writer and **33⅓** author

I'd probably try to take something that was new to me, and likely to reward a year's listening. Perhaps a year on a desert island would be enough to gain some understanding of the Ring cycle, or modern jazz, or Indian classical music. I'd bring a musical instrument and try to learn it.—**Sam Inglis**, Features Editor, *Sound On Sound* magazine

SONGS!?!?! I'm an album guy so this might be hard. But I'm gonna say: "Heartbreak Road," Bill Withers. I have listened to this maybe more than any other recording. I know I'll never get sick of it. "The Tracks of My Tears," Smokey Robinson and The Miracles. What a goddamn song.

"India," John Coltrane. I think you could keep trying to find the center of this song, and that could keep changing for you. Two objects: A huge box of micron pens and a huge box of blank notebooks. Novel: I actually think *Moby Dick* would be the prime pick. Just because I'd finally make myself finish it.—**Casey Jarman**, Managing Editor, the *Believer*

I once wrote a piece for Stylus (RIP) about Bonnie "Prince" Billy's *I See a Darkness* being the perfect desert island disc, and I stand by that!—**Matt LeMay**, senior contributor, Pitchfork

Three songs is pretty austere! "Visions of Johanna" (Dylan), "Days" (Kinks), "Chariots of Fire" (Al Green). That's off the top of my head. A guitar, to give me something to learn, and a typewriter, for the days I wanted to feel like I already knew what I was doing. And *Moby Dick*.—**Jonathan Lethem**, novelist

"To Here Knows When," by My Bloody Valentine, "When the Levee Breaks," by Led Zeppelin, and "White Clouds," by Aglaia (so I can get to sleep), my driver (golf club), boxing gloves and *Crime and Punishment.*—**Chris Ott**, 33⅓ author

Songs: John Coltrane "My Favorite Things" (live version from *Afro Blue Impressions*); My Bloody Valentine "To Here Knows When"; New Order

"Temptation"; objects: Swiss Army knife, lighter; novel: *Infinite Jest*.—**Mark Richardson**, Editor-in-Chief, Pitchfork

My three songs would be David Bowie's "Station to Station," Missy Elliott's "Let Me Fix My Weave" and Pulp's "Underwear." The objects would be Parliament's *Uncle Jam Wants You* and Isaac Hayes' *Hot Buttered Soul*—even if I can't play the LPs, the album covers inspire me to be my most indomitably resilient self.

Ulysses is my favorite novel but it's so social and urban it would make me miserable to read it on a desert island, so I'd bring *Finnegans Wake*, which I've been reading since 1988 without (obviously) even coming close to exhausting (or even comprehending). That's what I did for Hurricane Sandy—I holed up with some candles and *Finnegans Wake*. Then I blinked my eyes and a week had gone by.—**Rob Sheffield**, writer, *Rolling Stone*

Songs is too tough, so I'll do one album: Leadbelly's *Last Sessions*. A perfect and very personal collection of American folk music, and one that means a lot to me. Objects: A coffee maker and a really big can of coffee! Novel: Dickens' *Great Expectations* is my favorite, but I think I'd prefer one of the big Russian classics that I've never read, like *War and Peace* or *Anna Karenina*.—**Ben Sisario**, reporter, the *New York Times*

To be clichéd, the novel honestly would be *In Search of Lost Time* (so I could finally finish it). I can't imagine three songs I could listen to exclusively for a year without coming to hate them, but I would bring a guitar so that I could play the songs I remembered and write new ones. And a computer to write them on. You say there'd be no power for the computer, but then how would I play the songs anyway? In lieu of that, notebooks and pens.—**Carl Wilson**, Toronto-based writer and Slate.com music critic

Three songs: Randy Newman's "I Just Want You to Hurt Like I Do," Stephen Hartke's "King of the Sun" and The Beatles' "Let it Be." Two objects: A bowl and a knife. A novel: Amos Tutuola's *My Life in the Bush of Ghosts*.—**Ross Simonini**, writer, Editor at the *Believer* magazine, musician

Songs: Paul Simon: "Graceland"; Stars of the Lid: "Requiem for Dying Mothers"; Andrew Bird: "Masterfade." Objects: a large bell and a mallet. Novel: Albert Camus, *The Stranger*—**Scott Tennent**, 33⅓ author

Wow, we don't even get to do this with full albums any more, huh? OK. And I will not even cheat by bringing infinite media on one of the devices. Songs I'm always happy to hear: Prince's "Kiss," New Order's "True Faith," Stereolab's

"Jenny Ondioline." Objects: a ukulele (the kind with unbreakable strings) and a notebook (the kind that has lots of writing implements attached to its cover). A novel I've always wanted to read: *Gravity's Rainbow*.—**Douglas Wolk**, freelance arts journalist

Songs: "Power" by Kanye West, "Losing My Edge" by LCD Soundsystem, "Tenth Avenue Freeze-Out" by Bruce Springsteen. Objects: Laptop and a hoodie. Book: *Fear and Loathing on the Campaign Trail* by Hunter S. Thompson.—**Alex Young**, founder and publisher, Consequence of Sound

Songs: "This Year" by the Mountain Goats, "Game of Pricks" by Guided By Voices, "All I Could Do Was Cry" by Etta James. Objects: my dog, Chocolate, and my dog Chocolate's favorite toy, Birdie. Novel: *Mrs. Dalloway* by Virginia Woolf.—**Lindsay Zoladz**, Associate Editor, Pitchfork

CHAPTER 10
HOW IT SOUNDS

INTRODUCTION

Some of the keenest pleasure I've experienced reading about music derives not only from the work of brilliant stylists and prescient culture critics, but from nuts-and-bolts accounts teeming with facts, exhaustive chronologies, studio notes, and descriptions of musical instruments.

When I read Mark Lewisohn's remarkably comprehensive accounts of the Beatles' recording sessions at Abbey Road (*The Complete Beatles Recording Sessions*) or Andy Babiuk's compelling and meticulously researched book on the instruments the band used and the stories attached to them (*Beatles Gear: All the Fab Four's Instruments from Stage to Studio*; we include here an excerpt concerning the Mellotron that contributes the defining sound to "Strawberry Fields Forever") I often find more satisfaction reveling in pure information than I do following an extended interpretation or a complex aesthetic claim about a given song or lyric.

The focus and labor required to master so much information and the organizational acumen to present it in an appealing, accessible way are essential aspects of any worthwhile music writing. When hard facts undergird an emotionally or intellectually ambitious piece of writing, their solid presence provides a central and satisfying base on which to build ideas and opinions. This sense of solidity can also emerge when a writer describes the fundamental elements of a composition or performance in technical musical terms.

In conveying "how it sounds" whether by describing the conditions under which music was recorded, the way the musicians played their instruments, or the technical features that mark the music itself, the pieces collected in this chapter remind us not to neglect the power of basic facts and objective truths—writers need to know how to find and convey the facts about their subjects before discussing their significance or meaning.—MW

EXPERT ADVICE FROM OUR WRITERS

Knowledge accelerates understanding but softens surprise, perhaps. It helps you see under the hood, and notice details that might pass another writer by. But you still have to write about them well. (And there are lots of would-be musicians who attempt to write about music as a compensation for lapsed careers—they have superior knowledge but frequently write less well.)—**R. J. Wheaton**, Publisher, *Hazlitt* magazine; author of **33⅓** *Dummy*

There's a general inadequacy of written language to capture facets of the musical experience. What seems like an inspired sentence about music at the moment of writing usually, on later reflection, appears too rigid and dull. That said, this very elusiveness of music does often force the writer into more imaginative avenues than other objects of inquiry might—which is what makes it a rewarding task in the first place.—**Nick Attfield**, music academic

Elaborate descriptions of music will never come close to accurately describing the experience of listening to music. I prefer music writing that discusses the aspects that are suited to the act of writing and description and language.—**Ross Simonini**, writer, Editor at the *Believer* magazine, musician

When you're writing about the technical side of music, good style has more to do with clarity and precision than using a lot of adjectives. Nevertheless, the recording of album Y by Z routinely turns out to have been much more complicated than you might expect, so our features often run to many thousands of words. By dint of being especially ruthless with the adjectives, I got this one down to a slim two thousand or so.—**Sam Inglis**, Features Editor, *Sound On Sound* magazine

Technical knowledge about [music] does not translate to poetry in your prose. If you're profiling a musician, the most important thing is to capture their character and tell a captivating story. If you're reviewing, you should definitely know enough about music to not make foolish mistakes that would make even other non-musicians cringe (mistaking a conga for a bongo, for example, or a mandolin for a banjo). If you're going to employ any remotely technical term at all, do your research. You don't have to know how to play drums to know what a hi-hat is, or what it sounds like.—**Michael Barclay**, freelance writer/broadcaster, co-author, *Have Not Been the Same: The CanRock Renaissance 1985–1995*

I joke that most of the musicians I write about use three or fewer chords so there's not much technically that I need to be up to speed on. Yet it's true that the more I write about music the more helpful it is to have knowledge about basic stuff like chords and keys and notation and changes, styles of playing, the jamming/rehearsing ethos, and recording techniques. In my case, that knowledge is gleaned from talking to musician friends and by listening and reading.—**Joe Bonomo**, music columnist, *The Normal School*, and Associate Professor of English at Northern Illinois University

Recording one's impressions of a given performance need not engage the rarified lexicon forged and spoken by composers and arrangers. Increasingly, though, I do feel that a working knowledge of music technology and the ability to translate same for the lay reader is helpful. I've read a lot of music writing where the author clearly had little to no understanding of the recording process. Their efforts to describe what guitar pedals do, or how a producer contributed to the making of an album, usually amount to an extended malapropism. (Jimmy McDonough's *Shakey*, about Neil Young, exemplifies this shortcoming. By contrast, John Perry's **33⅓** monograph on Hendrix's *Electric Ladyland* does as good as job as one could want of rendering music technology understandable to a reader who might not truly comprehend all that's implied by a term like "feedback.") Ultimately, the great thought about all of this comes from my late colleague John Storm Roberts, who felt that a "universal language of music" was crap and, even if such a language existed, no one would want to learn it.—**Richard Henderson**, music writer and **33⅓** author

Ideally, you need to know about music to write about music. Learning to make music is one way of learning about music. Studying music theory is another, and I'd have thought it pretty much essential for anyone who wants to write about classical music. The most important thing of all is to be honest with yourself about the extent of your knowledge. When you know that you don't know, you can write around potential pitfalls. When you try to bluff, you'll get found out.—**Sam Inglis**, Features Editor, *Sound On Sound* magazine

Depending on the outlet you're writing for, you may need to know aspects of the craft. You probably can't write for *Billboard* or *Forbes* without knowing something about the music business. You probably shouldn't write for *Guitar Player* magazine without understanding how the guitar is played.—**Casey Jarman**, Managing Editor, the *Believer*

Technical dissections of pop music are absurd in the extreme. I regard the mathematical and textual approach to music as a kind of botany, giving names to things to create a self-reinforcing dialog familiar only to—exclusively to—the academics who have access to its practitioners. This may sound mystical, anti-intellectual or peripatetic, but assigning values to every aspect of art denudes it of all empiric beauty, and subsumes it in dialog. By binding art to external terms we imprison something that underscores the inert, creative impotence of its critics.—**Chris Ott**, 33⅓ author

I happen to be both a writer and a musician, but I don't put much stock in the old "if you can't make a better record, don't critique my record" canard. To me, good music writing speaks to how music does what it does from a listener's perspective, not from a musician's perspective. If anything, I often find myself having to tone down the more technical stuff in my writing because it will mean nothing to most readers.—**Matt LeMay**, senior contributor, Pitchfork

I studied music for a year at the Royal Academy of Music in London four years ago, after writing about music for over thirty years, to see what difference it would make to how and what I wrote about music. What would happen to my writing if I had a little technical knowledge about the architecture and history of music stretching back hundreds of years. It was a kind of test—would it ruin me as a writer to know more about the writing and theory of music or would it make me better? It didn't get in the way, and just made me think a little deeper, and write about things—Mozart, Bartok, Britten—I wouldn't have before. It confirmed that my instincts about why I liked and disliked certain music were correct, and that there was an intuitive response I had to lazy, corny, predictable, banal, formulaic music, or to brilliant, surprising, provocative music based not necessarily on the complexity or technical originality of the music but other factors. And as a writer about pop and rock you tend mostly to be talking about the sound of the music, and where it fits into the technological history of the music and the fashion of the times. Studying notation and the process and procedure of (classical) composition did make me realize that as a writer what I had been writing about for decades was not really the music—the notes, chords, instruments—but more the context around it, its basic cultural meaning, its emotional resonance, its psychic energy, its fashions and poses, its heroes and innovators, and what impact it had on my life and thinking. As a music writer I was not writing about music, I was writing about my emotions, how I responded to the music, how it fitted into cultural and social history, how it connected to other music, to art, poetry, cinema, theatre, show business, television, comedy, politics, how it moved things forward, how it made a difference in the wider world, how glamorous, strange, exotic it was, and what it was that fascinated, or repelled me, about the people who made, played and performed the music. I was writing more about adventure, intelligence, ideas, innovation, character—or lack of those things—and a search for meaning, than music.—**Paul Morley**, writer and critic

The best reviews are by critics who can recognize something going on in the song that produces a particular sensation in the listener—the way it was produced, how the instruments are working to produce a certain effect—so that readers can put it in a context of other music they've heard. Good reviews don't necessarily focus heavily on these things, but they know when and when not to reference the process. It's what gives music writers some authority to do what they do, and in my opinion the best music writers educate the reader about music without sounding like that's what they're doing.—**Evie Nagy**, *Fast Company* staff writer, former editor at *Billboard* and *Rolling Stone*

ANDY BABIUK ON THE BEATLES

The Mellotron and "Strawberry Fields Forever"*

Always searching for new sounds from different instruments, [John] Lennon became one of the first artists in Britain to acquire a unique new keyboard, the Mellotron. It was like 70 tape-recorders in a box. Pressing a key activated one of the pre-recorded tapes inside, loaded with sounds as diverse as pitched strings and brass, rhythm effects, and entire musical passages (although any held note would stop after ten seconds). In effect it was a forerunner of today's sampling keyboards. The Mellotron was in fact the younger brother to a US invention, the Chamberlin keyboard devised in the late 1940s by Harry Chamberlin. A Chamberlin representative, Bill Fransen, visited Britain in the early 1960s, ostensibly in search of tape-head manufacturers, but more likely on the look-out for a marketing opportunity. He stumbled upon electro-mechanical engineers Bradmatic in Birmingham, run by the Bradley brothers, Les, Frank and Norman.

Soon Fransen and the Bradleys collaborated—minus Henry Chamberlin—to form the British sales and distribution company Mellotronics, with the Bradleys set to manufacture a copy of the Chamberlin, the Mellotron Mark I, beginning in 1963. Changes were soon made to this prototype, and the Mark II appeared in 1964. It was this production version that Lennon saw.

Its retail price then was a phenomenal £1,000 (about $2,800 then; around £11,500 or $16,200 in today's money). The sometimes out-of-tune and eerie but always atmospheric sounds of the Mellotron became widely used by many later bands, including The Moody Blues and King Crimson. But despite Lennon's early enthusiasm, The Beatles would not use a Mellotron until the end of 1966 when they added some of its distinctive sounds to the recording of "Strawberry Fields Forever."

The song started out on November 24th with a basic rhythm track of guitars, bass and drums, quickly changing shape with the addition of the Mellotron. Lennon had acquired an early example of the new Mellotron Mark II keyboard back in the summer of 1965. He'd finally found time to experiment with the tape-replay instrument as he looked for a way to include its distinctive sounds on his latest composition. Ironically, it was McCartney who played the Mellotron on the recordings.

For this first take of "Strawberry Fields" McCartney played the brass setting on the Mellotron Mark II. The instrument had two keyboards, the right-hand one being the main section for playing melodies, the left split into rhythm parts and accompaniments.

---

*Babiuk, Andy. *Beatles Gear: All The Fab Four's Instruments, from Stage to Studio* (San Francisco: Backbeat Books, 2002). Used with permission.

Above the right-hand keyboard, pressing the second of six pushbuttons switched to Station 2, which selected the beginning of a particular 42-foot length of pre-recorded tape inside the Mellotron for each key. McCartney—or whoever was working the instrument—would then have moved to a further row of three buttons marks A, B or C, and chosen Track B. This would line up the "brass" portion of the tapes—a recording of close-miked trumpet, trombone and saxophone. Now, pitched single-note lines and chords could be played with this sound on the right-hand keyboard. "Brass" is the Mellotron sound heard throughout take one of "Strawberry Fields," as released on *Anthology 2*.

The sessions spilled into the following day with new versions being recorded, and various instrumental overdubs added along the way, such as Harrison's slide guitar, a piano, more Mellotron, maracas, and speeded-up vocals treated with Ken Townsend's ADT effect. On the 29th November the song was finalized, take 7 being the favored version, but by this time the Mellotron sound had been changed. The Mark II's "flute" sound was now used, selected by hitting Station 1 Track A, and most clearly heard at the very start of the official released version. Next the group started work on another new song, the vaudevillian 'When I'm Sixty-Four,' initially featuring McCartney on piano.

The group and George Martin then decided to remake "Strawberry Fields Forever," starting on December 8th. They went for a different approach, recording a fresh basic track for the song. This new version featured heavy use of backwards hi-hat cymbals, timpani, bongos, tambourine and a wild drum track played by Starr. "All right, calm down Ring," pleaded Lennon as the drummer created an enormous din.

The following day, Harrison added a new Beatles instrument to the developing retake of "Strawberry Fields," a surmandal (often misspelled as swordmandal). This Indian/Pakistani instrument is similar to a board zither, usually with about 40 metal strings played with a plectrum or plectrums, and provides something like the sound of a high-pitched harp. If the released version of "Strawberry Fields" is considered as starting with the song's chorus ("Let me take you down …") and having three subsequent verses in between (one: "Living is easy …," two: "No one I think …," and three: "Always know …") then the surmandal is prominently heard just before the start of verse two (1:18) and verse three (2:04), and also at the end of the song (from 3:06 and prominently from 3:15).

A week later, on December 15th, seven session musicians were hired to overdub trumpets and cellos on to the remake, playing parts that George Martin had written. With this second orchestral/drum version of "Strawberry Fields" now complete, work turned again to "When I'm Sixty-Four" with Starr adding orchestral bells. The Beatles were gradually increasing the input of studio musicians to help complement their sound, and on December 21st three more session players were called upon to add clarinets to "When I'm Sixty-Four."

Two complete recordings on "Strawberry Fields" had now been finalized—the take-7 Mellotron/guitar version and the later drum/orchestral version. The story goes that Lennon was still not completely satisfied with either, and that he simply asked George Martin for them to be joined together. According to Martin, the obstacle the producer faced was that the two versions were at different tempos and in different keys. In order to fuse them, tape speeds had to be manipulated using Abbey Road's frequency-control system. Various theories have been put forward based on the official and unofficial releases of "Strawberry Fields" in its various forms concerning the nature of the tape-speed manipulation. The take-7 Mellotron/guitar version released in its entirety on *Anthology 2* is two semitones higher than the official released version, which implies that it must have been slowed down. Accounts suggest that the drum/orchestral version was also slowed down.

Whatever the technical adjustments, Martin did an apparently remarkable job by bringing the two versions to the same tempo and pitch, and thus was able to satisfy Lennon's request. On the official released recording, about the first minute is the (edited) take-7 Mellotron/guitar version, the rest the drum/orchestral version. To achieve the blend Martin made two edits. The first occurs at 0:55 into the released version, chopping in from elsewhere in the Mellotron/guitar version the "Let me take you down cos I'm ..." phrase needed to provide the start of chorus 2. The at 0:59 comes the main edit, switching to the orchestral/drum version, which kicks in at "... going to Strawberry Fields...." Suddenly there are cellos!

At the very end of the track, coming in around 3:55, is a "re-entry" edit piece with more of the wild Starr drums and some swirling Mellotron. This time, McCartney played the Mark II's left-hand keyboard, selecting a tape of an entire passage of ensemble flutes. The passage was played in a random, repetitive fashion, without necessarily waiting for the internal tape to return to the start after releasing a key. The result sounds something like looped flutes, but is pure Mellotron.

Finally, "Strawberry Fields Forever" was complete, as much a complex studio construction as a new song. Where before the group had been interested in exploring new musical instruments to provide fresh inspiration, the studio itself was now fast becoming an instrument in its own right.

OWEN PALLETT ON KATY PERRY

Explaining the Genius of Katy Perry's "Teenage Dream" —
Using Music Theory*

In the days since Ted Gioia published his essay in the Daily Beast, alleging that music criticism has devolved into lifestyle reporting, with little or no attention paid to how the music itself works, I've been challenged by friends on Facebook to write a "not boring" piece that explains a successful pop song using music theory. My bet is that it'll be boring, but I'm going to do my best not to bore you!

I have picked Katy Perry's "Teenage Dream." Because: this song's success seems to mystify all the Katy Perry haters in the world. Why did it go to No. 1? Let's start by talking about the ingenuity of the harmonic content. This song is all about suspension— not in the voice-leading 4–3 sense, but in the emotional sense, which listeners often associate with "exhilaration," being on the road, being on a roller coaster, travel. This sense of suspension is created simply, by denying the listener any I chords. There is not a single I chord in the song. Laymen, the I chord ("one chord") is the chord that the key is in. For example, a song is in G but there are no G-chords. Other examples of this, in hit singles: Fleetwood Mac's "Dreams" and Stardust's "Music Sounds Better With You"; almost-examples include Earth Wind and Fire's "In September" which has an I chord but only passing and in inversion; same with Coldplay's "Viva La Vida."

Perry's voice is the sun and the song is in orbit around it.

"Teenage Dream" begins with a guitar sounding the I chord but an instant later, when the bass comes in, the I is transformed into an IV (an IV7 chord, to be exact). The I chord will never appear again. Notice, too, how Katy's melody begins on the tonic—tonic: the root note of the missing I chord, the same note that the key is in. She stays around the tonic, reinforces the tonic, and the vocal melody establishes the key so clearly that there is no doubt: Katy's voice is "home"; the rest of the song is oscillating around her. Even when the tonic note would clash with the chord (as it does over the V chord, on "feel like I'm living a") she hammers it home. Her voice is the sun and the song is in orbit around it.

The "feeling of suspension" I mentioned is an effect of this. The insistence of the tonic in the melody keeps your ears' eyes fixed on the destination, but the song never arrives there. Weightlessness is achieved. Great work, songwriters!

The second key to this song's Enormous Chart Success has to do with the weighting of the melody lines. Perfect balance of tension and release. Each line of the verses

---

*Pallett, Owen. "Explaining the Genius of Katy Perry's 'Teenage Dream'—Using Music Theory." *Slate Magazine*, March 25, 2014. Used with permission.

begin straight, on the beat, but end with a syncopation: [straight:] "you think I'm pretty without any" [syncopated:] "makeup on."

A brief aside: Dev Hynes (Blood Orange) is sometimes criticized as not "R&B" enough by some music writers—these writers often cite Dev's previous work in rock band Test Icicles as indicative of some illegitimacy of intention. But Dev's songwriting trademark—his supposed weakness—is rooted in this exact thing, the weighting of syllables. Unlike most R&B, Dev writes songs where the melody has no syncopation; they sound like hymns. Boring, perhaps, to you, but other people (myself included) hear a glorious religious calm, a stateliness.

Similarly, think about Black Sabbath's "Paranoid," where almost every note is off the beat. "FI-nished with my woman cause sheeee WOULDn't help meeeee WITH myyyy LIFE." It's kind of a bad melody, no? Doesn't suit the lyrics at all, has an vaguely ESL vibe, weighted all wrong. But the song is called "Paranoid" and he is singing about how you should enjoy life and how he wishes he could do the same but it's too late. It suits the material, works great.

Back to Katy. Her lyrics stretch into each subsequent bar: "You think I'm pretty without any makeup/ on, you think I'm . . ." etc. The "on" is more part of the next line than the proceeding one. Her lines dovetail elegantly into each other. This contributes to the feeling of suspension that I mentioned above. As listeners, we're waiting for her to get to the point. And here it comes!

As Katy moves out of introspective mode and starts using imperatives "Let's go all the way tonight! No regrets! Just love!" she gets straight, more serious, no syncopation. Then—genius—the chorus inverts the weighting that we heard in the verse. [Syncopated:] "You make me [straight:] "feel like I'm living a . . ." [syncopated:] "teenage dream!" And the gooey heart of the song, the "skin tight jeans" bit, is rhythmically entirely straight, voice tumbling out of the tonic-focused cage of the verse and chorus, like long-hair from a scrunchie released.

A particular point of pleasure: The title of the song ("Teenage Dream") is sung syncopated on the chorus, but straight on the bridge. Compare the two in your head. Do you hear that? How brilliant. The title of the song is rhythmically weighted two ways—it's like a flank attack. Two sides of the same face. You WILL remember the name of this song.

How'd I do? This analysis was an easy one, because the song is straight fours and its ingenuities are easy to describe. If I were going to talk about "Get Lucky" I'd probably have to start posting score. That is a complicated song.

SUSAN FAST ON LED ZEPPELIN

"Stairway to Heaven": Myth, Epic Ritual*

The music of each of these mythic/epic pieces like "Stairway to Heaven" deserves close analytical attention in order to determine how the mythological has been created through the use of sound. Here I want only to begin such a project through an analysis of "Stairway to Heaven." The fanfare in "Stairway" is a good place to begin exploring mythic, epic, and ritualistic aspects of Led Zeppelin's music. This fanfare taps into the mythological through the historic association of this musical genre with ceremony, pageantry, war, and other events of "deep" cultural significance. Within the context of the piece these associations are strengthened through the fanfare's position at a critical musical juncture: it signals a definitive break with the music heard up to that point and introduces the guitar solo (the guitar hero), the new central voice in the narrative. It is a kind of musical crossroads in a piece that has been marked, up to this point, by harmonic, timbral, and structural instability—a constant trying on and then calling into question of the chosen mode of discourse, features that may be what has led many, including John Paul Jones, to characterize the piece as a "journey."

Robert Walser notes that the opening phrases of the piece are "reassuringly square," and on the surface this is certainly true. The instrumental part uses a very traditional musical construction, which consists of four phrases, each four measures long, about as regular a formal design as is found in Western music. These four phrases of music are repeated several times, until, in fact, the electric guitar is introduced, at which time the music changes significantly. The rhythm of this opening music, predominantly straight eighth notes that occur regularly with almost no syncopation, reinforces this squareness and regularity. This formal and rhythmic design also suggests simplicity and, when the timbres of the instruments are considered (acoustic guitar and recorders), the pastoral and the archaic as well. When Plant enters after the sixteen-measure instrumental introduction of the piece, the melody he sings is simple, too. It consists of only one phrase, which is constantly repeated with only slight variations, and it reflects the square rhythmic and metric design of the rest of the music. Example 2.1 reproduces the first texted phrase of music in which these features are illustrated (measures 17–20 of the song); the instrumental part given in this example is essentially the same as that with which the piece begins.

---

*Fast, Susan. *In The Houses of the Holy: Led Zeppelin and the Power of Rock Music* (New York: Oxford University Press, 2001).

But the simplicity of the opening is deceptive. Just underneath the surface of the melodic and rhythmic squareness is a harmonic and formal openness and irregularity that is highly significant in terms of the semiotics of the piece. We can take the relationship between vocal and instrumental parts at the beginning of the piece as a first example of this irregularity. Example 2.2 maps the relationship between instrumental music and Plant's vocal line from the point at which Plant enters (measure 17) through what I would call the end of the first section of the piece (just before the first iteration of the line "ooh it makes me wonder"). Each horizontal numbered line represents a phrase of music, there being six phrases in this section altogether; this is the first departure from the regularity of phrase construction suggested by the opening four phrases of instrumental music and the four-plus-four phrase construction generally observed in tonal music.

The other feature of the relationship between voice and instruments in this section that I have tried to depict in the diagram is that even though Plant's melody repeats, there is no regular verse structure to the vocal line, and this creates an interesting disjunction between it and the instrumental part. In fact, some of the regularity of the instrumental music is undermined by Plant's irregular poetic construction, which at the beginning seems to consist of two lines ("There's a lady ..." and "When she get there ...") followed by a line that sounds as though it might become a refrain, although it doesn't return until the

Example 2.1. "Stairway to Heaven," first texted prase

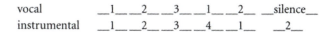

Example 2.2. "Stairway to Heaven," phrase relationship between vocal and instrumental parts, measures 17–40

end of the piece ("oooh, and she's buying a stairway to heaven"). This much takes up three phrases of music. The next line seems to begin a new stanza of poetry ("There's a sign on the wall"), but the instrumental part continues with the fourth phrase of music. In other words, the text seems to begin anew, but the music does not. This initial section of music then ends with one more line of text ("In a tree by the brook") and a reiteration of the first phrase of instrumental music: this time the music starts over while the vocal line continues. A final phrase of the instrumental music (the second phrase, cadencing on the tonic) brings this section to a close, but at this point of closure we simultaneously move ahead, since the guitar part changes, adding sixteenth notes to the texture. The verse form becomes more regular at this point: the refrain line "ooh it makes me wonder" alternates with two-line stanzas of text, all of which have the same poetic construction, up until the fanfare music.

The harmonic structure of this opening is also important to consider. The first two phrases of music cadence on the tonic, A, making them sound conclusive and "stable," but this stability is somewhat hard-won, since the harmonic progression that leads to the final cadence is built on a chromatically descending melody from A down to F♮ (these are the long-held notes heard in the acoustic guitar and recorder—see ex. 2.1). The chromatic scale is an unstable musical construct— it has no "center," no clear set of hierarchical relationships within it. Short segments of a descending chromatic scale also have a clearly established affective character that is as a musical signifier of lament in opera. Here the music also has a plaintive character, enhanced by the timbre of the recorders. This plaintiveness is important to the narrative, encoding the weightiness and uncertainty of spiritual journeys. In other words, this musical construction signifies struggle. The final cadence of each of these phrases is approached by a large leap—the long-held F♮ moving suddenly downward to a B, which quickly resolves to an A (see ex. 2.1). This is a jolting musical gesture, especially coming after the incremental movement by half tone that precedes it. It is as if the bottom has dropped out of the melodic line, forcing one to risk a leap to reach the safety of closure. There is also a great weightiness to this cadence— because of the large leap downward—which signals a kind of resignation to the inevitability of the tonic at this point. There are at least two semiotic readings of this cadence, then, one that views the leap to the tonic as daring, the other that views it as a gesture of resignation.

The third phrase cadences on the subdominant, D, leaving it tonally open, and the fourth phrase, which normally in such a "regular" kind of musical construction would bring another cadence on the tonic to balance the openness of the third phrase, cadences instead on an F major 7 chord, which creates a wonderful harmonic ambivalence (see ex. 2.3). F major 7 contains the complete tonic chord (A, C, and E) above its root, F, and one can really hear this tonic, but sounding displaced, its finality having been thwarted by the addition of the F underneath it. In the language of tonal theory, this kind of cadential movement, that is, to the sixth degree of the scale (F) instead of the tonic (A), is called deceptive because the harmonic movement that precedes it makes the listener expect the tonic. Here the deception is magnified by the addition of the seventh to the chord (E), so that we hear both the complete tonic and the submediant (F, A, C) sounding simultaneously. This doubleness of the cadence suggests choice as well as uncertainty; or, as Susan McClary has articulated it, "[the deceptive cadence can] rob the piece of certainty, yet create … [a] sense of nostalgia" or *desire*.[1] The changing cadential patterns of the phrases change the character of the repeated vocal line. For example, the cadence on D coincides with the repetition of the line "and she's buying a stairway to heaven," which, only one phrase earlier, cadenced definitively on the tonic. The refrainlike repetition of this line suggests that it should come with musical closure, but instead it has been musically recast, calling into question the certainty of its previous iteration, suggesting that there may be more than one way in which to interpret this lady and her quest. The line of text sung to the musical phrase that cadences on F is "Cause you know sometimes words have two meanings"; the deceptive movement of the music and the two ways of hearing the F major 7 chord underscore the sentiment of the text very effectively, by literarily painting its meaning in sound. But even without text, the cadential structure of these opening phrases is significant to take into account, because the tonal openness of the last two phrases and especially the deceptive movement and ambiguous nature of the last cadence point to a structural openness that supports the reading of this song as a "journey" or that might be said to fulfill the expectation of the hero-seeker of mythicological/epic tradition. Tonal closure indicates finality, a solution, an answer to a question; tonal openness suggests that there is more to come (or to learn), and the deceptive motion calls into question that which we think we know or can expect, challenges our assumptions, and forces us to open up to new possibilities.

The unexpected harmonic movements of the opening phrases are echoed later in the song in important ways. The fanfare begins with an unexpected harmonic move to the subdominant (D). Instead of continuing the two-measure progression III-VII⁶–i (C-B-A in the bass guitar), which has been used to structure the music for a considerable time (since the words "There's a feeling I get"), the tonic A is replaced by D, the subdominant. The structuring pattern and cadence on the subdominant are illustrated in example 2.4.

Earlier I called the fanfare a musical crossroads, the point at which the musical discourse changes irrevocably, so it makes sense that in addition to the music of a fanfare marking this point there should be a striking harmonic move to set the music off from what has come before, one that, once again, suggests a questioning

---

[1]Susan McClary, *Feminine Endings: Music, Gender, and Sexuality* (University of Minnesota Press, 2002), p. 157.

Example 2.3. "Stairway to Heaven,"
a) cadence on the subdominant, third phrase (measures 11 and 12)
b) "deceptive" cadence on F major 7, fourth phrase (measures 15 and 16)

of the status quo. This crossroads is also marked by a rhythmic questioning, if you will (see ex. 2.5). On one hand, there could not be a more decisive gesture than the rising triplet figure of the fanfare, all instruments playing it in sync, with a sweeping pickup to the downbeat of the measure, the melody rising in stepwise movement from D to G, suggesting a dominant–tonic relationship. On the other hand, there are constant metrical shifts that work to undermine the forcefulness of the gesture. In the notated score, the section has been transcribed as moving from $\frac{4}{4}$ to $\frac{7}{8}$ back to $\frac{4}{4}$ to $\frac{9}{8}, \frac{4}{4}, \frac{7}{8}$, and then finally resting on $\frac{4}{4}$ time. Basically, the addition and deletion of eighth-note beats here creates slight hesitancies or anticipations (someone holding back and then jumping the gun): in which direction do I move next? what turn do I take?

Finally with respect to harmony, there is one further playing with notions of closed and open between the grooves that accompany the verses leading up to

Example 2.4. "Stairway to Heaven," six measures before fanfare, piano and bass guitar parts only

the fanfare and that which follows it. Both involve three-note descending patterns, but before the fanfare the pattern ends each time on the tonic, A, suggesting closure (see ex. 2.4), while afterward, during the guitar solo and the verse that follows, the pattern begins on the tonic A, moving down through G to F (again, the sixth degree of the scale, on which deceptive cadences are built), moving outward from closure to openness (see ex. 2.6). The instruments end the piece, in fact, on the F of this repeated harmonic pattern, leaving Plant, alone, to bring final harmonic closure. The way the change in the riff is effected is worth noting. The three-note pattern prior to the fanfare is C-B-A. At the point of the fanfare, the movement is C-B-D, as noted earlier. At the end of the fanfare, the movement is from C down to B and then A, the closing note of the riff, but this A now becomes the first note of the new riff—A-G-F. The tonic is a kind of pivot in this construction, at once the closing or end point of the old riff and the beginning of the new one.

The harmonic, formal, and rhythmic instability just outlined are important ways in which a sense of growth or striving is achieved musically, in that a process of openness and questioning is constantly at work in the music. But there is another way, perhaps more obvious to the average listener, in which the concept of growth is constructed in this piece, and that is through instrumentation. *Rolling Stone's* Jim Miller has observed this concept of growth in the song, which he views as building intensity through the addition of instruments, the piece "finally ... blossom[ing] into an epic rocker," which he calls transcendent. While it is true that instruments are added—the recorders, voice, electric guitar, bass, and finally drums—it is also significant that instruments are "replaced" by the electric guitar. Although the acoustic guitar remains part of the timbre throughout the piece, the electric guitar *takes over* from it upon its entry—it dominates the timbre—and is responsible for reshaping the

313

discourse of the piece. The recorders drop out of the texture at the same time as the electric guitar enters. The electric guitar begins, upon its entry, with arpeggiated gestures

Example 2.5. "Stairway to Heaven" fanfare, opening measures

similar to that of the acoustic guitar (if slightly less complex), mimicking until it finds its own voice at the beginning of the solo. What happens, then, is a *replacement*, of the acoustic with the electric. Since this happens fairly smoothly, I would diverge from Robert Walser's opinion that there is a "narrative juxtaposition" of the two and that they "combine contradictory sensibilities without reconciling them." Rather, there seems to be an incremental movement away from the pastoral/ archaic toward the electric/contemporary (the instruments added after the electric guitar include electric piano, electric bass, and drum kit). Part of the journey, then, has to do with moving from the rural/folk/archaic to whatever we might equate with the electric instruments—certainly something more contemporary, technological, and perhaps also urban. There are several interesting implications in this reading. Eero Tarasti has suggested that in general, when references to "archaic" or "folk" music styles are overtly made in a contemporary piece, this points to the mythical in that it brings the "mythical" past into the present (again, this suggests the importance of the performative in mythology). Whether or not this is the case must depend on who is doing the listening. As a trained musicologist with a fairly good grasp of historical styles of Western music, I hear traces of sixteenth- or seventeenth-century Tudor music in the opening of "Stairway to Heaven," and this situates it not in mythological time for me but in a particular historical moment. The stylistic features that signal this to me are the timbres of the instruments (especially recorder), the contrapuntal lines, the quite static rhythmic texture (comprised primarily of straight eighth notes), with a few ornamental melodic gestures, the tonal and the square construction of the phrases. To many listeners, however, the opening of this piece may well suggest a kind of archaic music that is not linked to any particular time or place and hence may well signify the mythological. This is perhaps what Dave Lewis means when he writes about "Stairway" that "it has a pastoral opening cadence that is classical in feel and which has ensured its immortality." Here "classical" music of any kind signifies "timelessness," a characteristic of myth (as Ricoeur put it, "we can no longer connect [mythological] time with the time of history as we write it … nor can we connect mythical places with our geographical space"). The narrative that is suggested by this piece, then, becomes the movement

Example 2.6. "Stairway to Heaven" harmonic patterns, last two measures of the fanfare, and beginning of guitar solo

away from myth or mythological time into present time. Given the interpretation of this song as a journey with the implication, or the overt acknowledgment, that the journey is about "a search for spiritual perfection" or that it "seem[s] to embody the individual's prevailing quest for a spiritual rebirth," it is an interesting reversal, in musical terms, of the usual retreat into the archaic, away from the technological present, the past generally considered to have had more "depth" of spiritual force, especially for the counterculture.

In any event, the important mythological/ritualistic notion of transformation is certainly inherent in the formal characteristics of this piece. Spiritual/intellectual openness and questioning are suggested by the harmonic openness. Not only do we move from the acoustic to the electric (perhaps from mythological to historical time), but there is also the continual sense of growth through both the replacement and addition of instruments. Growth is also suggested by the unsettled form of the piece, the movement out of one music and into another, and, significantly, in never returning to the beginning. One might say, as Robert Walser does, that "Stairway" ends by "return[ing] to the solitary poignancy of the beginning," that is, with Plant's unaccompanied voice, but I would argue that this is not a very literal "return." Rather, because of the changes in the melody, the production, the complete lack of accompaniment (no acoustic guitar, no recorders, no "reassuring squareness" of the phrases), and the rubato way in which Plant sings (adding poignancy and a reflectiveness to the line), it is a clear indication of the transformation that has been undergone. One could argue that the idea of (extreme) transformation is also present in the drastic change in Plant's voice as he uses it after the guitar solo (from ballader to rock screecher). There is also a consistent textural movement away from counterpoint and toward homophony throughout the piece. In the first two sections

315

there are various independent voices that are intertwined (listen, especially, to the independent movement of the bass during the "ooh it makes me wonder" refrain in the second section of the piece). During the guitar solo, of course, a single voice emerges as predominant in the texture, but significantly, it does not remain unsupported for very long: a second electric guitar track is added toward the end of the solo, which repeats a simple four-note descending motive in answer to the final phrases of the solo. This accompanying gesture, a descendant of the baroque "sigh" motive, is full of pathos; it answers each phrase of the guitar solo with the same plaintive wail. Following this, in the final section of the piece, all the instruments play the riff together, in complete unity. These textural changes suggest movement from a kind of community individualism (a working together), to the extreme individualism of the guitar solo, to the extreme community (Ricoeur's mythological unity and connectedness) of the ending. One of the respondents to the fan survey, Cynthia Kasee (who holds a Ph.D. in American Indian studies), pointed to a way in which at least some of the musical changes that one might construe as "growth" in this song also correspond to rituals that "are intended to draw participants closer as they progress (such as rites of passage which seek to include participants in a new life-phase or 'society'); [these] sound/appear to get faster and either louder or higher-pitched" (Plant raising his voice an octave, the intensity of the groove that accompanies the guitar solo, and so forth).

Mary Douglas stresses that in ritual, "[e]vents . . . acquire meaning from relation with others in [a] sequence," and so it is important to consider that on the original LP "Stairway" was the last song on the first side of the album. This placement is significant to the semiotics of the piece because, on the one hand, it meant that the song was followed by silence that allowed for reflection—one had to turn the record over in order to hear any more music. But on the other hand, it is not the final song of the album—the last song of side 2—which might have been a logical positioning for the "gem" of the album. Getting to the end of the song that materializes the idea of the gnostic journey does not mark the end of the journey, only the midway point.

JOHN PERRY ON JIMI HENDRIX

33⅓ Volume #8*

All Along The Watchtower

In "Watchtower," Jimi chose a song whose lyrics are (at least, by the austere standards of *John Wesley Harding*) relatively open. "Watchtower" was much the happiest choice in harmonic terms too, its descending chord sequence far better suited to both melodic and dramatic guitar playing than either of the other songs [from *John Wesley Harding* he considered recording]. Hendrix stayed with Dylan's written key (although his detuning slightly lowers the pitch from C sharp) and preserved Dylan's chord sequence—C sharp minor to B, to A—altering it just once when the A chord beneath the word "joke" is replaced by the relative minor, F sharp.

Hendrix's famous, familiar opening guitar phrase at once demonstrates the melodic suitability of Dylan's chord sequence. After nine seconds stating the basic progression, the electric guitar enters with what has become one of the more memorable introductory phrases in rock. Riffs are easily remembered, because they repeat: memorable phrases are harder to come by. The same attention to detail is evident when you come to the main guitar solo—which makes pretty good sense: Hendrix would have known he could never top Dylan as a songwriter or singer, so the main statement would have to come from his strongest suit, the guitar.

A short guitar break separates the second and third verses (0:52), more a bridge than a solo. It's conventional, and there's no phrase distinctive enough to rival the opening hook, but at 1:43 comes the solo proper. Lasting just over one minute, it's divided into four distinct sections, each with its own tone and each built round a separate melodic idea. Notwithstanding its beauty as a piece of guitar playing, it's an object lesson in how to structure a single, a fine example of Keith Richards's production ethos for 45s: "hit 'em with something new every 10 seconds".

The first section of the solo (1:45–1:59) features a fairly clean-toned guitar gradually moving from the middle register into the high; it ends playing around with the same note (a ninth) that makes the intro hook so distinctive.

Section two (2:00–2:14) is arranged as a duet between the slide guitar and the bass (also played by Hendrix). The guitar tone is quite different from section 1—softer, and the playing more *legato*. What sounds like at least two types of echo are used to draw out the long sliding notes, creating a comet's tail behind the principal note. The bass guitar, which up until here has wandered around in best Jamie Jamerson style—the

---

*Perry, John. *Electric Ladyland*, 114–118. New York: Continuum, 2004. Reprinted with permission.

antithesis of Noel Redding's playing—now settles to a single repeated pattern. Root note, fifth, octave, (do-do-do, do-do-do, do-do-do, GAP) creating space for the slide guitar to slip around.

The fact that Hendrix played this section with a cigarette lighter opens the possibility that this portion was a spontaneous, on the spot, creation. If he'd been *planning* a bottleneck solo presumably he'd have brought a bottleneck with him? (I know from my own studio experience that the most effective soloing ideas often arrive in a flash, rather than after planning.) It's hard to be certain with Hendrix. On one hand, the demos for a song like "1983" indicate considerable pre-planning; on the other—and especially where a solo is concerned—an improvising musician as gifted as Hendrix could have plucked the idea out of the air as easily as he plucked the lighter from his pocket. All we can say with any certainty is that throughout its many incarnations, "Watchtower" always had 32 bars set aside for some sort of solo.

The third, the wah-wah section (2:16–2:32) is brought in with a cry of "hey," a fairly restrained commentary by some standards. The great Albert King, for instance, (along with Buddy Guy, Jimi's two favourite blues guitarists) was fond of inserting spoken remarks between notes. King liked to voice his solos in short staccato bursts, percussive two or three-beat phrases, each affirmed with *sotto voce* asides, sometimes fragments of the lyric, sometimes generic, "That's right", "Ohhhh", "Now watch this" etc., sometimes simply yelping.[2]

The wah-wah section comes closest to employing conventional triplets (the sort of over-used style of Clapton copyists, sometimes referred to as "widdling") but even when doing so Jimi chooses unusual groups of notes with which to widdle, and the phrasing makes formal sense in its contrast with the other sections. A short delay, added during the mix, causes the notes to "over-run" or bleed into each other.

For the fourth section (2:33–2:49), Hendrix selects phrases that shadow the chord progression, breaking them up with his dead-string scratching technique, before using unison bends to play a final ascending passage. This last phrase seems to be heading towards a natural resolution on the octave but in fact stops short before it reaches the obvious target: the final note is thus implied rather than voiced.

"Unison bends" are a way of articulating notes to make them sound more emphatic. Instead of playing a single note on a single string (the normal method), one plays a note—usually on the first or second string—at the same time doubling it on the string immediately below. The note gains "body" from being simultaneously played on two strings—but there's more. Since the note on the lower string is played by bending that string upward, its pitch is only approximate to the note on the higher string. Thus two notes are in near unison. When notes are so nearly in tune, a sort of psychoacoustic effect comes into play; a pulse occurs, at the places where the notes don't quite match,

---

[2] I refer the reader to "Crosscut Saw" or "Oh Pretty Woman" from the 1967 Stax album King recorded with Booker T & The MGs (issued under several names including *Laundromat Blues* and *Born Under A Bad Sign*).

which the ear hears as a sort of "boiling" sound. It's the equivalent, in visual terms, of doubling an image then moving one slightly out of true—the edges blur. A good player can direct the degree to which the note "boils" by controlling how far the second string strays from unison with the first. In this instance Hendrix keeps it pretty much in check: it simmers but never reaches the boil.

The key quality throughout the solo is restraint. We've become so used to "abandoned," all-in guitar solos (and so conditioned to the "wildman" image) that it takes a couple of close listens to appreciate how well within himself Hendrix plays. He achieves his effect without ever overstating the case.

WRITING PROMPT: ISOLATED TRACKS

Find online an isolated track from a song you know well (a few examples: Jimmy Page's guitar solo on Led Zeppelin's "Ramble On," James Jamerson's bass line on "What's Going On," Stevie Wonder's clavinet on "Superstitious," Keith Moon's drumming on "Won't Get Fooled Again"—it's harder to find tracks from less mainstream or more recent music, but while you're searching, don't miss David Lee Roth's vocal from Van Halen's "Running with the Devil," an instant viral classic of the isolated track movement).

Choose a specific section of the track and whether through your own knowledge of music theory, by conducting research, or asking a trained musician to help you, name its musical features in technical terms (time signature, key, playing technique, etc).

Next, determine if possible the actual instrument played on the track (Les Paul or Telecaster? Acoustic standup or Fender Precision bass?), the effects added to it, the way it appears in the mix. Does it sound as if it had been recorded directly or through an amplifier, close-miked or recorded at a distance, compressed, treated with reverb, or left natural?

Listen to the isolated track again, writing down five adjectives that describe what you hear. The adjectives should be specific but not technical, words that are able to convey the sound accurately to a general reader rather someone who can read music.

Listen again and write down five words that describe what the sound makes you feel, your sense of the track's emotional range.

Now that you've considered the track from all of these perspectives, listen to the complete song (with the isolated track taking its rightful place in the recording as a whole) and write a 500-word account of the track you focused on, working from your technical, factual, descriptive, and emotional responses to describe and discuss this element of the song and what it lends to its overall sound and impact.

WRITING PROMPT: WHAT'S IMPORTANT

In March 2014 Jazz critic Ted Gioia claimed that "music writing has devolved into lifestyle reporting[3] "and went on to argue that most contemporary music writers lack technical knowledge of music and therefore are failing to address the music itself. Chris Ott says "Technical dissections of pop music are absurd in the extreme." Read the pieces in this chapter by Owen Pallett and Susan Fast and formulate a response to Ted Gioia's claim that "music writing has devolved into lifestyle reporting." That is to say, argue for why you think it's important to have a technical understanding of music or not.

[3]Gioia, Ted. "Music Criticism Has Degenerated Into Lifestyle Reporting." *The Daily Beast*, March 18, 2014. http://www.thedailybeast.com/articles/2014/03/18/music-criticism-has-degenerated-into-lifestyle-reporting.html.

DO YOU NEED TO KNOW HOW TO MAKE MUSIC TO WRITE ABOUT IT?

Not really, but I think it helps to have a basic idea of the technology used, the instruments, how they work. Cursory knowledge is fine. For me, only when I was first writing criticism was it really about describing the actual sounds of the music, the qualities of it, per se, are often secondary for me as I write about the whole package. The image, the ideas, how it fits into contemporary music, America, masculinity, what the production tells us about what the artist is trying to communicate.—**Jessica Hopper**, Music Editor at *Rookie Magazine*, and Senior Editor, the *Pitchfork Review*

Not necessarily. If you want to write about musical texts/performances, it can be really informative and convincing to be able to express yourself using a performer's vocabulary. But this is only one vocabulary of many. An experienced and devoted listener can be equally hard-hitting as a writer.—**Nick Attfield**, music academic

Do you need to know how to make a soufflé to describe how it tastes?—**Michael Azerrad**, author, journalist and Editor-in-Chief of the *Talkhouse*

I think you need to know how to make music to succeed at all sorts of endeavors: dealing with the day's trivialities, wooing cuties, connecting with your fellow man. And even the understanding that there's musicality in acts as simple as humming or as tapping your fingers can only make you appreciate the musicality of more complex efforts. With that understanding and appreciation, you'll listen more closely, and take fewer things for granted.—**Phillip Crandall**, author of the **33⅓** book on Andrew W.K.'s *I Get Wet*

NO, but in that case you need to have a vivid way to describe what it feels like to experience the music as a listener, and a vivid way to illustrate the social or personal vision implied by a record, an artist, a performance or a scene. Knowing how to make music might help you describe certain technical components and is by no means to be discounted or pooh-poohed, but it's also not without its own attendant problems—i.e. having a "dog in the race" might impair your critical judgment, and no one wants to read you saying "If I was writing this song, I would …"—**Drew Daniel**, Assistant Professor, Department of English, Johns Hopkins University.

No—but you need to listen.—**Marty Davis**, comic book creator

For me, the impulses to write about music, to collect it, to play it and talk about it on college (and eventually national public) radio, and to make it in a series of garage bands that stretch from age 13 to the present all came from the same place, which I could never say better than the way Lester Bangs expressed it to me: *I always have been a fanatical fan with fanatical opinions to inflict on people.* While I joke that I am a drummer, not a musician, making music has been part of my life to the exact extent that I've wanted it to be—touring, recording, playing live—essentially as a hobby, the way a professional sports writer might cover a baseball team as his job but play softball or fun on the weekends. This is to say, I've never wanted to be a "professional" musician, or anything but a writer and teacher, and that hoary old line about "critics being frustrated musicians" be damned. I think having made music can bring a depth of experience to one's criticism that is lacking in the work of those who aren't musicians, but they may have a dozen other assets that are lacking in the music-making critic or journalist. There are no absolute musts for writing about music well, except for the passion to do it and do it right.—**Jim DeRogatis**, author, co-host of *Sound Opinions*, and lecturer at Columbia College Chicago

No. To me, music is like stage magic: I know that a process goes into it, and the result is an alchemical process that transcends the mechanical components that create it. I know something is happening, I don't fully understand it, and the results are something magical.—**D. X. Ferris**, Ohio Society of Professional Journalists Reporter of the Year, Professor, **33⅓** author

If you want to be a music critic, yes. If you want to cover music as entertainment, lifestyle, fashion or as an element of pop culture, no.—**Jim Fusilli**, rock and pop critic, *The Wall Street Journal*, Editor, ReNewMusic.net

There's value in a non-music-maker's (outsider) perspective. There's also value in knowing and understanding how to make music. I think non-music-makers may suffer credibility issues. When writing about vulnerable groups—and any artists who is putting their work out there to be judged is to some degree vulnerable—I think it's important to have shown your own vulnerability. If not, as the lyrics to a song I once wrote go: *You're just claiming a critique without being any part of the art.*—**Anthony Kwame Harrison**, popular music scholar, Virginia Tech

It can't hurt; it makes you both more knowledgeable and more sympathetic. But it's not absolutely necessary—go sing karaoke with a bunch of music writers and you'll note that the skill level varies pretty wildly.—**Rob Harvilla**, Deputy/Culture Editor, Deadspin

Not at all. There's no prerequisite required to share your thoughts about music, whether oral or written. Sure, it can be beneficial to know the mechanics of music, because it can reveal pretty easily how music manipulates and shapes emotion through harmony, melody, timbre, rhythm, etc. But not everyone has the luxury of knowing how to make music, and it's the cultural values associated with these musical combinations that produce their affects, not the other way around. There are plenty of other factors worth exploring that I find more interesting than the actual mechanics of music.—**Marvin Lin**, Editor-in-Chief, Tiny Mix Tapes

Absolutely not. It's somewhat fascinating to me that decades after the inception of rock journalism and the work of writers who don't make music but who still produce a wide range of sharp, insightful, stirring writing that some people still think that one should know how to make music in order to write about it. It certainly wouldn't hurt to become familiar with the language of musicians, both classically and non-classically trained. Just as important, though maybe more so, is to have some curiosity about what musicians deal with on a practical, everyday level—the social and economic worlds in which they exist, the sorts of professional paths one takes, how and why one becomes a musician at all instead of becoming, say, a teacher, a banker, or a lawyer. These things are far more compelling and necessary to me for making meaningful connections between where music comes from and the kind of public life it takes on. But when I think about the kind of writing that makes an impression on me, that sparks an interest, incenses or surprises me about an artist or a piece of music, it's not because it was written from the perspective of a musician or a non-musician. Good writing is good writing.—**Luis Sanchez, 33⅓** author

It seems like the parts of the brain that light up when making music are different from the parts of the brain that light up when writing about it. Some musicians are great at writing about music (cf. Questlove, Bono, Eno) but they're the exception. More commonly, some musicians are great writers when they discuss practically any topic *except* music—but working musicians tend to collect a lot of hurt feelings over the course of their careers, so it can be understandably tough for them to keep their professional grudges from limiting their music writing. Also, the rhythm of making music seems so different vs. the rhythm of writing. Performing is all about the gig, you know? The challenge in the gig is making something memorable happen in a short rush of time. You wait for showtime and then you *go*. That's not how writing works, because you have to do it over and over patiently until it's done. You can't get anything memorable written on gig time.—**Rob Sheffield**, writer, *Rolling Stone*

I don't think so—Robert Christgau is the great counterexample there—but it's astonishingly useful. (Learning to play guitar, even at a rudimentary level, probably did more to help me understand what I was listening to on pop records, and how to write about it, than anything else ever has.) **Douglas Wolk**, freelance arts journalist

It's not required, but it helps to understand how to play music, if for no other reason than to demystify that process. Musicians are not wizards—sometimes the coolest things they do are accidents.—**Scott Tennent**, **33⅓** author

CHAPTER 11
MUSIC SCENES

INTRODUCTION

The word "scene" suggests a simple concept but can, in fact, be a complicated term. Traditionally it's meant the backdrop for an event—as in "let's set the scene"—but more recently it's come to suggest the overall feel of a place and the people in it—as in "the scene down there is a mix of hardcore and punk." What makes a music scene a scene? Is it the people in that place and at that time? Is it the political ideals of those people? Is it the way they dress? Is it a response to the climate, geographical or social?

In Gina Arnold's far-reaching **33⅓** on Liz Phair's 1993 album *Exile in Guyville* we find Gina's perspective on the "scene" in the indie rock world of Chicago in the early '90s. Like Phair, Arnold calls this scene Guyville. It's a place where male indie rockers are dominant and don't want to make room for a singer and lyricist like Liz Phair, despite (or, finally, because of) the fact that Phair outstrips everyone else on the scene. Gina evokes a feel for the place and time that's smart, textured, and utterly convincing. She tells the reader what the people were wearing, what they were reading and most importantly what they were listening to. Guyville doesn't have a street address, but it's nevertheless a vivid reality in the author's brilliant account of it.

"Scene" is a term applied to an amorphous cultural moment by music critics to help distinguish one type of music from another. When you write about a particular scene think back to your high school days when different cliques and social groups defined the student population. What scene were you part of? What made your environment unique? Even in a small space, like a school, everyone's staking out turf. As geography expands from the utterly local, a scene often becomes synonymous with a style of music and a city. There's Detroit hiphop, DC hardcore, San Francisco punk and so many more . . . and that's just in the States. Ross Simonini treats us to a complete rundown of the particularly volatile scene that gave rise to Jamaican rude boys. His piece begins with a description of a particular moment but then expands to offer insightful, detailed accounts of the history (in this case a violent colonial one), people and cultural setting. Though the focus of Simonini's piece is the music itself, his prose reads like a dispatch from a war-torn country.

Describing a scene gives you a chance to be a true journalist. To capture the scene you need to explore the history, the setting, the key players, the politics and of course the sights and sounds. Interview people who were there at a particular show and try to get them to describe what it is they like about it. Can you get several differnet people to describe the same moment? Do their stories match up? Become a reporter and dig deep to find out what's really going on.—AJG

GINA ARNOLD ON LIZ PHAIR

33⅓ Volume #96 *Exile in Guyville**

[*Exile In Guyville*] was a real moment, and a real album. So it follows that Guyville is a real place, not a fictional construct stolen from a line in an obscure album called *Stull*. And that's OK, because for me, it is. You won't find Guyville on Google Maps, but for all that it exists in a more solid form than, say, Diagon Alley and the Hotel California, two noted fictional universes. Unlike those locations, Guyville is not merely a paracosm—that is, a distinctive imaginary world, with its own geography, history, and language—but the album *Exile in Guyville*, like Middle Earth and Hogwarts, may well be. That is to say, Guyville describes a real place in Chicago at a certain time, but the album *Exile in Guyville* merely provides a detailed description of imaginary scenes and places that are recognizable to listeners because they represent a certain kind of truth. They are, as Benedict Anderson, the author of the phrase "imagined community," once put it, "a complex gloss on the word 'meanwhile.'"[1]

The Chicago scene in particular prided itself on its insularity and lack of commerciality. It was a scene populated by amateur musicians or amateur critics, and surely, looking back at issues of these magazines with hindsight, their completely male-centric viewpoint is not only glaring—it's absurd. Indeed, some of the earlier issues of *SPIN* (like the Dando cover) have the same jarring effect as seeing 1950s advertisements for cigarettes or lingerie or cleaning products that feature babies smoking or women vacuuming in their bras.

The conclusion one takes away from glimpsing backwards is that in the 90s world of indie rock, sonic pleasure mimics visual pleasure and the microphone is always male. It looks male, and the sounds that come out of it are engineered to please the male, whether by conforming sonically to the codes that read as "good" in indie rock, or simply by providing him with something to gaze upon. In a snippet of an interview that ran in a *New York* magazine umbrella story on women in rock in 1996, Phair herself commented on the way that women fans at rock concerts may be presenting themselves as the subject of the male gaze, saying, "You go to the rock show because you want the guy to stare at you. You want to be singled out as an object." Phair goes on to suggest that the presence of women (like herself) on stage was changing the paradigm, but it seems more likely that more women on stage just means more male gazing—a process abetted by the journalism establishment: In the photo accompanying

---

*Arnold, Gina. *Exile in Guyville*. New York, NY. Bloomsbury, 2014. 5–6, 64–65, 98–101, 114–116.
[1]Benedict R. O'G. Anderson, *Imagined Communities: Reflections on the Origin and Spread of Nationalism*. (London: Verso, 1991), 20.

the article, Phair is portrayed as sultry and disheveled, under the caption "Post grad porn: Phair talks dirty and smart."[2]

I once heard Boston College professor Carlo Rotella compare "Stratford-on-Guy" to the opening passages of *Sister Carrie*, in which Carrie comes to Chicago. What Dreiser wrote is eerily similar in tone to the beginning of this song:

> To the child, the genius with imagination, or the wholly untravelled, the approach to a great city for the first time is wonderful thing. Particularly if it be evening—that mystic period between the glare and gloom of the world when life is changing from one sphere or condition to another. Ah, the promise of the night. What does it not hold for the weary! What old illusion of hope is not here forever repeated! Says the soul of the toiler to itself, "I shall soon be free. I shall be in the ways and the hosts of the merry. The streets, the lamps, the lighted chamber set for dining, are for me. The theatre, the halls, the parties, the ways of rest and the paths of song—these are mine in the night." Though all humanity be still enclosed in the shops, the thrill runs abroad. It is in the air. The dullest feel something which they may not always express or describe. It is the lifting of the burden of toil.[3]

Though written 100 years later, "Stratford-on-Guy" is about that very promise. The only difference is that Phair's approach to the city is from above. The song begins on an airplane flying into Chicago at night. In the song, Liz (the genius with imagination) is suddenly prompted to look down at Chicago from an airplane at sunset—that mystic period between glare and gloom—from which she is able to observe "the lake turn the sky into blue green smoke." And as she does so, she reimagines Guyville (that is, Wicker Park) when she sees it—literally—as a small point on the map, one where, as Dreiser said, she shall soon be free. Out of the farmlands, and into the grid, she waits as the cabin fills with in an unearthly glow. And suddenly, from 30,000 feet, she claims, she listens carefully, and she no longer hears the noise—she no longer hears the music. *The burden of toil is lifted.* In other words, from that vantage point, and in this song, she gains perspective on her life in Guyville.

It is a beautiful end to the story. Indeed, "Stratford-on-Guy" would be a great place to end a novel. But "Strange Loop," *Guyville*'s final song, is a better place to end a record. Listening to it right now makes me remember the limitations of writing about music: you can do whatever academic exercise you want on the stuff, but in the end, you'll never really be able to convey the power and beauty of a chord change, or why a particular record resonates. All you can do is listen to the words, which pay tribute to Liz's own insight into her problematic personality.

---

[2]Kim France, "Feminism Amplified." *New York*, June 3, 1995, 40.
[3]Theodore Dreiser, *Sister Carrie*. (Philadelphia: University of Pennsylvania Press, 1981), 21.

Exile in Guyville closes with the words "I only wanted more than I knew," a statement that sums up almost everyone's life at the age of twenty-six—as well as summarizing Liz Phair's personal ambition to compete with the Rolling Stones. Despite my dislike of the latter, deep down I don't actually think that *Guyville* is a better record than *Main St.*—I just think I like it a lot better. *Exile on Main St.* and *Exile in Guyville* each stand on their own merits. Each expresses something unique about its time and place and, more importantly, about its creator. Liz Phair may have been haunted by The Stones, but influenced by them? No more so than I was, all those years ago, when I bought a red satin scarf at Macy's and soon realized that it wasn't going to fit into my teenage wardrobe; that it would hang limply off a hanger until I went to college and finally threw it out.

That said, for me personally, Guyville was an apotheosis. It was a paracosm, an imagined community, an era, a neighborhood, and a total state of mind. There is no longer any doubt about why *Exile in Guyville* speaks so eloquently to me: it is because when I was coming of age in San Francisco in the 1990s I lived in a little corner of Guyville without even knowing its name. It wasn't Chicago. But for a long time after the record first came out, Liz Phair was always sort of hovering over our scene, being referred to by someone, or talked about, or dissed. It often felt like she was always just around the corner. A lot of the guys I knew bad mouthed that record: they said things like, "If she was a *guy* she wouldn't get so much attention," or, "She *slept* her way to being written about," or, "She can't play guitar!" or, "How come no one is writing about Tortoise, or Green, or Material Issue, or Big Black? They're way better than her!" I recall there was a lot of resentment, even before the record came out.

And yet, when I first heard *Exile in Guyville*, I couldn't believe it. A lot of it spoke to me so directly, and the parts that didn't—the weird experimental parts—were either hilarious or, at the very worst, no worse than anything I had to suffer through on every other indie record. I would have been way too shy to speak to her, or even say any of this, but deep down I was happy for Liz Phair. That people paid attention to her at all—that alone seemed like a miracle. There was no one else like her. That is why today, if I hear "Divorce Song" or "Stratford-on-Guy," or "Strange Loop," I am completely overcome with nostalgia for those days, whether in San Francisco or Chicago—for walking down Valencia Street on a hot summer night, or heading for the El for a late night cab ride through the snow, half drunk, with my ears ringing, for getting all dressed up with my girlfriends to go to a gig, for the sense we had, always, of absolutely owning that town.

And we *did* own the town, because we were young and foolish and had no expectations, because we didn't care about the sound quality or the commercial motivations of our favorite acts, because we thought, even then, that one day we were going to move on and become successful, because we knew—the way women always know—that life wasn't really about indie rock or music or the moment or the meaning, but that life was about *life*. And *Exile in Guyville* was about life, much more than *Exile on Main St.* is . . . that was what I loved about it, then and now, and why it's still one of my favorite records.

The Replacements, Pixies, Fugazi, Nirvana . . . the songs I once loved by those acts have faded entirely from the soundtrack of my past, but Liz's work still resonates in my mind. She is like one of my friends, her life laid out bare for me to participate in emotionally, any time I want to. Her art is my art in a way that I can't say about any other artist. Maybe that is one reason I don't miss Guyville, or Chicago, or my youth as an indie rocker, because I have that document of it, and I can immerse myself in it at will.

ROSS SIMONINI ON JAMAICAN RUDE BOYS

Clash of The Deejays: As The Line Between Reality And Performance Disappears, Kill Increasingly Means Kill*

On Boxing Day—December 26th, 2003—as the sun rose over the town of Portmore, Jamaica, the dancehall deejay Vybz Kartel (aka Adidja Palmer) took the stage at Jamaica's legendary Sting music festival. The annual concert, widely promoted as "The Greatest One Night Reggae Show on Earth," usually includes the most culturally visible artists in dancehall and ragga music, and has developed a reputation for hosting infamous on-stage clashes between feuding deejays (a term in reggae which refers not to disc jockeys or producers, but to MCs and vocalists).

His entourage surrounding him, Vybz dropped maniacal taunts about "wartime" and how "lyrics win war." Halfway into his set, he launched into his hits: *Gun Clown* and *Buss Mi Gun Like Nutten*, hype tracks that spout the same sort of vicious, self-aggrandizing lyrics popularized by gangsta rap in the States. But Vybz's songs weren't just vague anthems to violence; they were weapons aimed directly at his rival, Ninjaman (aka Desmond Ballentine) a senior deejay known for his criminal record and a history of onstage clashes. In his lyrics, Vybz called Ninja a crackhead, dug into him about some sexual-abuse allegations ("Him say him a bad man and a beat up woman and baby. Then if you beat up lady, that mean to say you a lady bad man and if you beat up baby that means you a baby bad man,") and then accused him of sodomy. When he finished, he called his dueling partner to the stage for a retort.

Ninjaman arrived to the clash in a graduation cap and gown (a visual jab about being in a higher "class" of deejay than Kartel). But Kartel was a local favorite, and after his strategic set of hits and disses, it seemed that he had pulled the 20,000 fans to his side. Ninjaman gave it his best shot, but after a few minutes of booing and bottle-flinging, Vybz returned to the stage to give him the lyrical knock out.

Then something happened that wasn't supposed to happen: Ninjaman pushed Kartel, giving him a clear shove on the shoulder (though differing accounts dispute who shoved who first: Ninjaman claimed, "Him chuck mi first, mi chuck him back"). Within moments, a fistfight was underway. Kartel and his crew threw Ninjaman to the ground and stomped on his ribs until a few security guards intervened. It was the first on-stage violence in the festival's 20-year history.

Because of the incident, Bounty Killer, a then-ally of Vybz's, canceled his performance as a form of protest against the goings on. The crowd didn't like this.

---

*Simonini, Ross. "The Clash Of The Jamaican Deejays." The *Believer*, July 1, 2009. Reprinted with permission.

Mobbing fans overtook the bar, attacked each another with thrown rocks, and fired guns into the air (a common dancehall show ritual). The *Jamaican Gleaner* reported: "Patrons in the VIP section of the crowd hid under the stage, sheltered behind buses and water tanks, and tore down chain-link fences as bottles fell like Old Testament hail from the sky." Twenty-three people were injured. Both Vybz and Ninjaman were incarcerated for assault and disorderly conduct, though Ninjaman was quickly released on a $15,000 station bail. Afterwards, the festival's promoters tried to extinguish the residual flames with an emergency peace-keeping meeting, but it didn't go so well: Ninjaman arrived with a bandaged face and refused to shake Kartel's hand.

How could these things happen on stage, in broad daylight, on national television, in the country that gave birth to Bob Marley, the Gandhi of reggae? Jamaica's reality, however, is one in which the gullies (ghettos) of its largest city, Kingston, post the highest murder rates in the world—1,574 people were murdered in 2007. Priests are shot in the head and left for dead in the street. The musical hero of the streets was never really Marley but the *rude boy* (the Jamaican criminal). A not-so-distant past of colonialism and slavery produced a strain of Jamaicans who bow to no one and who equate any form of submission with regression. Marley is the country's peace-loving rasta fantasy export, but consider Jimmy Cliff's cinematic masterpiece, *The Harder They Come* to witness the true Jamaican icon: a petty thief, crazy-eyed killer, and musician all rolled into one.

West Indian music feuds began back in the early '60s, before hip-hop was a glimmer in America's eye and before reggae emerged from the roots of ska. In the beginning, violence wasn't part of the feuding protocol. Like battles between hip-hop MCs, Jamaican feuds were and, for the most part still are, competitions of microphone prowess. Two deejays lyrically assault everything about each other—flow, fashion, family, masculinity, etc. Their voices float atop riddims (the production and beats behind the vocals) and their lyrics generally work on the same I'll-have–sex-with-your-wife-and-kill-you mentality that Tupac once aimed at Biggie, with a lot of additional racism, chauvinism and maternal insults. Looking back, the earliest feuds seem benign on the surface; but it's important to remember that obscene language is illegal in Jamaica, which gives a criminal weight to words that, in America, would be little more than a "sticks and stones" offense. Deejays are often arrested for letting a few curses slip out on stage. Acts of male homosexuality are also illegal (and are not accepted, even by criminals), thus hate lyrics about homosexuals are all the more titillating to the fans. It's clearly a testosterone-fueled art form, with terms like "bloodclat" (a tampon) and "faggot" qualifying as some of the harshest insults a Deejay can fling at an opponent. (A handful of dancehall artists have been banned from international venues for homophobia.)

In practice, feuds go on for months, years, or decades, and involve not only on-stage "clashes" but also interminable exchanges of radio singles called "diss tracks". Reggae music's use of riddims adds another layer to the conversation: producers build music tracks and allow multiple deejays (usually the biggest of-the-moment names) to overlay their own lyrics, melodies, and songs. During feuds, deejays will respond to each other's disses through riddims. This allows selectors (radio disc jockeys) to play half-hour long mixes of, say, the "Self Defense Riddim" or "The Beast Riddim" while interchanging each deejay's song, creating the effect of a seamless back-and-forth bickering opera.

In 1962, the same year as Jamaica's independence, one of the earliest feuds began when the ska producer Prince Buster took the upcoming artist Derrick Morgan under his wing. (In turn, Morgan would later mentor the great ska artist, Desmond Dekker.) But when Morgan switched to a higher-paying producer, Leslie Kong, Buster took offense and released a racist diss track called "Black Head Chinaman" taunting Morgan for stealing his musical ideas—specifically, a sax solo—and passing it to Kong, a half-Chinese, half-black producer. Morgan responded with "Blazing Fire," an attempted lyrical quelling—"Live and let others live and your days will be much longer/You said it/Now it's the Blazing Fire"—which led to Buster's "Watch It Blackhead," then Morgan's "No Raise No Praise," and so on.

As a general rule of competition, feuds go on until someone wins, either through superior lyricism, sales, crowd applause, or by forcing an opponent to back down. But with these feuds, "winning" isn't really the point. Everyone knows that clashes are just hyped-up WWF-style showmanship. The real goal is publicity. Pretty much all of the big-name deejays use rivalries to climb their way into the public eye.

In the case of Kartel, his career took a massive step forward after he "won" the feud against Ninjaman, not just because he was the dominant, more aggressive fighter, but because he'd vanquished an elder deejay (Ninjaman was 40, Kartel 27) more notorious than himself. Since then, he's been involved with a handful of increasingly violent feuds involving drive-bys and an incident where he threatened children with a machete—all of which has increased his popularity.

The dancehall economy, too, depends on seething conflict to keep fans attentive. Radio singles deliver retorts and inside puns about ongoing feuds, and fans follow the blow-by-blow like the arc of soap operas. And it gets juicier: Most of the feuds stem from a vast network of Mafioso-style connections between deejays. Allegiances constantly change, and betrayal, money, sex, and violence are always at work on Shakespearian levels. Two artists who are mentor and protégée—or *daddy* and *son*, in the parlance—for the first half of their careers might be feuding for the second half. Other feuds are passed down from *daddy* to *son*, from Corleone to Corleone, until it seems that these alliances between artists have almost nothing to do with artistic collaboration and everything to do with Grangerford-Shepherdson gang-style affiliation. The contemporary music scene in Jamaica is a big insular conversation, and even if a listener can pick up all the subtle cultural references and twisted slang of Jamaican patois, certain lyrics will make no sense unless you know who's feuding with whom. The whole thing creates intrigue for those who want a deeper dramatic story behind their music, and attempts to give an explanation to violence that otherwise appears to have no inherent meaning.

The Ninjaman vs. Vybz clash, for instance, was inspired by a legendary 15-year feud between two camps of dancehall artists, spearheaded by deejays Beenie Man and Bounty Killer. Beenie and Bounty, easily two of the biggest names in dancehall history, both emerged a little after the dancehall sound was born—which is generally considered to be 1985, with the release of "(Under Me) Sleng Teng" by Wayne Smith—as a part of a new generation of artists who generated gangsta lyrics about their lives in the appallingly poor shanty towns of Kingston. (The sound is also sometimes called *bashment* or *ragga*, because of its cultural connection to ragamuffin thugs.) These artists embraced the trend of *toasting* (i.e., Jamican sing-rapping), collaborated with American gangsta rappers such as Noreaga and Mobb Deep, and dropped hardcore violent lyrics. Bounty called his sound "gangsta music" and "hardcore social commentary," and wore the words, "cross, angry, Warlord" on his jacket.

Beenie vs. Bounty began in '93 when the artists engaged in their legendary first clash at the Sting music festival. Like Buster and Morgan, the feud began as theater, with the young, eager deejays dancing to cute rhythms in bright yellow baggy shorts. Beenie grinned in the sun and Bounty, in character, took himself too seriously, and there was no doubt that the clash was all part of the show.

But after a decade of ongoing conflict between the two artists, Bounty Killer brought the feud to the organized, pseudo-corporate level when he assembled a sort of deejay gang called The Alliance. The Alliance began monopolizing riddims, producers, selectors, and venues, excluding anyone who wasn't a part of their group. People outside the Alliance criticized it for dividing the industry and audience—not unlike the East Coast vs. West Coast rivalry in '90s rap. Ninjaman, Bounty's former *daddy*, was one of the primary critics of the Alliance. He challenged all the Alliance members to battles, threatening to "kill" them. Bounty's *son* Vybz Kartel accepted the challenge (so it was: *son* vs. *granddaddy*) and the whole thing came to head weeks later at the notorious Boxing Day shove-fight.

This fight, however, was more than just a turning point in the history of feuds. The threats and name-calling, which could once be laughed off as empty talk, became voyeuristic windows into real-life violence. The cultural problems moved from the dark corners of shantytowns to the public stage, and Jamaicans couldn't ignore that their most notable export (music) was exposing their island's nasty underbelly: The world's image of Jamaica as eternal Bob Marley Day was being replaced with gang warfare. Fans started questioning the necessity of feuds, feeling self-aware and perverse for listening to songs that portend the death of their favorite artists. The industry began to respond, and Sting banned violent and homophobic lyrics, attempting to end the festival's reputation as a host for feuds. Local selectors such as Colin Hinds refused to play the sort of "kill people music" that is "an open exhibition to shoot someone in (the) head"; and the island of St. Vincent banned the new, angry, uber-gangsta deejay named Mavado because he's a "potentially damaging influence on the island's youth."

Not that any of this makes much of a difference. The ongoing war attracts as many people as it repels, and so the musicians continue to outdo themselves, each one trying to reach the imaginary top of the violence pyramid. A few months ago, a knife fight between two young deejays broke out on a stage in Florida. And a gang of rival fans recently attacked Vybz with rocks in a gully, underscoring the fact that the gap between the stage and street has closed. In the earliest feuds, deejays fought in front of their audiences, then turned around and clinked Red Stripes, playing the whole scenario like the farce it was. Now, when Mavado sings, "Diss me and we take away ya life," he's not just trying to entertain a crowd or play up his image. He's issuing a warning.

"Spray—Kosovo"*

Beautifully confused

You understand that phrase that Kosovo is beautifully confused—the moment your plane touches down at Pristina airport, the corporate livery of your B.A. jumbo incongruous against the KFOR helicopters and the blue berets of the UN troops. Rowan switches on his mobile and a triplet of beeps acknowledge welcome texts from no less than three different territories—Kosovo, Albania and Serbia.

After a heavy night my head is also beautifully confused and I crash out until nightfall, woken by the wails from the minaret of a nearby mosque, calling people to prayer. Bersant Rizaj, owner of the club Spray, meets me in reception and drives us into the heart of Pristina. It's hard to envisage the horrors of full-blown war taking place in Europe within the last ten years, within these now quiet streets. But the Balkans is an ethnic frontline, where cultures (Slavic and Indo-European) and religions (Christianity and Islam) meet.

We hit July 2nd Street (the date independence was declared)—a short strip of bars and restaurants—with Bersant's cousin and fellow promoter, Genti. Genti orders a table full of gorgeous fish, steak and chicken (all Kosovan food is organic), washed down with a couple of glasses of peja. It's so relaxed, so full of new friends and smiles that it's hard to imagine the horror of what happened here—10,000 dead in a country of two million, towns burnt out, entire villages razed to the ground. Many people, such as Bersant and Genti, were outside the country during that period, returning only intermittently. "It was not a good place to live back then," says Bersant, a marked understatement. Outside on the terrace, we talk under the stars about repression and conflict, and how dancing is a release for people.

"Definitely," Bersant nods. "South East Europeans, and especially Kosovars . . . if you have a chance to see our weddings, it's crazy . . . people dance all night long. We have a saying . . . it's hard to make them start, but when they start . . . you can't stop them."

That festive spirit now infuses the club scene because Saturday night—as John Travolta once so beautifully espoused—is about checking your problems when you check your coat at the door, the dancefloor better than a psychiatrist's chair. And so to the club, swooping by the hotel to pick up the UK DJ Rowan Blades, who revels in

---

*Morrison, Simon A. "Around The World in 80 Discos: Number 27." *DJ Magazine*, 2007.

such gigs. One half of the phenomenally successful production duo Breeder (for a reference ask Sasha or Digweed), Rowan appreciates that there are gigs around the world where the money may not be right for the boss players, the club perhaps not showbiz enough or, in Kosovo, the territory too off-putting. These are the bread-and-butter gigs that he willingly mops up, as interested in the experience it engenders as the bank balance it swells. Sure there's an edge here, but who wants to live life flat? With no disrespect to that great city, we all know what Paris is about. This—being out in Pristina on a Saturday night—is uncharted territory.

Spray is outside of town in an industrial zone, a free standing, white-walled building on two levels. The club takes the upper level—a lush entrance gives way to the stairs and then the club itself—a big room that is almost all dancefloor. You can walk around the club's periphery, which allows a circulation of people—behind the booth and bar, into VIP rooms and out onto balconies that wouldn't look out of place in a Shakespeare play.

Bersant brings drinks, beaming with pride at his club. He worked three years straight for the money to buy the sound system, another for the lights. Named during a "eureka moment" in the shower, the club's courtyard will feature a water shower system in the summer months, cooling the clubbers. It's a labour of love for Bersant.

Rowan steps up for his main set and pulls no punches, spinning the kind of deep, underground music he would play anywhere else, affording the dancefloor the respect it deserves. The Kosovan spirit is indeed to party. 65% of the population is under 30. Apparently half of them are unemployed but that doesn't stop anybody, the dancefloor packed with funky Kosovars, sweating out their Saturday Night Fever.

After Rowan, residents Toton and Naka go back-to-back and keep the party pulsing—both extremely skilful mixologists. Meanwhile, the only thing I am able to mix is gin with tonic, joining Bersant out on the balcony, as the sun comes up over the distant mountains.

"It's beautiful," I tell him.

"Ah, but to many people it doesn't make sense," he replies, of a contrary country that loves football but has no national team, has no flag, no anthem. "It's beautifully confused."

It's the first time I hear the phrase and it captures Kosovo perfectly. Those of us who have been here need to bend perception when we return, replace those images of what happened here with positive impressions, so that Kosovo can truly become a part of the European family, become only beautiful, not confused.

Back inside the 1200 capacity club the only people present are Genti, and Toton and Naka, still playing back to back. Worryingly, even the bar staff have gone home. Rowan is spark out on a couch, beneath the club's retractable roof, bathing in new sunlight, his foot tapping gently to the music, even though he is clearly asleep. He soon snaps awake and asks if there's anything to eat.

I'm thinking Burger King, but our destiny lies further afield—out within the curvaceous beauty of the Gamia valley. There, beneath bright sunlight spilling through the trees, is a pine lodge, populated by couples, joggers, kids playing on swings. In the presence of such a purity I feel bankrupt inside and out, a feeling made manifest further up into the valley, where some Yugoslav barracks have been bombed into red brick rubble by NATO.

"It has always been a troubled place," Bersant says, looking around him. "And the population here are one of the most peaceful I know. They tend to forgive."

I have been to Serbia and have Serb friends, so I am aware of both sides of the argument. And it's with great sadness that you feel this story isn't yet over. Bush and Blair still push for an independent Kosovo (their diamond sat atop the steaming turd that is their shared foreign policy) but with Russia flexing, Serbia is once again bullish. In global realpolitik, as with playground bullying, it's all about who's got your back.

Then again, maybe the Kosovars have got deeper things to contend with. "For centuries Serbia has done a lot of bad promotion for this place," Bersant argues, and back in Pristina we realise just how true that is. Serbia has won the Eurovision Song Contest. Of course the irony is that this means the 2008 final will be held in Serbia and, if Kosovo achieves independence, as a European country it will be able put forward an entry. And perform it in Belgrade.

That's one party I want to be at.

WRITING PROMPT: MUSIC SCENES

Start with a band or musician you like and find out about the place where they made (most of or their) music.[4]

Become familiar with other bands and artists who were active in the same place and at the same time.

Learn about what defined this locale outside of music during that time (local papers are a helpful source).

Interview artists or fans who lived there at the time if possible or read accounts of their experiences on the scene if you can find them. Published interviews with musicians can be very useful here as well.

Once you have a more comprehensive sense of the particular "scene" you're researching and can describe its defining features, write a 3000-word essay that provides a context for the band that initially drew your attention to this place.

---

[4]The first volume of Mark Lewisohn's *Tune In: The Beatles: All These Years* (New York: Crown Archetype, 2014) provides an in-depth account of the Liverpool scene during the Beatles early years there and offers instructive use of primary material, interviews, and the music that developed in that place and at that time after the Beatles.

THE GO-BETWEENS

HOW HAS THE FIELD OF WRITING ABOUT MUSIC CHANGED?

There's both good and dreadful in the music-writing world, and I have to imagine both co-existed for years before the Internet made it easier to find both.—**Phillip Crandall**, author of the **33⅓** book on Andrew W.K.'s *I Get Wet*

Opportunities are better in some ways but that's just because I am working at a different level. I have been putting out consistent and original criticism for long enough that people usually say yes to my ideas, so I am lucky. That said, the per-word rate at every place I work for, save for Conde Nast, generally, had been halved or even quartered. What I get paid for work at alt weeklies is actually less than I made in 1993. The internet groomed a lot of people to work for nothing, it brought the entire market down—internet rates are always a tiny fraction of print. It's super depressing.—**Jessica Hopper**, Music Editor at *Rookie Magazine*, and Senior Editor, the *Pitchfork Review*

Well it's not new knowledge but the fact that print publications sell so much less these days means that there is so much less income for all types of writers. So that has changed the landscape and now a writer is more likely to do more than just write, which can actually be a very good thing because they then exist within a much wider and broader world which makes them less insular. They also generally get less money for what they do, which is, of course, very bad, but a difficult tide to turn.—**Pete Astor**, writer, academic, musician

We don't hear this often enough, but the written word and communications in general are in a period of seismic change unrivaled since Gutenberg built his printing press in the mid-1400's. Always hypercompetitive, the number of opportunities in dead-tree media continue to shrink, but this sad state of affairs (for people who'd like to get paid to write) arguably is offset by the ability to reach a larger audience than even the most prestigious print publication could offer in the past—to say something unique, in a colorful voice, which needed to be said, and to see it "go viral" with a reach far exceeding the front page of the *New York Times* or any other publication you could name. At the moment, that isn't necessarily paying. But the new media still are being invented, we have no idea what final form they will take, and we writers at least can hope for some profitable (as in sort of pay the rent) endeavor—or we can try to build it ourselves.—**Jim DeRogatis**, author, co-host of *Sound Opinions*, and lecturer at Columbia College Chicago

Well, to hone my flare for the obvious, there were a great many more record labels and record stores. There was a lot of money to be made from selling physical product through retail shops. In keeping with the physicality of all that, there were more, so many more magazines in print, magazines that made a profit and could pay writers. Nowadays, much writing for online sites resembles some attenuated form of internship.—**Richard Henderson**, itinerant stringer for the *Wire* (U.K.), with past writing having appeared in *Billboard*, *LA Weekly*, *The Beat*, *Escape*, *Soma* and *Murder Dog*

The possibilities are endless now. You can start a blog and become the most trusted music blog out there, if you're good at it. So I think a lot of the barriers have fallen and the tastemakers don't have access to a whole lot of music that you don't have access to. You can become an expert on Krautrock in like a week. I have met high school kids that know so much more than I do about entire genres of music, because they are sort of OCD and they have the internet. We are all music critics waiting to happen. (What a terrifying thought!)—**Casey Jarman**, Managing Editor, the *Believer*

In response to a question like this from where I am in time, I tend to say it is neither better nor worse since I started in 1976—it is just very, very different, for better or worse. The main difference is that there is now so many more people writing about music both professionally and not, and there is so much more music, and so much more music, even obscure music, being written about. It just becomes an unchecked, unremarkable, shattered deluge of words and recommendations and producer-consumers that lead to more and more playlists and more and more surface and less and less depth. It is the status quo rather than a determination to assassinate the status quo. The opportunity to make a real name as a writer has disappeared, even as it has seemed to have become easier—the move from print to online has diluted the cultural role original writing plays in helping to piece together the wider context of the music, and in a sense the position of the rock writer as a contributor to music history, in detecting patterns, selecting musicians to back as heroes and stars, interpreting moments, celebrating events, shaping opinion has been replaced not by contributors to the internet but by the internet itself. The context for popular music is now the internet—this is a good subject to write about, and

343

also the way that creates a kind of aftermath moment for pop music, but instead, the music is still written about as if the context and circumstances are the same as they were thirty years ago, as if there are still the charts, and there is still vinyl, and fame is not so mundane. I am waiting for a shift in the style of music writing to reflect this fundamental change in what pop music is, and how and why it appears in the world.—**Paul Morley**, writer and critic

It's better in some ways and worse in others, very difficult to say. There is less money now, and it's spread around a lot more people. So the good news is there are many more people writing about music, the bad news is an individual piece pays a lot less than it used to. The opportunity to work for weeks on end on one high-paying piece has mostly disappeared, but there's more opportunity to see your name in print somewhere.—**Mark Richardson**, Editor-in-Chief, Pitchfork

It's easier to write about music, easier to publish what you write, easier to reach readers, easier to find what's out there worth reading. (It's tougher to get paid, of course, but then it's always been tough to get paid for writing. Aside from the gold-rush years of the Nineties economic boom, only a tiny minority of music writers have gotten any checks out of it.) The main change has been the focus on timeliness—these days people are terrified of being late. They'd much rather be *wrong* than *late*. So it seems like there are huge new opportunities in terms of being late on purpose—taking your time to digest a piece of music and coming in a few weeks or months or years later with something new to say. Something that's not just recycling what everybody else was saying before the release date.—**Rob Sheffield**, writer, *Rolling Stone*

The music industry has definitely changed, even in the last seven or so years that I've been involved in the field. Several major publications have gone out of business, rates for freelancers continue to decrease, and there's more competition than ever before. That said, aspiring music writers have so many new resources at their disposal, from Tumblr to Twitter, and it's a lot easier to make a name for yourself today than it was seven years ago.—**Alex Young**, founder and publisher, Consequence of Sound

CHAPTER 12
CULTURAL CRITICISM

INTRODUCTION

Every semester my students research ten facts about the time a given song was released or the place from which it emerged—facts that have nothing directly to do with the subject they've chosen to write about. This prompt for writing about the cultural significance of a song sometimes seems to me too insubstantial, or even capricious. What happens when you ask seemingly unrelated facts, one at a time or in combination, to react with the song itself? Frequently nothing—cross those facts off the list. But at other times an unexpected influence, friction, or indication of the zeitgeist starts to make sense in the context of a song no one would have expected to have much cultural "relevance" at all. Even though the assignment usually leads to a lot of dead-ends before the writers find their direction, it never fails to spur a set of interesting essays as well as occasionally brilliant ones. So even though I'm perennially on the verge of swapping it out for another assignment and students routinely find it the most challenging work they undertake in the Writing Rock workshop, it remains the prompt that stretches them most as writers.

Last semester one student, Cody DeFalco, responded to the prompt by writing on "Song About Old Rollercoaster" by defunct Michigan-based post-hardcore band Bear vs. Shark. In his essay, the song by these Detroit-area musicians began to light up when Cody looked at it alongside Detroit's radical population decline, the European colonization of the site where the Motor City would later take shape, and the very hard fact that dumpsters now occupy the acres of what had once been a Cadillac assembly plant. The song's evocative, elliptical lyrics are anything but transparent, but in Cody's reading they start to suggest the way a song—one that may not be eager to "say something" directly about its time or place—allows us to understand a dynamic in the culture in a way no economic report or historical thesis can. Even cryptic lines like "Dig a trench with those megaphones, megaphones and pirates/Everything will change when you pull this boat ashore" start to signify, combining as they do a foreman's shouted order and the short-sighted ambitions of the "pirates," both the first European settlers and their descendants, those captains of industry whose will to power and a consuming appetite for material success caused the debilitating collapse, emotional as much an economic, that defines what the author calls the song's "dour energy." Like Cody's work, the essays by the writers collected in this chapter succeed in teaching us something about the way music can embody, recalibrate, and articulate aspects of the culture in revealing and surprising ways.—MW

CARL WILSON ON CÉLINE DION

33⅓ Volume #52 Let's Talk About Love*

Let's Do a Punk Version of "My Heart Will Go On" (or, Let's Talk About Our Feelings)

There's a portentous overture of bass, and then those flesheatingly familiar notes—*dah-dah-deee, yi-ee-da-doe-daah* . . . except that this time they are not tootling from a penny whistle but snapped out on electric guitar, like Jimi Hendrix unfurling his "Star-Spangled Banner." Then the guitarist stutters into power chords and the singer staggers into the lyrics in a noisey, melodic mewl: "Everrrrynightin*my*dreams! I *see*you! I *feel*you! ThatishowIknow you go-woah *awnnn!*" Chug-chug, chugchug, *kick*-drum, *kick*-drum.

Along with this one by Florida-bred mall punks New Found Glory, I know of at least five more punkish covers of "My Heart Will Go On" in circulation, by Australia's Screaming Jets, Nashville group Los Straitjackets (a twangy instrumental), Orange County's the Vandals, Los Angeles's snotty, "girlcentric" Switchblade Kittens and New Jersey spoof-metal band Satanicide (the closest to the original, since it just puts Céline's metal-on-estrogen back on testosterone). I bet many more have been done live by bands that never went so far as to record them. The rite of the punk or "ironic" cover goes back at least (not counting Hendrix) to the Sex Pistols covering the Monkees' "Stepping Stone," a middle-finger thrust at commercial disposability that's given a twist by the realization that the Pistols themselves were, like the Monkees, a "manufactured" band. The ironic cover might have come into full bloom when post-punk group the Replacements took to playing tunes by Kiss and other arena-rock bands in their early-80s club shows, as my friend Jake London claimed in a 1996 lost classic of rock criticism called "Sucking in the Seventies: Paul Westerberg, The Replacements and the Onset of the Ironic Cover Aesthetic in Rock'n'Roll." Jake, a Seattle musician and lawyer, thinks ironic covers allowed post-babyboom "underground" rock scenes to smuggle the repudiated music of their childhoods back into their lives: at first you'd ask if the Replacements were kidding or if they "really" liked Kiss, but with repetition, the jokey protective bubble would wear away, until Kiss seemed just plain *good* again, like they did when you were ten. It undermined the canons laid down by boomer rock criticism, and in time a lot of other outcast music was reclaimed this way: a band with the Midas touch of cool, like Sonic Youth, could overturn scenester vilification of Madonna just by releasing an EP of covers as Ciccone Youth.

---

*Wilson, Carl. *Let's Talk about Love: A Journey to the End of Taste*. New York: Continuum, 2007. 120–134.

Today the ironic cover's dominant form is the acoustic or rearranged version of a current hit—say, Kelly Clarkson's "Since U Been Gone." It still gets club crowds chuckling nervously, but there's a more charitable tone: at worst it says, "There's a good tune under all that cheese"; often it's just, "Fuck that, I love this song." Likewise, the punk cover's more high-tech successor, the mashup, often showcases the "good parts" of a hit, digitally spliced into a cooler song: when Christina Aguilera's "Genie in a Bottle" was mashed with the Strokes' "Can't Explain," it won her a lot of converts. Metacriticism in musical form, both covers and mashups help siphon the guilt out of guilty pleasures. But not for Céline. Punk covers of her acidly musicalize the vitriol she gets in the press. The only Céline mashup I've heard blends "My Heart Will Go On" with moody Icelandic band Sigur Ros, and the subtext isn't "look, Céline's okay," but "look, you stupid Sigur Ros fans, they're as boring as Céline Dion." Cover-version irony fails as a gateway to redemption because her music, much more than "dumb" rock, teen-pop or the cartoon-thug side of hip-hop, is exactly what hip defenses exist to guard against: it's sentimental.

For a century or more, sentimentality has been the cardinal aesthetic sin. To say a work of art is sentimental is perforce to damn it. To be sentimental is to be kitsch, phony, exaggerated, manipulative, self-indulgent, hypocritical, cheap and clichéd. It is the art of religious dupes, conservative apologists and corporate stooges. As kitsch, it is likened to fascist or Stalinist propaganda by Milan Kundera, Clement Greenberg, Harold Rosenberg, Dwight Macdonald and of course Theodor Adorno. The German novelist Hermann Broch wrote, "The producer of kitsch does not produce 'bad' art ... It is not quite impossible to assess him according to aesthetic criteria; rather he should be judged as an ethically base being, a malefactor who profoundly desires evil." The punk sneer pronounces the same verdict. And all things considered, perhaps because I'm a lyrics listener, sentimentality is also the most formidable barrier between Céline's music and me: it's not just that the Hallmark-card messages are unappealing, but a fear that yielding to them may turn my brain and principles to mush. Can that really be just learned prejudice, like so many other cultural filters?

To be sure, I can absolve sentimentality of the superficial charges fast. Manipulative? Manipulating listeners, *moving* them, is what music is supposed to do, skillfully. Phony? All art is fake. What matters is to be a convincing fake, a lie that feels true. Clearly Céline has her audience convinced. And is her soundtrack-to-your-life approach more "self-indulgent" than James Joyce's multilingual word games? Is that really a fault in art? Who else should the artist be indulging? As for hypocrisy: certainly, dressing Nazism up with rosy-cheeked mothers and children frolicking on German hillsides is disgusting, but what's wrong with rosy-cheeked mothers and kids if they're not Nazis? Taking mere mawkishness as propaganda is paranoid, absent a specific evil it's complicit in, unless you extend that indictment to any art not made explicitly as protest. (For a more rigorous rundown of these arguments, see the late American moral philosopher Robert C. Solomon's *In Defense of Sentimentality*.)

A more thoughtful question is one of proportion: is the problem that kitsch sentimentality (in musical terms, schmaltz) takes everyday hopes and affections and inflates them into life-or-death melodramas? Consider Zen scholar R. H. Blyth's elegant definition, "We are being sentimental when we give to a thing more tenderness than God gives to it." This is the antisentimentality John Cage enacted by composing music based on random rolls of dice, to subtract his own will from the outcome— his silent piece, *4'33"*, is just a frame to focus the ears and mind on the sounds of existence already in progress. His music is beautiful in its willingness to surrender itself to that objectivity. Like Cage's silence, God's love is unspeakable, implacable, its gaze matter-of-fact. But human love is something else: we love in excess of God's love if we love at all. We love by heaping meaning on objective fact. If I believed in God, I might imagine this is what He created humans for, to give things more tenderness than He granted them, amid nature's unblinking harshness and the cruelty of fate—perhaps we are here to make up for what Depeche Mode, in its Gnostic pop song "Blasphemous Rumors," called God's "sick sense of humor." God's love might sound like Kraftwerk, a sonic diagram of passing traffic, or the relentless electronic march of a disco track by Giorgio Moroder, but humanity is the Donna Summer vocal that cannot resist muscling in to overstate the obvious, to exalt the obvious in hallucinatory helixes, insisting over and over, "I feel love, I feel love, I feel love." God or no God, it's hubris to pretend to know the correct amount of tenderness it is ours to grant.

Aesthetically, too, excess seems an old-fashioned concern, unless excess tenderness is more reprehensible than the excesses of paint, noise, rage, monumentality, vocabulary, nakedness and more that art has rolled around in since modernism and especially since rock'n'roll, much to our delight. When a critic says Céline "bulldozes" a song, it's a plaint; when a critic says, "The Ramones bulldoze through a three-minute punk pounder," that's praise. Cliché certainly might be an aesthetic flaw, but it's not what sets sentimentality apart in pop music, or there wouldn't be a primitive band every two years that's hailed for bringing rock "back to basics."

Such double standards arise everywhere for sentimental music: excess, formulaism, two-dimensionality can all be positives for music that is not gentle and conciliatory, but infuriated and rebellious. You could say punk rock is anger's schmaltz—a notion reinforced by how easily, with "emo" punk, it is refitted to express personal angst. Punk, metal, even social-justice rock such as U2 or Rage Against the Machine, with their emphatic slogans of individuality and independence, are as much "inspirational" or "motivational" music as Céline's is, but for different subcultural groups. They are just as one-sided and unsubtle. Morally you could fairly ask what is more laudable about excess in the name of rage and resentment than immoderation in thrall to love and connection. The likely answer would be that Céline is conformist, quiescent, unsubversive. "Subversion" today is sentimentality's inverse: It is nearly always a term of approval. To show the subversiveness of a song, TV show or movie is tantamount to validating it, not just in pop criticism but in academic scholarship.

What is subversive? Transgression, satire, idiosyncracy, radicalism, asserting a minority identity, throwing noise into the signal, upending convention, generally mitigating for *change*. But as social critic Thomas Frank (*The Conquest of Cool*) has long argued, today those are values promoted by advertising, corporate-management gurus and high-tech entrepreneurs. Canadian authors Joseph Heath and Andrew Potter's entertaining polemic *The Rebel Sell* adds that anticonformist impulses are the octane of consumerism, seeking the cutting edge, the very soul of Bourdieuvian distinction, whether in designer couture, organic cuisine or "uncommodified" culture. Thus there is now, and maybe always was, a conservative vibration in the heartbeat of rock'n'rebellion. Corporate and government rhetoric mimics and migrates into rebel schmaltz. The kind of change implored in the music of strident sarcasm—freedom, equality, less authority—aligns handily with a "new economy" whose trade and labor-market needs require a more "flexible," mobile, multicultural social structure. Capitalism today cheers decentralization, deregulation and other conspicuous change that spikes short-term stock prices and justifies layoffs, unpaid overtime, third-world outsourcing and ubiquitous marketing, plus the organized violence that supports them. Naomi Klein's book *The Shock Doctrine* points to a continuum between economic, political, military and torture-room "shock therapy"—might the metaphor extend to the artistic "shock of the new"?

Music criticism's attachment to youth rebellion is not free of these myopias: what liberal critics label subversive seldom pertains to practical social reform. In fact, the few critics with larger political commitments often attend more sympathetically to mass culture, even the supposedly bland and sentimental sort, because their concerns involve human lives, not cultural one-upmanship. Which is not a bad yardstick to sort politics from revolutionary playacting.

Even in the ostensibly more serious realm of academia, notably Cultural Studies, the idea of "resistant" reading—that audiences make self-empowering, anti-establishment reinterpretations of mainstream culture—can be merely a reverse justification of personal taste. An academic who likes Kelly Clarkson will find cause to claim she offers more recoupably resistant material than Britney Spears. It may be that, as Bourdieu believed, aesthetics are mostly a disguise for political relationships. But to then use politics as a further disguise for your aesthetics is to build a hall of mirrors. Since power is a dynamic that permeates even the most microscopic interactions, you can find submission or resistance in any cultural figure or artifact if you look; but it can be misleading to do so selectively, and break pop culture down into quiescent versus subversive blocs.

Why, finally, should subversion be the *sine qua non*? Fans, after all, are not always busy resisting and recontextualizing their idols—they also support, defend and identify with them. If we disavow a Kantian formal aesthetic, a "disinterested" gaze, then whenever someone says an artwork is good or bad, it is reasonable to ask "good or bad for what?" What's the *usefulness* of Céline's music for her fans, if it is not about subversion? Lawrence W. Levine has written that appraising art by its novelty or radicalism is "a modern fallacy contradicted by the centuries of folk artists who saw their function as embodying the beliefs and meanings of their cultures in language that could be understood by their fellows." Sentimentality in popular art is one of the few vectors along which this "folk" function still can be fulfilled: "Art can just as legitimately stand near the center of common experience and give its audiences a sense of recognition and community."

In that light, mightn't Céline's music of everyday affirmation also have social value? Her songs are often about the struggle of sustaining an emotional reality, about fidelity, faith, bonding and survival—continuity, that is, in the destabilizing flux of late capitalism. While business and rebel-schmaltz stars alike tout self-realization, social negation and the delegitimation of traditional values, Céline's music (like Nashville country) tends to prioritize "recognition and community," connection and solidarity. Granted, she also promotes overwork, ambition and luxury, which is to say she's still a pop star. But in that matrix, sentimentality might be her greatest virtue.

That's a painful admission, because it implies that the shelter for oddness and dissatisfaction that maverick art and culture have offered in my life may be self-servingly segregating and undemocratic. It pours cold water on the hope that art that insists on its quirky independence fosters critical thinking, even models social change. Art's shock tactics do clear ground for cultural shifts, but what artists foresee is seldom what society gets. Certainly, celebrities like Céline can help advertise an American Dream cover story for a destructive hegemony by appealing to widely held desires and aspirations. But the transgressive individualism of modernism's heirs verges on directly emulating that destructive drive, while *jeering* at its victims' aspirations and desires. Maybe I have met the Ugly American, and he is me.

The most compelling indictment of sentimentality in art is that it distorts reality by expunging the darker side. In a famous passage in his novel *The Unbearable Lightness of Being*, Milan Kundera writes that kitsch is "the absolute denial of shit, in both the literal and the figurative senses of the word; kitsch excludes everything from its purview which is essentially unacceptable in human existence." But in much of modern, critically certified art, what happens is a denial of *non*shit, of everything that is *acceptable* in human existence. On a political level, one might ask if this equal and opposite distortion doesn't breed hopelessness and passivity. As Robert C. Solomon says, "Why should we *always* be made aware of flaws and dangers? . . . Should we make it a point never to have a nice thought without a nasty one as well?"

The very greatest art may ball all the shit and nonshit of existence together, the way it comes in life, but on the less exalted tiers, why must art that focuses mainly on what Solomon calls "the tender emotions" take a back seat to art that focuses mainly on the harsh ones? The hierarchies of antisentimentalism seem to end in a perverse reversal of values. As Canadian philosopher Deborah Knight suggests in her 1999 paper, "Why We Enjoy Condemning Sentimentality," one cause is macho rationalism. If the tender emotions are stereotypically feminine, cuddly, nurturing, then the sentimental, as she puts it, is "sluttish"—"indulgent, cheap, shallow, selfabsorbed, excessive." Philosophical antisentimentalism, she asserts, is a sentimentalization of rationalism, a pre-emptive strike against betraying any unseemly weakness for the illogical, girly side of human nature. (And it doesn't get much more girly than Céline Dion.)

And even if the gender bias is receding, it's not the only social ranking involved: mastering one's emotions is also a time-honored upper-class imperative. There's a reason cool is called "cool," and within its economy, it's not just, to swipe the title of a 1980s famine-relief anthem, that "Tears Are Not Enough," but that tears are almost always too much. If you put down "cheap thrills" today, you're a stuffy old snob, but you're far more free to vent distinctionalist contempt for sentiment's "cheap emotion."

It's often assumed that audiences for schmaltz are somehow stunted, using sentimental art as a kind of emotional crutch. As Solomon points out, there's no evidence for this slur: isn't it equally plausible that people uncomfortable with representations of vulnerability and tenderness have emotional problems? Sentimental art can be a rehearsal, a workout to keep emotions toned and ready for use. This doesn't dictate that those uses will be appropriate ones, and emotions alone are not solutions to issues, but sympathy and compassion are prerequisites to charity and solidarity. So between the sentimentalist and the antisentimentalist, who is the real emotional cripple?

Me, for one. The underlying reason I had such a bad time in Vegas was not that it was tacky: it was that the tackiness made me feel even lonelier than I already was, some six months after my marriage dissolved. For a moment in the Colosseum, beside the teary Filipino mom, Céline helped me feel that big, dumb emotion on a gut level. My usual, more "sophisticated" listening can help me reflect on such feelings, to scrutinize them from all angles, but I'm fine at that kind of analysis on my own. I am probably less skilled at just feeling an emotion without wanting to mess with it and craft it, to bargain with it until it becomes something else. Feeling emotions fully, bodily, as they are, may be sentimentality's promise, one too readily mistaken for a threat.

I'm not alone in that. At the same Pop Conference panel in which he made his faux pas about "black music, like Céline Dion," songwriter Stephin Merritt argued that "catharsis in art is always embarrassing." It's a common belief, though seldom so drolly expressed. He was partly drawing on Bertolt Brecht, who held that the purgative release of catharsis can defuse social criticism. But like many of us, Merritt transposed that political caveat to a personal one, a matter of style. His enjoyment, he claimed only half-joshingly, depends on having the embarrassment built into the art, as irony, which allows him to register emotion without the shameful loss of self-control involved in *feeling* it. Here we reach a crossroads where sophistication is just another word for paralyzing repression. It's as if we've mangled one nostrum of craft, which warns against artists "expressing themselves" by just blurting emotions out confessionally, into another (an)aesthetic principle that art should not be expressive or cathartic *for the audience*.

Kundera similarly rails against sentimentality for subjecting the sovereign individual to the humiliation of feeling human: "Kitsch causes two tears to flow in quick succession. The first tear says: *How nice to see children running on the grass!* The second tear says: *How nice to be moved, together with all mankind, by children running on the grass!* It is the second tear that makes kitsch kitsch." What he dismisses as self-congratulation here, as Solomon notes, is the way sentimental catharsis (like the tragic kind) might prompt contemplation of universal experience, arguably the starting place of philosophy. And Kundera's own self-congratulation practically reeks from the page.

What self-conscious aesthetes such as Kundera, Merritt and I might be guilty of sentimentalizing is ambiguity, that shibboleth of our postidealistic age. Which can make us dupes of another kind, prone to taking surface complication and opacity for depth, and apt to overlook the complexity that may lie even within the sentimental on more patient, curious inspection. It's a fault endemic, I think, to us antireligionists who have turned for transcendent experience to art, and so react to what our reflexes tell us is bad art as if it were a kind of blasphemy.

It's not that sentimental art can't be lousy. Nothing can convince me that the book Céline produced with photographer Anne Geddes, *Miracle*—full of color-saturated pictures of newborns lying limp in Céline's arms and in the pods of overgrown vegetables—is anything but grotesque, an unusual lapse into the total narcissism of which critics accuse her, which I can excuse only as the temporary insanity of new parenthood. (She and René had a lot of trouble conceiving, finally resorting to in vitro fertilization.) But what makes the book bad is not that it says babies are special. Babies *are* special: They represent continuity. They call for our protection. They present a mysterious otherness to the fallenness and compromise of socialized life. They're adorable. And Kundera be damned, it can enlarge our tolerance and fellow feeling to be reminded that other people, even real assholes, are mostly with us on the baby issue. What is wrong here is that the book makes the infants look like little dead space aliens laid out for autopsy in a prefabishly fecund Organic Garden of Eden.

It is what's done with sentiment, like any other inspiration, that can be an aesthetic liability, not sentiment itself. To muddle the two is to risk coarsening ourselves against, in Lincoln's phrase, the better angels of our nature. What's more, as Saul Bellow wrote, "Everybody knows there is no fineness or accuracy of suppression; if you hold down one thing, you hold down the adjoining." So what else, in pushing down the sentimental, might we lose access to? Anne Geddes's pictures will not deter us from cooing over real babies. But what of the fact that it is hard to imagine a male performer today having a hit by singing about his mother, at one time a regular occurrence in popular song? Is that topic inherently less artful than singing about fucking? No, but outside of country music, that last refuge of parlor-song verities, the spectre of sentimentality scares us off, and motherhood's exile from our music becomes one more way we take our moms for granted.

Canadian filmmaker Guy Maddin once said, "I think that melodrama isn't just life exaggerated, but life uninhibited." It's a provocative thought: that the melodramatic, the sentimental, might be a repressed truth of human feeling, inhibited by the modern imperatives of reason and ambiguity. Perhaps the dream content of the sentimental is today in need of liberation, the way that in the early twentieth century, Freud and the surrealists realized western society needed to bare and scratch the sexual, violent underbelly of consciousness. With inhibitions against them removed, the tender sentiments might unveil their unsuspected splendors.

For that, though, we would have to relax our constant vigil against looking or feeling ridiculous. Céline herself addresses that hurdle on the first single from her 2007 album *D'Elles*, "*Et s'il n'en restait qu'une*," with lyrics by French novelist Françoise Doiron. She sings that "if there remained only one person" who was willing to "stupidly" trace hearts in the sand, wish on stars, "envy the carousels where boys and girls have fallen in love since the beginning of time" and dream under the moonlight, she "would be that one." This song, which laughs at the clichédness of cliché but then defiantly embraces it, is Céline's rebuttal to the sneers of critics and punk singers—to, as Solomon puts it, "the enormous amount of sophistry that is devoted to making fun of and undermining the legitimacy of such emotions."

That barrage of ridicule can seem daunting, but remember that, in other instances, so frivolous a gesture as an ironic punk-rock cover has managed to melt scorn gradually into fond attachment. In his 2002 essay "On Being Laughed At," British psychoanalyst Adam Phillips writes: "We only laugh at those with whom we feel we have an affinity that we must repudiate. . . . We laugh to sabotage our feeling of being at one with; but the feeling of at-oneness has already happened. It is a question, as it often is, of imagined catastrophe; what, we must ask, is the imagined devastation that will occur if the mocker doesn't mock? If he isn't laughing at his victim, if he stops arranging his humiliation, what does he fear might happen? What might they do together? The so-called psychological answer might be, he will see too much of himself, too much of something about himself, in his chosen victim. The political answer would be, he would turn democratic. What mockery reveals, in other words, is the emotional terror of democracy. That what is always being ridiculed is our wish to be together, our secret affinity for each other."

One afternoon early in our relationship, my future exwife and I were lazing around her small apartment, listening to music. Testing boundaries, I began teasing her a bit about her music collection, mostly thrift-shop copies of 50s crooner and rock'n'roll records, a quaint-seeming fixation for a twenty-four-year-old downtown novelist. She went over to the suitcase record player and put "Oh Boy" by Buddy Holly under the worn-out needle: "All of my life I've been a-waitin'/Tonight there'll be no hesitatin'—oh boy! When you're with me . . ." And she sang along: "Stars appear and shadows are falling/You can hear my heart a-calling/A little bit of lovin' makes everything right/I'm gonna see my baby tonight!" She loved it, she said, because it was the truth. There was nothing more layered or contradictory to say. "Oh boy!" expressed exactly how she felt, right there and then, about me.

I don't think I have ever been more moved, even in our wedding vows, by a profession of love. I've seldom felt so honored, so human, so sure that merely human was enough. That it did not remain enough, that there would be a sadder side to the story, does nothing to mar it, nor to diminish one watt in my memory the soft autumn light that fell across her face as she sang Buddy Holly's words to me. All right, Céline, I'm ready. Bring it on.

My Eroding Generation Gap: On Eminem's Bizarre College
Football Cameo*

I had spent the day with my father at the hospital. He was not responsive and did not seem to recognize that I was there; I was actually hoping this was the case, since—if he had been conscious that I was in the room—it would likely mean he was equally aware of everything else that was happening, all of which was terrible.

That night I was back at my brother's farm, watching Notre Dame play Michigan. My dad loved Notre Dame football, so the game adopted a strange symbolic significance in my mind. I knew he wasn't watching it. I knew that was impossible. Throughout the first half, I wondered how many casual discussions I'd had with my father about which high school players Notre Dame was in the process of recruiting. It sometimes seemed like the main thing we talked about.

Tommy Rees threw a bad pick late in the second quarter and Michigan took a 27-13 lead. At halftime, I went into the basement to get more beer. When I returned, Eminem was on the television.

Mass media makes a lot of simple things confusing. One of these things is the recognition of age and maturity. Whenever I watch sports on TV, I always feel like I'm watching athletes who are somehow older than I am, even though this is almost never true (even when I watch golf). It infantilizes me. Meanwhile, seeing Eminem generates the opposite sensation: we're the same age, but it often feels like he's 15 years younger. When The Slim Shady LP was released in 1999, I was already a full-on taxpayer; his work was brilliant, but also juvenile. It was like Zappa. His worldview seemed like an inaccurate reflection of the generation we both occupied. I knew he was the most technically proficient rapper I'd ever heard (at least in terms of wordplay and verbal dexterity), but I did not relate to him in any context that wasn't a self-construction. This falls in stark contrast to my relationship with Brent Musburger, a stranger whose intertwinement with my existence is unnaturally deep. The number of raw minutes I've listened to Musburger speak aloud undoubtedly dwarfs the amount of time I've spent listening to almost anyone I know personally. (I mean, there just aren't that many non-cult scenarios in which it's normal to listen to the same person talk for three and a half straight hours on a weekly basis for 30 years.) I have a bizarre ongoing fantasy in which I randomly meet Musburger in a TGI Fridays and we end up

*Klosterman, Chuck. "My Eroding Generation Gap: On Eminem's Bizarre College Football Cameo." *Grantland*, December 2, 2013. Reprinted with permission.

watching a MAC game together on the bar television; I imagine Brent expressing enthusiastic opinions about the complimentary pot stickers. So now I'm watching this unnatural cultural collision (contrived by ABC for purposes of marketing), and I instantaneously find myself annoyed by the online reactions that have not yet been written. I know everyone is going to insist this interview is awkward and idiotic and hilarious. But I'm in the mind-set to be moved, so it moves me. I pretend like it doesn't, but it does.

Here is Eminem, placed in a situation where he knows he will be mocked if he doesn't make his discomfort obvious. He's promoting the use of "Berzerk" as weekly bumper music for college football, a song that (not coincidentally, I'm sure) samples a Billy Squier riff so familiar that it seems totally reasonable to hear it on prime-time network television. He knows he's actively re-branding himself as the classic-rock version of hip-hop, which is both his best commercial option and (almost certainly) an evolution he never imagined or desired. But he's being cool about it. When Kirk Herbstreit asks what about his new album makes him most excited, he gives two answers that are different versions of the same truth: His first response is, "Nothing." His second is, "To just be done with it." This does not seem like sarcasm; I believe it's how he really feels about this record, and maybe about his whole career. Still, he's trying to make this work. He's trying to build a weird bridge to somewhere reasonable. He forces his way through the publicity he knows is his responsibility, he sincerely compliments Brent on his broadcasting career, and he goes out of his way to note the passing of Pat Summerall. Musburger tries even harder: he drops Rick Rubin's name into the conversation and asks a needlessly specific gambling question that derives (for reasons unknown) from the state of Montana. Who are these anonymous Montana-based degenerates who want to know Eminem's take on an NFL point spread? And why is Eminem so reluctant to respond to that innocuous query?

I suspect it's because he actually cares about his answer.

People don't worry about the idea of a Generation Gap anymore. That notion has been replaced by a Technology Gap. The possibility of parents and children sharing the same cultural interests has increased dramatically over the past 25 years; today, the central bifurcation is how that communal culture is accessed and interpreted and experienced. Yet there are still certain chasms forged by the rudimentary passage of time. Musburger is, by all accounts, a deeply conservative guy (I love whenever he announces Cal home games, because he inevitably says something amusing and reactionary about the student body). It's hard for me to imagine him listening to a song like "Berzerk" without wondering what the hell happened to the world he helped create. But you know what? He's still engaged with that world. He still wants to know what Eminem thinks about the Detroit Lions. Sure, you could argue that he's just doing his job. But there is no condescension in his voice. There is no distaste with the assignment. What we have is an old man saying, "Look—I don't really understand what you do or why people care. But I don't need to understand it in order to know it has value." And what we have in response is a younger man saying, "I realize you have to treat me like a celebrity, because that's the reason I was pushed into this press box. But I am not your equal. That's not possible. I will never respect myself as much as I respect you."

The promotional segment ended and the game returned. Notre Dame mounted a comeback but failed in the fourth. I finished the rest of the beer, took an Ambien, and went to bed around midnight. Ten minutes later, my brother knocked on the door and said the whole family had to go back to the hospital immediately. So that's what we did.

Chuck Klosterman's Tips for Writers

1. Listen to other writers' advice, but don't unconditionally accept what they tell you. This includes the advice I'm giving you right now. People tend to retrospectively view their own personal experience as normative, particularly if they've had any degree of success. So whenever someone says, "You must do _____, you always need to _____," they're merely telling you what happened to them (while ignoring the fact that every other writer they've ever met has inevitably done things differently).

2. When writing a feature or a profile, don't get paralyzed by what you assume the story *should* be about. Don't immediately decide, "This is my thesis, and whatever I learn is just going to have to support this thesis." Be psychologically flexible. Immediately after you finish an interview, imagine the conversation that would happen if you randomly ran into your smartest, funniest friend on the sidewalk—if he or she casually asked you how the interview went, what would you tell them? That answer is probably the most interesting thing about whomever you're writing about.

3. People will tell you it's impossible to make money writing about music. This is not true. If you want to be incredibly rich (or if you have rich parents and assume "being rich" is "being normal"), then—yes—you should probably pursue a different career path. But you can definitely make a decent living as a music writer, assuming your intended audience is larger than the people you happen to know personally. Most critics only write for other critics. This has always been the case—and if other critics represent the readers you most want to reach, then you should absolutely do exactly that. But don't be surprised when no one wants to pay you for doing so.

4. Clarity is extremely important, unless you honestly don't care how people interpret your ideas.

5. It's impossible to anticipate what people will want or what people will like. They themselves won't know until they see it.

6. In essay writing, others will instruct you to never use qualifiers like "to a certain degree" or "almost" or "arguably." They will say this erodes your authoritative voice. But sometimes subjective ideas *need* to be qualified, because subjective ideas are not irrefutable. Accurately reflecting how you feel is more important than expressing an authoritative view that isn't genuine. Readers can see right through that.

7. In journalistic ventures, it's always tempting to interview your primary subject first and the secondary subjects later. However, it works way better if you do it the other way around.

8. If an interview subject isn't responding to your questions, ask them specific queries about their craft (i.e., "How did you tune your guitar to get that specific sound," "What is the initial step when writing a pop song?," etc.). Every artist enjoys explaining the technical minutia of what they do, as those details are usually overlooked. If that still doesn't work, directly ask them. "Why are you refusing to answer my questions?" You have nothing to lose by doing this.

9. Be aware of your own pre-existing biases. If you're inclined to be a left-leaning person, don't assume every album you love must therefore be politically progressive (and that any album you hate is therefore reactionary). If you're prone to conservatism, don't create an adversarial relationship with everything that's different and don't immediately gravitate toward sounds that seem familiar. Constantly question your own feelings, particularly when those feelings seem obvious and clear. Anytime you come to a critical conclusion, ask yourself, "But why do I *really* feel this way?" Continue asking yourself that question until there's nothing left to ask about.

10. There are exceptions to everything, but it's generally a bad idea to (a) respond to those who criticize your writing, and/or (b) take any compliment about your work seriously.

11. Social media distorts reality. Do not use it as a gauge for anything meaningful. And if you're going to promote your own work via these types of platforms, be selective about it. If you tweet a link to every single story you publish, it will eventually become no different than tweeting nothing at all. Also, people will slowly grow to despise you.

12. In 30 years, unless you're a genius (and probably not even then), no one is going to care about the quality of your work, and no one will accurately remember anything you published about some arcane album that

nobody listened to ... except you. *You* will care, and *you* will remember. So if you can't satisfy yourself, you ultimately can't satisfy anyone else. That said, nobody believes their own writing is brilliant; only crazy people think like that. So if you're insecure about your work and you lack confidence in your ability, it might just mean you're reasonable.

GREIL MARCUS ON CLARENCE ASHLEY

From *The Old, Weird America**

For thirty years people have listened to [Bob Dylan and the Band's] basement tapes as palavers with a community of ghosts—or even, in certain moments, as the palavers of a community of ghosts. Their presence is undeniable; to most it is also an abstraction, at best a vague tourism of specters from a foreign country.

As it happens, these ghosts were not abstractions . . .

Clarence Ashley was born in 1895 in Bristol, Tennessee; as a teenager he traveled with minstrel troupes and medicine shows ("I was always crazy about the show business"). By the 1920s he was a professional itinerant musician, playing in string bands, at fairs, on the streets, to miners as they picked up their money or their scrip. He died in 1967. In 1929 he was in his mid-thirties; he sounded seventeen, or one-hundred-and-seventeen, as if he'd died seventeen or one-hundred-and-seventeen years before. For "The Coo Coo Bird" he carried the tune as it appears throughout Lee Smith's 1992 novel *The Devil's Dream* sounding down through the history of a Virginia mountain family (which in its sixth generation of filial and fiddler mystery turns up a young woman studying semiotics at Duke), every time a beckoning to the will and a warning against fate, a sign of lust and mortal danger. Ashley's performance made one thing clear: however old the singer was, he wasn't as old as the song.

Like many of the numbers on the third volume of [Harry Smith's] *Anthology [of American Folk Music]*, "The Coo Coo Bird" was a "folk-lyric" song. That meant it was made up of verbal fragments that had no direct or logical relationship to each other, but were drawn from a floating pool of thousands of disconnected verses, couplets, one-liners, pieces of eight. Harry Smith guessed the folk-lyric form came together some time between 1850 and 1875. Whenever it happened, it wasn't until enough fragments were abroad in the land to reach a kind of critical mass—until there were enough fragments, passing back and forth between blacks and whites as common coin, to generate more fragments, to sustain within the matrix of a single musical language an almost infinite repertory of performances, to sustain the sense that out of the anonymity of the tradition a singer was presenting a distinct and separate account of a unique life. It is this quality—the insistence that the singer is singing his or her own life, as an event, taking place as you listen, its outcome uncertain—that separates the song, from which the singer emerges, from the ballad, into which the singer disappears.

*Marcus, Greil. *The Old, Weird America: The World of Bob Dylan's Basement Tapes*, Updated Edn., 2nd Picador edn. New York: Picador, 2011. 115–121. Reprinted with permission.

Just as it is a mistake to underestimate the strangeness of the cultures that spoke through folk-lyric fragments ("I'd rather be in some dark holler, where the sun refused to shine"; "My name I'd never deny"; "Forty dollars won't pay my fine"), it is also a mistake to imagine that when people spoke through these fragments, they were not speaking—for themselves, as contingent individuals. What appears to be a singer's random assemblage of fragments to fit a certain melody line may be, for that singer, an assemblage of fragments that melody called forth. It may be a sermon delivered by the singer's subconscious, his or her second mind. It may be a heretic's way of saying what could never be said out loud, a mask over a boiling face.

Ashley's singing—high, a voice edgy with the energy of musing, or wanting, of not getting, of expecting to get it all tomorrow—rises and falls, dips and wavers, playing off the rhythm his banjo makes like a tide eddying up to a bank again and again. There's a willful irascibility in his voice, a disdain for the consequences of any action the singer might take, or not take. The banjo could be from another song or another world. The music seems to have been found in the middle of some greater song; it is inexorable. The opening and closing flourishes on the banjo seem false, because the figures in the music make no progress, go from no one place to any other; the sound was here before the singer started and it will be here when he's gone.

In this mood, in this weather, the most apparently commonplace fragment in Ashley's "Coo Coo Bird"—the verse seemingly most unburdened by any shard of meaning—cannot be meaningless.

Gonna build me
Log Cabin
On a mountain
So high
So I can
See Willie
When he goes
On by

It sounds like a children's ditty only until you begin to realize the verse is made to refuse any of the questions it makes you ask. Who is Willie? Why does the singer want to watch him? Why must he put aside his life and embark on a grand endeavor (in versions of "The Cuckoo" closer to its protean, British form, the log cabin is a castle) just to accomplish this ordinary act? The verse can communicate only as a secret everybody already knows or as an allusion to a body of knowledge the singer knows can never be recovered; and Ashley only makes things worse by singing as if whatever he's singing about is the most obvious thing in the world. The performance doesn't seem like a jumble of fragments. Rather there is a theme: displacements, restlessness, homelessness, the comic worry of "a people," as Constance Rourke wrote of Americans as they were when the Civil War began, "unacquainted with themselves, strange to the land, unshaped as a nation." "We Americans are all cuckoos," Oliver Wendell Holmes said in 1872. "We make our homes in the nests of other birds." This is the starting point.

As long as seven hundred years ago, the English were singing that the cuckoo heralded the coming of summer, and yet the bird was hated. Its cry was reviled through the centuries as oppressive, repetitious, maniacally boring, a cry to drive you crazy, a cry that was already crazy, befitting a bird that was insane. The cuckoo—the true, "parasitic" cuckoo, which despite Holmes's choice of it for national bird is not found in the United States—lays its eggs in the nests of other birds. It is a kind of scavenger in reverse: violating the natural order of things, it is by its own nature an outsider, a creature that cannot belong. Depositing its orphans, leaving its progeny to be raised by others, to grow up as imposters in another's house—as America filled itself up with slaves, indentured servants, convicts, hustlers, adventurers, the ambitious and the greedy, the fleeing and the hated, who took or were given new, imposters' names—the cuckoo becomes the other and sees all other creatures as other. If the host bird removes a cuckoo's egg from its nest, the cuckoo may take revenge, killing all of the host's eggs or chicks; in the same manner as new Americans drove out or exterminated the Indians, when the cuckoo egg hatches the newborn may drive out any other nestlings or destroy any other eggs. As a creature alienated from its own nature, the cuckoo serves as the specter of the alienation of each from all.

If this is the theme of the song, then rather than the anti-narrative many find in folk-lyric performances, what is present in Clarence Ashley's performance—the axis on which Smith's *Anthology* seems to turn, or maybe the proud anthem of Smithville, sung every night at sundown—is a master narrative: a narrative of American willfulness and fatedness, a narrative implied but altogether missing, replaced instead by hints and gestures, code words and winks, a whole music of secret handshakes. Just as there is a certain historical impersonation on "Ballads,"[1] with Virginian Kelly Harrell singing as Charles Guiteau on the scaffold, recounting his assassination of President Garfield, and on "Social Music" there are no individuals, only townfolk indistinguishable from their fellows, on "Songs," where the premise is that one is singing as oneself, the mask goes on, the most profound mask of all, transparent and impenetrable. Who is singing? Who *are* these people? If you could put your hand through the mask you would feel nothing but air.

---

[1] Smith organized his *Anthology of American Folk Music* into three volumes: "Ballads," "Social Music," and "Songs." "Ballads" collected American versions of English folk ballads. "Social Music" included instrumental dance music as well as religious songs, and the selections on "Songs" range from those that offer what Marcus calls "a panorama of the uncanny" to "suites of tunes about marriage, labor, dissipation, prison, death."

WRITING PROMPT: CULTURAL CRITICISM

Carefully read the three samples of cultural criticism in this chapter. Consider how each author attempts to create a larger context for considering the music or musician in each case. While these essays *are* about music and musicians, each one makes sense of its subject through the dynamic of culture and by doing so comes to be about more than an artist or a song alone.

Choose a song by any artist that you'd like to write about in its cultural context. You don't have to write in the same way that Greil Marcus, Chuck Klosterman or Carl Wilson does, but you might think of the way such writers connect popular music to the culture around it as you write. You should choose a song that's rich enough to sustain the writing of a number of good pages about its significance beyond the immediate musical context though the song itself need not be directly political or offer a self-conscious statement of cultural importance. In fact, writing about music that doesn't have any particular ambition beyond being a good song often works best. The essay you write will be an exploration of the cultural context for the song you choose.

Research widely and eccentrically about the time and place from which the song comes and make a list of ten facts, events, and phenomena of that moment and locale that do not have anything directly to do with the song, the artist, or music in general. See what's happening in areas as distinct as philosophy, fashion, medicine, politics, and law—anything can prove a trigger. Make this list by relying on your intuition rather than attempting to link up the song in a logical way with the elements you choose. Don't despair at this point if you can't see a connection between the song and the facts.

Begin to write freely using the song and your list of facts as a starting point. You can conjure with the song's lyrics, imagery, instrumentation, arrangement, production values and sound as you consider the aspects of the time and place you've come up with. What connects the song to the culture of which it's part? Some of the facts will remain uncooperative and fail to "speak to" the song. Don't pursue those. Others—or perhaps only one—might provide an interesting cultural context in which to consider the song. Choose the connection that seems most promising and write an essay that explores that connection.

WORDS OF ADVICE TO THE LONELY MUSIC CRITIC

Critical Mass

Words of Advice to the Lonely Music Critic

By Tony Herrington

- Music criticism should wrap urgent dispatch (what is happening, where, when and who does it involve?) and instant philosophy (what does it mean?) into one volatile and unruly package.

- In music criticism, style (how you say something) is as crucial as content (what you say). Unlike the contributor to academic journals, who can count on the institutionalised compliance of a captive audience, the music critic must grab the attention of the laissez-faire reader and hold it rapt for the duration of their disquisition. For this reason, the music critic must make every sentence count, and dress it up accordingly.

- If the music critic has a duty to the musician it is to report the facts of that musician's endeavours without prejudice. If they have a duty to the reader it is to set up a process of knowledge transfer with regard to the nature of those endeavours. If they have a duty to themselves it is to have fun playing around with the stuff of those endeavours, even to the point of recklessness. These duties are not necessarily complementary. They are the petard on which the music critic will sooner or later be hoisted and roasted.

- The music critic should meet the pronouncement: musicians need support (pace Gertrude Stein), with the response: I am not here to be a crutch for anyone.

- The music critic must keep the musician at arm's length at all times while coaxing them into an intimate discourse regarding their philosophy and praxis.

- In deciding a work's true meaning, the music critic must be prepared to ignore what that work might mean to the musician who produced it. They should make every effort to discern the intention behind a work but must not be intimidated by the information those efforts might reveal. They must trust nothing but their own opinion. They should have the courage of their own convictions, and doubt everyone else's.

- The music critic has to decide immediately whether a work is inert or active, a closed circuit or a pathway to universality.

- The music critic must respond to local initiatives by thinking cosmically on their behalf. They should ask of them: do they expand and elevate existence, or do they diminish it?

- The music critic must at all times remain self-aware but never become self-conscious.

- The music critic should be aware of a work's world-historical significance, its cultural capital, and if that work has no such status, be prepared to construct a new world in which it will have.

- The music critic should be wary of canons. They have a habit of going off in the face and blinding the critic to the true meaning and actual value of individual works.

- The music critic should aspire to the status of the autodidact. They should eschew academic and systematic study in order to amass an idiosyncratic and syncretic personal cosmology from the stuff of the world around them as a way of both better understanding and negotiating a way through that world. This will result in an approach to the critical process that will by definition be non-doctrinaire, non-hierarchical and anti-dogmatic.

- Music critics are people too. It is beholden on them to remember that this is also sometimes true of musicians.

Tony Herrington is an editor at The Wire and one of the curators of Off The Page, a three-day literary festival for music. This piece was written for The Wire's February 2011 issue, in advance of the festival.

CHAPTER 33⅓
INTRODUCTION: HOW TO PITCH A 33⅓

INTRODUCTION HOW TO PITCH A 33⅓[1]

If you haven't caught on by now, **33⅓** is a series of short pocket-sized books about the best-loved albums of the past half-century. Every 18 months or so **33⅓** conducts an open call for new book proposals through the blog at http://333sound.com. This call for proposals is open to anyone. The potential authors can be any age, hail from anywhere and propose any music album. Of course factors like experience and qualifications weigh heavily when we make the decision but it is truly an OPEN call.

In September of 2014 Bloomsbury published the 100th volume in the series on Michael Jackson's 1991 album *Dangerous*. Its author, Susan Fast, had submitted a proposal for the project along with 471 other aspiring contributors in the spring of 2012. From those 471 pitches, founding series editor David Barker and I selected 18 to become books in the **33⅓** series.

What was special about Dr. Fast's proposal? Well, it was a perfect combination of an established author writing great prose about a popular album with a unique story. Susan Fast, a professor in the department of English and Cultural Studies at McMaster University, clearly has a firm grasp of popular music through her academic work which you can find in Chapter 10 of this book. There was no existing book in the series on Michael Jackson which seemed like an obvious oversight and one that we could remedy by publishing hers. *Dangerous* was perhaps an unexpected choice given the popularity of Jackson's other albums, but her proposal promised not only to examine the album, but to look at the cultural moment from which it emerged as well. The infamous album artwork and controversial music video also made this album a promising subject for the **33⅓** treatment. I've included Fast's proposal in this chapter as well as a successful pitch from Phillip Crandall.

There is no perfect formula for writing a **33⅓**. In 2014 I ran an open call and received 410 proposals out of which 14 books were selected. The authors ranged in age from their early 20s to early 60s and while most of them were full-time writers, a few had full-time day jobs completely unrelated to music writing or writing of any kind.

I receive hundreds of emails each year asking me which album I might prefer a book on or what approach would be best. My answers are almost always inadequate. I can't honestly say which Hüsker Dü album would make the best **33⅓**. You'll notice that many of the books in the **33⅓** series focus on albums that might not be the most obvious choice for a particular artist. Why Beastie Boys' *Paul's Boutique* instead of

---

[1]Reading this chapter does not guarantee that your **33⅓** proposal will be accepted, but it certainly can't hurt.

Licensed to Ill? Why Joni Mitchell's *Court and Spark* instead of *Blue*? Why Michael Jackson's *Dangerous* and not *Thriller* or *The Wall*?

The success of the **33⅓** series is based on the fact that the writers choose what album they want to write about. We have never made a list of THE BEST ALBUMS that need the **33⅓** treatment and that's often why the books themselves are richer than traditional music biographies. Of course, we can't please everyone and there are thousands of disappointed Black Sabbath fans out there who expected John Darnielle's book *on Master of Reality* to be an in-depth analysis and history of the album when what they got instead was a novella in the voice of a disturbed teenager (most readers we've heard from agree that Darnielle's volume is one of the most entertaining books in the series).

This is all to say that each approach is unique. In the same way that there are countless ways to roast a chicken, there are countless ways to pitch a **33⅓** proposal. But like roasting a chicken, there's a certain set of principles you must follow to succeed. To roast a chicken you'll need a chicken (preferably dead and de-feathered), some sort of fat, spices and a heat source. To pitch a **33⅓** proposal you'll need a great idea, lots of time and a bit of talent. Since I love to cook and write recipes I thought I'd share my special recipe for pitching a **33⅓** with you.—AJG

The Perfect 33⅓ Proposal

Serves 1

You will need: 1 word processing device, 1 month, 1 great idea, 5,000—7,000 words, 1 great proofreader, 1 up-to-date resume, 2 cups + 1 teaspoon patience, 1 teaspoon of inspiration and 5 cups of discipline.

Directions

1. Be sure to subscribe to 333sound.com and follow @333books on Twitter so you don't miss the next open call for proposals. It's also probably a good idea to familiarize yourself with some of the recent volumes published in the series. Once you are aware of the deadline for the next open call set aside at least one month of free weekends to craft your proposal.

2. Start with selecting an album and make sure that it hasn't already been covered in the **33⅓** series or elsewhere. Select an album you feel strongly connected to or select an album with a compelling untold history. Or pull a Carl Wilson and select an album you hate. The possibilities are endless.

3. Consider your selected album's place in the music stratosphere. Is it a popular album? How many copies has it sold? Is this an album people want to know

more about? **33⅓** is committed to publishing the best writing and the most interesting stories of albums but as a publisher, there's the simple need to sell books as well. If you've chosen a less popular album be sure to offer extra detail about why it should get the **33⅓** treatment. Is there a hidden audience? Are there thousands of fans of this album obsessively discussing it in the deep web?

4. Carefully read the requirements of the open call. Though they may change slightly each time, the basic requirements are always the same. You'll need to submit the following:

    1) Your professional CV/resume, including full contact details + a short biography (25–50 words).

    2) A draft annotated table of contents for the book. This should include chapter titles and a brief 50–500 word summary of each chapter. If you plan on deviating from a chapter structure, please explain why in 500 words.

    3) A draft introduction/opening chapter for the book, of around 2,000 words.

    4) A concise description of the book (up to 250 words). This needs to be clear, informative and persuasive. It should be suitable for use as the book's blurb. It should be written so that people who are unfamiliar with the album will understand what this book is about.

    5) Your analysis of the most relevant competing books already published (or forthcoming) about the artist in question or the scene surrounding that artist—and how your book will differ. Are there any films or film projects in the works? 500 words.

    6) At least 500 words about yourself and why you are qualified to write this book. How you would help Bloomsbury Academic market your book? Please list websites/forums/listservs you'd contact directly; any artist involvement you might expect; any college-level courses for which you think your book could be used, and so on.

    7) Which existing **33⅓** books or other types of music writing you like or dislike. Why? 500–1000 words.

    8) Describe the audience for your book. What are the fans like? Describe your target market. How large is this market?

As you can see, that's a lot of requirements and submitting a proposal is no small feat. Once you have selected your album, start outlining your book. The typical length of a **33⅓** is 30,000 words which generally translates to 7 or 8 chapters of 3,000 to 4,000 words each. Think about what sort of story you want to tell. Is the artist alive? Are you going to involve him, her, or them? If so, now is the time to initiate contact.

5. Set some time aside to work on the most important part of the proposal: the 2,000 word introduction. This is the heart of the matter, the chance for you to introduce your idea and show off your writing skills. This is also the part of the proposal that the series editor will pay special attention to. The rest of the proposal will fill in the blanks, but writing the introduction provides you with the single most important opportunity to stand out and make your case for contributing to the series.

6. Complete the rest of the requirements and make sure not to include any superfluous material like images or writing samples not related to the proposal.

7. Enlist the help of a good editor, friend or teacher to give your proposal a thorough once-over. In all likelihood you've been staring at the thing for hours on end and can't see the remaining errors. The series editor will understand that you are human but glaringly obvious typos are a red-flag (I'm sure many occur in this very textbook).

8. Make sure to submit your proposal at least 24 hours before the deadline. Almost half of the proposals come in at the last minute, stand out and get your proposal in early.

DESCRIBE WHAT IT WAS LIKE
TO WRITE A 33⅓

Working on the **33⅓** book was a terrific learning experience because it involved a whole set of conditions and freedoms specific to the project that I hadn't encountered before. When you're writing for an academic audience, you assume that that audience is familiar with the subject and has a baseline knowledge of theoretical underpinnings that you're working with; depending on your taste for density of language and the kind of dry witticisms that might click with a handful of people, this kind of writing nevertheless entails an intellectual distancing from the music. In my experience it rarely makes for the kind of writing that I enjoy reading. So on one hand, writing something for an academic publisher seemed like a good fit for somebody with my background; but at the same time the **33⅓** series is so wide-ranging and open-ended in the kind of work it's produced that I had to work through some challenges I hadn't experienced before. The last thing I wanted was for the book to read like an impersonal, dry scholarly study. The biggest challenge was working out how to take all the research I'd done on a band and an album that have had so much written about them and present a different perspective on all of it. In this case, that meant treating the album as an endpoint to a broader, looser narrative that perhaps hasn't been told before, at least not in the way I tried to tell it. In terms of having a specific workflow, it depends on the type of piece or project. For the **33⅓** book, I was fortunate to have a stretch of three months away from my day job to focus solely on writing; the majority of the research I'd already completed. So that meant mindfully putting myself into a more or less spartan routine that has seemed to work for me so far: get up in the morning, eat a substantial breakfast, drive to one of a handful of coffee shops in my neighborhood, set up shop and write for anywhere between three to five hours. For the rest of the day I'd try to reset my brain by reading things I found interesting, whether it was relevant to the subject of my book or not, jotting down passing thoughts or ideas I was working through, and getting a good night's sleep before starting over the next day. There's really nothing glamorous or romantic about any of this. The process of transposing your ideas into writing that communicates what you mean to say in the right way is a specific kind of hard work that requires a tremendous amount of focus and energy. I work best if I can keep my mind and general physiology on an even keel.—**Luis Sanchez**, **33⅓** author

A SUCCESSFUL PITCH: **SUSAN FAST** ON MICHAEL JACKSON'S *DANGEROUS*

Proposal Introduction

Dangerous is Michael Jackson's coming of age album. I know this is a grand claim to make, especially since many think his best work was behind him by this time. Let me explain. The record offers us Jackson on a threshold, finally inhabiting adulthood—isn't this what we wanted?—and doing so through an immersion in black music that would only deepen in his later work, yet he was unable to convince a skeptical public that he was either adult or interested in his black heritage. This tells an interesting story, about what will be tolerated, condoned, accepted and by whom; a story about what it's possible to see (and hear) and what gets distorted, as Wittgenstein put it, by the inability to create new mental pictures about the world.

The glimpse of adulthood that we get on this record finds Jackson struggling with some weighty stuff—love and lust, politics, and race—in ways hitherto unseen; he gives us a darker, less childishly optimistic vision of the world, one based more in realism than his characteristic theatricality (at least until the end of the record), one in which he seems, at times, at an emotional breaking point. Even the bright moments are surrounded by uncertainty, anger, or betrayal and taken as a whole, the album leaves little doubt that pain eclipses hope. In his review for *Rolling Stone*, Alan Light noted Jackson's new "assertive" sexuality and called his "best" work, here and elsewhere, that which "reveals a man, not a man-child," that his "finest song and dance is *always* sexually charged, tense, coiled," that "he is at his most gripping when he really is dangerous." Indeed. And he is more tense, more coiled on this record than he'd ever been. Joe Vogel recounts in his recent book on Jackson that some critics, like Light, seemed sympathetic to the new direction taken on *Dangerous*; one of them, Jon Dolan, even made the perceptive comparison to Nirvana's *Nevermind*, which toppled *Dangerous* from the number one spot on the *Billboard* charts and ushered in the age of grunge: "Jackson's dread, depression and wounded-child sense of good and evil have more in common with Kurt Cobain than anyone took the time to notice." While we're making ambitious statements about this record—*pace* rock aficionados—I've long toyed with the idea of *Dangerous* as Jackson's *Achtung Baby*, in many ways a similarly brooding, vulnerable leap into the breach. It isn't only lyrics that take Jackson down that road, but new ways of using his voice and a new allegiance to the sound of black music—past and present. Instead of producing another sleek crossover record full of hit singles, he offered up a table of gritty funk and gospel, punctuated by a dripping metal ballad (with one of the great, emotionally unbridled metal guitar players, Slash, in tow). Only "Heal the World" and "Black or White" follow the time-tested Jackson crossover formula, with "Gone Too Soon" a brief nod to his love of Great American Songbook style, and predictably, "Black or White" was his only number one single off the album. There were fewer top 10 hits on this record than he'd had since *Off the Wall*. Nor was his new direction blessed with the armful of Grammy's he was by now used to carrying home. But musically, it did have a significant impact. For one thing, Nelson George suggests that Jackson's new tense, clipped vocal style on *Dangerous* ushered in a whole new approach to r&b singing in the 1990's and beyond, a new approach, then, to making grown-up black music.

Significant as that may be, this album is one of Jackson's least celebrated, lumped together in that regard with *History* and *Invincible*, his last two records, perhaps some of the most substantive music ever to have been obliterated by personal scandal and professional missteps. My argument is that it is precisely at this moment, precisely when he enters maturity, that his aberrance becomes intolerable and that a critical blindness towards his music takes hold. Michael as quirky crossover wunderkind, fabulous; inhabiting adulthood as the dandy he was, with those looks, his love of kids and kid-like things, his failure to partner up, and making blacker-sounding music: good God. Here's what happens: first, he is admonished for his "violent" and sexually-charged dance sequence in the "Black or White" video—the first single released off the album and televised on national television, remember. The hoopla effectively silenced consideration of the artistic vision he presents in that piece. Next, his adult sexuality is considered improbable, not only *hetero*sexually improbable, but improbable in general, despite his often sizzling self-presentation during this period (calling this man "asexual" takes a willful blindness that could only be borne out of fear; missing his indebtedness to centuries of black dandyism mystifying). He is criticized for appearing whiter than ever, when in fact he begins to radically challenge ideas about race *and* gender through his constant metamorphosis (at the very least, why didn't the queer community like him?). He is deemed musically irrelevant in the wake of grunge and hip hop, without recognition that there might exist considerable congruity between these musical shapes and the ones he was laying down. And he is, finally, publically shamed with an allegation of child sexual molestation. What better metaphor could there be for society's rejection of him as an adult man, what better castrating gesture? *Dangerous* is the document that sets the wheels of his spectacular fall from grace into motion.

But let's try not to drift into this tragedy right now, a move so easy to make when thinking about Jackson, and one that so many writers indulge to the detriment of us learning anything new about his music; let's stay focused on the moment before it happened, the moment that started to open the door to a new Michael Jackson, a new artistic vision, a moment of considerable promise. Cut loose for the first time in his professional life from all his fathers (Joseph, Berry, Quincy: how many fathers can one kid take?), acting as his own executive producer on the project, authoring or co-authoring all but two tracks and working with hip, young producers like New Jack Swing Meister Teddy Riley, the album can be viewed as the culmination of his long struggle for artistic independence and control, for liberation from the guiding hand of paternal influence. Gone, at least from public view, are the chimp, crazy publicity stunts like the hyperbaric chamber and videos that pair him dancing with claymation rabbits or ghouls; these are replaced by images of him stepping out with Madonna, a steaming video with Naomi Campbell, a passionate on-screen kiss with Iman, the stunningly cathartic video dance sequence, a new charitable foundation, and a revealing interview with Oprah Winfrey (not the hippest choice, perhaps, but significant that Jackson chose, after his long silence, to speak to a black TV personality—he was always most honest and forthcoming to the black press, too).

After a long hiatus, I came back to this album through an odd coincidence in 2009, a few months before MJ died (maybe it was a foreshadowing of our collective return to his legacy as an artist). The last time I could remember thinking about his music before that was in the mid-1990's, when the greatest hits disk *History* came out and I was reminded how much I loved the incisive funkiness of tracks like "Wanna Be Starting Something." I was also struck by how Jackson had slipped into myth, his representation as a stone statue on the album cover symbolic of his passage out of the human realm altogether. (The release of *Invincible* in 2001 eluded me almost completely.) While his tunes lived on my Ipod, I didn't dial them up very often. Then, in March 2009, *American Idol* aired Michael Jackson week, certainly a cross-marketing strategy intended to promote his upcoming *This is It* concerts. The performances were categorically awful; I would realize after suffering through countless "tributes" in the wake of his death that it is all but impossible for other artists to sing his songs. They work because of the life he breathed into them, because of his intensity, his exquisite vocal colors, his phrasing, his rhythmic intricacy and precision. None of this seems to be replicable and trying to do it only points right back to Jackson's musical genius, his singularity as an artist. The only way to cover a Michael Jackson song is to blow it apart, turn it inside out, like Chris Cornell did with "Billie Jean." Even Adam Lambert, with his vocal histrionics, couldn't keep "Black or White" from sounding vaguely trite. The only performance remotely believable that night was Alison Iraheta's rendition of "Give Into Me." It awoke in me the memory of that ballad and Jackson's artistic shift into the world of adult pain. My brain was so used to associating him with "Beat It," and "Thriller" that I had forgotten the point in his work where he crossed from adorable into an emotional mess. Since I like my music bloody, this warranted a serious return to the source from whence this little gem sprang.

My trip back to *Dangerous* reminded me what a baroque album it is, from the ornate cover art by pop surrealist painter Mark Ryden, to its length (fourteen tracks, most of them five, six, even seven minutes long, stretching the capacity of the new CD format to its limits), and stylistic breadth, to Jackson's emotional and musical excess: an excerpt of the chorale finale to Beethoven's Ninth Symphony—really? The full-on Andraé Crouch choir in back-to-back songs? Far removed from the gleaming *Off the Wall*, the concise brilliance of *Thriller*, and the clean, theatrical synth-pop of *Bad*, *Dangerous* is messy, industrial, excessive. It all makes more sense if it's thought of as a concept album. Light criticizes the running order, commenting that "the sequencing of *Dangerous* often clusters similar songs in bunches when a more varied presentation would have been stronger," but the "clusters," give us a compelling narrative arc and delineate a number of themes Jackson wants to explore. The chapters in this book follow that arc, moving dialectically between song and the social.

Six Teddy Riley produced tracks open the album and they practically assault the listener with their hard, angular grooves. What has always fascinated me about this initial musical gesture on the album—a gesture that takes up fully *half* of the whole record offering the most stylistically congruent block of songs—is how black it sounds. The grooves are harder-hitting than any New Jack Swing Riley had previously created, perhaps deferring to Jackson's love of crisp, staccato, knock-you-down rhythm and allowing him to pay homage to his idol James Brown (the opening lick on "Can't Let Her Get Away," for example, replicates exactly the one with which Brown's "Sex Machine" starts). Jackson makes heavy distortion a principle in his singing on these tracks; he shapes this distortion in many different ways, but the fact is that this voice, equally capable of some of the most pristine, angelic timbres in the history of popular music, sometimes sounds as though it's going to disappear in the rasp. He's drawing on the long history of vocal distortion as a sound ideal in black music, from the blues, to r&b, to soul and funk, moving deeper and deeper into this sound world. He updates with the inclusion of elements from hip hop: others MC (except for a brief moment in "Can't Let Her Get Away" where he tries this form of artistic expression on himself—it's best left to others!) while he prefers to beat box. Perhaps the best moment from his interview with Oprah was when he spontaneously beat boxed the multi-layered groove to "Who is it," demonstrating a hip side of his musical personality that perhaps many didn't know existed; astonishing how he could just *produce* that groove without a moment's hesitation. Although "Black or White" offers what seems like a more direct testimonial about race, what Jackson does musically at the beginning of *Dangerous* is in fact a much bolder statement. When he could have chosen to stay in the shiny world of crossover pop, this kind of immersion in black music speaks loudly about where he wanted to locate his new, independent musical self. And he'd continue in this direction with *History* and *Invincible*, working with cutting-edge black r&b producers and singers right up to his death. It offers an interesting counterpoint to the even lighter skin tone that emerged with the release of this album; those who thought he was turning his back on black culture might have listened more closely to the new music he was making.

In these opening six songs, Jackson sings about the current hurtful state of the world ("Jam," "Why Ya Wanna Trip on Me"), and he gives us four different takes on love, from the lustful "In the Closet" and "She Drives Me Wild," to the nostalgic "Remember the Time," and the nervous "Can't Let her Get Away." All in all, these songs suggest that love is complicated and cruel—he's chasing it (her), but can't quite get it; he had it, but it slips away; he's got it, but it needs to be hidden. These songs are as much about desires of the flesh as those of the heart, a direction that Jackson had explored in more cinematic ways in songs like "Billie Jean" and "Dirty Diana;" even "She's Out of My Life" for all its poignancy seems like it belongs in a movie. Rather than playing characters and developing a plot as he does with those songs, thereby making it easier to perceive a gap between his own biography and the narrative, these songs feel more personal, more in the moment, more about a "regular" guy who's wrestling with his libido. Jon Pareles found this adult Jackson so improbable that he wrote in his review of the record: "of all the bizarre apparitions in current popular music, none is stranger than Michael Jackson singing ordinary love songs. He can barely choke them out." Pareles was rarely generous in his writing about Jackson, but here he really misses the boat: like the failure to read his allegiance to black music and style over the color of his skin, this is one of countless (mis)readings that refused Jackson as an adult, sexualized being, steeped in the sounds of black music.

Given Jackson's ability to inhabit different musical genres and styles, it's unsurprising that he didn't stick with New Jack Swing throughout *Dangerous*. This would have been too stultifying, too predictable. But the song with which Jackson chooses to break the flow is jarringly dissimilar, its sweetness next to what we've just encountered almost sickening. "Heal the World" appears at the very center of the album in an attempt, I'd argue, to make it the central message. Through it, Jackson tries to wash away the considerable world-weariness and relationship anxieties advanced at the beginning of the album, bringing him back to the (literal) voices and emotions of children, and it beautifully sets up "Black or White," a song (albeit an angry one) about racial harmony. This vision of healing and unity is all but shredded by the three ballads that follow, another "cluster" of songs that could only have been offered one after another to build and sustain a kind of emotional apocalypse. I find it difficult to listen to all three in a row—it's heartbreaking, gut-wrenching. "Who Is It" and "Give in to Me" are the album's most devastating songs of betrayal and wounded love, two sides of the same coin, one offered in the language of soul, the other metal. I'm not convinced that these songs are about romantic love, at least not entirely. Together with "Will You Be There," this trilogy has more to do with spirit than with flesh. On its own, "Will You Be There," sounds more hopeful than it does in the context of the album. The questioning tone of the lyrics suggests a doubt and wariness that even the gospel choir cannot overcome. "Keep the Faith" attempts to pull us back from the brink, but to no avail, not least because it's probably the weakest song on the album, just not a very believable call to be brave and keep strong. But maybe we need something so bland after the preceding turmoil. The tender ballad "Gone too Soon" devolves into the hardest, most industrial groove on the record, the title track "Dangerous," which brings Jackson back to one of his favorite subjects: the *femme fatale*. The record has come full circle, musically, back to another funky Teddy Riley track, but emotionally our protagonist has moved through his pain to a hardened place that views woman as suspect and threatening, even if he seems pretty ready to lose himself in the seduction.

My return to *Dangerous*, coupled with Jackson's sudden death, led me to a general reflection on how his difference played out in his adult life (I wrote a piece on this for

Popular Music & Society) and how, perhaps really starting with this record, his messages and his music could no longer be heard over the din of a body and its behaviors that did not square with American normal. Pitchfork's Rob Mitchum, like other critics, blamed Jackson himself for this, writing in 2002 that "Jacko" had waged "a twenty year campaign . . . to incinerate his artistic integrity." This is certainly true in a culture that likes to focus on weird behavior, but I also sense that it was largely the critics who chose to keep their attention on this rather than his work, who either couldn't keep up with the artistic shapes Jackson was throwing or lost interest and that, as Willa Stillwater offers in her book *M Poetica*, after a while they saw only what they wanted to see. I would say, back to Wittgenstein, what they *could* see, given the lens of normativity they were looking through. My question here is how Jackson's self-presentation as what we could perhaps consider a transgender, racially-questioning (not "post racial") "adult" in *Dangerous* contributed to this downfall: how much of the D.A.'s enthusiasm for bringing Jackson down in 1993 rested upon a fear—not only his, but society's—of an adult man who looked, moved and emoted like this? As Michael Awkward wrote shortly after this album appeared, "The best Afro-American man imaginable to racist white men and women was a dead, castrated, and therefore, according to androcentric notions, feminized man." That's a lot to unpack.

Proposal Annotated Table of Contents

Proposed date of delivery: September, 2013

Chapter 1

Jam

Postmodernism and Black Music

Jackson begins the album with a wide lens view of human relations; his vision is bleak. "Jam," in particular, gives us the fragmenting, marginalized surface self that characterizes postmodernity, especially as it was framed by thinkers of the time such as Frederic Jameson and Jean-François Lyotard. The African-American philosopher Cornel West suggested in the late 1980's that while postmodernism was being theorized by white thinkers through white texts, African-American musicians and artists had offered powerful examples of how to deal with otherness and difference for centuries. Jackson offers such examples at the beginning of *Dangerous*. Of course unlike his contemporaries, Prince and Madonna, whose work has been viewed as a self-conscious embrace of postmodernity, tempered with sufficient ironic distance, Jackson is wary, troubled by it (some have understood his reference to the schizophrenic trying on of different spiritual practices in "Jam" as a direct reference to Madonna, although her interest in Kabbalah came several years after the release of *Dangerous*). "Why You Wanna Trip on Me" has been viewed as one of Jackson's many diatribes against the tabloid press (a reading difficult to avoid, to be sure), but it can also be considered, together with "Jam" as a broader reflection on the intersections between private and public, on how systemic socio-cultural problems are eclipsed by trivialities. The lyrics refer to a litany of contemporary social issues, some of which can be very particularly located (the AIDS epidemic, the Rodney King beatings). Jackson situates his arguments within a musical language that connects them to the long history of soul, funk and, more recently, hip hop as vehicles through which struggles particular to black Americans have been articulated. The songs certainly need to be contextualized within that history; Jackson's crossover success has often remained the focus of attention over his later engagement with black musical styles, but his opening salvo on this record serves as a kind of history lesson in black vocal music, combining gospel-inflected r&b in the verses with James Brown's distortion in the chorus and the outro (the latter an homage to Brown to be sure) and including, for the first time, an MC, Heavy-D, who is given two solo spots on the song. Jackson's instruction to "jam" also situates solutions (or coping mechanisms) largely within the context of black vernacular culture, where the word has had special resonance (especially around the time of *Dangerous*, when hip hop DJ's regularly used the term as part of their moniker, including Run D.M.C.'s Jam-Master Jay, and Jimmy Jam); this positions Jackson firmly within contemporary, hip black music culture. Tracing some of the multiple resonances of this word, however, links it not only with music, but with larger ideas such as culture jamming (i.e. with interference). The focus of this chapter, then, will be to situate "Jam" and "Why You Wanna Trip on Me" at the nexus of Jackson's take on postmodernity and black music, linking his larger vision for the album to both.

Chapter Two

She Drives Me Wild?

Black Dandyism, Gender and Sexuality

In her historical study of black dandyism, Monica Miller writes that "the [black] dandy manifests an evolving series of debates about racial formation, class mobility, gender assignment, sexuality and nationalism." From the time of slavery, when dandified young boys were turned out in fine dress as "luxury items" by their owners, to the sartorial dimension of black spiritual practice, to the ubiquitous and varied displays of dandyism in the entertainment industry, which Miller calls "de rigueur," black dandyism has "embodied the construction and deconstruction of masculine identity relative to the negotiations of race, sexuality and class." Although Jackson was the quintessential dandy, he's never really been considered through this lens ... even by Miller! The discourse on his appearance has been squarely centered on his mutability, his desire for constant self-transformation, the eventual singularity of his appearance; writers have often either condemned him or tried to salvage him from some perceived wreckage, rather than thinking through how it all might relate to larger social ideas about black identity and style. His "stylin' out" in regal garb was as much a statement about class as it intersects with race than it was about gender or sexuality (a subject that has also never received due scrutiny); nevertheless, his sexuality—particularly his believability as the slightly macho hetero figure he wants to sell in songs like "In the Closet," "She Drives me Wild," "Remember the Time," and "Can't Let Her Get Away,"—becomes less problematic if thought through in the context of black dandyism, not to mention the long history of sexually hot white androgynous figures in music, like the castrato Farinelli, to whom Jackson has been compared. Jackson's androgyny, or what in the current context might be thought of as a transgendered identity, doesn't need to be neatly pigeon-holed into a hetero framework, but it seems that his desire to do so, along with his insistence on staying single in the public eye (he stated that he didn't want to be seen as paired up because that would shatter the illusion of his availability to his female fans) created confusion and anxiety about his gendered and sexual identity. Margo Jefferson wrote that Jackson, "the performer, has never offered portraits of black or white masculinity that are at all realistic, or better conventional." Her correction is significant, for what exactly *is* a "realistic" portrait of masculinity? The anxiety isn't about what's real, it's about what's normal.

Chapter Three

Heal the World

Children, Charity and Race

Maybe "Heal the World" is a sappy ballad, but Jackson claimed in an internet chat with his fans in 2001 that if he could only perform a few of his songs for the rest of his life, this would be one of them. It doesn't sound like an ironic statement. Elsewhere he said that when he hears this song in his head, children are singing it. I believe that "Heal the World" and "Black or White" were both written primarily *for* children, as well as putting children—that is, the next generation—squarely at the center of two weighty issues Jackson takes up on this record: racial equality and the search for unity and healing. It's nearly impossible to reconcile songs written for children and/or young adults with the rest of *Dangerous*, but that's probably the point. The musical simplicity and directness of these songs, as well as the introduction of children's voices (for the first, but certainly not the last time on a Jackson record: they appear on his later albums at points where he needs healing, or where he feels healed, too), radically shifts the tone of the album, jerking the listener away from adult concerns to an uncomplicated, or what has been viewed by some as a downright corny and unrealistic vision of world peace and unity. I would argue, however, that finding a place for children on an album otherwise occupied by adult concerns is a bold move, perhaps one that only Jackson, with his multi-generational appeal, could have pulled off: imagine children appearing in the middle of *Achtung Baby*! This move actually opens the album up to address concerns other than Jackson's own struggles with the world.

In these songs he gives children the first and last words. On "Heal the World," his voice *gives way* to a child's at the end of the song and in the video for "Black or White" the child actor Macaulay Culkin ventriloquizes the recorded rap that is clearly in an adult man's voice. These frames work to decenter/destabilize not only adults in general, but Jackson himself from the songs' messages; his complete absence from the video for "Heal the World" is a striking statement, as is the relative balance in that video between images of black, white and brown children (Jackson can't really be accused of a vision that posits those in the Global North as the saviors of those in the Global South, like so much charity and charity rock in particular, including his own "We Are the World"). Within the context of the album, "Heal the World," offers a moment of respite, something we don't ever get on albums like *Achtung Baby* or *Nevermind*: happiness, like tricks, is for kids. And this is exactly the point: we have to understand Jackson's sentiments here as possible *only* through the voices of children; this is the only means through which he can imagine the future he wants. Suddenly, perhaps, these songs sound less hokey and utopian and more wistful. While "Heal the World" maintains this vision until the end, "Black or White" only holds onto shreds of this hopeful simplicity through it's catchy riff, rap and chorus. Jackson's already pissed off by the bridge (is he actually going to take on the KKK?) and the extraordinary dance that he created for the end of the video has nothing to do with childish visions of unity or anything else.

This chapter will further unpack Jackson's complex engagement with race (he didn't "become" white so much as liquid with respect to his skin color), in part by revisiting some of the first writings on Jackson by African-American journalists and academics in the late 1980's and early 1990's; by thinking through his relationship to generation (the lines between childhood and adulthood); and both of these as they relate to charitable work and celebrities: "Heal the World" was, after all, intended as the song with which he would launch his charitable foundation of the same name.

Chapter Four

Will You Be There

"Secular" Spirituality

In an article written in the early 1990's, Michael Eric Dyson argued that "central to Jackson's career is an abiding spiritual and religious consciousness that is expressed in his body of work as a performer." Two of Dyson's unlikely, and less than convincing choices for analysis include the videos to "Thriller" and "Bad;" but his description of Jackson's performance of "Man in the Mirror" at the 1988 Grammy Awards is powerful. At the end of this he writes:

> Jackson's performance revealed a crucial aspect of his vocation: a theatricalization of spirituality, a festive choreography of religious reality that is often present in

his live performances . . . He increases the influence of black religious experience and practices by articulating ... his brand of African-American secular spirituality and institution-transcending piety, rife with appropriate religious and cultural imagery. He also transforms the stage into a world-extending sanctuary on which he enacts rituals of religious ecstasy, moral courage, and spiritual passion that mediate substantive concerns about love, peace and justice. . . .

This might sound a bit over-the-top. It could easily be argued that pop music concerts in big venues often have the air of a religious service, regardless of who's performing. Yet a lot of Jackson's music, many of his videos and live performances are infused with a spiritual, perhaps even quasi-religious sensibility that seems to operate quite differently from your average arena gig. How does this work, and how can it be linked to larger narratives of music as salvation? From moralizing stories told through lyrics and film, to music deeply infused by gospel, to the evangelical feel of his concerts, Jackson was interested in the idea of art as transcendent. In fact he was regularly criticized because a lot of it seemed simplistic and the rest seemed tied to his own ego. The martyred "Christ-like" pose with which he often ended a segment of his concerts was thought to be particularly self-serving (you know the one: white shirt blown open by a fan, arms outstretched, head back, beams of white light raining down on him from above). You can only buy images like these if they're placed within the larger contexts of his performances—what leads up to this image to make it powerful, believable, less about him than him channeling a big idea?

This chapter will explore what Dyson calls Jackson's "secular spirituality," beginning with a group of four songs on *Dangerous*, another "cluster," in which he wrestles with the spirit, where he seems to feel betrayed, alone, and questions whether comfort and community are available at all. I'll move from there to a consideration of the dance sequence in the "Black or White" video (which belongs to this discussion, rather than, or at least in addition to, the one about race) and of elements of his live performance on the *Dangerous* tour that constructed this spiritual or religious vibe. While "Who Is It" and "Give into Me" seem, on the surface to be about love of and betrayal by a woman, I think the lyrics are sufficiently vague in places to call the identity of Jackson's subject into question: Jackson seems to borrow Bono's rhetorical trick that makes the word "she" deliciously ambiguous—referring, as Bono has often said, to the Holy Spirit, as much as an individual woman. The opening angelic chorus of "Who Is It," which is swept away by the hard groove, frames the song with what sounds like sacred polyphony that comes right out of the Italian renaissance; it's a white church that's evoked here. This theme tries to return throughout the song—fragments of it appear in the violins, cellos, the voices return for a moment, but it can't really ever break through again. The lyrics can certainly be read as conventional romantic betrayal, but there's also room for a move into the spiritual: he is damned, dead; he uses archaic, quasi-biblical language ("woe unto thee;" "I pray this punishment would have mercy on me"); he talks about the will; his soul is wounded (not that romantic love can't have these devastating effects, of course). Read from this perspective, lyrics such as "And she promised me forever that we'd live our life as one" might be referring to the hereafter rather than the here and now. And betrayal by brothers and friends suggests betrayal located in the earthly church. "Give into Me" works in a similar way, sometimes locating love in the specifics of a romantic relationship in which Jackson has, again, been betrayed, but also seeming to move in and out of a spiritual realm, this time drawing on a long tradition of blurring the boundaries between sexual and spiritual love (like those medieval mystics who burned in their love of Christ). The short films that Jackson made to accompany these films restricted and, in some ways, trivialized, what I read as a more profound significance in both the lyrics and music. "Will You Be There" continues the emotionally-draining journey, now placed squarely in the realm of the spiritual. It's musically connected to "Who Is It" through a similarly angelic opening, preceded by a musical quotation from the chorale finale of Beethoven's ninth symphony. The excerpt that Jackson chooses centers on these words:

> Embrace each other now, you millions!
> The kiss is for the whole wide world!
> Brothers—over the starry firmament
> A beloved Father must surely dwell.

Not only is the last line infused with doubt, but it's set to music that ends on an unresolved chord, leaving a question hanging in the air. Jackson's doubt, exhaustion, and loneliness in this song are gut-wrenching. It's interesting that at his lowest point, he turns to the musical language of black gospel and black gospel singers as his community.

Chapter Five

Dangerous

The Femme Fatale

Billie Jean, Dirty Diana, the anonymous woman in "Dangerous," later Susie ("Blood on the Dance Floor"); even Annie in "Smooth Criminal" might be considered one of Jackson's *femme fatales*. His return to this character throughout his career is one of the reasons he has sometimes been labeled a misogynist (although some critics thought the way he hassled his girl in the "Thriller" video, or his pursuit of his girl in the video to "The Way You Make Me Feel" qualified, inexplicably, as misogyny). On his History tour in the late 1990's, he began performances of "Dangerous" by circling around a woman dressed in a suit that had dozens of spikes protruding from it; as he touched one of them he said, ironically, "Oh yeah ... just the way it should be." And in the film that was to preface his performance of "Smooth Criminal" in his *This Is It* concerts, he warily watches Gilda, one of Hollywood's classic *femmes fatales*, dance seductively.

Jackson's *femmes fatales* are always situated within a cinematic musical narrative, and I think his interest in this character came out of his love of classic Hollywood movies, where the *femme fatale* is a constant presence. Mary Ann Doane explains in her classic study of the *femme fatale* in Hollywood cinema that this character first appears in 19th century literature and painting, in response to "fears and anxieties prompted by understanding sexual difference." It is a moment, she argues, when "the male seems to loose access to the body and the woman then comes to *overrepresent*." She ties this to the emergence of Freudian psychoanalysis, in particular the new concept of the unconscious: "the *femme fatale* is an articulation of fears surrounding the loss of stability and centrality of the self, of the 'I'." The character is also found in Western opera of the nineteenth century and much has recently been written about the ways in which she almost always had to be eradicated—knocked off—or found mad in the end in order for the male protagonist to gain back control. Rob Walser also talked about how this character functions in metal of the 1980's (woman as just downright dangerous and threatening). This chapter will situate Jackson's fascination with the *femme fatale* in these larger contexts, and examine how his narratives correspond with, or diverge from, classic *femme fatales*. Especially given his own gendered identity and the centrality of his own much worked on body in both his life and art, how does the idea of the *femme fatale* as overrepresenting the body, and the male's loss of access to the body, work? Finally, Jackson's retreat into theatricality, to the presentation of stylized characters (including his own) at the end of *Dangerous* safely distances him from the world of hurt he has explored throughout the record.

Relationship to other books in the 33⅓ series

The book in the series I most wish to emulate is Carl Wilson's *Let's Talk About Love*. The best writing about music, in my opinion, moves outward from individual songs, albums and artists, to capture how these both reflect and produce culture. Wilson links Dion's record with a number of different cultural issues, from notions of what constitutes "authenticity" in popular music, to the particular cultural location out of which Céline's penchant for sentimentality comes (Québécois culture, Italian opera). I especially like the complexity that he introduces, finding multiple and diverse locations for Dion's musical style. I appreciate how Wilson challenges his own ideas about music in the process of writing about Dion's album and its enormous commercial success: the fact that he doesn't understand it is what prompts him to write in the first place and he ends up looking deeply into ideas about music to which he previously had no emotional or intellectual connection (such as "schmaltzy" music, or over-the-top sentimentality). I also appreciate the ways in which Wilson weaves cultural theory, such as Pierre Bourdieu's important study on taste, into his arguments, in a way that is neither patronizing to those who might know about this kind of work, nor alienating to those who don't. Years ago musicologist Rob Walser wrote that those of us who study music can either dismiss the stuff we don't like and call people who love it "stupid," or we can try to find out what their investments are about and maybe, in the process, also contextualize those investments for the fans themselves. This is exactly what Wilson's book does. Writing for different communities (fans, journalists, academics) is difficult to do—I think my proposal is probably still tilted too much towards the academic side, a discourse I'm most comfortable with, but which I'm interested in tempering to reach a wider audience—but Wilson has negotiated these different territories extremely well. What he doesn't do, very much, is address the details of the music: since I'm a musicologist, I have an interest in looking closely at musical details—not in a way that is overly technical, but that connects specific gestures, forms, timbres, turns of phrase, etc. with larger cultural ideas. Wilson does this in a more general way, focusing more on style and genre instead of the particulars of songs.

I think the introduction to Eric Weisbard's book on *Use Your Illusion* offers a good model for how to situate an album within the moment of its release. Weisbard surveys the state of "rock" and UYI's place within a genre that was waning from its previous position of authority and power; he talks about the idea of the blockbuster album as a dying creature; and he surveys the state of the music industry. His review of G&R criticism in the third chapter is helpful in recounting the reception of the band: the journalistic discourse about an artist or particular album forms a significant part of the way that document is received as well as historicized (thinking that records exist in some cultural vacuum and that they can be thought of only through consideration of what some call "the music itself," whatever that is, is highly problematic). That being said, I do appreciate it when Weisbard starts writing more about individual songs, giving some musical details as well as situating these songs within stories about particular performances, what the band liked or didn't about them, etc. I realize he's offering a particular kind of narrative, working *towards* his own reconnection with the actual music.

It's precisely because there is so much detail about the music in both Weingarten's book on Public Enemy and Janovitz's on *Exile on Main Street* that I also find these books good models. Weingarten in particular, brings together incredible detail about the music, situating this in the context of contemporary rap music and the politics surrounding its early production (such as the controversy over samples "ripping off" the original artists). It's impressive how he weaves details about the music through the larger narrative about hip hop. I like the organization of Janovitz's book into an opening chapter that situates the album historically, followed by a separate section for each song on the record. Since these books are about albums, I like the idea of treating the album as a whole, of presenting the songs in their original sequence: this probably makes more sense for some albums than for others; as I argue above, it seems to make a lot of sense for *Dangerous*.

A SUCCESSFUL PITCH: **PHILLIP CRANDALL** ON ANDREW W.K.'S *I GET WET*

I Get Wet

By Phillip Crandall

Approximate completion date: Spring 2013

PROPOSED TABLE OF CONTENTS Introduction – INK

- Explain intent to contextualize album as whole, not to over-intellectualize songs
- Public opinion / criticisms of Andrew W.K.
- Brief description of chapters

Chapter One – JUICE: AWK, before *I Get Wet*

- His musical tastes and tendencies as teen
- Encouragement (financial, otherwise) leading up to *I Get Wet* recording
- How noise scene and self-produced work evolved into *I Get Wet*-style

Chapter Two – SWEAT: The Making of *I Get Wet*

- The songs as they materialized and evolved
- The players he corralled (through NYC scene and fan-letters) and their roles
- The new Wall of Sound
- How the "thousands of hours" were spent in studio
- The sounds/songs they were trying to emulate
- How overdubbing and effects avoided becoming muddled
- The "Who Is Andrew W.K. / Steev Mike" controversy
- The roles of anonymous players on *I Get Wet*
- The impact, if any, of that ambiguity
- The album's artwork

Chapter Three – BLOOD: The Bond We Share

- Reception of *I Get Wet*
- Promotional / commercial use

386

- Tours
- How lyrics create a shared experience
- Effect of narration in song
- Impact on emotions, connection to song
- Perception as bubblegum metal
- How pop-tendencies speak to its universalness

Chapter Four – CHAMPAGNE: AWK, after *I Get Wet*

- AWK today
- How subsequent albums utilized / ignored the Shared Experience
- Impact of AWK's musical evolutions on subsequent albums
- *I Get Wet*, 10 years later

Works Cited

I Get Wet

By Phillip Crandall

Introduction: Ink

"It is not the critic who counts; not the man who points out how the strong man stumbles, or where the doer of deeds could have done them better. The credit belongs to the man who is actually in the arena, whose face is marred by dust and sweat and blood . . . who at the best knows in the end the triumph of high achievement, and who at the worst, if he fails, at least fails while daring greatly, so that his place shall never be with those cold and timid souls who neither know victory nor defeat."
– Theodore Roosevelt, *Citizen of a Republic*

"Hey you! / Let's party!"
– Andrew W.K., "It's Time To Party"

The House of Blues Los Angeles offers 600 square feet of stage, and on November 23, 2003, Andrew W.K. is taking advantage of every inch. The band—which consists of the mic-clutching and occasional keyboard-pounding Andrew Wilkes-Krier, three guitarists, a bass player, and only one drummer because they wouldn't get around to adding a second drummer until the following spring—is in the midst of its third circling of the United States in six months, but the first full tour (and West Coast show) since the follow-up to *I Get Wet* was released in September. Hyperactive as ever, Andrew W.K. is growling the chorus to "Your Rules," a new track that, when performed on *Late Night with Conan O'Brien* weeks earlier, was introduced by Andrew W.K. as a song "for anybody who has ever believed in music." Tonight's lineup is a slightly different one from that performance, however; before heading west, one of Andrew W.K.'s guitarists was fired over musical differences. Thankfully, a trusted guitar tech was ready, willing, and able to jump in the mix, ensuring stages would remain as packed as usual for the rest of the tour.

"We will never listen to your rules," screams the leader, uniting an L.A. crowd that, throughout the set, will climb up onto the stage and prance about the ever-shrinking hallowed ground in a frenzied scene still a trademark for AWK shows. Chorus completed, Andrew W.K. leaps around some more, charging himself up for his second-verse cue. In doing so, he accidentally wraps his microphone cable around his leg. As he explains on his website days later:

> This happens all the time, and I usually just dance my way out of it, but this time when I came down from the last jump and started walking over towards Gregg [Roberts, the band's bass player], I got more tangled in his bass cable and I got my foot pulled out from under me. At the same time that happened my foot got rolled and crushed and twisted and I fell over.

Feeling a sharp pain but thinking nothing of it—"twisted my ankle . . . happens every now and then"—Andrew W.K. powers through the rest of the concert on pure adrenaline, no one the wiser. It's only when the lights come up and the rush wears off that the subtle pain becomes a siren. Partying produces yet another battle scar for Andrew W.K., joining the head injury he sustained while filming the "We Want Fun" video with the *Jackass* guys and, of course, the nose he purposely crushed with a brick for that iconic *I Get Wet* cover image.

Loaded into the ambulance, the hobbled showman keeps the driver idling so he can sign every last autograph request, a common post-show gesture he would years later push to its extreme in a 24-hour marathon signing session in Tokyo. Once at the hospital, X-rays show he shattered his right foot. His options: cancel the tour's remaining shows and rest at home for two months, or perform while confined to either a bench, crutches, or a wheelchair. Gnarly stage-wheelies are envisioned, and shows, including the Anaheim show less than 24 hours later, only get rowdier.

"I just lock the wheels, and then hold on for dear life as I try to whip myself back and forth with all the power I have," he would explain. A national audience got to witness this wild ride eleven days after the injury when the band performed at the 2003 Spike Video Games Awards show, cranking through a medley that gets its largest response when Andrew W.K. declares, "When it's time to party, we will party hard"— the inviting intro line to his debut's breakout anthem, "Party Hard."

Viewers at home didn't know it, but they were almost denied the opportunity. "When they saw I was in a wheelchair they just wanted me to cancel," he told England's *The Guardian* in this unedited, British-ized interview. "They said: 'No it doesn't look good, there's a reason why you don't see people in wheelchairs performing on telly!' I was just baffled by that and then I realised, holy smoke, you really *don't* see people in wheelchairs on television! Why the fuck is that? Afterwards the guy apologised, he said he was wrong, the show was amazing and thanks for doing it. I realised if you're injured it's not just getting around that changes, it's the whole way you're treated."

No rock cliche—lesson learned the hard way, collateral bodily damage, the show having to go on—has ever resulted in such incredible footage, as Andrew W.K.'s live concert DVD attests. Edited in a process called sync-staking, where clips from many different shows were spliced together to create what sounds like one seamless performance, the interwoven wheelchair antics feel like a compilation of greatest spins, slams, and spasms. His charismatic vessel, compacted by his own reckless abandon, develops an even stronger gravitational pull.

"I didn't know if people we're going to like it," he confessed online, "but me and the band just slammed it as hard as we possibly could. In honor of everyone who never gets the chance. In honor of everyone who has to be in a wheelchair forever."

"In honor of all those left out and discriminated against and told no, we slammed."

*   *   *

"It's Time To Party," the first track off of *I Get Wet*, opens with a rapid-fire guitar line—nothing fancy, just a couple crunchy barre chords to acclimate the ears—repeated twice before a booming bass drum joins in to provide a quarter-note countdown. A faint, swirling effect intensifies with each bass kick and, by the eighth one, the ears have prepped themselves for the metal mayhem they are about to receive. When it all drops, and the joyous onslaught of a hundred guitars is finally realized, you'll have to forgive your ears for being duped into a false sense of security, because it's that second intensified drop a few seconds later—the one where yet more guitars manifest and Andrew W.K. slam-plants his vocal flag by screaming the song's titular line—that really floods the brain with endorphins, serotonin, dopamine, and whatever else formulates invincibility.

*   *   *

A pianist sits down to his instrument and plays an original piece. When the song is over, a man approaches the pianist and says, "Tell me about the song and what it means to you."

Without saying a word, the pianist simply begins playing the song again.

Andrew W.K. likes to offer this anecdote when asked about his music's meaning or message. Perhaps "playing the song again" is just his practical, albeit less-punchy spin on that old "dancing about architecture" chestnut. Or perhaps it's gentlemanly tact directed toward an enquirer who wants to know what a song entitled "Party Til You Puke" *really* means. The purpose of this book will be to provide context for the *I Get Wet* experience as a whole, not to over-intellectualize its individual songs (a quarter of which, yes, do have the word "party" in the title). The album was a polarizing sensation when it debuted in 2001. It didn't capture the zeitgeist of rock at the turn of the century; it captured the timeless zeitgeist of youth, awesome and as stupid as ever, and that created immediate deriders. Interpreting and implying some unspoken political message to the album now wouldn't reaffirm polarized positions; it would drive both polarized camps to disgust.

Pitchfork gave *I Get Wet* an abysmal 0.6 rating when it came out—"Maybe Y2K really was Armageddon," the reviewer wrote, "and maybe Andrew W.K. is just the first of four pending horsemen"—then, at the end of the decade, named it one of their Top 200 Albums of the 2000s. Even talking about Andrew W.K. seemed to breed polarization and, interestingly, self-reflection. Three gentlemen debated "the death of irony" for *Ink 19*, an online music magazine, shortly after *I Get Wet*'s release. Christopher R. Weingarten, the topic's broacher, a self-described "cultural eviscerist," and eventual 33⅓ author, cited Andrew W.K.'s "Party Hard" lyrics and asked, "If he is indeed being ironic, should he be reviled for being a gimmicky jape? Or revered for being a brilliant appropriation artist? If he is indeed as serious as he says, should he be lauded for creating visceral body music? Or derided for cock-rock arrogance?" The rebuttals painted Andrew W.K.'s music as "icky bubblegum metal (with umlauts over the 'u')" and unworthy of any conversations, period. Eventually, the debate broke down over its impenetrable layers of arguing about irony arguments—"I made no argument whatsoever as to whether the work of AWK is or is not ironic," wrote rebutter M. David Hornbuckle. "My main point is that he sucks"—but Weingarten's questions about post-modern enjoyment based on artist context are still interesting, especially since Andrew W.K.'s celebrity only got larger in the decade that followed *I Get Wet*.

Andrew W.K. sends out "Party Tips" to his thousands of Twitter followers. He helped a fan throw a birthday party on one of the television series he hosted. He opened a nightclub called Santos Party House in New York City. He gives slightly re-phrased, often verbose mission statements to anyone who will give him a microphone—"My goal, my life's work is not only to discover myself, but to discover what that self of my own is meant to do, and so far, and I could be wrong, it is to party"—then resorts to Caps Lock simplicity for his online profile ("ANDREW W.K. = PARTY"). If the man didn't have such a defined outer shell—unwashed white jeans, unwashed white T-shirt, unwashed hair—you'd envision him wandering the streets with nothing but a megaphone and a sandwich board with "Party Party Party" spray-painted in blood red on both sides.

What makes Andrew W.K.'s "play the song again" anecdote such an odd, yet beautiful sentiment is that he does have a crystal-clear message *outside* the confines of the *I Get Wet* vinyl groove, one he seems absolutely hellbent on sharing with the world. Man-at-the-piano Andrew W.K. is in the camp that music should speak for itself, regardless of context, but to even be aware of that opinion, you would have had to read an interview with the artist, the mere intake of which is proof that artist-contextualization is unavoidable. The only music without any context is an unlabeled

CD, left at your doorstep by an anonymous stranger. At least contradictory beliefs cannot be the driving force of Andrew W.K. conversation; with the exception of one controversy we'll address shortly, Andrew W.K.'s extracurricular messages have been consistent and complementary to any superficial readings of his lyrics, with charisma in lieu of melody driving it home. What G.G. Allin did with feces, Andrew W.K. does with fiesta. Asking whether that "doing" is serious or ironic says more about listener expectations than artist intent.

*　*　*

In Chapter 1 of this book, Andrew W.K. will guide us through the music he created prior to *I Get Wet*, including his teenage percussion work in the Ann Arbor noise scene, the song of unrequited love that earned him a restraining order, and the EP that would hint at the bedlam to come.

Chapter 2 will take an in-depth look at the recording of *I Get Wet*. Andrew W.K. told *Rolling Stone*, "Thousands of hours were put into making sure that the songs didn't sound like they had thousands of hours put into them." What resulted was a focused, singular sound that never decrescendos, with effects and overdubs more ambitious and far cleaner than the metal genre had ever heard. Ionian and mixolydian scales have been used to pop-ify metal for years, but *I Get Wet*'s unrelenting use of bright keyboards and massive guitars to carry the blissful melodies is its irresistible signature. Its layered sound confronts in terms of volume and texture, but not in distortion or face-contorting guitar solos. It gets labeled as metal, but there's clearly something distinct about his particular brand which seems to eschew the defining guidelines. The derider in the above debate called it "icky bubblegum metal," and if you ignore the subjective four-letter adjective, he couldn't have been more right.

The bubblegum descriptor carries with it damning connotations of being easily consumed and easily disposed, appealing to those with yet-to-develop tastes and overflowing piggy-banks. That's not necessarily an incorrect sentiment, but it's not the complete picture either. "Unlike all the astral-planing acidwreck dreck you were soon burning out to, bubblegum laid all its cards out, not disguising itself as anything (i.e. "smart") it wasn't," wrote Chuck Eddy in the pages of an 1987 issue of *Creem*. "You didn't have to study these hooks paramecium-like under a microscope or anything; they were so blatantly cute on the surface you just wanted to tickle 'em under the chin. Which is fine, because rock's not supposed to require much thought."

Tellingly, *I Get Wet* shares some of bubblegum music's more subterranean, shadowy characteristics as well. The genre exploded in the late '60s with songs like "Sugar, Sugar," written and created by faceless writers and musicians who could remain hidden behind the cartoonish characters (literally and figuratively) that made up the bands; in this case, The Archies. Not to gloss over the "controversy" of who exactly Andrew W.K. really is—which, depending on how deep you dig, is either the most banal question in the history of bookshelves or the only reason you've cracked this spine—but he has admitted that anonymous people did contribute to *I Get Wet*.

Abbreviations and obvious aliases abound throughout the album's liner notes, but the real names, no matter how juicy, are not as important as the roles that were played. (Especially if—and this has been posited, conveniently around the time other AWK albums were being released—those anonymous contributors are hiding behind the collective name of Andrew W.K., the name credited as the album's singer, songwriter, producer, etc. This book will attempt to clear up the roles of any such contributors and, if necessary, re-address any impacts on the question of serious vs. ironic enjoyment.)

If nothing else, the endless AWK-dichotomies (and occasional stunts) only breed further hyperbole about his public persona, indomitable spirit, and resulting music. When taken in their proper dosages, both the hyperbole and the post-modern brain-wrinkling are vital to deconstructing *I Get Wet* for the purpose of experiencing it completely.

*   *   *

Every time, without fail, the brain has to weather the same flood of sound, chemicals, and emotions when confronted with that first "It's Time To Party" declaration. As the brain takes a second to find its aural orientations, Andrew W.K.'s second line is an even more insistent growl. "Hey you! / Let's party!" With this invitation, you, the listener, have hereby joined forces with Andrew W.K. on the party front. And you are not alone.

Despite the first-person singular pronoun in the album's title, the *I Get Wet* experience is a shared one between artist and audience. You've been invited right off the bat and, in the first verse, told "don't even try and deny it / 'cause we're gonna have a party tonight." If Andrew W.K. were yelling that at someone he didn't want to party with (say, a neighbor who always calls the cops), his sentiment would have been something to the effect of "don't even try to stop *us* . . .." But the us-and-them dynamic isn't the narrative device here; it's us for the sake of us, "we" for the sake of "we." That mentality finds its way into most tracks literally and all tracks collaterally, and Chapter 3 of this book will explore the uniqueness of this shared experience as well as the psychological nature of how such narratives work. Chapter 4 will look at how it has carried over into his post-*I Get Wet* ventures, musical and otherwise.

"We" isn't a revolutionary narrative device, but in the hands of Andrew W.K., there is no exclusivity to who can join. Queen is actually responsible for two of the most famous examples. "We Are The Champions," which unites victorious fans at sporting events and even the socially persecuted at the end of *Revenge of the Nerds*, may have ended up with the masses, but initially, singer Freddie Mercury claimed it to be, "the most egotistical song I've ever written." Guitarist Brian May says he was "on the floor laughing" the first time he heard the song, shocked by lyrics he thought would patronize people (envisioning, no doubt, those words being belted by a self-assured man wearing a crown). As it were, May says "We Will Rock You," the b-side to "We Are The Champions," was written with audience participation specifically in mind.

In a *New York Magazine* profile of Santos Party House, Andrew W.K. revealed he'd much rather be the party's organizer than the reveler; part of the group as opposed to the literal life of the party. And while party may be an all-purpose, universal word applied to whatever topic Andrew W.K. happens to be talking about, "we" is not. "We" is specific. "We" are those that find our place with the daring, non-timid souls who only know victory.

Books This Would Be Competing Against

No book has ever been written about Andrew W.K. He has "authored" a book in Japan—a compilation of advice columns he wrote for a music magazine there—and his father co-wrote the renowned casebook *Property*, but law-speak may as well be Greek (which may as well be Japanese) to most of us, so they should not be considered direct competitors.

If you put Andrew W.K. in the metal genre, where juicy tell-alls currently rule, than it would be a disservice to readers if I didn't at least try to get some *Dirt*-level debauchery out of the party-impresario. Robert Walser's *Running With The Devil* and its academic look at metal as a whole may not be considered a direct competitor, but I was impressed with his deconstruction of the genre and would look to emulate his technical breakdown of song.

One close competitor might be Chris Handyside's *Fell in Love With a Band: The Story of the White Stripes*. He was a writer for a Detroit alt-weekly and wrote this first-hand account of the band and its surrounding scene. Like Jack White, Andrew W.K. represents Michigan music that gained traction at the turn of the century. As it were, Handyside even mentions Andrew W.K. in reference to a White-written call-and-response. "It would take fellow Michigander Andrew W.K. four years to top that kind of open-hearted, open-chorded absurd openmindedness." While he had the advantage of, well, being there, I have no doubt that my dogged interviews with those closer to AWK's Ann Arbor scene will help paint my picture of AWK's humble beginnings and the hometown influences / co-conspirators he was working with.

Should all go to plan, I'd like a fair deal of this book to be about AWK's in-studio obsessions. There are three Phil Spector books—one I read, two I skimmed—that touched upon his in-studio set-up and practices, attention to sonic detail, and console obsession; none of them went into the fine detail I'd love to get out of Andrew W.K.

33⅓ Books I Would Be Emulating

Speaking of in-studio workings, the book whose discussion of the process I will most try to emulate is Hank Shteamer's *Chocolate and Cheese*. I enjoyed his breakdown of the recording of the album—not to mention the comparisons of recordings prior and since—but would hope to add more technical information about Andrew W.K.'s in-studio techniques and choices.

At first, I wondered if Dai Griffiths had it right eschewing artist input in his academic-style analysis of *OK Computer* (which I would emulate to an extent with some of AWK's songs) but *Double Nickels on the Dime* and *Zaireeka* convinced me that it can be a rewarding venture. The overall tone of Michael T. Fournier's book really reflected the Minutemen's econo attitude too, and I would hope *I Get Wet* could do the same with AWK's spirit.

Random critique: With the exception of *Let's Talk About Love*, I always find myself slightly put off when that "I was first introduced to this band/album" story comes out. Maybe I'm missing something and will figure it out in time to write my own though . . . who knows?

Which brings me to *It Takes A Nation of Millions To Hold Us Back*. If there's investigating to be done for *I Get Wet*, I will absolutely be aping Christopher R. Weingarten's ethic. What impressed me most about his book is how well-written it is WITHOUT an abundance of signature (and also incredible) Weingartenisms. It's his energy and intellect I hope to capture by "sampling" his quotes in my intro . . . and I'm not just saying that because we're pals and he used to be my editor in college and he was actually in the store—sharing his critical-approval of the Andrew W.K. CD that I was walking to the register—when I first experienced *I Get Wet* in 2002.

There. My "first time" story. It's out of my system.

PHILLIP CRANDALL REVISITS HIS 33⅓ PROPOSAL

I caught up with Phillip Crandall in August of 2014, more than two years after he submitted this proposal and just about a year after he submitted his final manuscript for the 33⅓ that would eventually become #89 in the series, *Andrew W.K.'s I Get Wet*. I asked him to look back on this proposal . . .

WHAT WAS THE HARDEST PART OF PUTTING TOGETHER THE PROPOSAL?
The biggest mistake I made when I began working on my proposal was putting my stack of beloved 33⅓ books right next to my computer. What I had hoped would provide early inspiration to think smarter was instead driving me to write in an unnatural voice and venture off on convoluted tangents I was in no way equipped to explore. Put simply, my impression of our favorite 33⅓ writers was shit! My reverence for the series had instead become a hurdle, and I woke up one morning realizing I wouldn't even want to read the book I was hoping to write. Once I stepped back to consider what I wanted in a book about Andrew W.K. and *I Get Wet*—and not what I foolishly thought would make for an accepted 33⅓—it was easy to delete all text that would get in the way of making that book. With focus came a reenergized spirit, and that stack of books eventually represented enthusiasm. I no longer wanted to write a 33⅓ book; I wanted to write *this* 33⅓ book.

I probably spent more time whittling away at making my proposal's Table of Contents tighter and more laser-focused than I did actually writing the sample introduction. Besides some of the chapter-divides coming in at different places, the final product shows little change from that backbone. Almost all of this writing sample remained in the book's introduction as well, save for a passage that was moved to the end and a poop analogy that was pinched entirely.

WHAT CHANGED FROM PROPOSAL STAGE TO MANUSCRIPT STAGE?
The biggest change between my proposal and manuscript was in regards to how I handled a track-by-track lyrical analysis. From the beginning, I was taken by two choice words Andrew W.K. sings that creates the album's triumphant, inclusive vibe, and I had wanted to thoroughly deconstruct all of the tracks to get the full effect of those words. The more I talked to Andrew and the people associated with him and his music, the full effect of those two simple words illuminated the *I Get Wet* spirit so wholly and incredibly that a more detailed analysis of the text was actually counterproductive. It was as if the further inward I explored, the farther away I felt. Fortunately, 33⅓ shared my allegiance to the proposal's spirit rather than be beholden

to some letter of its law. I don't even think I asked their permission to stray from this idea; it just made big-picture sense, and we all knew it.

DO YOU HAVE ANY ADVICE TO OFFER HOPEFUL 33⅓ AUTHORS?

I'd suggest simplifying whatever ideas you have into a concept you're entirely comfortable thinking about and overly enthusiastic writing about. You'll have ample time to explore what incredibleness comes out of that nugget, but if you seem in over your head from the get-go, your best strengths will be obscured. For all the rookie-writer anxiety and stress I started with—and that totally came rushing back once the proposal was actually chosen—my confidence in the proposal's simple idea was unbreakable precisely because it was one I wanted so badly to explore.

WRITING PROMPT: THE 33⅓ PITCH

So you've read close to 400 pages of some of the greatest music writing out there. You've listened to our experts talk about their process, where they find inspiration and what tools they use. Now you are ready to produce a substantial piece of music writing. Select an album of music that you want to cover for the **33⅓** series and write a complete pitch. Set a deadline and make sure to include all of the requirements listed below.

Complete the following:

1. A short biography of yourself (25–50 words).

2. A draft annotated table of contents for the book. This should include chapter titles and a brief 50–500 word summary of each chapter. If you plan on deviating from a chapter structure, please explain why in 500 words.

3. A draft introduction/opening chapter for the book, of around 2,000 words.

4. A concise description of the book (up to 250 words). This needs to be clear, informative and persuasive. It should be suitable for use as the book's blurb. It should be written so that people who are unfamiliar with the album will understand what this book is about.

5. Your analysis of the most relevant competing books already published (or forthcoming) about the artist in question or the scene surrounding that artist—and how your book will differ. Are there any films or film projects in the works? 500 words.

6. At least 500 words about yourself and why you are qualified to write this book. How would you help the publisher market your book? Please list websites/forums/listservs you'd contact directly; any artist involvement you might expect; any college-level courses on which you think your book could be used, and so on.

7. Which existing **33⅓** books or other types of music writing you like or dislike. Why? 500–1000 words.

8. Describe the audience for your book. What are the fans like? Describe your target market. How large is this market?

THE GO-BETWEENS

WHERE DO YOU FIND INSPIRATION?

Other great writing of any sort, foremost. Didion is great for learning about economy. I didn't go to college, so I learned to develop my writing from reading.—**Jessica Hopper**, Music Editor at *Rookie Magazine*, and Senior Editor, the *Pitchfork Review*

Oh, books of every stamp: a particular favourite is Geoff Dyer's *But Beautiful*. I was also formatively very influenced by the *NME* writers of the mid 70s (Nick Kent, Charles Shaar Murray, Mick Farren) and their delight in language and music, although I hope some of their most purple, Gonzoid qualities have been assimilated and tempered in my own writing.—**Pete Astor**, writer, academic, musician

From many sources: essays, memoirs, songs, abandoned buildings, movies, road trips.—**Joe Bonomo**, music columnist, *The Normal School*, and Associate Professor of English at Northern Illinois University

From music! I don't think I'd have gotten involved in this strange, generally underappreciated activity except through being moved and excited by the joy and conviction that great—and sometimes just *pretty good*—songs and records can embody, whatever their genre or historical period.—**Franklin Bruno**, 33⅓ author

I'm not a great believer in inspiration. It's really more a matter of getting your ass in the chair every day. That's really the blunt truth. There's no other way to get better. That said, if I hit a wall, I'll go over to my bookshelves, find a book that I think might be sort of similar to what I'm going for, take it to my desk and flip through it a while. Sometimes that'll spark something; other times I'll spend fifteen, twenty minutes reading the book, which is all right too.—**Bryan Charles**, writer and **33⅓** author

I have a mental list of friends and their inspiring qualities that I think of when I want to channel an idea or convey a feeling. Something along the lines of, "What would _____ find interesting here?" It's weird to say, but I also find inspiration in the stuff I own. So long as my wife allows me to shelve books and records and movies and toys and shirts and whatever other collectibles fit my dumb fancy, I'm going to be driven to create so that my tactile contributions might end up on someone else's shelf.—**Phillip Crandall**, author of the **33⅓** book on Andrew W.K.'s *I Get Wet*

I read a lot of poetry, fiction, other kinds of cultural criticism, essays etc. They're all potential inspiration. Critics should read as widely as they listen. For example, the psychoanalyst, essayist, cultural critic and historian Adam Phillips is a major influence on me. I often read a few paragraphs of his when I want to ground myself, for the calm musicality of his prose.—**Carl Wilson**, Toronto-based writer and Slate.com music critic

I read other sorts of culture writing—TV, movies, books, video games—and try and keep up with, you know, the news.—**Rob Harvilla**, Deputy/Culture Editor, Deadspin

I like talking to musicians about what inspires them and about what their lives are like. So I'm just inspired by people and their stories, I guess.—**Casey Jarman**, Managing Editor, the *Believer*

This will sound awful, but the critical theory I read in college definitely helped me to write about what things *mean*, as opposed to just what they *do*.—**Matt LeMay**, senior contributor, Pitchfork

I considered Arthur Rimbaud and Gertrude Stein to be the Godfather and Godmother of rock journalism. For me there is now far too much music writing that is only influenced by other music writing, by all the reviews that now get posted, and stuck where they are, not by writing itself and the idea of what you can do to and with the imagination with writing—very few music writers appear directly influenced by David Foster Wallace, who wrote about life and all that comes with it and from it and to it in the way I always liked my music writing, and therefore are influenced by Thomas De Quincey, Herman Melville, B. S. Johnson, David Lynch. Where truth is angular and fractured not measured and coherent. This being influenced within a very narrow range reflects a lot of current pop and rock music, which is more and more influenced only by other music, not by things outside music, and consequently gets more and more visible, animated and comforting and more and more restricted and familiar in its concerns.—**Paul Morley**, writer and critic

Other kinds of writing and other types of voices are key. I don't think "music writing" should be thought of as its own thing—it's writing that happens to be about music, but you still need to engage and inform and entertain and make people think, and no one topic has a monopoly on that.—**Evie Nagy**, *Fast Company* staff writer, former editor at *Billboard* and *Rolling Stone*

I find a lot of inspiration from non-music writing. The way tech writers, or film writers approach their work is fascinating to me. It doesn't always translate, but there's definitely a lot to be taken from those sectors.—**Oliver Primus**, Site Editor, *The 405*

Ralph Waldo Emerson (especially *Representative Men*), Walter Pater (especially *The Renaissance*), William Butler Yeats (especially "The Happiest of the Poets" and "The Philosophy of Shelley's Poetry"), Oscar Wilde (especially "The Decay of Lying" and "The Critic As Artist"), Virginia Woolf (especially *A Room of One's Own*), Mario Praz (especially *The Romantic Agony*), Thomas Weiskel (especially *The Romantic Sublime*)—these are the critical essays that matter most to me as a reader and critic. My favorite novel is *Ulysses* and my favorite poet is Wallace Stevens—nothing I write is uninflected by them, no matter what I'm writing about.—**Rob Sheffield**, writer, *Rolling Stone*

I've told a few budding critics to read Luca Turin and Tania Sanchez's "Perfumes: The A–Z Guide"; I don't even know or care anything about perfume, but that book is some of the best critical writing I've ever read.—**Douglas Wolk**, freelance arts journalist

When I was first experimenting with how to weave together criticism and more personal "subjective" writing, my biggest inspiration was the French filmmaker Agnes Varda, who has made these really inventive films that are hybrids of documentary and "personal essay" style filmmaking. I found it very inspiring the way she playfully plucked elements from different genres and invented her own structure to express herself; I remember thinking that I wanted to do that in writing.—**Lindsay Zoladz**, Associate Editor, Pitchfork

First of all, from music. The only reason that people get into this is because they love music, and you need to constantly rekindle that and find music that truly moves you and intrigues you and makes you want to learn about it. But music isn't everything. I read novels, history, journalism, and anything else that interests me; I absorb lots of films, and enjoy reading good criticism and scholarship of film. Politics, philosophy and other forms of scholarship and cultural history also interest me and teach me a lot about the world we live in.—**Ben Sisario**, reporter, the *New York Times*

I think reading other music writing is often a trap. You can read Robert Christgau or Lester Bangs or keep up with Pitchfork or what have you, but likely that will force you, consciously or not, into accepting a canonical perspective that is a complete fabrication. Even reacting against that canon is a form of accepting that canon. I encourage writers instead to read good writers, period. Become a great writer, and listen to music while becoming so. You'll learn more about writing by reading Saul Bellow or Donald Barthelme than you ever will from reading Lester Bangs. If you know your way around the rhythm, pace, and musicality of prose, then you will be able to handle any topic, music included.— **Scott Tennent**, 33⅓ author

WANT MORE?
WE'VE GOT A COMPANION WEBSITE

For course materials, further readings, playlists and more information please visit:
http://333sound.com/howtowriteaboutmusic

ALSO AVAILABLE IN THE 33⅓ SERIES:

65. *Radio City* by Bruce Eaton

66. *One Step Beyond . . .* by Terry Edwards

67. *Another Green World* by Geeta Dayal

68. *Zaireeka* by Mark Richardson

69. *69 Love Songs* by L. D. Beghtol

70. *Facing Future* by Dan Kois

71. *It Takes a Nation of Millions to Hold Us Back* by Christopher R. Weingarten

72. *Wowee Zowee* by Bryan Charles

73. *Highway to Hell* by Joe Bonomo

74. *Song Cycle* by Richard Henderson

75. *Kid A* by Marvin Lin

76. *Spiderland* by Scott Tennent

77. *Tusk* by Rob Trucks

78. *Pretty Hate Machine* by Daphne Carr

79. *Chocolate and Cheese* by Hank Shteamer

80. *American Recordings* by Tony Tost

81. *Some Girls* by Cyrus Patell

82. *You're Living All Over Me* by Nick Attfield

83. *Marquee Moon* by Bryan Waterman

84. *Amazing Grace* by Aaron Cohen

85. *Dummy* by R. J. Wheaton

86. *Fear of Music* by Jonathan Lethem

87. *Histoire de Melody Nelson* by Darran Anderson

88. *Flood* by S. Alexander Reed and Philip Sandifer

89. *I Get Wet* by Phillip Crandall

90. *Selected Ambient Works Volume II* by Marc Weidenbaum

91. *Entertainment!* by Kevin J.H. Dettmar

92. *Blank Generation* by Pete Astor

93. *Donuts* by Jordan Ferguson

94. *Smile* by Luis Sanchez

95. *Definitely Maybe* by Alex Niven

96. *Exile in Guyville* by Gina Arnold

97. *My Beautiful Dark Twisted Fantasy* by Kirk Walker Graves

98. *The Grey Album* by Charles Fairchild

INDEX

Page numbers in *italics* refer to the writing excerpts found within each chapter.

Index

Index

Index